Echoes of Discontent

Echoes of Discontent

Jesse Jackson, Pat Robertson, and the Resurgence of Populism

Allen D. Hertzke
University of Oklahoma
Carl Albert Congressional Research and Studies Center

A Division of Congressional Quarterly Inc.
Washington, D.C.

Cover design: Ben Santora
Cover photographs: Jackson photo by Dudley M. Brooks, *Washington Post;* Robertson photo, Christian Broadcasting Network

1414 22nd Street, N.W., Washington, D.C. 20037

Printed in the United States of America

Library of Congress Cataloging-in-Publication Data

Hertzke, Allen D., 1950-
Echoes of Discontent : Jesse Jackson, Pat Robertson, and the resurgence of populism / Allen D. Hertzke.
p. cm.
Includes bibliographical references and index.
ISBN 0-87187-744-9 (hard) -- ISBN 0-87187-640-X (pbk.):
1. Presidents--United States--Election--1988. 2. Presidents--United States--Election--1984. 3. United States--Politics and government--1981-1989. 4. Populism--United States--History--20th century. 5. Christianity and politics--History--20th century. 6. Jackson, Jesse, 1941- . 7. Robertson, Pat. 8. Electioneering--United States--History--20th century. I. Title.
E880.H47 1992
973.927--dc20 92-29842
CIP

To my parents

Contents

Preface

The "rich and powerful" took a rhetorical beating in the 1992 presidential campaign. Vice President Dan Quayle railed against "cultural elites" in Hollywood for flouting cherished family values. Democratic nominee Bill Clinton, in turn, castigated the "millionaire friends" of President George Bush. From Jerry Brown to Tom Harkin to Ross Perot, we also heard rumblings of disquiet and anger at entrenched elites. But this kind of language is not new. We heard it before in the 1988 presidential campaigns of Jesse Jackson and Pat Robertson. It is the language of populism, expressing discontent with those perceived to wield economic and cultural power. One cannot understand contemporary American political parties or presidential politics without comprehending the forces tapped and unleashed by the Jackson and Robertson crusades. Indeed, the 1992 election campaign shaped up as a contest between the economic populism of the Democrats and the cultural populism of the Republicans. In this book on the Jackson and Robertson movements I have examined the origins and effects of the politics of discontent in the United States.

My study began as an account of the role of churches in political mobilization. Like many scholars and commentators, I was fascinated by the phenomenon of two ministers campaigning for the presidency, employing church networks and biblical imagery in their quest to mobilize followers. In the course of observing and interviewing, however, I discerned a common theme of discontent in the two camps that was largely lacking among other Democratic and Republican partisans at the time.

In probing the reasons for this discontent, I concluded that "populism" is the term that best describes the two movements and illuminates their commonalities. Both Jackson and Robertson campaigned as populist outsiders. Their followers, who often perceive themselves to be on the periphery of economic and cultural life in America, feel ignored by elites with power to determine the destiny of the nation. These themes of discontent, resentment toward elites, and faith in charismatic leadership were all found in earlier movements in American history, and they continue to reverberate through our political system today. We even see the populist blend of radical economics and traditional moralism in the messages of Jackson and Robertson. Notwithstanding this interpretation, I have tried to be faithful to the unique dynamics of the Jackson and Robertson crusades. I am well aware that it may be jarring for some to see Jackson and Robertson linked. But my objective here is scholarly, to see what we can learn by comparing such seemingly different individuals and movements.

This study, in part, followed an approach that uses extensive interviewing and personal observation.[1] One primary aim was to understand the movements from within—in scholarly parlance, to take an ethnographic or phenomenological approach. Field research, which began in February 1988 with the Iowa caucuses, continued through mid-1992. I observed firsthand the insurgent movements in several states, went to both national party conventions in 1988, and subsequently observed state, district, and national party meetings. I also attended functions sponsored by the two leaders in the first half of 1992. During this research I interviewed Jackson's and Robertson's national campaign managers (Jerry Austin for Jackson, Marc Nuttle for Robertson), along with campaign aides, state coordinators, grass-roots activists, ministers, delegates, caucus attenders, journalists, and other scholars following the campaigns. In addition, I interviewed officials in George Bush's and Michael Dukakis's campaigns to gain insights about how they perceived and dealt with the insurgents. In 1991 and 1992 I completed field research by interviewing Jackson and Robertson and the political directors of their organizations (Frank Watkins for the Rainbow Coalition, Ralph Reed for the Christian Coalition).

In addition to interviews and observation, I drew upon the rich biographical and archival material available on Jackson and Robertson to examine their lives and messages. I analyzed data from opinion surveys of their followers; these polls tended to corroborate my impression that the campaigns mobilized two distinct communities of discontent in the United States. As I sought to understand the common historical threads in the discontent experienced within these communities, I was led to a serious inquiry into the history of American populism. The populists, I discovered, combined economic radicalism and religious piety and at the same time issued a powerful communitarian critique of "destructive individualism" that had no moral constraints. Like the populists, who saw themselves harking back to an earlier "republican age" in American history—when individualism supposedly was restrained for the good of the community—I looked back to historical scholarship to trace this communitarian element in American life. My broader argument about the tension between classical liberalism and populism arises from this analysis.[2] Jackson's and Robertson's campaigns, at least on one level, can be understood as continuing populist protests by Christian communities against perceived corrosive or exploitive individualism in economics and culture.

An ethnographic approach tends to produce a sympathetic treatment of its subjects, since the objective is to understand the events from the perspective of the partisans.[3] Because of this tendency, my approach may seem oversympathetic to some. But, as the reader will note, I explore the problems and limits of religious charisma in politics as well as its value. Although I came to appreciate the unique gifts of both ministers, I recognize that they are imperfect vessels, bringing various strengths and weaknesses to their tasks as movement leaders. Those who see their roles as God-ordained may be good at registering discontent but ill-equipped to govern. Both ministers have proclivities that militate against efficacy in actual governance: Jackson can be a gadfly populist with a seemingly overweening ego; Robertson has a tendency to weave conspiracy theories.

Some readers, accustomed to depictions of populists as demagogues or backwater nativists, may find my treatment of populism more positive than they might expect. In response, I make two observations. First, the wholly negative portrayals of populists characteristic of historian Richard Hofstadter have been largely refuted by nearly three decades of new evidence and fresh interpretation. The populists of the late nineteenth century now seem prescient in their appreciation of the economic consequences of the emerging industrial order. Moreover, the reform energies they unleashed played a role in the Progressive era and the New Deal. Second, even if populist uprisings cannot "govern," they may be viewed as a societal gauge, registering pressures that build up whenever the commonweal fails to negotiate the challenges of the times. One does not have to agree with populist prescriptions, or approve of their attacks on elites, to sympathize with their disquiet.

In analyzing the roots of these two campaigns, I became aware of disjunctions in the scholarly literature that should be addressed. The literature on black protest politics, for example, long ago discarded psychological explanations that tended to minimize the genuine grievances of protesters. Today protest movements are viewed as arising when people with authentic grievances shed fatalistic habits of thought (in what is termed "cognitive liberation") to take advantage of new opportunities to organize in their interest.[4] The civil rights movement is explained by the emergence of new opportunities to vent grievances, combined with a liberating sense of hope in potential success. In contrast, the literature on moral crusades remains fixed in a more critical "status politics" school that draws heavily upon psychological models. It hypothesizes that the declining social status of a group leaves members suffering from "status anxiety." They respond by striking back, at times irrationally and meanly.[5] Why can we not apply the insights of scholarship on black insurgency to moral protests? In other words, we can understand religious conservatives to be using newly created opportunity structures to express authentic grievances. They, too, may experience cognitive liberation as hitherto undreamed possibilities emerge. Certainly, that is the impression I gained after following Robertson's campaign. In this study I treat both Jackson's and Robertson's campaigns as movements that are airing legitimate grievances, taking advantage of favorable opportunities and resources, and embodying a measure of cognitive liberation in the ecstatic dedication of their followers.[6]

By taking an ethnographic, interpretive, and historical approach, I hope to have purchased a broader theoretical explanation than a behavioral approach would have allowed. My analysis does not test, in a scientific sense, theories about the evangelical right or the black protest left. Instead, it attempts to discern what may be common in such distinct social movements and to comprehend broader forces at work. After all, here were two Baptist ministers running for president—one black, one white—trumpeting moral renewal, chastising elites, mobilizing congregations, and challenging their respective parties. The similarities are more than superficial. Populism, as a historical and theoretical framework, provides us with the best anvil on which to forge an explanation of their commonalities. Whereas a behaviorist interpretation might view populism as a variant of status or protest politics, a historically rooted analysis sees populism as the broad cultural stream with diverse protests as some of its eddies.

In the chapters that follow I will develop this thesis. Chapter 1 reviews the features of Jackson's and Robertson's campaigns, discussing their populist rhetoric, their church bases, and their charismatic ability to mobilize those who experience discontent. Chapter 2 traces the origins of nineteenth-century populism and shows that populists sought to reclaim Christian and republican communitarian values, which often clashed with individualistic trends, from the colonial period onward. To illustrate the populist blend of moralistic religion and radical politics, I examine the life of William Jennings Bryan, who combined evangelical faith with progressive economic views. Chapter 3 focuses on the lives and rhetoric of Jackson and Robertson, comparing their messages with the messages of populists in the past and discussing their religiously inspired critiques of elites. Chapter 4 shows how churches became vital political resources in 1988 and presents the drama of a presidential campaign from the inside. In Chapter 5, I show how the two major parties assimilated the activists mobilized by the two ministers into their ranks. This chapter describes the political battles that ensued and offers conclusions about the continuing legacy of the Rainbow Coalition and Christian Coalition in American politics. Chapter 6 uses survey data to profile the voters who backed the two populist candidates. Responses to the surveys reveal unexpected similarities between voters often considered to be on opposite ends of the political spectrum. In the last chapter, I chart the rise of populist politics and sentiment from 1988 through 1992, showing how the campaigns of Jackson and Robertson seemed to signal a coming tide of populist outbursts. The central argument—that populism is a reaction to an ascendant individualism in economics and culture—is developed more fully. Finally, I look at the weaknesses and unsavory aspects of populism and discuss some of the troubling church-state implications of religious politics.

The metaphor in the title of this book—"echoes of discontent"—shows how themes and concerns of earlier populists in American history were echoed in Robertson's and Jackson's movements. In another sense, it shows how real-world problems echo through the sound chambers of church networks and charismatic leadership. Finally, it suggests that the concerns of the 1988 campaign will reverberate into the future. Jackson and Robertson motivated religious communities to express their frustration with historical tides that simultaneously threatened the economically vulnerable and the morally traditional. Thus contemporary populist movements have much to teach us about the cultural and economic challenges of the age in which we live.

It is humbling to realize how much of one's work is the product of the time, talent, and treasury of others. So it is with this book, which represents an enormous investment by many institutions and individuals. *Echoes of Discontent* was made possible through the support provided by the Carl Albert Congressional Research and Studies Center. Ronald M. Peters, Jr., founder and director of the center, offered encouragement, discerning criticism, and financial backing throughout research for this book. A number of able graduate fellows at the center assisted me at various stages; they included Nancy Bednar, Bill Granstaff, Karen Kedrowski, Robin LeBlanc, David Rausch, and Jean Shumway Warner. Several talented undergraduates affiliated with the center also worked extensively on this project. Among them were Steve Van Winkle, who researched the literature on populism; Smruti Patel, who helped with survey analysis; and Chris Schultz and Brad Welsh, who spent countless hours assisting me during the last stages of editing the manuscript. My work was facilitated by the center's top-flight administrative staff, led by LaDonna Sullivan and including Karla Feist, Carma Hurst, and Kathy Wade.

My research was also supported by the Graduate College of the University of Oklahoma, which provided me with a summer fellowship, and the Department of Political Science, which reduced my teaching load. I am especially grateful to Donald J. Maletz, chair of the Department of Political Science, and to my colleagues in the department and the university for their encouragement and support.

My work on this book has been blessed immeasurably by the contributions of a national community of scholars, many of whom read and criticized various parts of this manuscript. CQ Press reviewers C. Anthony Broh and James L. Guth offered detailed suggestions on my research prospectus. Ken Wald and an anonymous reviewer did extremely thorough reviews of an early draft. Their detailed comments, along with those of my colleague Ron Peters, improved the book in a major way, especially in helping to provide more balance in the analysis. I am deeply grateful to my mentor, Booth Fowler, whose attentive reading of a later draft helped me strengthen the theme and qualify my assertions. Special thanks also go to Gary Copeland, John Green, Matt Moen, Duane Oldfield, Corwin Smidt, and Clyde Wilcox; each of them read various parts of my work and shared their insights. I am grateful to Lucius Barker, who advised me early on to hit the road and interview key black preachers, and to Ronald Walters, whose insights into black presidential politics benefited me greatly. I am also indebted to Hubert Morken for generously sharing his voluminous files on Pat Robertson and for long and fruitful discussions about the campaign.

To the people of CQ Press, especially to Brenda Carter, David Tarr, and Shana Wagger, I offer thanks. Their faith in this project helped to sustain me when I had doubts. The final editing of this book was done by Ann Davies. Her remarkably meticulous and discerning editing cleaned up a number of mistakes and helped make this book more lucid and accessible. My thanks also go to Kate Quinlin and Jackie Davey for their fine work in marketing this book.

Jesse Jackson's and Pat Robertson's generosity in sharing their time with me greatly enhanced the texture of my analysis. I am indebted to their top aides, who offered many insights, and to numerous others involved in the campaigns who told their stories.

Closer to home, my wife, Barbara Norton, and our two sons, Patrick and Simon, endured with equanimity the bouts of angst that accompany the enterprise of writing. Barbara was a source of constant encouragement when I occasionally became overwhelmed with the enormity of the task. I can only express my love and devotion.

Finally, exploring the community needs of free individuals has deepened my appreciation of my own roots—of family, farm community, and church. Thus it is to my parents, Luverne and Annie Hertzke, that I dedicate this volume.

NOTES

1. This "soak and poke" approach is characteristic of the work of Richard Fenno. See the appendix in Richard F. Fenno, Jr., *Home Style: House Members in Their Districts* (Boston: Little, Brown, 1978).
2. The argument of this book can be stated in formal scientific language: the dependent variable (the thing to be explained) is the outbreak of populist politics in the late 1980s and early 1990s; the independent variable (the thing that explains) is the ascendant liberal order in economics and culture; the intervening variable (what links the dependent and independent variables) is religion, or, more specifically, the strategic resources of charisma and tightknit churches that serve to mobilize and channel discontent.
3. Fenno observes that researchers can come to like and identify with their subjects and thus, in a sense, can lose scholarly objectivity. Just as Fenno, in his celebrated study of House members, admitted that he came to "love them all," I came to appreciate and sympathize with the supporters of Jackson and Robertson and with the ministers themselves. The benefits of this close examination, in my judgment, outweigh the dangers. I compensated for any potential loss of scholarly detachment by analyzing survey data, studying extensive critical scholarly and press commentary, interviewing adversaries of the two ministers, and responding to several reviewers' trenchant criticisms.
4. See especially Doug McAdam, *Political Process and the Development of Black Insurgency, 1930-1970* (Chicago: University of Chicago Press, 1982).
5. See especially Seymour Martin Lipset and Earl Raab, *The Politics of Unreason*, 2d ed. (Chicago: University of Chicago Press, 1978); for a more recent synthesis of the literature and an empirical test, see Kenneth D. Wald, Dennis E. Owen, and Samuel S. Hill, Jr., "Evangelical Politics and Status Issues," *Journal for the Scientific Study of Religion* 28 (1989): 1-16.
6. By accepting the premise that both movements are airing legitimate grievances, I take seriously the communitarian critique of individualism, from both the right and the left. I do so, however, not as one who believes in a grand alternative to the emerging liberal order but as one convinced that its atomistic tendencies constitute one of the major challenges of our day. For a fuller exploration of this theme of atomistic culture, see the introductory essay in *The Atomistic Congress: An Interpretation of Political Change*, ed. Allen D. Hertzke and Ronald M. Peters, Jr. (Armonk, N.Y.: M. E. Sharpe, 1992).

1

Religion and Populism in America

It is Easter Sunday, 1988, and presidential candidates are in Denver on the eve of the Colorado caucuses. Rather than delivering the usual campaign rhetoric, two ministers weave Easter themes into their addresses to ecstatic congregations. Receiving standing ovations at four evangelical churches, Republican presidential candidate Pat Robertson compares the despair of early Christians on Good Friday with the discontent of contemporary Christians in America. To a chorus of "amens" he proclaims, "It looks like the bad guys are winning in this country, but so did it look that way on Good Friday. . . . It looked as if Satan had beaten Jesus on that day." And just as Jesus rose from the dead, Robertson declares, so will moral Americans eventually prevail.[1] Democratic candidate Jesse Jackson also sees an Easter message in the political signs of the times. Before an unusual combined service of prominent black and white churches, an emotional Jackson likens "the Good Friday Crucifixion to the onset of the Reagan administration" but promises "an Easter-like political resurrection for the nation's downtrodden." "Hope has been unleashed," Jackson intones. "It's Easter. Not ruffled dresses, not eggs. . . . The *real* Easter is going on." At Our Lady of Guadalupe, a predominately Hispanic church, Jackson likens Reagan to the Roman leader who condemned Jesus: "Pilate was in power; Pilate had credentials, but he couldn't make a decision. He said, 'I think Jesus is innocent, but he might be guilty. . . . I think he's right, but the crowds say he's wrong. So let me wash my hands.' We don't need no more hand washing. We need leaders who will stand in a moment of crisis."[2]

Clearly, something remarkable was afoot, as presidential politics brought simmering forces in American society to the surface, challenging conventional politicians to respond. Capitalizing on black desperation and pride, the Reverend Jesse Jackson mobilized a formidable network of black congregations and ministers to serve as the vanguard of his "rainbow" challenge to the Democratic party establishment. Pat Robertson, exploiting a religious broadcasting network to activate charismatic evangelicals, brought moral conservatives into a direct clash with Republican regulars. More like ongoing social movements than political campaigns, these two crusades endured into the 1990s.

On the eve of the 1992 presidential campaign, Robertson's Christian Coalition brought together a thousand conservative ministers and activists from across the country to plan strategies to register voters, mobilize turnout, and influence the Republican party. Coalition members have girded themselves for local, state, and national struggles over abortion, secularization in the schools, and libertine popular culture they expect to last throughout the decade. Similarly, in January 1992 Jackson's Rainbow Coalition hosted a forum at which all the announced Democratic presidential candidates subjected themselves to a grilling by the coalition's leaders. Jackson declared his intention to traverse the country, organizing a fifty-city effort to increase voter registration by 25 percent, principally among African Americans. Both ministers remain in the headlines, speaking, writing, hosting television programs, and building their organizations for what they both view as a long-term struggle for "the soul of America."

These two forces seem at first glance confusing and contradictory. How can we make sense of the fact that both of these leaders champion movements on the extreme ends of the political spectrum—Jackson on the far left, Robertson on the far right? How can we generalize about such different contexts as black churches and white charismatic congregations? How can we reconcile the fact that discontent and urgency were expressed far more by supporters of Jackson and Robertson than by other party activists? The answers lie in the radical nature of the Jackson and Robertson movements. Radical ideas imply that problems are fundamental and thus are unsolvable through incremental tinkering. Drawing upon the prophetic biblical tradition, Jackson and Robertson argue that the nation is beset by fundamental problems that demand a profound reordering of thought and action.[3] Their messages resonate with followers who are deeply discontented with the country's condition. The most important story of the 1988 campaign, therefore, was not necessarily the immediate outcome. Rather, the blend of religion, populism, and political charisma that erupted in 1988 continues to swirl on the edges of the mainstream, perhaps telling us more about the stresses of contemporary life than conventional politics can.[4] Indeed, the populist idea of "politics from the outside" that emerged in 1988 foreshadowed a growing disenchantment within the

American electorate that became the dominant theme in 1992. Thus we should try to comprehend some of the forces behind this discontent.

Much has been written about the two minister-candidates, their campaigns, and their constituencies, but no one has attempted a major analysis of both as part of a broader picture. The explanation for this is simple: scholars of African American politics are separate in their approach and theoretical focus from those who study the religious right. Moreover, uttering the names of Pat Robertson and Jesse Jackson in the same breath is shocking to some and repugnant to others. Although I do not intend to equate the moral claims of Jackson and Robertson, I believe that insights might be gained by comparing them. For example, Jesse Jackson is often profiled as the quintessential liberal in textbooks on government and in journalistic treatments, while Pat Robertson is portrayed as the classic conservative. Yet comparing their messages and movements reveals some surprising commonalities (as we will see in Chapter 3). I did not expect Robertson to describe Jackson as a "good friend" and "a strong Christian," explaining away his leftist tendencies to "radical" aides. I did not expect to hear Jackson seriously proposing the Ten Commandments as the solution to the crisis in the inner cities, a sentiment more commonly associated with the religious right. I did not expect to find, as I did, black ministers speaking kindly of Robertson and his work with black inner-city churches. I did not expect to discover the sizable overlap between Jackson supporters and Robertson supporters in the electorate nor the unusually favorable view of Jackson by Robertson backers. Nor did I expect to learn that Robertson is more highly regarded by blacks than by whites. I was intrigued by the extent to which both candidates appeal disproportionately to women voters, perhaps indicating women's sense of the threat of economic and cultural change. Finally, in these supposedly secular times, I was struck by the combination of "prophecy and politics" that distinguishes these two candidates from others. Jackson does not merely speak to his followers; he preaches with the seeming authority of an Amos or Micah. Robertson, in turn, offers his own mix of political analysis with the charismatic "gift" of prophecy. Religion, in short, remains a salient variable in understanding "politics from the outside."

How then can we comprehend these crusades? My thesis is that we can understand Jackson and Robertson as manifestations of American populism—in this case a kind of "gospel populism" articulated most cogently through tightknit churches.[5] As the enduring quest of people "to claim politics as something of theirs,"[6] populism evokes a rich legacy from nineteenth-century America. It also enjoys currency today, not only in the United States but around the world. As a political style populism commonly describes mass-movement politics based on the idea that elites are not responsive to the popular will. Scholars often portray populism as a clash between those who feel themselves on the "periphery" and those perceived to be at the "core" of economic and cultural life. Charismatic leadership and rhetorical celebration of "the people" are also key aspects of the populist style. In an ideological sense, on the other hand, populism describes a distinct blend of economic progressivism and social conservatism.[7] Both the stylistic and ideological usages are valuable: the first captures the tenor of the Jackson and Robertson movements; the second, their ideological mix.

Jackson's populism takes the form of prophetic outrage at the economic exploitation of the poor by the rich; Robertson's is vented against cultural elites who undermine traditional moral values. Both leaders share other elements of populism: they present a moralistic challenge to complacency, they emphasize crisis and charisma, they celebrate common people and castigate elites, and they hold a polarized view of society.

An important difference between Jackson and Robertson lies in their perception of which elites are most responsible for the state of society. Jackson casts the elites in left-wing terms as heirs of the robber barons. He castigates multinational corporations that export American jobs, investment bankers with no concern for the commonweal, wealthy exploiters of the laboring classes, and Republican plunderers of the government. Robertson's elites comprise the "new class" of secular educators, media moguls, "snooty artists," liberal academics, government bureaucrats, ACLU attorneys, and feminists bent on destroying the family. Both men's conceptions of elites are rooted in perceived sources of discontent among their followers: in the black community an economic crisis, for conservative Christians the threat of secular domination. Although contemporary populism has to a degree thus split into left-wing and right-wing variations, the characteristic blend remains. Jackson's progressive economic and foreign policy platform commingles with a strong dose of religious fervor and moral traditionalism. Robertson's moral conservatism is mixed with a populist distrust of financial interests, banks, and the Federal Reserve.

A contemporary analysis of populism is needed because a simple liberal-conservative reading of politics is inadequate to capture the dynamics now afoot. Increasingly, scholars are finding that the populist blend of pietism and progressivism does not fit neatly into a left-right political spectrum. One study, for example, found that working-class folk are more populist than middle-class people, who tend to be libertarian.[8] Moreover, it found populism to be the predominant ideology among nonwhites, leading to the conclusion that "candidates who present moralistic or religious themes in their public positions (Jimmy Carter in 1976 and Jesse Jackson in 1984) provide a better representation of black views than do traditional liberals."[9]

Unfortunately, terminology can be a stumbling block to understanding. Take the word *liberal* used in the above quotation. In current parlance its connotations are so unsavory that Republican candidates fling it as a negative epithet against their Democratic opponents. In this book, however, I generally use *liberal* in its broad, classical meaning. "Classical liberalism" suggests a blend of free-market economics and protection of individual liberty—a posture embraced by most Democrats and Republicans today. Especially rooted in the American story, liberalism now seems ascendant around the globe. We speak of "liberalization in the communist world" to describe the rejection of command economies and the freeing of dissent and individual expression. Liberalism, so understood, embodies and promotes individualism. But as we will see, populists often perceive the excesses of this individualism as a major source of their problems.

While acknowledging the obvious historical and social differences between followers of Jackson and followers of Robertson, I propose that there may be a common source of discontent. Both Jackson's indictment of economic power and Robertson's critique of moral decline can be seen as criticisms of the rather chaotic, laissez faire individualism that characterizes American cultural and economic trends. Interviews I conducted with the two ministers and their followers revealed similar concerns about the drift of social and economic change. Both sides complained of excessive greed in contemporary life, the collapse of community and family, the loss of a moral compass, and a coarsening of attitudes. Echoes of these concerns, as we will see in Chapter 2, reverberate throughout American history. From the eighteenth century onward we find periodic outbursts against the effects of excessive or exploitative individualism, whether in the economic or cultural realm. Herein lies the link between the strands of populism today. Certain modern forces that reflect the triumph of classical liberalism—expanding global markets in economics and increasing moral individualism in cultural affairs—simultaneously threaten the economically vulnerable and the morally traditional.

Church communities, as mobilized by the Jackson and Robertson crusades, gave voice to this sense of threat. To understand why this occurred, we must probe more deeply the cultural context of the politics of discontent.

CULTURE, POLITICS, AND RELIGIOUS LIFE

Few issues in political inquiry breathe with such timeless vitality as the link between culture and politics. From Plato's *Republic* to Tocqueville's *Democracy in America* to more recent treatments of civic culture, we see the interweaving of cultural life and political institutions.[10] Aaron Wildavsky, one of the most prolific scholars in this field, argues that three cultural modalities—egalitarian, individualist, and hierarchical—compete, blend, and ultimately shape the American polity. Defining culture as "shared values that justify social relations," Wildavsky contends that all politics are underpinned by these cultural forms.[11]

Insightful as this line of research is, however, it misses something. Much of Wildavsky's work suggests that broad cultural forms exist independent of, or at least are deeper than, religious traditions and practices. Yet religion, as we know, profoundly molded American culture and politics in the past, and churches have been at the center of a number of the great political movements in the nation's history, from the abolitionist crusade to the civil rights revolution.[12] With 60 percent of all citizens regular attenders, religious institutions today dwarf the membership of other private associations, unions, or groups in the collective society.[13] Mounting evidence also charts the pivotal role of religion in the formation of political attitudes, voting behavior, and social action.

We can better appreciate the significance of religious organizations when we examine the broad cultural tendencies that undermine community structures. Although Wildavsky emphasizes the power of the egalitarian culture in politics, other scholars for at least four decades have pointed to the weakness of community-based politics in a liberal political culture that stresses individual autonomy. In the 1950s Robert Nisbet suggested that the vacuum created by weakening ties to family, village, and parish would be filled by a quest for some national community, which he viewed as inevitably futile. Echoing Nisbet, Richard Merelman argued thirty years later that Americans had become so loosely attached to social institutions that citizens were stripped of effective avenues for cohesive group action. Similarly, Robert Bellah warned against an individualism (bordering on atomism) that corroded the civic virtue necessary to a healthy community life and national policy.[14]

To be sure, scholars may have exaggerated these trends, writing more of their own academic (and heavily bicoastal) culture than of the one manifest on Sunday morning, when civic responsibility is still preached in many churches and apparently is even practiced. But powerful modern forces—mobility, mass media, and cosmopolitan education—have uprooted people from local social realms and weakened communal solidarity. The real world of political power, however, is about collective action.[15] To gain leverage in politics, we must make common cause with one another, a process increasingly undermined by contemporary atomizing tendencies.

American churches, however, are a notable exception to the prevailing depictions of atomistic contemporary culture. Of course, where religious commitment is tepid or where churches are themselves sapped by trends in the broader culture, the likelihood of an intense political following is dim. Yet there are some tightknit churches whose members seem willing to sacrifice for the faith. Different though they are in many respects, predominately black congregations and conservative charismatic churches have one thing in common: the church is profoundly central to the life of its members. For the black church this centrality has roots in the legacy of slavery and segregation.[16] For charismatic churches the commitment is often explained by psychological forces[17] and the dislocations of modernity.[18]

As ministers steeped in religious traditions and rooted in church communities, Jackson and Robertson understood this spiritual commitment and sought political capital in its bosom. Neither leader can be understood, consequently, apart from his connection to a religious tradition. A comparison of the Jackson and Robertson campaigns will help us to understand the power, and the limits, of church-based social movements. More important, it will illuminate the barriers to political action in our increasingly individualistic culture, where traditional means of collective participation, such as local parties or unions, no longer provide most citizens with a meaningful venue. "Gospel populism," in a sense, rushed into the expanding vacuum left by the weakening of these local political institutions. Church-based politics, with all the baggage it can bring, thus can be viewed as a symptom of the civic malaise and as an attempted cure.

THE WELLSPRINGS OF DISCONTENT

Presidential campaigns, more than routine interest group action, sometimes serve as barometers of American society, registering the frustration of particular constituencies. Buoyed by support in the churches, Jackson capitalized on the sense of crisis in the black community to alter the political configuration of the Democratic party. Robertson, similarly, mobilized religious conservatives threatened by cultural change to confront the GOP establishment.

To understand my cultural explanation of these phenomena, we must explore the intimate connection between liberalism (in its broad, classical definition) and modernity. With the collapse of communism has come an intellectual appreciation of the global power of liberal ideas. Nations once committed to the socialist vision have concluded that defying the logic of capitalist economics is like defying the law of gravity; one does so at one's peril. But as individuals now celebrate their new-found freedom, they also experience the cultural and economic dislocations that flow from this entrance into the marketplace of commodities and lifestyle choices. So powerful are these global forces that some have equated the ascendant liberal order with modernity itself.[19] Although perhaps overstated, such a formulation makes some sense. In economics, for example, the metaphors for the global village dovetail with the ideas behind capitalist liberalism: we hear terms such as international competition, perpetual innovation, consumerism, and creative destruction. In cultural circles, too, the metaphors of modernity often are linked with the strengths and weaknesses of liberal culture: freedom, rights, and individual autonomy but also hedonism, narcissism, anomie, and dysfunctional families. In literary circles rootless individualism evokes such phrases as "all that is solid melts into air" and "the unbearable lightness of being." Even some liberals reluctantly acknowledge liberalism's less than savory elements. Theodore Lowi, for example, boldly defines liberalism as embodying individualism, capitalism, greed, antimorality in public discourse, and collective association by contract alone (versus religious visions of community).[20]

That many people accept the ascendance of liberal modernity in no way minimizes their feelings that it is fraught with moral perils or physical disruptions. Thus parochial, religious, or more ancient discourses continue to compete with or complement the language of liberalism. We still hear, especially from Jackson and Robertson, such words as fidelity, community, sacrifice, sin, redemptive suffering, and moral obligation.

Our analysis of populism, then, will be based on understanding how modern forces clash with the ideals embedded in religious communities. Economically, the modern global marketplace leaves little room for egalitarian visions. Just as nations must compete in the global market, so must individuals fail or prosper on the basis of what they have to offer the international economy.[21] Once-thriving communities can decay, and whole regions of the country can lapse into depression as the effects of international events are felt throughout the economy. The Marxist (and some might argue Christian) vision—"from each according to his ability, to each according to his need"—appears more and more utopian and impractical as the rotting communist regimes collapse. For many African Americans, vulnerable from the legacy of slavery and discrimination, the economic shifts have been particularly problematic.

Ill-positioned to respond easily to the high-tech "perpetual innovation" of the global marketplace,[22] many black workers struggle to stay afloat. These same forces operate to some degree for all working-class and middle-class Americans, from formerly affluent factory workers to small-town merchants, who may see their fortunes quickly decay. Jackson's indictment of multinational corporations that destroy communities by exporting jobs and his demand that the commonweal be strengthened reflect the threat posed to the vulnerable and unprepared by the dynamic global marketplace.

What is not well appreciated is that the effect of the ascendant marketplace in morals is equally profound and threatening to moral traditionalists.[23] Indeed, the unbridled free-enterprise system so extolled by "conservatives" does radical things: it uproots people, fosters a youth culture hostile to parental authority, undermines traditional communities, and pummels consumers with seductive appeals to the seven deadly sins. Religious leaders around the world are keenly aware of these tendencies, from Islamic clerics, who want the technological benefits of modernity without the moral baggage, to the Roman Catholic pope, who has warned Eastern Europeans against losing their faith in mindless consumerism. In the United States, one of the most liberal and individualistic of all nations, these market forces are exceedingly powerful. After all, what do we export as well as the seductive promises of our advertising and our mass entertainment? Although some religious populists may seem ignorant of the capitalist sources of their discontent, we occasionally see glimmerings of awareness in their desire to boycott businesses and advertisers who make a buck by exploiting the young.

The marketplace in morals has influenced our very language. In a process so subtle that it almost eludes consciousness, we have adopted the language of "values" to describe what once was the province of ethics and morals. The word *value*, which economists use to compare consumer preferences (I value ice cream, you prefer cookies), has been transmuted into "moral values," suggesting that moral or ethical judgments are merely a matter of taste. In such a marketplace the perceived threat of moral chaos infuses religious conservatives with a sense of urgency, though they are often unaware of where the threat lies.[24] But political progressives such as Jesse Jackson have also sounded the clarion about the collapse of moral order. How, they ask, can racism or poverty or injustice be fought without a transcendent moral basis? As Jackson and Robertson both suggest, transcendent family and community mores, which they view as under siege, may be essential for the economic advancement of the vulnerable.

It is not surprising that the protest against cultural and economic trends should come from churches, which by their existence confront the individualistic assumptions that drive the broader society. Jackson's economic prophecy and Robertson's moral jeremiad can be seen as communitarian responses to an ascendant liberal order that celebrates the self above family, community, or tradition. Because this celebration of self comes in both right-wing forms ("deregulate the entrepreneur") and left-wing forms ("uncensor the artist"), we should not be surprised that populism might appeal most successfully to the economically vulnerable and the morally traditional (groups not necessarily mutually exclusive, as we shall see in Chapter 6). The dual strands of populism in the 1980s, in a way, offer a distinct challenge to the drift of secular modernity.[25]

Yet how can we account for the fact that other tightknit communities—Jewish, Catholic, and perhaps others—do not conform to this picture? How can we distinguish between communities that serve to vent discontent and those that do not? Perhaps Jackson and Robertson mobilized those religious communities that felt most vulnerable to imploding forces. We know that Robertson's support comes not from rural evangelical environs but from suburban churches, where charismatic faith presumably collides most clearly with atomizing modernity.[26] Jackson's support arguably arises from communities in which people most keenly perceive economic dislocation or decline.

The question remains: to what extent can politics ameliorate problems that arise from the very nature of powerful trends? If the answer is only to a limited extent, then the sources of discontent will remain to pique the complacency of elites for some time to come. Perhaps this is one reason that the crusades of Jackson and Robertson endured beyond the 1988 election.

CAMPAIGNS AS SOCIAL MOVEMENTS

Jesse Jackson and Pat Robertson view their crusades as the culmination of political and social developments whose immediate origins can be traced to the 1960s. To begin understanding the two movements, therefore, we can look to the tumultuous decade that produced both the civil rights movement, so central to black politics, and the counterculture and sexual revolution that ultimately galvanized the religious right.

Jesse Jackson sees his Rainbow Coalition as the logical extension of the efforts begun by Martin Luther King, Jr., through the Southern Christian Leadership Conference and the Poor People's Campaign. What has changed is the relative clout of the black electorate. Lyndon Johnson's embrace of civil rights solidified black loyalty to the Democratic party,[27] but it was Jackson's campaigns that forged that constituency into a powerful bloc within the party.

On the other side, the Democrats' association with the radicalism and counterculture of the 1960s created an opportunity for Republicans to appeal to culturally conservative Roman Catholics and evangelical Protestants. At the height of the counterculture, while the media effused over the sexual revolution, women's liberation, and gay rights, a largely unnoticed religious movement was gaining strength. Evangelical churches were growing, conversions to "born again" religion mounted, and a charismatic movement blossomed across denominations, even among some Catholics. A new cultural divide was emerging, at least in white America, between moral and religious traditionalists and those turned off by pietist faith.[28] While one part of the nation rushed headlong into the modern age, the other clung to the rock of ages. But the American public adhered to (and still does) a remarkably durable and orthodox set of religious values.[29] As liberalism became associated with alternative lifestyles, loose morality, and hostility to religion, Republican campaign consultants made hay. Not surprisingly, the last Democrat to win the White House since Lyndon Johnson was Jimmy Carter, a born-again southerner who received support from both Jesse Jackson and Pat Robertson, a fact more startling now than it appeared then.

Many conservative evangelicals felt betrayed by Carter's liberal White House, and the religious right burst on the scene in 1979, just in time for Ronald Reagan to sweep conservative Christians into the GOP under his appeal to "traditional values." Reagan's strategists also promoted racial polarization in the South. This strategy, coupled with his supply-side attack on activist government, alienated many black voters.

The stage was being set for the church-based politics of discontent that appeared in 1988. Among traditionally Democratic groups, blacks in particular suffered from the economic and social tides of the 1980s. A massive literature cataloged the growing crisis.[30] Blacks were particularly ill-positioned to benefit from Reagan's supply-side revolution, the rise of the service economy, and the transformation of the global marketplace. Many African Americans, dependent upon inner-city industrial jobs and with little capital to cushion them, saw their economic position stagnate during the go-go years on Wall Street. The flight of capital and industrial jobs from the cities deepened the cultural crisis; out-of-wedlock pregnancies, inner-city violence, and lagging educational attainment left many young blacks vulnerable and alienated. Disturbing trends were noted by scholars and the media. Nearly 60 percent of all black children were born out of wedlock (in the black underclass nearly all children were so afflicted); 72 percent of them would live in a household that received welfare at one time before they were eighteen. As inner-city families collapsed, welfare workers began to speak of zero-parent households: more than 10 percent of black children were cared for by neither their mother nor their father. College attendance by black students actually dropped in the 1980s, after peaking in 1975. Young black men were more likely to be incarcerated or on parole than in college. The situation in the inner cities remains desperate. In Washington, D.C., an appalling 70 percent of all young black men will have been involved in the criminal justice system by the age of thirty-five. A lost generation fills the nation's jails.

In the 1980s, as a sense of crisis grew in the black community, intense debate occurred over the black underclass, the "vanishing" black male, and the weakening black family. In response, the Reagan administration attacked affirmative action. Although not happy with Reagan, many other Democratic groups, in contrast with the embattled African American community, nonetheless seemed to have it pretty good.

Business interests, of course, reaped the most tangible benefits from the policies of the Reagan revolution, in the form of tax cuts and deregulation. Morally conservative evangelicals, despite their loyalty to Reagan, got mostly rhetorical support and won few tangible victories. Abortion endured, pornography survived, TV became trashier, and public schools seemed increasingly hostile to those of traditional faith.[31] In many ways the New Christian Right failed miserably in the 1980s,[32] and the concerns that animated the movement remain as intense as ever. Ironically, the deregulatory emphasis of the Reagan years may have led to the excesses in the marketplace that traditional Christians find so disturbing, such as increased violence and commercial exploitation of children's television. Indeed, some cultural conservatives chastised corporations for promoting immorality, hedonism, and violence in their advertising appeals and sponsorship of trash TV.[33] Thus if blacks expressed the greatest discontent within the Democratic coalition, white conservative Christians were the angriest of the Republicans. The soil had been fertilized for decades, but the seeds of the Jackson and Robertson crusades were planted in the Reagan era, which represented a profound threat to blacks and a promise unfulfilled for white evangelicals.

Each political party thus was challenged by an insurgent Baptist minister who exploited church networks and made religious appeals to activate his followers. The common thread in these challenges is the sense of crisis experienced within the respective communities and evoked by the two leaders. On the Republican side, Robertson supporters—in contrast to business elites and "country club" types who had little to complain about in the Reagan-Bush years—felt their way of life was threatened by collapsing moral codes and secular trends. Compared with the feel-good, "morning in America" themes popular with Republicans in the 1980s, Robertson's campaign ads painted a dark picture of America. In the ads he described a place where children were victimized by pornographers, misled in undisciplined schools, and manipulated by greedy marketers of glitz, lust, and sloth. He spoke of the need to return America to "greatness through moral strength," suggesting that the nation had fallen—an image that Bush was clearly uncomfortable with. Within the Democratic coalition, similarly, Jesse Jackson represented the anguish of the African American community and linked its fortunes with a coalition of the "forgotten" and "disinherited." Chastising those who embrace the politically expedient, Jackson challenged his fellow candidates to reach for the "moral center," the godly response to the economic crisis.

In 1988, consequently, two distinct "communities of discontent" seemed ripe for mobilization. The question was, what political avenues were available to redress these grievances? Apparently, a number of leaders and followers concluded that conditions were ripe for presidential mobilization as a means of registering discontent. To paraphrase a popular book on Jackson's 1984 campaign, many partisans apparently felt that their "time had come." [34]

THE CANDIDATES AND THE CAMPAIGNS

No other national black leader can match the galvanizing effect achieved by Jesse Louis Jackson, with his intimate knowledge of the black church, his mastery of religious imagery, and his prophetic approach to politics. Jackson was ideally positioned to articulate the economic and cultural crisis in the black community, having focused on those two elements in his ministry for more than a decade. Indeed, his message was as much cultural as it was economic or racial. Throughout the 1980s Jackson dominated black politics, and despite the emergence of new black leaders, he continues to be a major player. Not only did all presidential candidates court him in 1992, but at least a couple implied that he would be an excellent running mate. To understand the power of Jesse Jackson and his role, one must appreciate that he is a product of the distinctive African American religious heritage.

It is an ironic legacy of slavery and Jim Crow that the black church emerged from the Civil War as the one institution "owned and operated" by black people themselves,[35] a fact that was to shape profoundly the revolution of the 1960s. For a century before the civil rights movement, the all-black congregation (primarily Baptist or Methodist but decidedly evangelical) was the social center, the refuge, the place where messages of comfort for the afflicted and judgment for oppressors could be heard. Tremendously diverse, black churches nonetheless produced a unique religious heritage, a combination of pietistic enthusiasm and prophetic witness. If America was the new Israel for the Puritans, it was Pharaoh's Egypt for many American blacks; thus biblical themes of liberation and the Promised Land possessed special poignancy and power. The centrality of the black minister was due in part to his economic independence from the white power structure, but it also owed something to his dynamic oratorical powers, a legacy of the evangelical heritage of the black experience. The combination of these elements produced a faith so strong among blacks that, when asked how important religion is to them (on a scale of 1-10), their mean response was greater than 9. This response surpasses that of every other group Gallup has surveyed worldwide. More blacks than whites, in fact, say they are active church members.[36]

Before the civil rights movement the political potential of this tightknit community structure was only intermittently realized, but the black church, often conservative and cautious before the revolution, would never be the same. It is now the most highly politicized sector of religious America. Black ministers endorse candidates from the pulpit, something even highly political white fundamentalist ministers usually avoid. They mobilize voter registration drives, raise money, and solicit volunteers for campaigns. Thus, although Walter Mondale complained about mixing religion and politics in 1984 (in reference to the religious right), 29 percent of his voters in Alabama (most of them black) had been urged by their preachers to back him; only 9 percent of Reagan's voters heard similar appeals.[37] Any political consultant would covet the formidable national network of churches led by forty thousand black ministers and bishops, most of whom campaigned actively in Jackson's behalf in 1988, serving as local and state coordinators, delegation leaders, and fund-raisers.

It is an understatement to say that Jackson capitalized on this resource: black congregations anchored his presidential crusades and remain the financial backbone of his Rainbow Coalition. A group of churches even provided Jackson's family with economic support during the campaign.[38] Jackson was able to capitalize on this resource only because his life was rooted in the prophetic tradition of the black church. As one black minister put it, "He is one of us. And I don't mean just that he's black."

Born the illegitimate son of a teen-age mother, Jackson in his quest for legitimacy found vent in his gift for blending the spiritual and the political. As we will see, he discovered the power of his own life as a religious metaphor of hope for the despairing. His roots in the religious tradition consequently allowed him to give eloquent voice to a broad critique of the smug politics of the 1980s. In an era of chic investment bankers and leveraged buyouts, Jackson represented the voiceless and dispossessed. In his speech at the 1988 Democratic Convention, he pleaded with the nation not to forget those who clean the bedpans and wash the commodes, who "catch the early bus" but cannot afford to stay in the very hospital beds they change. His message was profoundly religious and moral: the community had an obligation to care for the least of its brothers and sisters. To do otherwise was contrary to God's will.

Jackson strives to develop an alliance between his core black constituency and other disparate elements of the "left out" in American society. Financially supported by a flow of "love offerings" from black congregations, the peripatetic Jackson travels from one "point of challenge" to another. On one day he may travel to West Virginia to picket with striking coal miners; on another he will march with welfare recipients cut from public assistance rolls in Michigan. He expresses outrage with foreclosed farmers in Iowa; organizes a voter registration drive in response to the jailing of the black mayor of Birmingham, Alabama; sleeps in a homeless shelter in California; and ministers to dying AIDS patients in New York. Crisis and urgency: these are the watchwords of the Rainbow Coalition.

This sense of crisis and urgency is what unites Pat Robertson's politics with Jackson's. As host of "The 700 Club" (one of the most popular religious programs on television), Robertson cultivated a constituency for years, blending upscale technology with faith-healing charismatic practices to create what scholars term a "parachurch." To understand his appeal, and its limits, one must understand the place of charismatic churches within the broader evangelical world.

During the nineteenth century Protestant faith dominated American culture. Most believers adhered to orthodox Christian doctrine, with an emphasis on personal conversion and a passionate commitment to the Great Commission to evangelize the world. By the turn of the century, however, the advance of science and its application to biblical criticism split Protestant America into theological liberals, who embraced modernity, and theological traditionalists, who clung to the fundamentals of the faith. Distinct among the traditionalists was a group of charismatics, who emphasized emotional worship, faith healing, and gifts of the Holy Spirit. Many charismatics formed local independent churches, but some banded together in new Pentecostal denominations, such as the rapidly growing Assemblies of God, founded in 1914. For people who found modern life shallow and mainstream churches compromising, charismatic religion was a refuge. It attracted a sizable number of blacks as well as poor whites.

Remarkably, as liberal social and political changes rocked American society in the 1960s and 1970s, Pentecostal denominations experienced dramatic growth, blending with a contemporary charismatic renewal movement that spilled over into the mainline Protestant churches and became popular with Roman Catholics as well. As a protest against "rationalist" modernity, paranormal practices such as glossolalia, or "speaking in tongues," separated the faithful from the broader culture.[39] Morally puritanical, fervently religious, devoted to traditional values, and threatened by "libertine" popular culture, charismatics felt misunderstood or ignored by media moguls and political leaders. Yet their numbers swelled, and by 1988 they were ripe for political mobilization.

Marion G. "Pat" Robertson, son of a prominent U.S. senator from Virginia, experienced a religious conversion that changed the direction of his life and brought him into the heart of the charismatic fold. Abandoning a traditional career in law, he purchased a defunct television station that was the forerunner of the nation's first Christian television network, CBN. Unlike Jerry Falwell, who as an old-time fundamentalist eschews "Pentecostal excesses," Robertson brought the gifts of the Holy Spirit into prime time, cultivating a large and loyal following. As one of the pioneers of religious broadcasting, he honed the fund-raising techniques necessary to keep paid television ministries afloat. In the process he developed a formidable list of followers. Like St. Augustine, Robertson confesses to have lived a life of "wine, women, and song" before his born-again experience. Thus he can argue persuasively about the need for, and the power of, the religious revival he trumpets. Robertson's years as a minister have enabled him to sharpen his message—a withering critique of the chaos of a modern culture cut adrift from its moral and religious moorings.[40]

Each minister, in his own way, spoke to the moral yearnings of people in the midst of atomizing cultural and economic forces. As we will see in Chapter 4, this message was combined with political strategies based on the unique resources of churches in contemporary politics. Robertson stunned Republican party regulars, first in Michigan in 1986, when his backers seized control of the party organization. In Iowa in 1987 he won a straw poll and went on to defeat George Bush, the party's standing vice president, in the caucuses. Raising enormous sums of money and organizing newly registered Republicans, Robertson's campaign sparked intense battles with "country club" Republicans nationwide. This cultural clash was as intense as anything between the parties.

Although his campaign ultimately collapsed, Robertson unleashed a new cadre of Christian activists, many of whom plan to stay involved in politics (as was clear during the 1992 Republican National Convention).

Claiming that his Christian Coalition is the fastest growing independent political organization in the nation, Robertson envisions a struggle throughout the decade. Although related to other right-wing expressions, the Robertson campaign remains distinct in its constituency and message. For example, Pat Buchanan's presidential quest in 1992 attracted antitax and nativist voters (disproportionately men), whereas Robertson's appeal in 1988 was primarily to fervently religious women concerned about the breakup of the family, children at risk, and the like. Into the 1990s we continue to hear "regular" Republicans plaintively asking, "Who are these people anyway? What are we going to do with them?"

Jackson, in contrast to Robertson, had gained valuable experience as a candidate in 1984, and he capitalized on that experience in his 1988 campaign. Scoring respectable numbers in largely white Iowa, Minnesota, and New Hampshire, Jackson was able to ride a crest of increasing excitement into the South on Super Tuesday on March 8. With his popularity at its height in the black community, and with black churches as his organizing and fund-raising base, Jackson turned Super Tuesday against its creators. Designed to increase the clout of moderate and conservative Democrats in the nomination process, the coordinated southern primaries and caucuses instead rewarded Jackson with big wins in six states and gained him a host of delegates.[41] Jackson then stunned the Dukakis campaign with a smashing victory in Michigan, organizing black parishes as precincts and combining his support by African Americans with that of liberal activists and Arab Americans. Although the campaign finally stalled in Wisconsin and New York, Jackson never let up on Dukakis, demanding that his constituents not be taken for granted and that he be treated with respect. Dukakis was never able to handle these demands gracefully. By 1992 all Democratic presidential candidates seemed to acknowledge that respect was indeed owed to this leader and his followers. Clearly, the barometer of populist pressures increased in the 1980s and influenced politics into the following decade.

POPULISM AND CHARISMA

What enabled Jackson and Robertson to capitalize on popular discontent was an intangible but potent resource: religious charisma. Unfortunately, in modern parlance the word *charisma* has been shorn of its religious connotations. Yet no review of populists would be complete without an appreciation of the profound link between populism, religion, and the kind of charisma that the great sociologist Max Weber had in mind when he coined the term. Populist leaders are "spellbinders," leaders who sway their followers through religious signification. The complex blend of discontent and religious hope that often produces populist upheaval can be understood, in part, by probing into the nature of charismatic leadership.

It is helpful here to look at Ruth Ann Willner's penetrating study of political charisma, which draws upon Weber to illuminate the origins and characteristics of this kind of leadership.[42] In Jackson and Robertson, the populists of the 1980s, we find striking commonalities with other charismatic leaders. Charismatic leadership is intensely personal, resting on "devotion to the specific sanctity, heroism, or exemplary character of an individual person." [43] Followers "believe their leader to have superhuman qualities or to possess to an extraordinary degree the qualities highly esteemed in their culture." [44] The leader's special gift evokes blind loyalty from the followers, who invest in him an unqualified emotional commitment.

Willner notes the obvious religious implications of charismatic leadership. In a fascinating account of the rhetoric of Franklin D. Roosevelt, for example, she found FDR's oratory replete with allusions to the poetic King James Bible and evocations of classic religious literature such as *Pilgrim's Progress.* Roosevelt, the prophet and moralist, chastises "obeisance to Mammon" and the "money changers." He calls for the faithful to "abandon false prophets" so that they can "give light to them that sit in darkness." He makes sacred the political mission: "We of the Republic pledged ourselves to drive from the temple of our ancient faith those who had profaned it." [45] It is hard to imagine any contemporary Democrat, other than Jackson, who could speak in such terms (with the possible exception of Mario Cuomo, who evoked the name of St. Francis as the "true democrat" in his 1984 address to the Democratic National Convention). Charismatic spellbinders, in contrast to more conventional leaders, attempt to distill the mystic chords of memory into powerful tools of leadership. Although perhaps not so eloquent as Jackson in his rhetoric, Robertson also draws upon a rich biblical literature as a source of his power.

If we review the characteristics Weber attributed to charismatic leadership,[46] we find notable similarities with those of Pat Robertson and Jesse Jackson. First, the charismatic leader is "called" (in a sense by God), not chosen through some political or bureaucratic process, to embark on the historic mission. Both Jackson and Robertson approached their crusades as anointed missions. Neither had previously held elective office; both approached the political system from the outside. Jackson's fiery preaching, rooted in black Baptist culture, signified that he had received the call from God, that he had the gift. Robertson, who also viewed his political involvement as a divine mandate, suffered much abuse by political cartoonists as a result.

A second attribute of charismatic leaders, according to Weber, is that they gain recognition from their followers through a special "sign" or miraculous achievement. Robertson, for example, claimed that his run for the presidency was by divine appointment. As a charismatic Christian, he views life through the lens of the "secret kingdom" of spiritual signs that pierce the visible world.[47] Thus he unabashedly sought signs from God to clarify his calling to politics. As he described the famous prayer in 1985 to turn back Hurricane Gloria from Virginia Beach, Robertson placed what happened firmly in a biblical context. He "put out a fleece," just as the Old Testament leader Gideon had done. As recorded in the Book of Judges, Gideon, a simple man, was greeted by a messenger from God commanding him to lead Israel into battle. Gideon, seeking to test the authenticity of this call, asked for confirmation from God by a sign—a wet fleece on dry ground or a dry fleece on wet ground. Gideon put out a fleece, and God provided the sign. Robertson argues that he did not pray to turn back the hurricane out of spiritual hubris. Instead, as he recounted it,

> At 9:15 I knelt on the floor of my small dressing room and poured my heart out to the Lord. "Father," I said, "if I can't move a storm, how can I move a nation? Father, I am laying a fleece before You. If this storm hits our area, I am out of the presidential race completely." [48]

At 4:00 the next morning, Robertson writes, he awoke to find that the hurricane had suddenly veered away from the region before hitting land. "God had answered our prayers. Our region had been spared, but I was back in the presidential race. Only now I had been labeled the nut who thinks he can pray away hurricanes." [49]

But what of Jackson? Within his cultural context there is a striking indication of this seeking of signification. For Jackson that moment came when Martin Luther King, Jr., a modern-day Moses, was shot in Memphis. Claiming to have cradled the dying leader in his arms, Jackson played Joshua to King's Moses, and he wore the blood of the fallen leader as a sign of his charismatic succession. The national press, in this case, aided in the signifying. For Jackson the signifying continues. His prophetic style emphasizes "being there" at any point of challenge, exposing himself to the painful realities ignored by others. It is this style that explains his supporters' devotion to him—not only black ministers and elected officials but also the white leader of striking mine workers and former Texas agriculture commissioner and populist firebrand, Jim Hightower. Jackson alone, in person, championed their cause with them.

A third characteristic of the charismatic leader, according to Weber, is that he seems to his followers to be endowed with superhuman strength, energy, wisdom, or cunning. We find evidence of such attributes in Jackson and Robertson. Jackson arguably is one of the most energetic and natural campaigners ever born on American soil. Aides marvel at his sense of history, his courage, his timing, his flare for the dramatic, his energy. Jackson does nothing to subdue such talk. Comparing himself with the other candidates, he once remarked, "If we six were dropped anywhere in the world with no money, who do you think would lead the others out?" Robertson, too, has been welcomed by his followers as a religious figure as much as a political one. "He is anointed," said one of his followers during the caucuses.

A fourth characteristic noted by Weber is organizational style. Organizations run by charismatic leaders tend to operate loosely and unconventionally, depending on the support of gifts—almost to the point of extortion. Criticisms of the finances of Jackson's Operation Push in Chicago confirm the organization's "charismatic" quality. Moreover, anyone who has watched either Jackson or Robertson raising money marvels at the way charisma can call forth financial sacrifices from their followers.

Finally, Weber stresses the instability of charismatic leadership. Charismatic leaders must continually prove themselves through religious signs and achievements; without these outward signs their leadership will likely decay into a routine form of authority. Perhaps this explains the almost desperate peripatetic quality of Jackson's work, as he seeks to maintain his charisma. It may also explain Robertson's oscillation between "charismatic" and more routine leadership. His writings still evoke gifts of prophecy, yet he has deemphasized faith healing on "The 700 Club," offering instead financial and family advice, all the while building his broadcasting empire.

The temptations—some might say dangers—of charismatic leadership also are visible in the two movements. Robertson's tendency to invent "funny facts" during the 1988 campaign arose perhaps from an overconfidence in himself as God's vehicle. Similarly, Jackson's proclivity to interpret even the most mundane public policy issues in gospel terms at times wears thin, even to the admiring.[50] Both Jackson and Robertson, moreover, come from milieus that invest them with nearly unchallenged authority. These points raise questions about how they might actually govern in the less self-contained Washington environment.

But governing aside, Jackson and Robertson succeeded in mobilizing their followers by assuming the extraordinary qualities of the God-anointed. Throughout his career Jackson has explicitly identified himself with biblical figures. According to Barbara Reynolds, "The messianic motif is nurtured by his own comparisons of himself to Jesus, Ezekiel, or David fighting off Goliath. He often portrays himself as a black Moses opening up the Red Sea." [51] Jackson's messianic language abounded in his speeches as early as 1969,[52] and he frequently identifies his own struggle with Jesus' redemptive suffering. Whatever the forum, Jackson liberally sprinkles biblical allusions. Robertson, too, embodies a religious charisma in his "gifts of the spirit": he healed, prophesied, and was touched for special mission by God. Both leaders are united in a "premodern" religious vision that emphasizes spiritual legitimation rather than legal, rational, or bureaucratic forms of authority. As we shall see, Jackson and Robertson both reached out to their followers through religious and community identifications that transcend mundane politics. Their followers responded with almost a religious devotion: "Jesse is a balm in Gilead;" [53] "Pat is a man of God." And as we shall see, there is a link between the courses of their lives and their identifications with their followers. Leaders are, in part, made by the dilemmas and needs of followers.[54]

SUMMARY

Discontent, like hope, is inherent in the human condition. At times it finds mass political expression. Periodically throughout American history movements have registered the discontent of particular communities. In the late nineteenth century rapid economic and social changes inspired a movement that spread through the prairie states like the proverbial windswept fire. Adopting the populist mantle, William Jennings Bryan seized the presidential nomination of the Democratic party in 1896 and twice again thereafter. Bryan denounced "capitalists," who exploited the poor, with the same vigor that he castigated demon rum and the doctrine of evolution. Weaving biblical themes into his speeches, he could sound like Karl Marx one minute and a pietist preacher the next. But the common thread of his oratory was a critique of elites whose greed, materialism, and libertarian immorality undermined the economic well-being and moral fiber of common folk.[55] This blending of moral traditionalism with economic radicalism was not uncommon in the American past. In contemporary politics, however, the populist heritage is split. Both sides of the political spectrum must contend with discontents in the ranks. When Jesse Jackson champions the dispossessed and afflicts the comfortable, when Pat Robertson trumpets moral renewal and chastises cultural elites for flouting traditional values, we hear echoes through American history, echoes of discontent.

NOTES

1. Drew Digby, "Robertson Vows to Push Quest Until He Wins," *Denver Post*, April 4, 1988, 1A.
2. Mark Obmascik, "Wide Spectrum Crams Churches to Hear Jackson," *Denver Post*, April 4, 1988, 1A.
3. The word *prophetic* is often misunderstood. Its richer biblical meaning involves a God-inspired critique of the times; it does not simply connote prediction. A biblical prophet called upon the people to live up to God's plan and commandments. Often prophets warned of what would happen if the people did not turn from their wicked ways. In this sense they "predicted" the future.
4. Extensive scholarship has documented the structural factors and party dynamics that produce divided party government. So strong are these forces that even considerable popular frustration does not seem able to upset the trend. Voter alienation and electoral decay seem apt descriptions of the current state of affairs.
5. Marshall Frady, in a masterful three-part series on Jesse Jackson in the *New Yorker*, coined the phrase "gospel populist" to describe Jackson. See "Profiles: Outsider, I—The Gift," Feb. 3, 1992; 36-69; "II—History Is upon Us," Feb. 10, 1992, 41-75; and "III—Without Portfolio," Feb. 17, 1992, 39-69.
6. Peter Worsley, "The Concept of Populism," in *Populism: Its Meaning and National Characteristics*, ed. Ghita Ionescu and Ernest Gellner (London: Macmillan, 1969), 248.
7. One textbook on American government explicitly employs this definition as contrasted with both conservatism and liberalism. See Jack E. Holmes, Michael J. Engelhardt, and Robert E. Elder, *American Government: Essentials and Perspectives* (New York: McGraw-Hill, 1991), chap. 1.
8. See William S. Maddox and Stuart A. Lilie, *Beyond Liberal and Conservative: Reassessing the Political Spectrum* (Washington, D.C.: Cato Institute, 1984), which classifies populists as those whose beliefs embrace economically progressive and morally traditional elements. Drawing upon survey research, the authors conclude that the electorate is distributed in the following fashion: liberals, 24 percent; populists, 26 percent; conservatives, 17 percent; and libertarians, 18 percent. The 1980 distribution of nonwhites found 47 percent of the nonwhites to be populists, 30 percent liberals, and only 5 percent each libertarians and conservatives; the remainder is unclassifiable.
9. Ibid., 92.
10. See especially Gabriel Almond and Sidney Verba, *The Civic Culture* and *The Civic Culture Revisited* (Newbury Park, Calif.: Sage, 1989); and Robert Bellah et al., *Habits of the Heart* (Berkeley: University of California Press, 1985).
11. See especially Michael Thompson, Richard Ellis, and Aaron Wildavksy, *Cultural Theory* (Boulder: Westview Press, 1990); and Aaron Wildavsky, "Choosing Preferences by Constructing Institutions: A Cultural Theory of Preference Formation," *American Political Science Review* 81 (March 1987): 3-21.

12. The literature on the religious influence is voluminous. See especially Sydney Ahlstrom, *A Religious History of the American People* (New Haven: Yale University Press, 1972); Andrew Greeley, *The Denominational Society* (Glenview, Ill.: Scott, Foresman, 1972); Will Herberg, *Protestant, Catholic, Jew* (New York: Doubleday, 1955); Sydney E. Mead, *The Nation with the Soul of a Church* (New York: Harper and Row, 1975); A. James Reichley, *Religion in American Public Life* (Washington, D.C.: Brookings Institution, 1985); and, of course, Alexis de Tocqueville, *Democracy in America,* trans. George Lawrence, ed. J. P. Mayer and A. P. Kerr (Garden City, N.Y.: Anchor, 1969). Two recent texts summarize nicely the broad influence of religion on American politics. See Robert Booth Fowler, *Religion and Politics in America* (Metuchen, N.J.: Scarecrow, 1985); and Kenneth D. Wald, *Religion and Politics in the United States,* 2d ed. (Washington, D.C.: CQ Press, 1992).
13. See George Gallup, Jr., "Religion in America, 50 Years: 1935-1985," Gallup Report 236, May 1985.
14. Robert A. Nisbet, *The Quest for Community* (New York: Oxford University Press, 1953); Richard A. Merelman, *Making Something of Ourselves* (Berkeley: University of California Press, 1984); Bellah et al., *Habits of the Heart.*
15. This point is stressed by E. E. Schattschneider, *The Semisovereign People* (New York: Holt, Rinehart, 1960); and by Mancur Olson, *The Logic of Collective Action* (Cambridge: Harvard University Press, 1965).
16. See especially C. Eric Lincoln and Lawrence H. Mamiya, *The Black Church in the African American Experience* (Durham, N.C.: Duke University Press, 1990); and Fowler, *Religion and Politics in America.*
17. Dean M. Kelley, *Why Conservative Churches Are Growing* .(New York: Harper and Row, 1972).
18. See Mickey Crews, *The Church of God: A Social History* (Knoxville: University of Tennessee Press, 1990); Margaret M. Poloma, *The Assemblies of God at the Crossroads: Charisma and Institutional Dilemmas* (Knoxville: University of Tennessee Press, 1989); and George M. Marsden, *Fundamentalism and American Culture* (New York: Oxford University Press, 1980).
19. Francis Fukuyama, " The End of History?" *National Interest* (Summer 1989). See also Fukuyama, *The End of History and the Last Man* (New York: Free Press, 1992).
20. Theodore Lowi, Rothbaum Lectures, University of Oklahoma, Norman, November 1991.
21. See especially the argument by Robert B. Reich, *The Work of Nations* (New York: Knopf, 1991).
22. Don Kash, *Perpetual Innovation* (New York: Basic Books, 1989).
23. Daniel Bell, *The Cultural Contradictions of Capitalism* (New York: Basic Books, 1976).
24. Ibid.
25. Bruce B. Lawrence, *Defenders of God: The Fundamentalist Revolt against the Modern Age* (San Francisco: Harper and Row, 1989).
26. John C. Green, "Pat Robertson and the Latest Crusade," *Social Science Quarterly* (forthcoming).

27. Earl Black and Merle Black, *Politics and Society in the South* (Cambridge: Harvard University Press, 1987).
28. Robert Wuthnow, *The Restructuring of American Religion* (Princeton: Princeton University Press, 1988).
29. Gallup, "Religion in America."
30. See Gregory D. Squires, "Economic Restructuring, Urban Development, and Race: The Political Economy of Civil Rights in 'Post Industrial America,'" *Western Political Quarterly* 43 (March 1990): 201-217; and Jewelle Taylor Gibbs et al., *Young, Black, and Male in America: An Endangered Species* (Dover, Mass.: Auburn House, 1988), on industrial flight from the inner city; William Julius Wilson, *The Declining Significance of Race* (Chicago: University of Chicago Press, 1980), and *The Truly Disadvantaged: The Inner City, the Underclass, and Public Policy* (Chicago: University of Chicago Press, 1987), on related measures of cultural crisis and lagging economic attainment; Ann M. Nichols-Casebolt, "Black Families Headed by Single Mothers: Growing Numbers and Increasing Poverty," *Social Work* (July-August 1988): 306-313, on out-of-wedlock births; Bill McAllister, "The Plight of Young Black Men in America," *Washington Post National Weekly Edition*, Feb. 12-18, 1990, on college attendance; Jane Gross, "Collapse of Inner-City Families Creates America's New Orphans," *New York Times*, March 29, 1992, 1, on "zero-parent households"; AP wire story, "One out of Four Young Black Men in Justice System," *Daily Oklahoman*, Feb. 27, 1990, on black incarceration rates; and Jason DeParle, "Suffering in the Cities Persists as U.S. Fights Other Battles," *New York Times*, Jan. 27, 1991, on welfare rates among children. For a disturbing portrait of self-destructive behavior in a Washington, D.C., ghetto, see Leon Dash, *When Children Want Children: The Urban Crisis of Teenage Childbearing* (New York: Morrow, 1989); on the stark situation in the inner cities, see the editorial by Mortimer B. Zuckerman, "The New Realism," *U.S. News and World Report*, May 25, 1992, 94.
31. Allen D. Hertzke, "Christian Fundamentalists and the Imperatives of American Politics," in *Religious Resurgence and Politics in the Contemporary World*, ed. Emile Sahliyeh (Albany: State University of New York Press, 1990).
32. This point is made by Robert Booth Fowler, "The Failure of the New Christian Right" (Paper presented at the Ethics and Public Policy Center Conference on Evangelicals, Politics, and the Religious New Right, Washington, D.C., Nov. 14-15, 1990); and by Steve Bruce, *The Rise and Fall of the New Christian Right* (New York: Oxford University Press, 1988).
33. Bob DeMoss, "Help Your Kids Learn to Discern," *Focus on the Family Citizen*, Aug. 20, 1990.
34. Lucius J. Barker, *Our Time Has Come: A Delegate's Diary of Jesse Jackson's 1984 Presidential Campaign* (Urbana: University of Illinois Press, 1988).
35. See Fowler, *Religion and Politics in America;* and Reichley, *Religion in American Public Life.*
36. Gallup, "Religion in America."
37. Reichley, *Religion in American Public Life,* 284.

38. According to the Rev. James Holley, close friend and campaign organizer for Jackson in Detroit, Mich., a group of churches pledged to provide Jackson's family with monthly sums in lieu of his lost salary during the campaign. (Holley, interview with author, Detroit, December 1991.)
39. See Poloma, *Assemblies of God at the Crossroads.*
40. Pat Robertson, *America's Dates with Destiny* (Nashville: Thomas Nelson, 1986).
41. Jackson won the South Carolina caucuses the weekend before Super Tuesday; he then marched to victory in five other southern states the following Tuesday.
42. Willner consciously applies Max Weber's formulation of charismatic authority in analyzing what made diverse figures, such as Franklin Delano Roosevelt, Adolf Hitler, Fidel Castro, and Mohandas Gandhi, "charismatically" powerful. See Ruth Ann Willner, *The Spellbinders: Charismatic Political Leadership* (New Haven: Yale University Press, 1984).
43. Max Weber, quoted in ibid., 4.
44. Ibid., 6.
45. Ibid., 154-156.
46. Ibid., 202-203, 8.
47. Pat Robertson, with Bob Slosser, *The Secret Kingdom* (Nashville: Thomas Nelson, 1982).
48. Pat Robertson, *The Plan* (Nashville: Thomas Nelson, 1989), 64.
49. Ibid, 66-67.
50. See Frady's account in his *New Yorker* series.
51. Barbara A. Reynolds, *Jesse Jackson: America's David* (Washington, D.C.: JFJ Associates, 1985), 13.
52. Georgia May Swanson, "Messiah or Manipulator? A Burkean Cluster Analysis of the Motivations Revealed in the Selected Speeches of the Reverend Jesse Louis Jackson" (Ph.D. diss., Bowling Green State University, 1982).
53. Reynolds, *Jesse Jackson,* 43.
54. James MacGregor Burns, *Leadership* (New York: Harper and Row, 1978).
55. Paolo Coletta, *William Jennings Bryan,* 3 vols. (Lincoln: University of Nebraska Press, 1964, vol. 1, and 1969, vols. 2 and 3). See also Willard Smith, *The Social and Religious Thought of William Jennings Bryan* (Lawrence, Kan.: Coronado Press, 1975).

2

Echoes of Populist Discontent: The Historical Legacy

Profile 1: As a Christian evangelical, he filled his quixotic presidential campaign with gospel fervor, which he used to mobilize an army of followers across the nation. He was criticized for bringing a pietist's simplistic view of moral absolutes into political battle, yet he firmly believed that the nation yearned for moral leadership. His railings against the secular teaching of evolution and condemnations of those who wanted to relax moral laws made him the target of East Coast urban elites. Believing that the strength of the nation lay in its religious heritage, he wanted to reestablish America's rootedness in biblical truths.

Profile 2: As one of the great orators of a generation, he tirelessly crisscrossed the nation in his crusades for the dispossessed, impoverished, and forgotten. Although some Democrats viewed him as a spoiler in his repeated presidential campaigns, he saw himself as the conscience of the party. Through the force of his personal charisma he galvanized crowds with "prophetic" and egalitarian messages in behalf of the downtrodden—though many continued to see his remedies as unrealistic. Viewed as naïve, even pacifist, on foreign policy, he called the nation to live up to its highest ideals, to put faith in dialogue and respect for human rights rather than in force.

Readers who recognize Pat Robertson and Jesse Jackson in the two profiles may be surprised to find that these portraits accurately describe a single figure: the great turn-of-the-century populist William Jennings Bryan, who was nominated three times for the presidency by the Democratic party. Bryan was not unusual in his blend of religious traditionalism and economic radicalism, though perhaps he was one of the most dramatic examples. Nineteenth-century populists, in fact, commonly united progressive economic ideas with traditional cultural and religious values. What knit these populist stands together was their concern with the destructive consequences of unchecked individualism, particularly the avarice or immorality of powerful elites. The slave master, the robber baron, the banker, the saloonkeeper—these images of destructive (though powerful) individuals focused the outrage of a generation of reformers, including the populists.

In this chapter we will see how local religious communities have served in American history to vent periodic discontent with the perceived excesses of individualism. One cannot fully appreciate the place of Jesse Jackson or Pat Robertson in American history without understanding the role of this communal element. Indeed, the celebrated "liberal tradition" in the United States—individualistic, skeptical, pragmatic, capitalist—has coexisted with communal practice and religious vision. Populist leaders, for example, interpreted the massive impoverishment of farmers in the late 1800s as a failure of the nation to live up to its "republican" and religious ideals rather than its liberal and individualistic ones. As farmers began to organize politically, populist thinkers offered an intellectual critique of the emerging liberal order with its perceived greed and selfishness. The populists harkened back to an era of perceived communitarian Christian values and republican virtues, when individuals worked for the good of their brothers and sisters, not just for selfish gain. In analyzing the source of misery and dislocation, they spoke to a timeless tension in American life between liberal, individualist, and materialist realities and Christian, republican, and communitarian visions. In Jackson's and Robertson's crusades we hear distinct echoes of this tension.

Religious faith, because it embodies transcendent moral obligations, has often served in the United States as a repository of communal habits and visions. Not surprisingly, churches and religious leaders periodically become vehicles for the expression of popular discontent with perceived deleterious tendencies in the evolving liberal order. To see this clearly, however, we must broaden our view of societal cleavages beyond the Marxist category of economic class to include the cultural dimension. What we discover is that average citizens may object just as much to the perceived hegemony of cultural elites as they do to economic exploitation—or that the two are often blended. If humans do not live by bread alone but by spiritual hungers as well, populist discontent may rise, as we will see, from either source.

THE INDIVIDUAL AND THE COMMUNITY: THE PURITAN DILEMMA

A dilemma lies at the heart of the American experience, perhaps at the heart of any liberal culture that promotes individual freedom and striving: what is to ensure that destructive individual selfishness will not undermine the community structures that nurture and sustain individuals?[1] Although this question deeply vexed the earliest Puritan thinkers, it breathes with a special urgency in the modern age. Scholars from diverse fields have noted the emergence of a new kind of individualism eating away at the body politic.[2] Uprooted from traditional communities and thrust into the maelstrom of perpetual change, modern individuals are at once freer and more autonomous than ever before. Yet that freedom seems to have brought with it the breakup of families and communal bonds once thought essential to a healthy society. From the social sciences to literature, the picture of this new autonomous individual is less likely to emerge as a Jeffersonian yeoman (or even a Nietzschean *übermensch)* than as a "dysfunctional" sufferer of anomie, rootlessness, and alienation. As we will see in the next chapter, both Jackson and Robertson articulate a conscious critique of this kind of self-possessed individualism.

Given this contemporary crucible, the ways in which past societies worked through this problem may tutor our modern, liberally ascendant world. Few struggled as mightily with the dilemma of the "free individual in community" as the much-maligned Puritans of the seventeenth and eighteenth centuries. Embarking on an "errand into the wilderness," they sought to build a holy commonwealth in which the freely consenting individual's liberty was to do "that only which is good, just and honest." [3] But the vastness of the wilderness meant that individuals whose private visions differed from the community's could claim their own errand, if not in Boston then in Rhode Island or Pennsylvania. The Puritans' quest to retain the intensity and purity of the original mission was doubly difficult; they had to contend with a seemingly natural waning of religious fervor and with the challenge to authority represented by alternative communities.

American history, consequently, has been marked by a recurrent, perhaps natural, social cycle: a period of intense religious life is followed by neglect and declension, which is followed by calls for renewal and awakening.[4] The Puritan heritage, after all, began as a passionate denunciation of lax churches, complacent leaders, and immoral society—a vision that shook seventeenth-century Europe and inspired settlements in the New World. But then as day-to-day commerce prevailed and religious intensity waned, fresh calls emerged to reclaim the purity and vision of former days. Perry Miller recounts that barely thirty years into their mission the Puritan divines sensed the imminent demise of their experiment if corrupting trends were not quickly reversed. Indeed, by 1679 Puritan leaders were cataloging in vivid detail the sins of the people "destitute of civic spirit." They cited land speculation, sharp business practices, and crowded taverns. They noted a "shocking extravagance in attire," "an increase in swearing and a spreading disposition to sleep at sermons," and a rising rate of "bastardy." [5] Jesse Jackson's warning of an "ethical collapse" in contemporary America and Pat Robertson's call to "return America to greatness through moral strength" are reminiscent of these concerns.

Calls for reform, even stirring movements of revival, are a central part of the American experience.[6] As William McLoughlin argues, religious awakenings arise when daily life in society deviates too far from moral and religious understandings that legitimate authority.[7] Complex though they are, great cultural movements spawned by religious revivals have profoundly shaped American society and, by fallout, have influenced American economic and political institutions. McLoughlin contends that periodic religious awakenings are both fruitful and necessary for the culture to adapt to the traumas of social change. The Revolution of 1776, the abolitionist movement, and other sea changes in American history are impossible to understand without appreciating the religious revivals that led to them. For example, McLoughlin echoes A. James Reichley's contention that religious renewal in the colonies sowed the seeds of discontent with English rule.[8] McLoughlin also points to the antislavery societies that sprang up in the wake of frontier revivals as testament to the way changes in religious consciousness and practice created tension with existent life.

It is perhaps not too disingenuous or circular to say that, at a fundamental level, discontent appears to drive this process of declension and renewal. By definition, the contented and self-satisfied are not disposed to enthusiastic movements or social unrest. Take, for example, the religious revolution in the 1730s and 1740s, known as the Great Awakening, which began the process that transformed austere Calvinism into American evangelicalism and served as a defining experience for the emerging nation.[9] What Jonathan Edwards, George Whitefield, and other evangelists ignited was nothing less than a populist and emotional pietism that threatened established elites. Miller observes that by 1740 the educated and upper classes on the seaboard "tired of the squabbling of the seventeenth century, and turned to the more pleasing and not at all contentious generalities of eighteenth-century rationalism." But this left "the spiritual hungers of the lower classes . . . ordinary folk" unsatisfied. In short, according to Miller, "The Great Awakening in New England was an uprising of the common people who declared that what Harvard and Yale graduates were teaching was too academic." [10] Thus preaching that departed from scholastic reasoning and directly appealed to the emotions of listeners seemed to resonate with the raw wilderness experience. As a byproduct it produced a new form of popular leadership:

> What he [Edwards] realized . . . was that a leader could no longer stand before the people giving them mathematically or logically impregnable postulates of the eternally good, just and honest. That might work in 1640 or in Europe . . . but not in the American Wilderness. . . . By 1740 the leader had to get down amongst them, and bring them by actual participation into an experience that was no longer private and privileged, but social and communal.[11]

By his identification with, and excitement over, popular religious movements, Edwards, no less a Calvinist than earlier Puritan divines in his understanding of human sinfulness, nonetheless helped to forge an optimistic, democratic, and characteristically American view of the potential for social renewal and moral transformation. He also helped to legitimate a more populist church response to the exigencies of life in the expanding nation. In a way both Jesse Jackson and Pat Robertson—in their stirring calls for moral renewal, in the pietistic fervor of their movements—embody a similar moral and religious response to the exigencies of modernity.

We see here another echo of our own age. As educated and urbane Protestants in colonial America adopted a more liberal and "enlightened" theology, they found themselves out of touch with the spiritual yearnings of common people. In the three decades before the American Revolution, churches led by these liberal, rationalist clergy had rapidly declined in membership while evangelical churches thrived.[12] The political significance of this popular religious revival was that it prepared the way for the break with England by creating a society of people who saw themselves as increasingly distinct and invested with a prophetic mission.[13] This revival set the stage for recurring movements of transformation and reform as Americans continued to measure day-to-day conditions of life against the standard of religiously inspired ideals.

This evangelical contribution to democratic ideals and practice was as "baffling" to deists such as Benjamin Franklin as it is to many historians and political scientists today.[14] Yet Eldon Eisenach has documented "strong correlations between radically democratizing political beliefs and evangelical religion in the 1750s," from Connecticut and Massachusetts to the southern states.[15] Members of churches formed or transformed by the Great Awakening consistently backed more "radical" democratic state constitutions. "In the South as well as the North, the most democratic features of the first state constitutions were often proposed by the same groups which insisted on oaths asserting the truth of biblical revelation and belief in the trinity."[16] This tendency carried over into the nineteenth century; Baptist and Methodist revivals were central in democratizing the culture and polity of the new nation.[17]

We can see that a kind of religiously inspired populism began to emerge early in the American republic. To be sure, this populism could take a mean turn, but its contribution to majoritarian democracy should not be minimized. As Robert Shalhope observes, throughout the period before the Revolution and shortly thereafter, Baptists, Shakers, separatists, and other evangelicals found themselves persecuted, from Boston to Virginia—whipped, thrown in jail, their churches closed down—because their popular moral fervor threatened the social hierarchy of the established religious and political elites. With the Revolution, however, the gentry's position was undercut by its necessary embrace of republican rhetoric against monarchy and privilege. Cosmopolitan elites who opposed the king, consequently, found themselves dependent for support on rural Christians whose revolutionary enthusiasm was fueled more by the millennialist fervor of evangelical religion than by classical republican theories. Still, republican virtues of courage and sacrifice dovetailed nicely with Christian faith, and for a moment at least individualistic behavior was submerged nationally in the communalist imperative of revolutionary sacrifice.[18]

The tension between populist, majoritarian democracy and liberal individualism, however, emerged again in the constitutional era, when fear of the demos by elites led to the construction of institutional structures that would protect individual liberty against the "passions" of the majority. Not surprisingly, this era was a time of religious declension. Again a wave of religious revivals at the century's end infused the small-town and rural folk with a renewed populist conviction that they must be heard. Ironically, Thomas Jefferson, a deist who predicted wrongly that the next generation would become Unitarian, captured the presidency in part because he channeled the popular uprising of Baptists and other evangelical dissenters against the more cosmopolitan Federalists.[19] Because the population of the new nation was pervasively rural, a certain continuity emerged in a localist culture, which continued to stress evangelical piety, majority rule, and communalist norms despite national trends that would chip away at this vision. To understand better the clash of this culture with the emerging liberal order, we must look at the contrasting interpretations of the founding era.

POPULIST TENSIONS IN THE NEW NATION

Writing in the 1950s, Louis Hartz argued that from its inception the American experience was dominated by a liberal consensus: a commitment to individual autonomy, materialism, and a truncated vision of community and state.[20] Adherents to this school of interpretation suggest that individualism left America "without a sense of moral community" or a sense of the public good.[21] Because liberalism blessed selfish striving, it produced in America "a democracy of cupidity rather than a democracy of fraternity."[22] Moreover, the liberal tendency to equate liberty with property or material pleasure led Americans from the Founders on to view the individual as little more than "an atom of self-interest."[23] Thus the Framers abandoned any hope for civic virtue as a support for the new Republic, placing their faith instead in mechanisms that channeled self-interest into publicly benign ways. The American republic, then, was rooted in such liberal motifs as private property, individual moral autonomy, and pursuit of self-interest.

Contrasted with this view is one of the most remarkable trends in American historiography: the revival of the so-called republican tradition. Challenging Hartz's claim that self-interested liberalism dominated the national drama,[24] republican theorists have mounted an impressive case that early Americans understood virtuous citizenship as the foundation of the new Republic.[25] Fired by revolutionary fervor, Americans of various stripes came to associate certain sturdy virtues—courage, integrity, frugality, temperance, industry—with the survival of republics, which history told them were fragile and subject to moral decay. As J. G. A. Pocock put it, "The fear of encroaching corruption helped drive the Americans to the renewal of virtue in a republic and the rejection of the parliamentary monarchy from which, all agreed, some measure of corruption was inseparable."[26] Americans shared the conviction that the "sacrifice of individual interests" to the common good lay at the heart of the quest to preserve the revolutionary moment.[27] In contrast, social distinctions, selfishness, and the love of luxury were viewed as inherent underminers of the new republic.

This scholarship impressively documents the power of republican thought, especially during the historic moment when Americans enjoyed the unique opportunity to create a republic.[28] Educated Americans embraced the Greek and Roman classics, while the less literate received their republicanism filtered through "plays, newspapers, orations, and charges to grand juries."[29] The "manly" virtues of courage, fortitude, and devotion to the public weal were promulgated through these means, as Americans drew moral lessons from Shakespeare's *Julius Caesar* and other plays that contrasted republican virtues with selfish corruption.[30]

There are, of course, enormous complexities in this scholarship that relate to regional and class differences and interpretations of language. Republican virtue might have meant one thing to the yeoman Baptist in

Virginia and another to the Anglican gentry; it might have meant one thing to the Boston merchant and another to the small-town separatist in the Connecticut Valley; and it could have meant still another thing to the Pennsylvania Quaker. Moreover, the historical conflict between the republican ideal of manly virtue and the Christian ethic of meekness was submerged in revolutionary unity. Otherwise, it is hard to imagine how such a pervasively religious society could have countenanced a Machiavellian republicanism hostile to Christianity. Finally, republican theorists themselves have observed that the moment was short-lived, rooted in a unique historical context of revolution and statecraft that would soon be overwhelmed by the emerging commercial reality.[31] In his magisterial study, Gordon Wood describes the end of classical politics as coming in the wake of the Constitution.[32] And Forrest McDonald, while acknowledging that Americans readily adopted republican rhetoric and symbols during the revolutionary era, suggests that republican commitment was shallow and ephemeral.[33] Thus James Madison's imprint on the American Constitution—a dependence upon the structure of political institutions to protect the Republic—while clothed in republican language, had abandoned the vision of a virtuous citizenry for "auxiliary precautions." [34]

In light of these complexities, some scholars have recently suggested that a synthesis of the republican and liberal traditions would more accurately depict the founding era. They argue that classical liberalism is misinterpreted when shorn of its supporting precepts based on Christianity and natural law. As McDonald notes, John Locke believed that natural law placed strict limits on property-holding free individuals,[35] and Locke himself used powerful religious metaphors to describe the corruptions of money and endless acquisition. That rendering of Locke, McDonald notes, better "accorded with the goals of the Patriots of 1776" than the materialistic and individualistic Locke of Hartz. Similarly, although Adam Smith is now interpreted as a champion of the unfettered individual, his work assumed that ethical codes or moral sentiments would underpin a society of free individuals—an understanding shared by Jesse Jackson and Pat Robertson. Moreover, Smith was read and understood by revolutionary Americans as supporting a republican check on monarchs and their mercantile corruption.[36] To people living at the time, academic distinctions, of course, often would have been meaningless. People simultaneously could have been devout Christians, striving individualists, and nurturers of republican virtue in their young. Thus it was not inherently contradictory, as James Kloppenberg observes, for citizens in colonial America to embrace Locke and Smith (as libertarians) and yet to continue operating their communities under strict religious mores and through republican exhortation.[37]

The liberal order we experience today, with its moral relativism, is far removed from the one early Americans might have embraced along with their Christian faith and their republican ideology.

In this historical debate, however, we often fail to appreciate fully the extent to which the lives of many citizens were rooted in religious conceptions that, strictly speaking, conformed to neither the liberal nor the republican view.[38] To be sure, the Protestant ideas of covenant theology, the priesthood of all believers, and work as a calling did support aspects of the emerging liberal order.[39] And religious views about duty and citizenship fortified the classical republican virtues of courage and sacrifice for the broader good.[40] But the religious vision, first Puritan, then evangelical, remained distinct from either school of thought, as indicated by the fact that both republicans and liberals are often ambivalent about the contribution of orthodox piety to the new order.[41] For example, McDonald suggests that religious language and culture were deeper than republican argot and that they were synthesized in infinite ways to support the republican moment. Indeed, republicanism often looked like a secularized form of Puritan public virtue. Thus, although John Adams promoted a "passion for the public good," his "republicanism seems little more than John Winthrop's puritanism revisited." Adams wrote to his wife Abigail that he labored to produce a free government, not so that his children could live in "ease and elegance," but that they might "live upon thin Diet, wear mean Cloths, and work hard, with Cheerful Hearts and free Spirits." Moreover, in Virginia the most "extreme" republican sentiment was found in those places where the Baptist Great Awakening "had its strongest impact."[42]

Why has this religious and communitarian motif been given little attention? One explanation is simply that we have misread the founding era and have applied contemporary interpretations to such concepts as liberty and individualism, interpretations that diverge significantly from what eighteenth-century citizens had in mind. Ronald Peters, in a compelling analysis of the Massachusetts constitution of 1780, argues that the individual was ultimately subordinate to the community in the understanding of those who created the social compact in Massachusetts.[43] Popular sovereignty, as embodied in majority rule, fostered an expansive, some might say intrusive, concern with the public good. Liberty was understood to mean not exclusively individual rights (common parlance today) but the right of the community to self-government. A reading of state constitutions and other documents suggests that a rich and religiously infused conception of the public interest prevailed before the formation of the national Constitution. State constitutions admonished citizens to espouse the virtues of moderation, temperance, and frugality.[44] The religious elements of that conception are evident in the constitutional provisions for publicly supported religious and moral education as a means of tempering destructive individualism and fostering the republican virtues of sacrifice, courage, and service to community and country.

Liberalism, understood as the pursuit of individual self-interest, can thus be contrasted with both the republican and the Christian conceptions of a human telos achieved in a nurturing or restraining communal context. But it was local Christian communalism, rather than the more expansive communalism of the republican tradition, that sustained this vision into the nineteenth century.[45] When populists in the nineteenth century challenged individuals to rise above self-interest, they clothed their republicanism with a religious garment. My analysis, though not intended to minimize the insights of liberal or republican historiography, highlights the importance of an independent religious motif in the shaping of American history.

Cosmopolitan Culture versus Local Citizenry

In attempting to understand this religious motif, it is helpful to contrast the more cosmopolitan culture that shaped the national Constitution with the more parochial rural citizenry who often held sway in the state governments. Cosmopolitans might be "conservative" wealthy merchants and Anglican clergy who "valued social stability, fostered capitalistic economic relations, and believed in their own political stewardship." Or they might be "liberal" ship captains, craftsmen, and small manufacturers who embraced commercial life but also held egalitarian ideas such as equality of opportunity.[46] Challenging both kinds of cosmopolitans were the locals, who clung to a communal vision of a "moral" economy and culture. Although diverse and amorphous, the locals drew their "meaning and identity" from "family, church, and community." Baptists in Virginia, for example, "sought an orderly, moral community, a system of social control in the people themselves."[47] Therefore the same people who sought to control drunkenness and gambling also pushed for debtor relief, to the horror of more elite lenders.

Most Americans, it must be remembered, continued to live in isolated rural communities throughout the eighteenth and early nineteenth centuries. These citizens largely "drew meaning in their lives from a traditional corporate world rather than the entrepreneurial individualism of those advocating a market economy and a more open, competitive society."[48] After the Revolution, not surprisingly, the political interests in most states were polarized into cosmopolitan and local factions. The Constitutional Convention, in part, can be interpreted as a response of national cosmopolitans to the "excesses" in states controlled by locals. In a sense, the convention was a liberal attempt to protect the cosmopolitans' cultural and economic freedom from morally intrusive local interference. Considerable evidence suggests that at least one of the major divisions between the Federalists and the Anti-Federalists centered on this cultural dimension. The Anti-Federalists were far more comfortable with communitarian republican and Christian notions of virtue, while the Federalists had come to embrace the nascent individualism of the commercial era.

Both the cosmopolitan Framers and the parochial Christians, of course, believed in the selfishness of the individual. But for rural Christians there were cultural means—face-to-face, morally nurturing, or intrusive sanctions—to ensure that individuals would achieve their better nature. The cosmopolitan Framers, who were less sanguine about such communal checks, produced instead "auxiliary precautions" in the form of institutional machinery that would channel and check the selfishness of majorities and leaders alike. In doing so, however, the Framers abandoned the inculcation of republican virtue or Christian ethics as means of sustaining the Republic. Thus they legitimated self-interest and failed to substitute a compelling, or even adequate, vision of the public good, assuming that somehow the public interest would emerge from the dispersion of power and competition between factions.[49]

Populists, we are beginning to see, could trace their lineage to a cultural split that was emerging in eighteenth-century America. From his copious reading of documents from the mass culture (small town, Protestant, rural), Barry Shain concludes that most Americans did not share the liberal and individualistic assumptions of the elite Founders. Shain has explored sermons and other sources evocative of popular culture to show that "liberty" was understood in orthodox Christian terms as the freedom to pursue God's will within the context of a morally restraining and nurturing community—what Richard Neuhaus calls "ordered liberty." [50] For at least two centuries, Shain contends, most Americans adhered "to the vision of a community as essentially a corporate ethical project whose purpose was fulfilled through structuring and promoting the achievement of its individuals' uniquely human telos." Morally intrusive communities, in this Protestant cultural context, were viewed not as a barrier to individual freedom but as a necessary condition of its achievement. From the pulpits of the land the word *slavery* was used to describe an individual's captivity to his own selfish pleasures, a sentiment we hear echoed in Jesse Jackson's powerful denunciation of drug addiction and promiscuity. A person was freed from this slavery to sin by the guidance of the community. Thus there existed a communal public philosophy "in opposition to the ubiquitous and seductive contemporary appeal of egoism and rampant materialism." An individual was "understood to be an ethical being with a transcendent nature, who lives most fruitfully outside himself in family and community." For most eighteenth-century Americans living in small rural communities, freedom implied a positive nurturing of the individual, in contrast to the prevailing view that it was understood in negative terms (freedom from government intrusion, for example). "Communalism, deep religiosity, face-to-face-relations, and charity" were the predominant life modalities.[51]

Because 95 percent of Americans in the founding era lived in villages of 2,500 or fewer people, this localist tradition deserves our scrutiny. Echoing Shalhope, Shain suggests that localist values were communitarian, Christian, and democratic, while the cosmopolitan elite represented nationalist, liberal, individualist, and secular values. And contrary to our accustomed way of thinking, the morally intrusive rural Protestants hewed to a relatively egalitarian social structure, while the liberal elites, suspicious of mass democracy, rooted their efforts to structure the national government in hierarchical soil, attempting to protect individual liberty from the intrusions of the majority. This analysis helps us to see the extent to which liberalism (either in the economic marketplace or in personal lifestyles) can be at odds with populist democracy,[52] as we see dramatically in the late nineteenth century and in our own time.

Conflict of Ideals and Behavior

The bifurcation in eighteenth-century political culture could work in part because it was understood that the national government would not interfere with the cultural, religious, or political concerns of the states and local communities. Theodore Lowi suggests that the federal structure of the government allowed national "liberals" and "conservative" locals to coexist.[53] Shain echoes this: "No matter how America's parochial and Protestant communalist people understood the construction of this admittedly secular and national experiment, it must be noted that they did not believe that the national regime's values (or lack thereof) could, should, or would be applied to the real units of corporate ethical and political life—the local communities and states." Although liberal national elites had abandoned the "long tradition of submerging the self in the public good" and accepted instead "the understanding that men had a right to decide what their own happiness was," local culture (as Tocqueville showed later) provided the mores necessary to sustain the experiment. Thus a dynamic balance existed between a national elite that "spoke for individuals" and a local mass that "lived in communities." [54]

It is beyond the scope of this discussion to trace fully the lineage of this cultural split, but historical evidence suggests that something of the division continued. As Edward Countryman noted, "Well into the nineteenth century, small farmers in the interior were still organizing their lives around the lineal family, not the isolated individual, and around exchange for the sake of community, not trade for the sake of gain." [55] Tocqueville, of course, spoke of the Christian mores that guided the lives of Americans in the early nineteenth century.[56] This perception that national elites somehow do not share the localist heritage has continued from the Jacksonian era through the Populist movement to our own age. In his celebrated historical analysis of Andrew Jackson, Marvin Meyers observed, "Thus Jackson gives to the party contest the aura of a class struggle, distinguishing the classes not by their economic position as such, but primarily by their moral orientation." To Jackson, Meyers notes, "real people" ("the people" of the populists) are yeoman-republicans, while the aristocracy are irresponsibly adventurous enterprisers. Government should govern least only because then would society "realize its own natural moral discipline." In the United States, "Jacksonians announced, the people were the true conservatives," and aristocracy could be blamed for the erosion of republican communitarian social values.[57]

This localist communal tradition, because it was largely oral, lacked an adequate means of expressing itself comparable to the cosmopolitan culture that passed its heritage through the written word. The nativist excesses and irrational violence that periodically erupted from these popular communal forces—documented so extensively by scholars such as Richard Hofstadter and Seymour Martin Lipset—may be attributed to this inadequacy.[58] Still, in one sense, as Shain observes,

> It became the unsought responsibility of average small-town Americans and inhabitants of urban ethnic neighborhoods, with their continued commitment to a traditional (17th and 18th centuries) understanding of liberty and to communal values, to sustain, albeit most imperfectly, the central values of Classic and Christian political thought that had guided Western civilization for the previous 2,000 years." [59]

Shain overstates this case. Other interpreters have noted that many people in these communities were finding themselves increasingly drawn into the competitive marketplace, where their communal or Christian values were strained by their own self-possessed behavior.[60] To be sure, the potentially destructive tendencies were held in check for a time, allowing people to enjoy their new freedom in an atmosphere of cultural certitudes. Or as Tocqueville put it, liberalism told the man he could do as he pleased, while religion told him he should not do that which was destructive to his family and the community. Such a delicate balance, however, could not be long sustained. The forces of commercial modernization and the atomizing tendencies of a highly mobile population would chip away at the republican and Christian visions of the good society. Thus the tension between ideals and behavior increased through the nineteenth century: "Most Americans still clung to a harmonious, communal view of their society even while behaving in a materialistic, competitive manner." [61]

That the behavior of many Americans did not square with their professed ideals, however, does not completely undercut the power of those ideals—especially during times of rising discontent—as an intellectual basis for political mobilization. The point is that the populists had a genuine tradition to draw upon. The blend of republican virtues and Christian faith that gave meaning to parochial communities was there to be distilled, remembered, and reified. Thus our excursion into American history is central to understanding how nineteenth-century populists viewed their political mission. When rural farmers banded together to battle the powerful economic forces emerging in the late nineteenth century, they consciously attempted to reclaim the communitarian language of republican ideals and Christian sacrifice, all the while engaging in the practical work of forming agricultural cooperatives and farm organizations. Creating cooperative ventures, moreover, required individual sacrifice if they were to thrive.[62] The populists' criticism of the selfishness they saw emerging in the liberal order had its origins both in the contemporary situation and in American political traditions. Together these explain the populist blend of economic progressivism and moral traditionalism to which we now turn.

THE RISE OF THE POPULIST MOVEMENT

The term "populism" evokes a rich legacy of nineteenth-century America, but it enjoys currency in contemporary political parlance as well. Certain presidential candidates are described as populists. Columnists speak of the populist revolt against public school bureaucracies. Boris Yeltsin, the champion of the "Second Russian Revolution," is frequently described as a populist who challenged the entrenched Soviet elite. Scholars of comparative politics use the term "populist" to describe a variety of people's movements in developing nations.[63] One connotation of populism, as we have noted, suggests movement politics based on the celebration of "the people," whose virtues contrast with the exploitative greed or libertine immorality of the powerful. Ideologically, populism describes a distinct blend of economic progressivism (tax the rich, regulate business) and social conservatism (support for traditional moral values).[64]

Populism is driven by discontent, but what is not fully appreciated is the extent to which populist analysis is rooted in a communalist understanding of society, over and against an individualist one. Indeed, some scholars see these distinct and contrasting approaches as the major traditions in the American polity. There are "two traditional American rhetorics," observes Bernard Wishy. "One is the rhetoric of populism, the other a rhetoric of individualism." [65] William Riker, the theorist of social choice, also contrasts these two traditions in his defense of liberalism against populist democratic aims.[66] We can trace the lineage of populism back to early Protestant rural communities, follow it through the nineteenth-century revolt, and note its reemergence in the contemporary reaction against liberal modernity, both on the right and the left. To explore the legacy of nineteenth-century populism, let us look for a moment at the climate and conditions that produced it.

Hard Times in the Gilded Age

The rise of agrarian activism in the late nineteenth century arose from the rapidly deteriorating economic condition of the western and southern farmer.[67] After the Civil War settlers flocked to the West, motivated by hunger for land, spurred by banks with money to lend, and lured by the extravagant claims of railroad agents. This boom in western settlements led to farm indebtedness, overinvestment, and surplus production. Huge tracts of land were brought into cultivation, fueled by borrowed money. For a short while the fragility of the system was hidden by unusually good weather and a rising demand for farm products. But by 1887 reality had set in; the weather turned sour, bank notes came due, and "hard times settled down upon the whole frontier, not to be shaken for a decade." [68] In the South the problem was not speculation but the breakup of plantation agriculture, which produced a system of tenant farmers dependent on absentee landowners. Here, too, overproduction sent the prices of commodities such as cotton down precipitously, and impoverished tenants found themselves paying debts with deflated money.[69]

The monetary deflation was devastating for debtors, while lenders enjoyed enormous, and usurious, returns. Railroads held a monopoly on freight, and eastern banks reaped huge profits from currency deflation. Powerful economic trusts were emerging, and conspicuous consumption among the wealthy became fashionable in what has become known as the Gilded Age. The United States was experiencing the development of the capitalist market, with the vast dislocations that entailed. The shape of this new industrial state threatened the ideal of rural and small-town communalism, materially as well as ideologically.

A new set of ideas gained currency: the success myth, the gospel of wealth, social Darwinism, and laissez faire individualism. The old ideal of the individual rooted in a religious cosmos and constrained by fixed moral codes was transmuted into the new, unfettered, superior individual of the sort extolled first by Nietzsche and later by Ayn Rand. Although Darwin's theories of natural selection threatened religious world views, they were embraced by the new class of capitalists whose wealth in the midst of poverty was justified by the doctrine of "survival of the fittest." One cannot overstress this point. Darwin's theories, as popularized by Herbert Spencer and William Graham Sumner, gave to the robber baron a "scientific" justification for his plunder; he was central to the evolutionary progress of humanity. The wealthy owed nothing to the poor, who were merely examples of the less "fit" by virtue of their abilities and habits. As Gene Clanton put it, "The captains of industry were indeed fortunate to have begun their great work at a time when Charles Darwin had shocked a quasi-religious age with his *Origin of Species* (1859) and Herbert Spencer had begun to popularize his rendition of the social counterpart."[70] The liberal interpretation of individual freedom thus could not adequately deal with its offspring, the rapacious individual. The acceptance of the Spencerian idea of unchecked individual freedom in the marketplace, Hofstadter argued, paralyzed "the will to reform."[71]

The populists were keenly aware of the threat of this new ideology to their livelihood, and they located the underlying problem in the unbridled individualism that knew no moral or ethical bounds. Echoing the earlier communalist understanding of human telos, populist thinkers condemned the gospel of wealth and heaped scorn on social Darwinism as antithetical to Christianity, democracy, and justice. "The plutocracy of today is the logical result of the individual freedom which we have always considered the pride of our system," stated an editorial in the *Farmers' Alliance*. Yet, the editorial continued, this unchecked individualism fosters monopoly capitalism in which the "corporation has absorbed the community." Another editorial charged that "a reigning plutocracy with the masses enslaved, is the natural development and end of individualism."[72] The threat of industrial capitalism to communal norms was keenly perceived,[73] in part because it married enormous economic power with an ideology that glorified its exercise: might makes right. Even as Nietzsche was calling for a rejection of Christian charity, populists saw in the robber barons individuals who had "reversed the code of morals. . . . They have the power to impoverish the farmers, make millions of good men tramps; to reduce their employees to silent slaves; to ruin great cities; to plunge a happy and prosperous nation into sorrow and bankruptcy." [74]

Evangelical Faith and Populism

The evangelical flavor of populism, its camp meetings and stirring speeches, is captured by this description of the times: "The upheaval that took place . . . can hardly be diagnosed as a political campaign. It was a religious revival, a crusade, a Pentecost of politics in which a tongue of flame sat upon every man, and each spake as the spirit gave him utterance." [75] The religious flavor was more than symbolic. Many populists were comfortable with the broader religious aim of a moral structuring of society, as reflected in the temperance movement. Indeed, some Populist party leaders called for close cooperation with the Prohibition party, and Ignatius Donnelly, a well-known Populist leader, remarked, "I am sure that ninety-nine out of a hundred Populists are Temperance men." [76] During the 1896 presidential campaign Populist organs unabashedly identified themselves with the cause of creating a "grander" moral society. As we shall see, this vision of a moral commonweal would animate the crusades of both Jesse Jackson and Pat Robertson.

Profound discontent in the late nineteenth century thus was wedded to a great hope that society would be transformed and renewed by the efforts of the great mass of citizens banding together. Scholars largely agree that in addition to expressing anger over their economic distress populists relied on a communalist analysis of what makes a good society work. As Bruce Palmer argues of the southern populists, their belief was "that the only decent society was one in which each person looked out for every other one . . . accepted responsibility for every other, rather than a society in which each watched out for his or her own interest and the Devil took the hindmost." [77] The enormous threat posed by capital-owning individuals with their anti-Christian ideology, populists concluded, required that a democratic, majoritarian government act with increased vigor and authority. Initiatives for state regulation of business—even nationalization—though radical, seemed necessary in this new environment. As simply stated by Populist governor Lorenzo Lewelling of Kansas, the government must protect the weak, "because the strong are able to protect themselves." [78]

Thus the desperate plight of the farm community was linked to a broader societal force in the emerging dominance of laissez faire ideology and exploitative banks, railroads, and robber barons. Industrial capitalism, to populists, represented shattered communities and families, alienated workers, and a Hobbesian world of competition between individuals. "The tendency of the competitive system is to antagonize and disassociate men.... The survival of the fittest is a satanic creed.... The actual state of society today is a state of war.... Deny it if you can. Competition is only another name for war." [79]

There is a close historical tie between populism and the rise of charismatic churches and Pentecostal denominations, which sprang from the same rural waters. The Pentecostal Church of God, for example, arose contemporaneously with the Farmers' Alliance, the People's party, and other expressions of the Populist movement. The Church of God appealed to the same people as the populists, offering a spiritual rather than a worldly response to the "chaotic changing world." Many of its ministers were subsistence farmers, and the church attracted many blacks. The new church arose in part as a reaction to the perceived declension of the Methodists and Baptists, who were relaxing moral codes and "taboos against worldly amusements." What united the Pentecostal and Populist movements was a communal vision, the idea of a "cooperative brotherhood." Thus "the Church of God minister delivered his message with a dual purpose in mind: denouncing sin and encouraging the community," a theme that also can be found in the populist energy devoted to creating communal institutions such as cooperatives and farm associations. Furthermore, "members of the Church of God, like populists, were antagonistic toward the new order of American society which had arisen as a consequence of industrialism. They believed that the industrial trend toward depersonalization and reliance on profit in ordering social values would destroy Christian morality." The task of the church, in this new industrial order, was to "promote the gospel of Christ as providing the only means of moral emancipation, not only from personal sins, but also from worship of the 'almighty dollar.'" The Church of God's critique of the emerging order was similar to that of the populists, especially in its concern about the effect of "industrialism on personal morality and collective community." Moreover, the new Pentecostal church emphasized the moral community in much the same way that the populists did. "Church of God members believed that the only decent society was one in which people assumed responsibility for each other. In short, such religion resulted from the desire to produce a more egalitarian society." [80]

Often, historians see this link between populism and "fundamentalist" religion as just another piece of evidence for their conclusion that populism was deficient, that it suffered from nativism, xenophobia, racism, and envy of urban life. There were, to be sure, elements of all these characteristics, especially on the fringes of the movement. Anti-Semitism clearly was prevalent; scorn for bankers easily degenerated into contempt for Jews as age-old personifications of the usurious lender.[81] But some populists, remarkable for their time, attempted to build alliances with southern blacks,[82] just as the lower class Pentecostal churches were open to black members.[83] Indeed, the Pentecostal churches were terrorized by the Ku Klux Klan, which burned homes and destroyed church buildings. Similarly, women found themselves welcomed into the Pentecostal church, even in leadership roles, just as they were in the Farmers' Alliance and the People's party.

The populist and religious critique of the unfettered market, as we see here, was combined with a moralist denunciation of social Darwinism. Fashionable leftists in the academy today delight in denouncing the antievolutionists,[84] but to many economic radicals of the nineteenth century the teachings of Darwin were a profound threat, justifying as they did the dominance of those who succeeded in the marketplace by ruthless cunning.[85] What modern scholars do not appreciate enough, consequently, is that rural evangelicals objected to the economic, communal, and social implications of Darwinism as well as to its theological implications. We shall see how these populist doctrines played out in the life of William Jennings Bryan.

THE POPULISM OF WILLIAM JENNINGS BRYAN

As one of the most eloquent and tireless defenders of the people against the trusts, William Jennings Bryan should be secure in his credentials as a populist. During his lifetime, however, there were doubts. In the 1896 presidential campaign many in the People's party were troubled by his excessive reliance on silver coinage as the means to redress complex economic problems, and a fierce debate ensued over whether Populists should "fuse" with the Democrats under Bryan. But if Bryan was not pure enough for the People's party, his style, rhetoric, and concerns were populist. "He could picture the wrongs of a suffering people as they had never been portrayed before."[86] He earned the sobriquet the Great Commoner.

Bryan is valuable to our study because in his story there is a blend (not uncommon among populists but jarring to modern analysts) of political progressivism and moral traditionalism. It is hard for some to appreciate how he could be a radical in politics and economics but a conservative in religion. Even some of his contemporaries could not see the link between his tireless campaigning for progressive causes and his religious "fundamentalism." So Bryan's life was neatly divided into stages—young progressive, old reactionary—allowing his crusades against Darwin or drink to be written off as an old man's futile attempt to hold back the tide of modernity.[87] To understand Bryan, one must see his life as a seamless garment of Christian witness rather than as a journey from progressive to reactionary.[88]

Bryan's life (1860-1925) spanned a time of enormous cultural change, from McGuffey's Readers through the Jazz Age, and he witnessed the dramatic secularization of elites so nicely chronicled by Daniel Bell.[89] Toward the end of his life the theories of Darwin, Freud, and Nietzsche became fashionable among cosmopolitan elites, and traditional religion was viewed as passé by intellectuals. But Bryan saw in the attack on the foundations of traditional moral codes a dangerous ethical relativism, individualism, and materialism that threatened his vision of social justice. He was repelled by the rapacious struggle implied in the "survival of the fittest," which he did not feel could be reconciled with the Christian ideals of love, mercy, charity, and community.[90]

Bryan's critique of social Darwinism resonated with a progressive social gospel as much as it did with religious fundamentalism. And he actually had read Darwin, not just the social Darwinists. After reading *Descent of Man,* Bryan told a professor that such teachings would "weaken the cause of democracy and strengthen class pride and the power of wealth." Bryan saw that social Darwinism arose more naturally from Darwin's ideas than many progressives, then and now, appreciated. He quoted passages from Darwin likely to make modern liberals cringe. For Darwin spoke approvingly of savages allowing the natural "elimination of the weak in body and mind" and contrasted their behavior with civilized ways that forestalled the progress of the race, including relief for the poor and "asylums for the imbecile, the maimed and the sick." Medical advances and vaccination, Darwin argued, "preserved thousands who from weak constitutions would have succumbed to small pox. Thus, the weak members of civilized society propagate their kind. No one who has attended to the breeding of domestic animals will doubt that this must be highly injurious to the race of man." [91] These kinds of sentiments were presented as scientific fact in the famous biology text on evolution that Bryan attacked in Tennessee. Responding to this scientism, Bryan strove to maintain humanity's distinctive moral status, which he thought impossible without a theistic underpinning. "Is man a brother or a brute?" he frequently asked.

In Nietzsche, Bryan saw the doctrine of "might makes right" advancing, because the philosopher "carried the Darwinian theory to its logical conclusion." In the wake of the devastation of World War I, the pacifist Bryan argued that Nietzsche had "overturned all standards of morality, eulogized war as both necessary and desirable, praised hatred because it leads to war, denied to sympathy and pity any rightful place in a manly heart and endeavored to substitute the worship of the superman for the worship of Jehovah." [92] In his later years Bryan saw plenty of evidence that these new ideas were making their mark. These were years when "positive eugenics" enjoyed a certain vogue; this was an age when Margaret Sanger, a leader in birth control education, could criticize breeding by minorities and the lower classes and call for forced sterilizations. In the seedbeds of the emerging secular society, Bryan saw no check on plutocracy, privilege, materialism, and a coarsening of life (this was a future that Jesse Jackson and Pat Robertson also seem to fear).

A related element in Bryan's crusade was his occasionally apocalyptic tone. "Thundering righteousness," his "appeal was articulated in the cadence and with the same Biblical allusions and apocalyptic vision that had long characterized pietistic Protestantism." Viewing the moment as a "crisis in human affairs," he put the struggle simply: "We have arrayed on either side the great forces of society. Against us are . . . money, the corporations and the high positions in politics and society, but on our side . . . is simply justice." Not surprisingly, Bryan was accused by his Republican opponents of waging a campaign "of envy, discontent, riot, and anarchy," which was "fomenting class struggle." [93] But if there was danger to the people, the apocalyptic vision also promised redemption for the faithful. Bryan's populism blended discontent with religious hope. This belief that the good will triumph is a theme that echoes resoundingly among modern-day populists. "Keep hope alive!" is Jesse Jackson's recurring refrain.

Electoral evidence suggests that Bryan's evangelical style resonated with a particular stratum of society. As Kleppner's careful analysis of voting behavior demonstrates, Bryan's campaign in 1896 cut across longstanding partisan identifications, splitting urban from rural and pietists from secularists. As a Democrat Bryan did better than expected among pietist Republican voters, but he fared worse among liturgical Democrats (Catholics and Lutherans, for example), who were not comfortable with his evangelical politics. As Kleppner notes, the Democratic party under Bryan ceased to be the party of "personal liberty" and became the party of "imperialistic pietism," a place where groups interested in a moral reconstitution of society could pursue their goals. Kleppner stresses that Bryan's religious perspective was vital to his political efforts. It was impossible for Bryan to distinguish between "political" and "religious" activities, something we hear explicitly from Jesse Jackson. "To him these were not two unrelated spheres of endeavor, but two aspects of the same battle, the battle between good and evil, between the Christian and the sources of temptation that abounded in his social environment." The pietist's conviction of the need for a morally restraining and nurturing community naturally flowed from this perspective, and Bryan was warmly received by those who shared his evangelistic views and understood the "Biblical allusions that permeated his rhetoric." Bryan's Republican opponent, William McKinley, "did not perceive the same inexorable relationship between religious attitudes and secular activity that characterized Bryan's perspective." More modern in that sense, McKinley was able to appeal to voters put off by the morally intrusive pietists, and, at least for a while, he helped to transform the GOP from the "party of piety" into the "party of prosperity." [94]

Describing the Democrats and Republicans of a generation earlier, Abraham Lincoln likened them to two drunk men who got into a brawl and in the process exchanged their coats. Something like this happened in 1896. The Republican party under McKinley ceased being the "agency of rapid evangelical Protestantism that it had been for the temperance, sabbatarian, and abolitionist crusaders of the 1850s." Instead, it became the carrier of an emergent entrepreneurial, market liberalism. On the other hand, the Democratic party that in 1894 had been characterized as the party of "saloon interests," "corruption," and Catholicism became the "party of piety" in 1896, an instrument "aimed at the creation of a moral social order." [95] Bryan and the Democrats, of course, lost, but the people's cause was picked up to an extent by the progressives and reified by Franklin D. Roosevelt, whose New Deal embodied a vision of a caring "national" community that restrained rapacious "economic royalists." Far more than many historians acknowledge, Roosevelt's rhetoric rang with the religious cadences of the populists as he pledged to "drive the money changers from the temple of democracy." [96]

Like contemporary populists, perhaps, Bryan had blinders that kept him from broadening his appeal; his pietist politics did not sit well with Catholic farmers or with urban workers. The 1896 election is not the end of the story, however. Bryan continued to crusade for social causes, then for peace. Taking the Sermon on the Mount as his guide, he never wavered in his political progressivism. He fought for child labor legislation, women's suffrage, the graduated income tax, government aid to farmers, public ownership of railroads, federal development of water resources, government guarantee of bank deposits, and laws to prevent profiteering. Nonetheless, Bryan's fate among the intelligentsia was sealed by his antievolution crusade, which culminated in the Scopes Trial in 1925. This circus was devastatingly reported by H. L. Mencken and popularized by the play and movie *Inherit the Wind,* which caricatured the man.

Yet just three years before his ill-fated intervention in the Scopes Trial, Bryan had excoriated (in characteristically progressive terms) a Supreme Court decision striking down child labor legislation: "It has been hailed as a victory for states' rights but it is no such thing; it is a victory for capitalism whose greed coins the blood of little children into larger dividends."[97] Unmatched in his eloquence in behalf of the vulnerable, Bryan was at heart a descendant of the tradition described by Shain, a man who believed individuals were created in God's image for a defined purpose that was realized in a communalist context. Bryan exalted authority in religion as the surest, perhaps only true underpinning to freedom in politics and a just ordering of society.[98] His critique of modernity, in which anything goes in morality as well as in business, rings more prophetically today than the cognoscenti of his day might have realized.

PROPHETIC RELIGION AND THE AFRICAN AMERICAN HERITAGE

The question of race is central to our understanding of the dynamics of populist politics. Critics of populism, for example, see racism flowing from the same rural waters that nourished the Southern Alliance or the People's party.[99] Many who flocked to the Populist banner in 1896 might easily have joined the Ku Klux Klan, they argue, if not at the time, then a decade or two later. Depicting Jesse Jackson as a populist seems odd in this light. Yet on another level, Jackson's populism rings true to an authentic tradition within the African American experience.

The legacy of African slavery is so complex that any attempts to describe it briefly must oversimplify. My purpose here is not to suggest that the black experience in America can be fitted neatly into an analysis of populism, for surely it cannot. Still, there is a story here that deserves continued scrutiny. We know that African slaves retained vestiges of their tribal religions, which were blended with the Protestant faith dominant in the South. And we know that, as an oppressed people, they heard the liberationist messages of the Bible with special keenness, producing a distinctive mix of evangelical pietism and prophetic faith. We know that African American religious practice produced a cadre of gifted and influential ministers, whom W. E. B. Du Bois called a unique American creation.

Most important for our analysis, though, is that by the end of the Civil War African Americans constituted a Protestant rural population whose community life centered on the Baptist or Methodist church.[100] As late as 1900, 90 percent of America's blacks lived in the South, and most of them were in rural communities or small towns. Segregation heightened the isolation and ironically increased the centrality of the church as social center and refuge. And, as we know, the religiously rooted cultural system, nurtured by the black minister, emphasized traditional (even Puritan) moral codes. Blacks, in short, lived in communities in which morally intrusive norms prevailed, not unlike the pattern described earlier. The political context, of course, was radically different from that of colonial Protestants, but the moral and religious foundation was similar. God's mercy and judgment, not secular or individual interpretation, were viewed as normative. Indeed, slavery and the oppression that followed placed African Americans in a vivid biblical context in which their identification with the prophetic themes of captivity and liberation was vital.[101]

How was freedom understood in this context? An analysis of black cultural life from Reconstruction onward would likely reveal that freedom was interpreted not in contemporary liberal and individualist terms but in biblical and communalist ones. This legacy of the early black church continues today, generating a barely discussed tension between national black political leaders, who are socially liberal, and local ministers and lay members, who hold traditional views on many issues pertaining to individual autonomy. As one black state senator put it to me, "On family issues, prolife, women's place, prayer—you won't find a more conservative lot than some black ministers." Yet culturally conservative black ministers could ignore Jackson's advocacy, say, of gay marriages, because Jackson also represents the heritage of black pride and liberation. And, frankly, voting for Jesse Jackson was a way to stick it to the SWABs—"smart-ass white boys." How else can we explain that such prominent ministers as E. V. Hill and T. J. Jemison supported Jackson in the primaries but backed Reagan or Bush in the general elections?

Thus, in the setting of rural communalist life, blacks developed their own blend of moral traditionalism and economic radicalism, a tradition more enduring than that of whites. During the late nineteenth century black tenant farmers were among the worst off, and populist politics held special appeal to them. And for a while southern populists openly sought to build a biracial coalition based on economic lines. The Colored Farmers' National Alliance and Cooperative Union, for example, was a closely coordinated appendage of its white counterpart, the Southern Alliance. Remarkably, in the context of the post-Reconstruction South, white populists called for a common crusade with former slaves: "Your race today, like ours, is groaning under . . . oppression. . . . Under the present administration, the fruits of your labor, like the fruits of ours, instead of going to make our homes happy and comfortable, go to pay tithes to the money lords of Wall Street." [102] Such figures as Tom

Watson, a prominent Populist in Georgia, acknowledged that political rights for black voters were a part of the Populist platform and occasionally acted with considerable courage on that premise. The poisonous politics of race undermined attempts at lasting alliances, however, and blacks were ultimately shut out.[103] Sadly, Watson later abandoned his biracial efforts and adopted Jim Crow. But, as Vann Woodward notes, the astonishing thing is that he maintained that early vision as long as he did.[104]

Populism retained its resiliency in the black community in part because African Americans' condition never improved substantially. When the agricultural economy prospered again in the early 1900s, black farmers were not positioned to take advantage of the boom. Thus while some former white populists got rich, blacks got Jim Crow. Perhaps this is why a latter-day populist like Jesse Jackson can rouse the black community as no other.

THE DIFFUSION OF POPULISM IN THE TWENTIETH CENTURY

By the early twentieth century the Populist movement had found its energies diffused in a variety of directions, not all of them compatible. Some former populists moved with alacrity into the Progressive movement and later joined the New Deal; others veered into the Klan. Some retreated into a fundamentalist religion that shed the evangelical Christian ideal of a moral economy, which had become tainted by its association with "apostate" liberal theology.[105] Still others became linked in the 1920s and 1930s with a nascent American fascism, in which hatred of cosmopolitan elites by the lower middle class was transmuted into faith in the iron leader who would protect tradition and economic livelihood. The unsavory images of populism—anti-Semitism, anti-intellectualism, and demagoguery—in part spring from this legacy.

But the enduring concerns of the populists—fear of concentrated power and the quest for community and moral economy—remained. These concerns animated the likes of Huey Long and Father Charles Coughlin, who rallied millions during the Great Depression in insurgent movements that demanded protection of the livelihoods and communities of the common people. Although later associated with pure hatred and demagoguery, Long and Coughlin evoked distinctively populist themes. As a powerful Louisiana senator, Long might have challenged Roosevelt in 1936 with his radical share-the-wealth platform, had he not been assassinated in 1935. Father Coughlin gained a huge following as a radio commentator who heaped vituperative attacks on international banking conspiracies (a populist tradition Pat Robertson echoed a generation later).

Their appeal was to poor farmers, small shopkeepers, and urban workers who saw their world undermined by social and economic tides. As Alan Brinkley notes, Long and Coughlin spoke to genuine concerns about the rise of laissez faire individualism in economics and culture that had inspired the earlier populists. Both leaders bemoaned the decline of the local merchant, symbol of the tightknit community, who was being run out of business by the concentrated wealth represented by the chain store. Like earlier populists, Long and Coughlin made "an affirmation of the ideal of community" a central theme in their rhetoric.[106] Money-changers, plutocrats, and international bankers became the embodiment of forces undermining local communities. Their movements, however, did not have the practical focus of the earlier populist crusade, in which farmers actually created cooperatives. This shortcoming arose in part because economic and social modernization had outpaced the insurgents' ability to comprehend and respond. In some ways populists today face that same dilemma.

Before turning to the resurgence of populism in the 1980s, it is instructive to note the odyssey of another populist heir, former Alabama governor and third-party presidential candidate George Wallace. Beginning his career as a somewhat progressive southern populist, Wallace learned early that to win he had to descend, like Tom Watson, to race baiting and segregation. But once he sought a national stage in his presidential campaign in 1968, he picked up populist themes again, especially cultural ones, in his attacks on "pointy headed intellectuals." When desegregation and enforcement of voting rights enfranchised black voters, he renounced his racist past, embraced economic populism, and recaptured the governorship with a remarkable biracial vote. Among the visitors to the governor's mansion was none other than Jesse Jackson, who received some advice from Wallace about how to mount a populist campaign: "Pitch your message so low even the goats can get it." [107] This advice was like teaching a fox to hunt, for Jackson's rhyming cadences, homey metaphors, and biblical allusions perfectly fit Wallace's advice. The meeting of the two sons of the South was fateful in a number of respects. Wallace's renunciation of racism appealed to Jackson's religious belief in redemption as well as his hope for a new South. But one senses that the two adroit politicians also understood each other, sharing an intuitive grasp of the power of populist themes in American society.

SUMMARY

An account of populism infused with religion becomes more meaningful when we trace its lineage through history. We find that many populists harken back to a preliberal discourse that emphasizes classical or Christian ideas, such as community, duty, and sacrifice. Although some scholars argue that these ideas constitute authentic "conservatism,"[108] in fact they can also infuse progressive or leftist politics with the solidarity necessary to confront powerful interests. Thus the populists of the nineteenth century, once dismissed by liberal historians as backward looking, are increasingly seen by revisionist scholars as prescient in their appreciation of the threat posed by the emerging industrial and capitalist order.[109] Many revisionists, however, tend to ignore the cultural and religious conservatism of the populists, a tradition that puzzles many historians but can be understood as part of a seamless communitarian fabric. The same wellsprings that produced agricultural cooperatives, the Farmers' Alliance, and the People's party also energized the crusade against alcohol and the ferment for moral rectitude. Populists at the time viewed these seemingly contradictory elements as complementary.[110] The moral zeal of the populists, their sense of justice, arose naturally from the rural evangelical milieu in which many farmers lived.

Today the forces of change seem tremendously complex, but they can be viewed as a culmination of the economic and social tides that activated the populists of the nineteenth century. Contemporary populists, faced with a marketplace of global impersonality and buffeted by atomizing cultural trends, resemble those of the past—in their discontent as well as in their religious hope. The distinguishing characteristic of modern populism is that it seems to have split into left-wing and right-wing variants, represented here by Jesse Jackson and Pat Robertson. Yet residues of each tradition remain in the other. Although Jackson seeks to galvanize the economically dispossessed, he continues to stress traditional values and moral codes. And while Robertson champions religious traditionalists, he also criticizes Wall Street and banking interests. The ideological chasm between the two leaders masks more similarities than the followers of either man would acknowledge. What unites many populists on the right and the left is a repugnance for the moral hollowness and atomizing tendencies of liberal culture and politics. To understand modern populism and its communitarian critique of the ascendant liberal order, we now turn to the lives and messages of the two ministers.

NOTES

1. Edmund S. Morgan, *The Puritan Dilemma: The Story of John Winthrop* (Boston: Little, Brown, 1958).

2. Robert Bellah et al., *Habits of the Heart* (Berkeley: University of California Press, 1985); and Mary Ann Glendon, *Rights Talk* (New York: Free Press, 1991).
3. Perry Miller, *Errand into the Wilderness* (Cambridge: Harvard University Press, 1956), 149.
4. Eldon Eisenach, "The American Revolution Made and Remembered: Cultural Politics and Political Thought," *American Studies* 20 (Spring 1979).
5. Miller, *Errand into the Wilderness,* 8.
6. Mark A. Noll, *One Nation under God? Christian Faith and Political Action in America* (San Francisco: Harper, 1988), argues convincingly that the periodic engagement of American Christians in politics has been characterized by a passionate, revivalist temperament, often treating politics as a spiritual struggle between good and evil.
7. William G. McLoughlin, *Revivals, Awakening, and Reform: An Essay on Religion and Social Change in America, 1607-1977* (Chicago: University of Chicago Press, 1978).
8. A. James Reichley, *Religion in American Public Life* (Washington, D.C.: Brookings Institution, 1985), 74.
9. Ibid, 68-74.
10. Miller, *Errand into the Wilderness,* 156-157.
11. Ibid., 163.
12. Eisenach, "American Revolution Made and Remembered," 77.
13. Although Jon Butler depicts a more multifaceted Great Awakening than do Reichley and others, his analysis generally supports the argument that revivals were central to American history. See Jon Butler, *Awash in a Sea of Faith: Christianizing the American People* (Cambridge: Harvard University Press, 1990).
14. Eisenach, "American Revolution Made and Remembered," 78.
15. Ibid.
16. Ibid., 74.
17. Nathan O. Hatch, *The Democratization of American Christianity* (New Haven: Yale University Press, 1989).
18. See Robert E. Shalhope, "Republicanism and Early American Historiography," *William and Mary Quarterly* 39 (April 1982): 334-356; J. G. A. Pocock, *The Machiavellian Moment: Florentine Political Thought and the Atlantic Republican Tradition* (Princeton: Princeton University Press, 1975); and Forrest McDonald, *Novus Ordo Seclorum: The Intellectual Origins of the Constitution* (Lawrence: University of Kansas Press, 1985).
19. Shalhope, "Republicanism and Early American Historiography."
20. Louis Hartz, *The Liberal Tradition in America: An Interpretation of American Political Thought since the Revolution* (New York: Harcourt, Brace, 1955).
21. John P. Diggins, *The Lost Soul of American Politics: Virtue, Self-Interest, and the Foundations of Liberalism* (New York: Basic Books, 1984), 5.
22. Richard Hofstadter, quoted in ibid.
23. Diggins, *The Lost Soul of American Politics.*
24. Theodore Lowi argues that Hartz was half-right, that at the national,

cosmopolitan level, liberalism dominated, while at the state and local level what he calls true conservatism held reign. Of course, the traits Lowi defines as conservative—the individual subordinate to a moral code, need over greed, restraint of wants, morality in public discourse, community over contract—overlap significantly with what American historians have termed republican virtues. (Theodore Lowi, "Before Conservatism and Beyond: American Ideology and Politics in the 1990s," Cornell University, unpublished manuscript, 1992.)

25. Bernard Bailyn, *The Ideological Origins of the American Revolution* (Cambridge, Mass.: Belknap Press, 1967); Gordon S. Wood, *The Creation of the American Republic* (Chapel Hill: University of North Carolina Press, 1987); Shalhope, "Republicanism and Early American Historiography"; Pocock, *Machiavellian Moment;* James T. Kloppenberg, *Uncertain Victory: Social Democracy and Progressivism in European and American Thought, 1870-1920* (New York: Oxford University Press, 1986); Thomas L. Pangle, *The Spirit of Modern Republicanism* (Chicago: University of Chicago Press, 1988); and McDonald, *Novus Ordo Seclorum.*
26. Pocock, *Machiavellian Moment,* 546.
27. Robert E. Shalhope, *The Roots of Democracy: American Thought and Culture, 1760-1800* (Boston: Twayne, 1990), 44-45.
28. Pocock, *Machiavellian Moment.*
29. McDonald, *Novus Ordo Seclorum,* 69.
30. Ibid.
31. Shalhope, "Republicanism and Early American Historiography."
32. Wood, *Creation of the American Republic.*
33. McDonald, *Novus Ordo Seclorum.*
34. *The Federalist Papers,* No. 51, with an introduction by Clinton Rossiter (New York: Mentor, 1961).
35. McDonald, *Novus Ordo Seclorum,* 63.
36. Shalhope, "Republicanism and Early American Historiography"; Kloppenberg, *Uncertain Victory.*
37. Kloppenberg, *Uncertain Victory.*
38. A third branch of scholarship emphasizes the Puritan, Baptist, and evangelical contributions to the founding moment of the Republic and to the ethical impulses of the citizenry. See Reichley, *Religion in American Public Life,* chap. 3.
39. Max Weber, *The Protestant Ethic and the Spirit of Capitalism* (New York: Scribner's, 1958).
40. Richard Vetterli and Gary Bryner, *In Search of the Republic: Public Virtue and the Roots of American Government* (Totowa, N.J.: Rowman and Littlefield, 1987).
41. McDonald, *Novus Ordo Seclorum.*
42. Ibid., 72.
43. Ronald M. Peters, *The Massachusetts Constitution of 1780: A Social Compact* (Amherst: University of Massachusetts Press, 1978).
44. Philip B. Burland and Ralph Lerner, eds., *The Founders' Constitution* (Chicago: University of Chicago Press, 1987).

45. Barry Alan Shain, "A Study in Eighteenth Century Political Theory: Liberty, Autonomy, Protestant Communalism, and Slavery in Revolutionary America" (Ph.D. diss., Yale University, 1990).
46. Shalhope, "Republicanism and Early American Historiography," 340.
47. Shalhope, *Roots of Democracy,* 32.
48. Ibid., 46.
49. Susan Zlomke, "From Private Interests to the Public Interest: A Neglected Theme in the Framing of the American Constitution" (Ph.D. diss., Stanford University, 1991).
50. Richard John Neuhaus, *The Naked Public Square* (Grand Rapids, Mich.: Eerdmans, 1984).
51. Shain, "Study in Eighteenth Century Political Theory," 11, 40, 16.
52. See especially William Riker, *Liberalism against Populism* (Prospect Heights, Ill.: Waveland Press, 1982).
53. Lowi, "Before Conservatism and Beyond"; and McDonald, *Novus Ordo Seclorum.*
54. Shain, "Study in Eighteenth Century Political Theory," 14-15, 35.
55. Edward Countryman, quoted in ibid., 8.
56. Alexis de Tocqueville, *Democracy in America,* trans. George Lawrence, ed. J. P. Mayer and A. P. Kerr (Garden City, N.Y.: Anchor, 1969).
57. Marvin Meyers, *The Jacksonian Persuasion: Politics and Belief* (Stanford: Stanford University Press, 1957), 31.
58. Richard Hofstadter, *The Age of Reform* (New York: Vintage, 1955); Seymour Martin Lipset and Earl Raab, *The Politics of Unreason,* 2d ed. (Chicago: University of Chicago Press, 1978).
59. Shain, "Study in Eighteenth Century Political Theory," 11.
60. Shalhope, "Republicanism and Early American Historiography"; and Kloppenberg, *Uncertain Victory.*
61. Shalhope, "Republicanism and Early American Historiography," 50.
62. We forget that these organizations required individual members to perform real sacrifices to make them work. Mancur Olson did not invent the "free rider" problem; he only identified it. See Mancur Olson, *The Logic of Collective Action* (Cambridge: Harvard University Press, 1965).
63. Ghita Ionescu and Ernest Gellner, *Populism: Its Meaning and National Characteristics* (London: Macmillan, 1969.)
64. *National Journal* divides congressional members into four categories: liberals, conservatives, populists (who are liberal on economic issues and conservative on social issues), and libertarians (who are the reverse of populists). In the 101st Congress *National Journal* found eleven populists in the Senate and thirty in the House, versus twelve libertarians in the Senate and thirty-four in the House. (The remaining members in both bodies were divided equally between liberals and conservatives.)
65. Bernard Wishy, quoted in Shain, "Study in Eighteenth Century Political Theory," 37.
66. Riker, *Liberalism against Populism.*
67. See Lawrence Goodwyn, *The Populist Moment: A Short History of the Agrarian*

Revolt in America (New York: Oxford University Press, 1978); John D. Hicks, *The Populist Revolt* (Lincoln: University of Nebraska Press, 1961); Norman Pollack, *The Populist Response to Industrial America* (New York: Norton, 1962); Norman Pollack, *The Just Polity* (Urbana: University of Illinois Press, 1987); Gene O. Clanton, *Kansas Populism: Ideas and Men* (Lawrence: University of Kansas Press, 1969); and Bruce Palmer, *Man over Money: The Southern Populist Critique of American Capitalism* (Chapel Hill: University of North Carolina Press, 1980).

68. Hicks, *Populist Revolt*, 31.
69. Palmer, *Man over Money*.
70. Clanton, *Kansas Populism*, 9.
71. Hofstadter, *Age of Reform*.
72. Cited in Pollack, *Populist Response to Industrial America*, 19.
73. See Clanton, *Kansas Populism;* Pollack, *Populist Response to Industrial America;* and Willard Smith, *The Social and Religious Thought of William Jennings Bryan* (Lawrence, Kan: Coronado Press, 1975).
74. Pollack, *Populist Response to Industrial America*, 21.
75. Elizabeth Barr, quoted in Hicks, *Populist Revolt*, 159.
76. Paul Kleppner, *The Cross of Culture: A Social Analysis of Midwestern Politics, 1850-1900* (New York: Free Press, 1970), 354.
77. Palmer, *Man over Money*, 5.
78. Pollack, *Populist Response to Industrial America*, 18.
79. Ibid., 26-27.
80. Mickey Crews, *The Church of God: A Social History* (Knoxville: University of Tennessee Press, 1990), 7, 8, 13, 14.
81. Hofstadter, *Age of Reform*.
82. C. Vann Woodward, *Tom Watson: Agrarian Rebel* (New York: Holt, Rinehart, 1955).
83. Crews, *Church of God*.
84. Phillip E. Johnson, *Darwin on Trial* (Washington, D.C.: Regnery Gateway, 1991).
85. Clanton, *Kansas Populism*.
86. Paolo Coletta, *William Jennings Bryan*, vol. 3 (Lincoln: University of Nebraska Press, 1969), 288.
87. The temperance movement, criticized though it was by liberal historians such as Hofstadter, was closely linked with other progressive causes, including women's suffrage, workmen's compensation, the enactment of child labor laws, and the direct election of senators. It could be so linked because alcoholism was a serious social problem, and the saloon was a symbol of unregulated capitalism, as destructive to the fabric of families and communities as the sweatshop. See Norman H. Clark, *Deliver Us from Evil: An Interpretation of American Prohibition* (New York: Norton, 1976); and Hofstadter, *Age of Reform*.
88. Smith, *Social and Religious Thought of Bryan*.
89. Daniel Bell, *The Cultural Contradictions of Capitalism* (New York: Basic Books, 1976).

90. Smith, *Social and Religious Thought of Bryan,* 13.
91. Ibid., 38, 189.
92. Ibid., 191.
93. Paul Kleppner, *Continuity and Change in Electoral Politics, 1892-1928* (Westport, Conn.: Greenwood, 1987), 110, 112.
94. Kleppner, *Cross of Culture,* 338-339, 341-342, 345, 347, 369.
95. Ibid., 258, 339, 375.
96. Roosevelt's populist and religious rhetoric is well cataloged in Ruth Ann Willner's fine study of charisma; see *The Spellbinders: Charismatic Political Leadership* (New Haven: Yale University Press, 1984), chap. 7. This imagery echoes Ignatius Donnelly's *Caesar's Column: A Story of the Twentieth Century* (Cambridge, Mass.: Belknap Press, 1960), as well as the speeches of Bryan.
97. Smith, *Social and Religious Thought of Bryan,* 14.
98. Coletta, *Bryan,* vol. 3, 298.
99. See Gerald H. Gaither, *Blacks and the Populist Revolt: Ballots and Bigotry in the New South* (Tuscaloosa: University of Alabama Press, 1977); and Robert M. Saunders, "Southern Populists and the Negro, 1893-1895," *Journal of Negro History* 54 (July 1969): 240-261.
100. Robert Booth Fowler, *Religion and Politics in America* (Metuchen, N.J.: Scarecrow, 1985).
101. C. Eric Lincoln and Lawrence H. Mamiya, *The Black Church in the African American Experience* (Durham, N.C.: Duke University Press, 1990).
102. Palmer, *Man over Money,* 51.
103. Gregg Cantrell and D. Scott Barton, "Texas Populists and the Failure of Biracial Politics," *Journal of Southern History* 55 (November 1989): 659-692.
104. Woodward, *Tom Watson.*
105. George M. Marsden, *Fundamentalism and American Culture* (New York: Oxford University Press, 1980).
106. Alan Brinkley, *Voices of Protest: Huey Long, Father Coughlin, and the Great Depression* (New York: Knopf, 1982).
107. Jackson has recounted this story to reporters numerous times.
108. Lowi, "Before Conservatism and Beyond."
109. Goodwyn, *Populist Moment.*
110. Clark, *Deliver Us from Evil.*

3

The Spiritual and Political Development of Jesse Jackson and Pat Robertson

> Profile 1: In 1992 this minister denounced the "ethical collapse" and "moral degeneracy" infecting American society, in particular rebuking its "Sodom and Gomorrah sex ethic." He called for stronger family life, prayer life, ethical education, and a return to the Ten Commandments.[1]

> Profile 2: In 1991 this religious leader expressed his disdain for the greed and immorality of bankers who pile debt on developing countries and American farmers and then impose hardship to collect the interest. Why not forgive the debt and save everybody a lot of suffering?[2]

Who is who? Contrary to what we might expect, the first profile is of Jesse Jackson; the second of Pat Robertson. In Chapter 1 we saw that populists often blended traditional moral beliefs with radical economic ideas, fearing as they did the threat of unfettered individualism in economics and culture. Jackson and Robertson echo these themes. Jackson combines an egalitarian economic message with "conservative" moral views, while Robertson's "traditional values" commingle with some historically populist, and quite radical, views about economics and debt. By analyzing the lives and messages of these two men we can more vividly see the contours of populist discontent in the contemporary United States.

THE POLITICAL ODYSSEY OF JESSE JACKSON

Jesse Jackson was nurtured in a morally traditional, communalist setting, though his political odyssey would take him, in some cases, far afield of that heritage. Born in Greenville, South Carolina, in 1941, Jackson was the object of scrutiny in the morally intrusive environment of this small southern town. As Jackson biographer Barbara Reynolds recounts, "Southern black communities were communal in a literal sense." Children were not allowed to "grow up through happenstance as they do in Northern urban areas." Instead, a "life plan for them [was] interwoven through the institutions of church, home, and school." Social mores were reinforced in these interlocking institutions so that "when Jesse was disruptive in class, he was disciplined at school, 'wupped' at home, and the preacher—that autocratic figure who dictated to the community—would publicly rebuke Jesse in church." When his behavior was a problem, "it was not unusual for the preacher and his teachers to converge on Jesse at his home." [3]

In this communal environment the individual would achieve his proper character through the nurturing and restraining bonds of the community. In repeated, mutually reinforcing messages Jackson and the other young people were told that the individual's obligation was to the community, not to the self. This message was especially poignant in the context of life in the segregated South. Yet one is struck with how much the experience of the southern black community resonates with the depictions of Puritan villages in colonial America or rural communities in nineteenth-century America or even the "morally suffocating" small towns depicted by a generation of writers. It was this communalist context, Reynolds argues, that provided the crucible through which Jackson would develop as a leader. Exhibiting bravado at an early age, Jackson made jokes about whites when most African Americans were too intimidated to dream of such behavior. But Jackson's bravado was backed by habits of diligent study, hard work, and discipline inculcated by morally nurturing community institutions—habits that have served him well. He was not raised by "antinomian" individualists.[4]

Jackson's burning ambition invites psychological speculation.[5] Born out of wedlock to Helen Burns, a teen-ager still in high school, Jesse grew up in a time and place in which an unwed mother still incurred gossip. Even more scandalous, Jesse's father, Noah Robinson, a married man with children, lived next door to Burns and made no attempt to disguise his paternity. Although Burns eventually married another man, Charles Jackson, young Jesse was preoccupied with his natural father and could be seen gazing into the window of the house next door, presumably trying to catch a glimpse of Robinson.[6] He watched with some envy as his half-brother, Noah Junior, freely moved in higher social circles than he could aspire to.[7] He endured the taunts of other children: "Jesse ain't got no dad-die. Jesse ain't got no dad-die. . . . You ain't nothing but a nobody, a nobody, nothing but a nobody." [8] One does not have to stretch far to understand the significance of this illegitimate son's famous refrain, "I am somebody."

Indelibly as such pain might be imprinted in a child, Jesse's character was also forged in the humiliating racist environment of the segregated South. But, as Reynolds suggests, where others were crushed Jackson became steeled: "The small town malice that tore at his birthright and the racism that denied him his human right actually fired his determination."[9] Jackson's natural talent and nerve put him in conflict with the white establishment more than once. When Jesse was eight years old, a store owner put a gun in his face to chasten him for his impudence. But Jackson's fierce pride was undaunted. A gifted athlete, he was recruited by the New York Giants baseball organization. He contemptuously turned down the offer when a white counterpart (a player he had struck out) received an offer of $95,000 to Jackson's $6,000. Later Jackson left the University of Illinois, where he had a football scholarship, because he felt the environment to be racist and he was not given the opportunity he desired—to be quarterback. Leaving Illinois, he enrolled in a black college, the Agricultural and Technical College of North Carolina at Greensboro. He graduated in 1964, after earning tremendous respect as a campus leader and star athlete. The theme of respect weaves throughout Jackson's life, asserting itself along with the struggle for dignity and racial justice. Michael Dukakis only dimly understood this need, when, during tense negotiations with Jackson in the summer of 1988, Jackson kept demanding respect, both for himself and as a sign to black voters that the presidential nominee recognized their aspirations.

Jackson's decision to enter the ministry came naturally from the church-based, African American community he grew up in. Jackson speaks fondly of the great preachers who influenced him and of the black congregations that helped shape the American story. Each one of those he recalls as influential in his formative years was a minister, and many other ministers later played a role in his decision to run for the presidency. As a college student, however, Jackson was ambivalent about the ministry. Fired to do civil rights work, he was at first attracted to law; he saw lawyers as "very well trained" and worldly wise, in contrast to many preachers who seemed to him "one-dimensional." But as Jackson describes it, one of the major influences on his going to seminary was Dr. Sam Proctor, a minister who headed A&T. Proctor told him that "law is much more limited than theology. . . . Seminary is the great books, history, law, theology, philosophy, systematics, world history. Law is a tiny component of that." Proctor persuaded Jackson to heed the "call" to ministry, and upon graduation in 1964 Jackson entered the Chicago Theological Seminary.[10]

JACKSON'S EVOLVING PROPHETIC STYLE

Jackson combined religious studies with political activism during those early years, honing his ability to find the sacred message in the secular event. In a way, the Christian message was ideally suited to Jackson's "gospel populism."[11] Like William Jennings Bryan, Jackson came to view the birth of Christ as one of the great political events in world history. God's son, born in a lowly stable, came to offer hope to the poor, justice to the oppressed, judgment to the powerful. "A new world was born in a manger," he said, "not in Herod's house." But Jackson's theology also merged naturally with his own story. His lowly birth would become a sign of his religious charisma and a metaphor of his populist identification with "the people." While acknowledging the presumption of calling oneself a prophet, Jackson views his ministry as part of that biblical, prophetic tradition.[12] A potent, if not altogether harmonious, blend of ambition and christic identification shaped Jackson as a powerful political figure.

The civil rights revolution that swept the South in the 1960s was a defining experience for Jackson. As an undergraduate he led a lunch-counter sit-in, after which he was arrested and spent a night in jail.[13] In 1965, as a Chicago seminarian, he would lead a delegation of students to the march in Selma, Alabama. Through sheer ambition and grit Jackson worked his way into the circle around Martin Luther King, Jr. In typically brash fashion the young Jackson implored King to move north to attack the segregation and racism found there. Never fully accepted by King's tight circle of aides, Jackson nonetheless helped to orchestrate King's northern campaign in Chicago; eventually he headed Operation Breadbasket, an affiliate of the Southern Christian Leadership Conference.[14]

What catapulted Jackson to a position of preeminence among blacks was King's assassination and Jackson's anointing by the media as the heir apparent. The details of these events are well known, but their interpretation is still disputed. Reynolds paints an unsavory picture of twenty-four hours of raw ambition in Jackson after King's murder. Soon after King was shot, Jackson was on the networks claiming to have cradled the dying man in his arms; in fact, Ralph Abernathy held King. Jackson also appeared at a Chicago city council meeting wearing a turtleneck sweater said to be smeared with King's blood. This act incensed other King confidants. Some claimed that Jackson could not have got blood on his sweater accidentally.[15] Garry Wills's depiction is more charitable; he explains the sweater (Jackson was standing below the balcony and blood spattered everywhere) and some of the statements (Jackson may have been the last person to speak with King, who was shot just after speaking to Jackson and the Rev. Samuel Kyles in the parking lot below). But Wills, uncharacteristically, seems to go out of his way to rationalize Jackson's behavior, in a portrait hardly less flattering to its subject than the children's biographies of Jackson.[16]

Nevertheless, Wills draws an important insight from these hazy circumstances: Jackson would continue to be "illegitimate in his claims"; he would remain "of ambiguous paternity where King is concerned, just as with his first two fathers." This "illegitimacy," in the eyes of many in the old civil rights establishment, would extend to his role as outsider and troublemaker in the Chicago Democratic party.[17] And finally, it would extend to his two presidential campaigns, in which he made herculean efforts to gain recognition as a legitimate leader to be reckoned with. His drive for legitimacy, for respect, would continue to propel him.

What distinguishes Jackson's drive, however, is his gift for translating his experience into a means of empathizing with and inspiring others who feel the sting of rebuke, failure, and crushed self-esteem. Jackson's life recalls Erik Erikson's classic biography of reformation leader Martin Luther, which probes the way individuals grapple with the psychological consequences of childhood suffering. According to Erikson, childhood suffering produces in the young adult an intense need, manifested in a kind of "patienthood" in search of a cure. A few extraordinary individuals, however, are able to translate their own painful experiences into a universal cause—into a struggle for others similarly afflicted—and in doing so they shape history:

> Now and again . . . an individual is called upon (called by whom, only the theologians claim to know, and by what, only bad psychologists) to lift his individual patienthood to the level of universal one and to try to solve for all what he could not solve for himself alone.[18]

In Jackson's leadership, then, we see the merger of religious wellsprings and psychological drives. Jackson's life has been a self-conscious quest to use his own struggle and triumph as a metaphor for the experience of the dispossessed. In his work with children through Operation Push (which focused on motivating inner-city students to excel in education), he leads them to recite the familiar litany:

> I am *(Jackson)*
> I am *(Kids)*
> Somebody *(Jackson)*
> Somebody *(Kids)*
> I may be poor
> I may be poor
> But I am somebody
> But I am somebody

> I may have lost hope
> I may have lost hope
> But I am somebody
> But I am somebody
> My mind's a pearl
> My mind's a pearl
> I can learn anything
> I can learn anything
> in the world
> in the world
> I am somebody
> I am somebody.[19]

Jackson self-consciously identifies his struggle with adults as well. In one of the most moving passages of his speech to the 1988 Democratic National Convention, he imagined what those without hope might be thinking: "Jesse Jackson, you don't understand my situation. You be on television. You don't understand. I see you with big people. You don't understand." But then Jackson engages in a remarkable litany of psychological self-revelation:

> I understand. You're seeing me on TV, but you don't know what makes me me.... They wonder what makes Jesse run, because they see me running for the White House. They don't see the house I'm running from.... I have a story.... I was born to a teen-age mother who was born to a teen-age mother. I know abandonment and people being mean to you, and saying you're nothing and nobody, and can never be anything. I understand. Jesse Jackson is my third name. I'm adopted.... I understand when you have no name.... I understand work. I was not born with a silver spoon in my mouth. I had a shovel programmed for my hand.... I really do understand. Every one of these funny labels they put on you, those of you who are watching this broadcast tonight in the projects, on the corners, understand. Call you outcast, lowdown, you can't make it, you're nothing, you're from nobody, subclass, underclass—when you see Jesse Jackson, when my name goes in nomination, your name goes in nomination. I was born in the slum, but the slum was not born in me. And it wasn't born in you, and you can make it. Hold your head high, stick your chest out. You can make it.[20]

Throughout the 1988 campaign Jackson gave rhetorical voice to these sentiments and tried to live them as well. He moved effortlessly from the role of prophet to that of minister, attending farm foreclosures to offer spiritual solace to families in crisis or praying with AIDS patients. Trained as a minister to deal with suffering and death, he exhibited no discomfort or embarrassment in situations that other candidates naturally would shun. As Wills notes, it was Jackson's ministerial persona that broke down barriers during his 1988 campaign: "In Iowa, when Jackson, the urban black activist, first talked to white farmers, he was somehow less menacing, less alien, because he shared their language on Sundays. Staying overnight in voters' homes, he said prayers before meals." [21]

The bond between Jackson and his core followers may seem obvious enough: He is an articulate black man speaking to black concerns. And, indeed, that is how many journalists treated his campaign. But there is a deeper dimension, as we have seen. Jackson's "transforming" leadership,[22] forged in a communal and moral context and fired by powerful psychological drives, was given vent by a religious vision that sees suffering as redemptive and sacrifice as Christ-like. Only in this light can we comprehend Jackson's undeniable charisma, attested to by his followers interviewed throughout this research.[23]

During one interview, for example, a minister from Detroit struggled to describe Jackson's charismatic bond in the community: "He is one of us . . . and by that I don't mean just that he's black or a minister. I mean he is ONE OF US . . . and he is a genius!" Delegates at the Democratic convention would assert, "He is our leader," in a kind of identification seldom found among the Dukakis supporters. Jackson followers across the nation noted again and again how he delivered the sermon at their church or spoke to a local high school about drugs or joined a local struggle. They spoke to his remarkable gifts, his athletic prowess, his debating skills, his fiery oratory, his prophetic witness, his redemptive suffering. More than anything else, they spoke with pride—pride in what he had accomplished, pride in how he had shown whites that a black man can win a debate with any white leader alive.

We cannot understand Jackson's life and message, then, apart from the context of African American politics. For our purposes, what is important is that the 1980s marked a watershed for African American politics, and events pushed the black electorate to the forefront of populist insurgency. The nation elected Ronald Reagan as president, a man ideologically committed to reversing civil rights gains. (As governor of California he had opposed the civil rights and voting rights acts of the 1960s.) Reagan's election coincided with a perception of cultural crisis in the black community. In the 1980s many African Americans, dependent upon industrial jobs and with little capital to cushion them, were unable to respond easily to the upheavals in the global marketplace. Moreover, there was little to stop multinational corporations from withdrawing capital and closing plants in the inner cities, thus deepening the economic disparity between blacks and whites.[24] This economic plight exacerbated the growing crisis of out-of-wedlock pregnancies and single-parent (or no-parent) households that left many young blacks even farther behind.[25]

In a way Jackson was ideally positioned to speak to the economic and cultural disturbances afflicting portions of the black community because he had addressed these dual crises for much of his adult life. As Roger Hatch notes, Jackson's message has long combined the populist blend of progressive economics and conservative cultural values. Government and corporate policies, Jackson contends, must expand economic opportunities to those at the bottom of the ladder; simultaneously, those at the bottom must develop moral character and disciplined habits to allow them to take advantage of expanded opportunities. "Both opportunity and effort are essential," and, as Hatch observes, Jackson "rarely emphasizes one element of the dialectic at the expense of the other.[26]

JACKSON'S POPULIST MESSAGE: ECHOES OF BRYAN

A detailed analysis of Jackson's message illuminates its populist themes. His message blends a vision of the "moral economy," which those on the left see eroding, with a vision of the "moral community," which those on the right characteristically see under siege. Although he is associated with left-wing populism, his life has exhibited a strong element of the culturally conservative themes found in right-wing populism. The exigencies of campaigning within the Democratic party, however, pushed him toward an accommodation with the cultural left that in the past he had eschewed. Still, the populist themes in Jesse Jackson's presidential campaigns, replete with attempts to capitalize on the distress and anger in the farm belt, suggest that we are not completely off the track in including the black revolt of the 1980s within an analysis of populism. Indeed, his campaign staff sent him "wherever there was suffering," to meet striking workers or angry farmers. And he continues to function as a traveling prophet with a bruising schedule only slightly less frenetic than a presidential candidate "campaigning to change the country." [27]

Jackson's speeches and writings reveal striking echoes of Bryan and other nineteenth-century populists. Jackson condemned the doctrine of "might makes right" in exactly the same terms that Bryan did. Like Bryan, he saw his political efforts as rooted in a moral context: "In my preaching, teaching, and activism over the past quarter of a century . . . I have tried to illustrate that the issues of life flow primarily from the heart, not from the head, and that at the center of every political, economic, legal, and social issue is the spiritual, moral, and ethical dimension." Just as Bryan viewed his political crusades as an extension of Christian witness, so did Jackson see his public work flowing from his faith. "My religion obligates me to be political, that is, to seek to do God's will and allow the spiritual Word to become concrete justice and dwell among us." Both Bryan and Jackson liberally sprinkled biblical allusions into their speeches and conversation. And even when Jackson does not directly quote Scripture, we hear the inevitable biblical cadence: "Weeping may endure for a night, but joy is coming in the morning." [28] Like Bryan's oratory, Jackson's allusions do not vaguely evoke civil religion or deistic providence; they are unabashedly Christian and specific. Calling the nation to a higher moral purpose, Jackson preached in his 1988 speech to the Democratic convention, "As Jesus said, 'Not my will, but thine be done.'"

In the populist tradition both Bryan and Jackson identified suffering people as special in God's sight and as carriers of true democracy. Bryan, accused of demagoguery because he spoke in behalf of the masses, made this response: "The Bible tells us that when Christ preached, those who 'devoured widow's houses' would have turned him away, but the common people heard him gladly." Since the "deceitfulness of riches" chokes the truth, Bryan sermonized, reforms in society "never come down from the well-to-do." Rather, "the common people of this nation are the only ones who will defend Democratic institutions." [29] Jackson, fond of speaking for the "disinherited, disrespected, and the despised," shares that populist view: "Jesus was rejected from the inn and born in a slum." [30] This explicit identification of Jesus with the "movement" is characteristically populist. Bryan spoke often of the Nazarene who championed the common people. Jackson too spoke a christic language to depict his movement. In calling his party to reclaim its roots, Jackson was as unabashed in his Christian witness as the Great Commoner, and he was an equally deft word merchant: "Jesus said that we should not be judged by the bark we wear but by the fruit we bear. Jesus said that we must measure greatness by how we treat the least of these." [31] Jackson's economic populism, moreover, touched a nerve in the same heartland that had nurtured Bryan. At the Nebraska state legislature he received a standing ovation for remarks redolent of past struggles: "If there must be a fight, let that fight be at the plant gate that closed without notice. Let that fight be against farm foreclosures. . . . Then we will be known as the generation that did justice and had mercy and walked in the way of God." [32]

People who suffer, according to Jackson and Bryan, are God's chosen, while the rich likewise are judged by biblical standards. Bryan celebrated the "struggling masses" who produced the wealth but who were "despised and spit upon" by "idle holders of idle capital." "What pains me more than anything else," Bryan intoned, "is to find the common people, who are always the most law abiding people of the community, denounced as anarchists by those who override the law, defy the government and dispute authority with Jehovah himself." [33]

Similarly, Jackson eloquently championed those whom others forgot, the working poor:

> They catch the early bus. . . . They raise other people's children. . . . They drive dangerous cabs. . . . They work in hospitals. . . . They wipe the bodies of those who are sick with fever and pain. They empty their bedpans. They clean out their commode. No job is beneath them, and yet when they get sick they cannot lie in the bed they made up every day. America, that is not right. We are a better nation than that.[34]

Bryan rebuked those who would give encouragement to the poor but would leave "the brother or sister naked or destitute." [35] So Jackson spoke. "We are not a perfect people. Yet we are called to a perfect mission: to feed the hungry, to clothe the naked, to house the homeless, to teach the illiterate, to provide jobs for the jobless." [36] Jackson saw himself as the conscience of the Democratic party, calling the party back to its populist roots. So, too, did Bryan see himself a century earlier: "The Democratic Party cannot serve God and Mammon; it cannot serve plutocracy and at the same time defend the rights of the masses." [37] And as Bryan saw great political potential in the populist mobilization of the alienated, so did Jackson:

> When I was a child . . . the Reverend . . . would quote Jesus as saying, "If I be lifted up, I'll draw all men unto me." When I was a child I didn't quite understand what he meant. But I understand it a little better now. If you raise up truth, it's magnetic. . . . We must raise up a simple proposition: feed the hungry, and the poor will come running; study war no more, and our youth will come running . . . put America back to work . . . the unemployed will come running.[38]

To both populists the concentration of wealth was a great economic and political evil. Bryan asked, "If it is alarming that thirty-six thousand people own one-half of the wealth of the country, is it not also alarming that these same people are uniting to control legislation in order that they may continue to dominate the politics of this country?" [39] Jackson, similarly, chastised the Reagan administration for increasing the disparity between the rich and the poor. Both Bryan and Jackson offered similar critiques of the economic theories guiding the Republican administrations they opposed. In condemning the "supply side" economics of his day, Bryan argued:

> There are two ideas of government. There are those who believe that, if you will only legislate to make the well-to-do prosperous, their prosperity will leak through on those below. The Democratic idea, however, has been that if you legislate to make the masses prosperous, their prosperity will find its way up through every class which rests upon them.[40]

In similar terms Jackson scorned the trickle-down economics of the

1980s: "Reaganomics. Based on the belief that the rich had too little money and the poor too much. . . . So, they engage in reverse Robin Hood—took from the poor, gave to the rich, paid for by the middle class." [41]

If Bryan could catalog the sufferings of people as no other in his day, Jackson has inherited that legacy. At a Rainbow Coalition meeting in January 1992, Jackson reminded listeners not to forget the struggling working people of America. Then he told the painful story of one working woman that summarized so well Jackson's analysis of the forgotten American:

> We must ask about Cynthia Chavis Wall. Mrs. Wall was a single mother. She worked for thirteen years at a textile factory near Hamlet, North Carolina, making $8 an hour. She was fired when she stayed home to care for a daughter threatened by pneumonia. Desperate for a job, she went to Imperial Food Products Company, Hamlet's largest employer. There she worked long hours making chicken parts for fast-food restaurants. She worked near fryers with oil heated to 400 degrees in a factory with few windows and no fans. She returned home drenched in sweat, her fingers cut and bleeding. She worked an eight-hour shift, receiving one-half hour for lunch and two fifteen-minute breaks. She worked with pregnant women, six and seven months pregnant, who had two bathroom breaks a day, sometimes unable to hold their water. The doors were locked from the outside to guard against the theft of chicken parts. . . . On September 3, a fire broke out at Imperial Food. Panicked workers ran into locked doors and could not get out. Of ninety people on the shift, twenty-five died and over fifty were injured. Mrs. Cynthia Chavis Wall's body was found that afternoon.[42]

Jackson then aimed the sad story at the "aristocratic" George Bush:

> George Bush never met Mrs. Wall. Surely if he had, he would not have vetoed the first minimum wage in a decade. If he had met her precious daughter, he would not have vetoed the family leave act, which would have given Mrs. Wall the right to unpaid leave to care for her daughter without losing her job. If he had visited Imperial Food Products, surely he would not have turned his head as OSHA [Occupational Safety and Health Administration] enforcement budgets were slashed over the last decade.

The speech ended with a populist flourish:

> The president breakfasts with the wealthiest people in the world, but he has not shared eggs and biscuits with the working people of Hamlet. . . . If he did, he might learn what it means to live on $115 a week, working full time on the hardest jobs, unable to afford health care. . . . We need a program for working Americans that is commensurate with the size of our problems.[43]

Even in their campaign styles we see haunting similarities between these two populists. Driven, energetic, and committed, Bryan practically invented the modern presidential campaign, traveling an astonishing number of miles in primitive conditions to give an estimated six hundred speeches to several million people.[44] Vastly outspent by his Republican opponent, he was one of the great campaigners of his day. Jackson, too, is a masterful campaigner, one of the best in this century according to Richard Nixon, a "natural" in politics. With his charismatic appeal in the black churches and his ability to keep himself in the news, Jackson had no need for paid commercials. "We are a poor campaign with a rich message," he liked to say.

Jackson's specific proposals called for greater public investment in housing, health care, and infrastructure. These initiatives would put the unemployed to work, provide job training and experience, and bolster the long-term health of the economy. Jackson proposed a national investment bank to be funded through the vast pool of national pension funds. The twenty-five largest pension funds hold $500 billion in potential investment capital; Jackson believed these funds were not being invested in a manner compatible with making the United States globally competitive. He hammered away at the theme "investing in America," by which he meant "investing in the community structures that keep this country at work—vital projects like roads, bridges, ports, harbors and water treatment." [45] To Jackson there is something morally and economically wrong when people are out of work and lacking in job skills, while the country's bridges, roads, and public housing are crumbling. He continued to articulate this theme even when he announced that he would not run a third time for the presidency. Pointing his finger at a boarded-up apartment building in Washington, D.C., Jackson challenged the nation to train and employ bricklayers, plumbers, glaziers, and carpenters to combat urban decay. Notably, several presidential candidates in 1992 made Jackson's theme of "investing in America" a core plank in their platform.

The legacy of race in America adds special poignancy to Jackson's populist message. Hatch observes that "as a result of this country's 350 year history of slavery, segregation, and discrimination black Americans find themselves behind in nearly every area of American life that is desirable and ahead in nearly every area that is undesirable." Thus racial justice is the "starting point of Jackson's analysis." [46] To Jackson justice for American blacks demands true power sharing and economic reciprocity as well as "opportunity." Justice calls for "our share," not welfare; trade, not aid. This progressive racial vision, moreover, has become linked in Jackson's mind with the plight of all others left out of the American dream. To Jackson African Americans will always be in the vanguard of progressive politics because they understand better than others the failures of the politics of smugness. Once again, we hear echoes of the Great Commoner as Jackson articulates this theme:

> As I look out over the landscape of America and see 10 million able-bodied men and women who are actively seeking employment but unable to find jobs; as I read with sorrow about the record number of foreclosures on homes and farms because people who have worked all their lives are unable to make the mortgage notes; as I behold families sleeping in automobiles and under bridges and standing numbly and shamefully in cheese lines because they have no food in the wealthiest nation on earth; as I see schools being closed and jails being built, teachers being fired and jailers being hired; as I watch our national tax code become increasingly regressive, unfair, and full of wasteful, unjustifiable subsidies for big corporations and wealthy individuals; as I watch the leaders of the nation's largest corporations use windfall tax breaks for foreign investment, conglomerate mergers, acquisitions, and other fast-buck schemes which add nothing to our national levels of employment, productivity, or output . . . it is clear to me that if America stands before the mirror of justice it must answer Ronald Reagan's question "Are You better off today than you were four years ago?" with a resounding "No!"[47]

At the end of the nineteenth century Democrat William Jennings Bryan and Republican William McKinley offered the nation vastly different visions. In a way Ronald Reagan and Jesse Jackson were the true protagonists of the 1980s. Reagan saw America from above through romantic, nostalgic eyes; Jackson viewed it prophetically from the suffering below. Jackson's entrance into presidential politics was a reaction to Reagan's ascendance. While other political leaders rose and fell from prominence, these two graced the list of the ten "most admired men" in America throughout the decade. In 1984 Jackson was third on the Gallup honor roll, behind Reagan and Pope John Paul II; by 1991 he was ninth, just behind Reagan.[48]

Admiration for Jackson rested on more than racial pride or economic populism (for, as we shall see in Chapter 6, many white charismatic Christians said he inspired them as well). What distinguishes Jackson from other progressive politicians is a moral and religious traditionalism that cuts across ideological lines.

JACKSON'S CRITIQUE OF LIBERAL CULTURE

If Jackson exemplifies economically populist themes, his life and message also display a cultural and moral conservatism suggestive of Bryan's crusades against alcohol and libertine morality. As a minister and heir to a morally traditional culture, Jackson had built his career with Operation Push on the basis of the message—hammered home in speeches at hundreds of schools—that young people had to develop discipline, a strong work ethic, and sexual self-control for their own welfare and for the good of the community. This emphasis places Jackson in tension with a number of liberal cultural trends in the broader society. As Robert Booth Fowler observes, a liberal culture fosters moral relativism, in part because it promotes skepticism about spiritually revealed codes of behavior.[49] Although some leftists may celebrate the morally unrestrained individual, Jackson, as a minister, believer, and moralist, will not brook such an idea. In pondering the tension between freedom and morality, he articulates a critique of what he calls "boundless liberalism."[50] Because he is convinced that God's moral truths are knowable and that they demand a public response, he is not uncomfortable with a language of moral certitude, which most liberals find unseemly. When he condemns drug abuse and sexual irresponsibility, or when he chastises the media for promoting hedonism among the young, he does so with the same moral conviction that he shows when denouncing racism and economic injustice. Jackson's populist and moral vision, then, shapes his views about liberalism.

Liberalism and the Moral Center

At the heart of Jackson's thought is the concept of the "moral center," a phrase he uses in speeches and conversation to describe his conviction that a clear moral dimension exists on every issue. Although others may attempt to "move toward the political center," to get more votes, Jackson seeks to discern and champion the moral center, a vision that shapes his progressive economics and idealist foreign policy views. Whether the issue is foreign trade or inner-city aid, race relations or welfare, Jackson pursues the moral center. Not surprisingly, this mission guides his criticism of the moral excesses of a liberal culture.

To be sure, in many respects Jackson remains a devout liberal and an ardent foe of conservatism, at least as these terms are commonly understood. "Conservatives," he says with grimacing face, "are people who want to keep people like me out." Conservatives, Jackson notes, shrink back from inviting others into their orbit for fear that their world view will be challenged. "They have a very narrow view" and thus are threatened by change. In historical terms, Jackson says, conservatives resisted all the major reforms now understood as simple justice. Conservatives supported slavery and segregation, resisted civil rights and voting rights, opposed unions and worker rights. Liberals, on the other hand, "support expansion and inclusion" and are open to change. On ideas and learning, Jackson says, "Liberalism means read any book as opposed to only a few books. . . . Conservativism means you could not read a book about communism, or can't read Karl Marx; liberalism meant read all of it, and conclude that a godless ideology cannot prevail very long. Liberal freedom meant 'Free to read; you know, FREE.' "[51]

Jackson tempers his support for liberalism, however, believing that abuses occur when people practice freedom without limits. He criticizes both "boundless liberalism and static conservatism." Because liberalism means unfettered freedom for individuals to "expand, grow," it can lead to destructive behavior if not restrained by moral limits. Thus in Jackson's view "boundless liberalism" can degenerate into "every drunken festival," with people "smoking pot, drinking liquor, and engaging in all kinds of Sodom and Gomorrah behavior." Similarly, free speech can become "abusive speech." Reflecting upon the blossoming of the 1960s, Jackson draws a sharp distinction between the civil rights struggle and the counterculture. Liberalism, with "real integrity and meaning," meant "taking a strong position against racial segregation; it didn't mean walking around with a Sodom and Gomorrah sex ethic." [52] Beginning with his work in the 1970s with Operation Push, Jackson has consistently preached cultural and moral restraint in his message. To Jackson the counterculture, which reveled in drugs, promiscuous sex, and sloth, should not be lumped together with the disciplined, sacrificial, and hard-fought civil rights movement. As his longtime aide Frank Watkins put it, civil rights workers suffered courageously to gain fundamental justice for black Americans, while upper middle class white college kids wanted the "right to make love in the park." Freedom to Jackson does not mean the "freedom to be decadent." [53]

With a religiously rooted understanding of timeless principles, Jackson articulates a clear sense of the potentials and dilemmas of a society that celebrates freedom. "Freedom," Jackson says, "involves choices and also consequences. . . . You're free to step out of this plane. But you also accept the consequences when you land. And when you land, you do not break the law of gravity; you prove the law of gravity." [54] Thus in Jackson's view abuse of freedom leads to "destruction." And he unabashedly invokes the religious meaning of that destruction: "The wages of sin is death." [55]

Drugs and the New Temperance Crusade

A dramatic example of Jackson's understanding of destructive freedom is his position on narcotics. In few areas has Jackson expressed such consistent and passionate conviction as on drug abuse. A century ago temperance reformers, including Bryan, saw alcoholism as a scourge that left families broken, children destitute, and industry sapped.[56] In terms strikingly similar to those used by nineteenth-century crusaders, Jackson has denounced the scourge of dope, condemning economic and cultural elites alike. He has condemned bankers who launder billions of dollars in drug money, but he has also reproved those in entertainment who glorify drugs. In 1986 Jackson declared war on the drug trade in his eulogy for Don Rogers, the football star who died of a cocaine overdose. Listen to the echoes of the temperance movement a century earlier:

> Today we're in a war where the enemy is disguised as our friend. . . . Terrorism is camouflaged as terrific. . . . Yet the KKK . . . and the rope have never killed as many of our young people as the pusher of dope. Pushers are terrorists and death messengers. . . . Drugs are the hound of hell for this generation. . . . When drugs attack, our minds go, our morals go, our morale goes, and pretty soon the hound of hell takes our liberties and our life. . . . The transmitters of our culture—our artists, athletes, television, radio, video, and music—are glorifying and adding glitter to the poison, which is making it socially acceptable as entertainment, a personal right and privilege, and inoffensive. . . . Today we declare a state of emergency. The living of our generation have been summoned to declare war on a plague.[57]

Just as reformers implored an earlier generation to take the temperance pledge, so did Jackson urge such a radical response to the epidemic of alcohol and drug abuse. In many speeches to school audiences, Jackson pleaded with students to get off dope, to substitute hard study for passive TV watching, and to end the cycle of "babies making babies." Gail Sheehy's account of these exhortations to high school students demonstrates Jackson's remarkable charisma and influence with young people. Jackson always gives his inspirational speech, then employs a variation on the Baptist altar call: "Stand and come forward if you are today renouncing drugs." By the end of the assembly, scores, perhaps hundreds, of students—tough kids, many weeping—have come forward to admit their sinfulness, much to the astonishment of teachers and parents.[58] Critics charge that the results are ephemeral, but one cannot imagine another political figure even attempting such a feat.

An Urban Policy from Moses

If liberalism is agnostic about the reality of fixed moral truths and tolerant of alternative ethical ideas, Jackson lives in tension with it; he remains convinced that timeless moral laws exist. One of the most striking examples of this conviction is his analysis of crime and community breakdown in the inner cities. Although he calls for institutional and policy changes to address the economic and racial oppression that afflicts the inner-city poor, Jackson stresses the moral dimension with equal vigor. Surveying the specter of lawlessness in the inner cities, for example, he concluded that it reflects a profound moral and religious collapse. Speaking at a Rainbow Coalition meeting in

January 1992, he lamented the senseless violence ravaging the cities. People are not stealing from hunger, he said, because they are not stealing bread. They are not killing out of self-defense, he argued, because drive-by shootings are just plain "mad dog crazy." Look at the staggering cost of crime, he implored his audience, think of how our neighborhoods could be revived if crime were reduced. Later, on March 12, Jackson offered his "ten-point urban policy plan":

> I spoke at Harvard last night, at the Kennedy School. . . . After I gave my political analysis, I said I would convene the mayors [of the fifty top cities] to increase registration by 25 percent, reduce crime by 25 percent, and reduce illiteracy by 25 percent. Crime is not mandatory, it's predatory, and it's growing. But I am convinced that the policy by which you change this is a ten-point plan Moses brought from the mountain.[59]

Elaborating on the need for the Ten Commandments, Jackson suggested that the people in the inner cities have lost their way much as the Israelites had. At first, after their liberation from bondage, the people of Israel lived "with this sense of unity, common feel, common love, common faith." Then they foolishly abused their freedom:

> They lost their way, disobeying God, disregarding their parents, laying with each other's husbands and wives, lying and stealing, worshiping idols.
>
> Moses said, "Stop this."
>
> They said, "Moses, you've got to understand. When you were a young preacher, young liberator, you could rap—you were with the real deal then. But you too old—you too old to dance."
>
> Moses did the only thing an old preacher knows to do. He went to the mountaintop, which was his prayer room, and told God all about it. "They're rebelling against you, against me, against everybody."
>
> God said, "Take 'em back this urban policy plan."
>
> No committee. No budget . . . ten-point plan.[60]

The crisis of crime, Jackson argued, "is not economic, it's ethical." Sounding much like a modern-day John Wesley, Jackson observed that if people "increase their ethics it'll also increase their economics because crime costs, it doesn't pay, it costs." He continued, "You want to shift from jail budgets to school budgets. You want to raise the value of neighborhood property again, neighborhood stores to come back, drug stores to come back, stop paying so much money for bars on their houses, stop paying so much for security, pay for child care or something—ten-point plan." Jackson then went down the list of commandments to show how they related to community health:

> People who respect their creator . . . behave differently. There's a sense of . . . healthy fear and trembling in his presence. Even if you do wrong, you feel uneasy; you're not likely to make right wrong and wrong

> right. If you won't honor the creator, you're not likely to honor the preacher, your mother, your father. . . . If you won't honor your mother and father, you won't honor your sister and brother. If you won't honor your sister and brother, you'll rape mine and steal from mine. All on down the line.
>
> So, do not be jealous of what other people got. So much of killing is jealousy, greed, want a bigger house, better house, more car than I can drive, more, more, more. Don't commit adultery. A lot of preachers preach around the commandments . . . to preach the laws [they] can comply with and then beat everybody else to death with 'em. . . . The preaching at its best is a willingness to face the two-edge sword, when you cut the sin in the congregation you cut the sin in yourself at the same time. So even if you do wrong, even if you disobey the law, don't bring it down and make it a doormat. Let it remain a chin bar. If you fall short, ask forgiveness but keep on reaching.[61]

Linking ethics to economics, Jackson then cited the enormous cost of the breakup of the family—so much of it caused by simple adultery—and its effect on child welfare. He cataloged the staggering costs of building prisons and housing the burgeoning prison population. "It costs twice to go to jail than Yale." An ethical revolution not to "lie and kill or commit adultery" would reap huge economic benefits for the community.

Of course, Pat Robertson has offered much the same analysis, though one expects that he might have received a different reception from Harvard. Jackson, told that his prescription sounded rather conservative, responded in this way:

> It may be the fallacy of labels. Moses was a social revolutionary, emancipator. The ten ethical laws are really liberating laws, they liberate culture. Now one might call those ten ethical laws "conservative" in that they are worth conserving. But Republicans act as if the Ten Commandments is their platform. That's Moses' platform; it's not a Republican platform. It preceded American politics.[62]

In some ways Jackson must struggle to reconcile his traditional moral vision with the demands of maintaining his progressive Rainbow Coalition. He acknowledges that there is some "tension" between his moral views and at least a contingent of the gay community that does not wish to accept moral limits on sexual promiscuity. On no issue, however, does Jackson remain as deeply ambivalent as on abortion, in spite of his publicly stated abortion-rights position.

The Agony of Abortion

Throughout the 1970s Jackson spoke vigorously against abortion; he addressed prolife rallies and even issued an open letter to Congress. In 1977 he wrote an essay for the *Right to Life News,* condemning abortion in philosophical terms that would have made outspoken Illinois Republican Henry Hyde proud. "Human life," said Jackson, "is the highest human good and God is the supreme good because he is the giver of life. . . . Everything I do proceeds from that religious and philosophical premise." He likened the dehumanizing language of racism to the language of prochoice advocates, who "never talk about aborting a baby because that would imply something human. Rather they talk about aborting the fetus. Fetus sounds less than human and therefore can be justified." With characteristic prophetic language Jackson reflected on the implications of an abortion culture. "What happens to the mind of a person and to the moral fabric of a nation that accepts the aborting of the life of a baby without a pang of conscience? What kind of person—what kind of society—will we have in 20 years hence if life can be taken so casually?" [63]

As a presidential candidate in 1984, however, Jackson reversed himself to embrace the prochoice position. Since then he has spoken at abortion-rights rallies and criticized antiabortion politicians. Commenting on this dramatic reversal, columnist Colman McCarthy argued that the old Jackson would have trounced the new Jackson in a debate. Jackson's support of abortion rights, for example, led him to echo the common argument that "it is not right to impose private, religious and moral positions on public policy," [64] an assertion clearly contrary to Jackson's prophetic style of political witness on other issues.[65] In contrast, he had this to say a decade earlier: "If one accepts the position that life is private, and therefore you have the right to do with it as you please, one must also accept the conclusion of that logic. That was the premise of slavery. You could not protest the existence or treatment of slaves on the plantation because that was private and therefore outside your right to be concerned." [66]

In spite of his declared position about abortion during two presidential campaigns, Jackson remains troubled by the issue. "I've really tortured my soul about the abortion question," a reflective Jackson observed in the spring of 1992, "I'm clear that under delicate, extenuating circumstances—life of the mother's at stake, incest—I'm clearer on abortion in those instances than I am abortion as birth control. That's not right to me." Jackson suggested that his views have changed because he is willing to "wrestle with the complications of life," because he allows experience to influence his thinking, because he searches to "make room for people." [67]

In a long discussion about abortion, Jackson demonstrated that he had thought about the nuances of the issue. Some antiabortion advocates would allow abortions in cases of rape or incest, but Jackson noted that the "complications of life" can lead to contradictions. "In a lot of societies with arranged marriages, relatives marry relatives . . . as in first cousins. That's incest, by our definition." And the issue of rape is painful for "those of us who came off plantations. . . . In so many ways a whole race of people—African Americans, and now of course many native Americans—come directly out of situations where we're the sons and daughters of relationships between the raped and the rapist. So even when you say rape, even that takes on a different light when you think about that. You get my point?" [68]

Privately, Jackson criticizes the extremes in both camps. "Some use abortion as a form of birth control; others use it to beat other people across the head unconditionally." Criticizing the antiabortion movement, Jackson noted that "some people love the fetus but show no comparable regard for the baby once it's born. Once the baby's born—can't afford day care. They even resist prenatal care. All they know is that they're against abortion. It's like giving them one little peg to hang on to." He resists punitive legislative attempts to reduce the number of abortions. Instead, he believes that "sex education and sex discipline on the front side for a young woman" and "more education and job opportunities on the back side" would significantly reduce the need for abortions. The more the young are provided with sex education and training in sex discipline, the less likely accidental pregnancies will occur. If a young woman gets pregnant, however, and "knows that pregnancy does not mean for her the end of education opportunities or a job, she may have the baby. So if you want to radically reduce abortions, then radically increase opportunities." [69]

Jackson admitted to having "the same fear and trembling" about abortion, in part because of his personal history. During his prolife phase, he often implied that had his mother conceived in a time more accepting of abortions, he might have been a victim. "I was born out of wedlock and against the advice that my mother received from her doctor." [70] Now he is less likely to put the matter so graphically, but he still notes how personal the issue is to him. "Tension? Born to a teen-age mother, I really understand that, feel it deeply." [71]

Perhaps there is some truth in Pat Robertson's assertion that Jackson's aides have turned him around on the issue. Frank Watkins recalled that Jackson's prolife position was one of the few differences he has had with the "reverend." Watkins noted, however, that Jackson "finally came around to my point of view on abortion." Still, he acknowledges that Jackson "has relapses now and then. . . . We've had to remind him that there is a difference between one's personal views and public policy." [72] Jackson apparently resisted these arguments until his presidential quest, when he actively sought feminist support for his Rainbow Coalition. Perhaps Jackson continues to struggle with abortion because he senses that political "expedience" may have moved him away from his previous conviction about the "moral center" of the issue.

TENSIONS IN THE DEMOCRATIC CAMPAIGN

Before his presidential campaigns in 1984 and 1988 Jackson's brand of populist politics puzzled some black intellectuals on the left, who saw Jackson as the reincarnation of a Booker T. Washington selling bourgeois values. The thought of Jackson leading the "progressive" movement was, to some leftists, repugnant and laughable. But Jackson's strength was his keen insight into the black community and his appreciation of the populist blend of economical radicalism and moral traditionalism often found in the black churches. Still, as Jackson's presidential ambitions grew and his political antennae tuned into the dynamics of the Democratic party, he adapted his message to appeal to those to whom he had previously shown little favor: feminists, gays, abortion-rights activists. As Manning Marable describes the campaign, it was Jackson who was "adopted" by the left and transformed by it.[73] He grew, according to Marable, because he broadened his message to pull together the disparate forces of the left—radical trade unionists, angry farmers, socialists, environmentalists, gays and lesbians, antinuclear activists, Sandinista enthusiasts, and Arab Americans. But in some ways this "growth" moved Jackson far afield from his ministerial roots. Jackson shifted from favoring laws against abortion to supporting public funding for abortions. He came out in favor of homosexual marriages. He joined a protest at Stanford University against the core curriculum, leading the chant, "Hey, hey, ho, ho, Western civ has got to go"—quite a change for a minister steeped in the poetry and imagery of the Bible.

Jackson's presidential campaigns thus were marked by a tension between his cultural heritage as a Baptist minister and the realities of Democratic politics. He retained the populist call to represent the voiceless and dispossessed, but he was increasingly ready to embrace what has been called the antinomian legacy of the 1960s, a libertarian rejection of the morally intrusive communalism that shaped his childhood. According to Edward Shils, antinomianism represents the radical individualism that seeks liberation from the burden of any obligations, "a life of complete self-determination, free of the constraints imposed by institutional rules and laws and of the stipulations of authority," a selfish freedom primarily for the gratification of any immediate desire, however destructive to the community.[74] It is hard to reconcile, though Jackson tried, the religiously inspired, community-based vision of black politics with the more libertarian elements of left-wing politics. The influence of these antinomian forces in the Democratic party, reflected again in the 1992 national convention, helps to explain why the populist heritage bifurcated in the late twentieth century. By default, in many cases, populists on the right gave voice to a growing cultural anxiety that those on the left refused to acknowledge as legitimate. Thus when Pat Robertson castigated elites, he often found them firmly ensconced in liberal politics.

THE SPIRITUAL JOURNEY OF PAT ROBERTSON

Born to privilege and worth millions through his broadcasting empire, Pat Robertson is a peculiar apostle of cultural populism, as he himself acknowledges. Asked during an interview whether he is a populist, he responded that he is an unlikely candidate for such an appellation:

> After all I'm a Yale law graduate, my father was a committee chairman of the United States Senate. . . . I harken back to a couple of presidents in my background and signers of the Declaration of Independence. So by the term "populist" I'm really not one of them. By heritage I'm more of the Eastern establishment.[75]

Yet Robertson added that by "inclination" he is "more aligned with the regular guy on the street." If Jackson identifies his constituency as the dispossessed, Robertson identifies his as the "unappreciated":

> The people who were coming to my rallies [for the 1988 presidential primaries] were just plain folks. They were farmers and they were shopkeepers and they were factory workers. I won in Dubuque, Iowa. . . . It was a Democratic factory town, and I was the only candidate, Democratic or Republican, to go into the big John Deere plant. . . . I really love people, and these people were responding to me.[76]

Still, Robertson resisted the populist label because in his mind populism suggested radical politics. "I'm traditional in what I believe, but traditional now is considered 'far right.'" At a deeper level, however, his argument about the struggle for the soul of America and his conviction about the failure of elites evokes the moralistic concerns and crisis language of the populists. Moreover, Robertson's denunciation of profligate banks, the savings and loan bailout, and the Trilateral Commission's domination of U.S. foreign policy sounds much like what a populist might say. The key to his own brand of populism, as we will see, lies in his spiritual journey.

Robertson, born the pampered son of a Virginia senator in 1930, seemed destined to a comfortable life as a well-connected lawyer.

Educated in prep schools, he entered Washington and Lee University at the age of sixteen and was graduated magna cum laude. As his biographer David Harrell recounts, Sen. Willis Robertson promised that if Pat made Phi Beta Kappa he could spend a summer in Europe. He did so when he was nineteen and spent the summer at the University of London as a student of fine arts. He also "traveled to France and Italy, drinking in culture and good times, a carefree, spirited young man." [77] Robertson then did his stint in the military, during the Korean War, where he was dubbed the "division liquor officer" by his buddies. At least some of his fellow marines resented his "privileged" position as a senator's son, a fact that would later haunt his presidential campaign, when former representative Pete McCloskey, R-Calif., aired the charge that the senator had used his influence to keep Pat out of combat. After Robertson's time in the marines his father rewarded him with another tour of Europe, just before he enrolled in Yale law school. His tastes centered on the Riviera and the bistros of Paris.

Some knowledge of Robertson's background is critical in understanding the radical turn of events that would produce this unlikely prophet against sin. While at Yale Robertson continued to "wing his way through life on charm and the casual use of his native abilities." Harrell summarized those years: "He was glib, charming, and a smashing poker player and casanova. 'Whiskey and women,' recalled one classmate, 'he was way out on the point there.'" This hedonistic life apparently caught up with Robertson. His law school performance suffered, he flunked the New York bar exam, and he abruptly married Adelia Elmer (Dede), a nursing student at Yale, ten weeks before their first child was born. These events seriously strained Robertson's relationship with his father. Yet although he began to show signs of introspection, he remained, by his own admission, arrogant, "cocksure, and self-centered." [78] After graduating from Yale he joined the New York investment company W. R. Grace, hoping to make a quick fortune. He resigned less than a year later to start his own company, which foundered.

Robertson's story reveals a profoundly discontented young man, often in conflict with his imposing father, living, according to his own account, a roguish life, yet spiritually hungry. He also seemed unable to achieve the kind of worldly success expected of a senator's son. Because his business failed to support his lifestyle, Robertson went deeply into debt, mostly to his parents. "He brooded over his series of failures. At home Dede observed that he was restless, pacing and drinking beer, filled with thinly veiled anxiety." Yet he and Dede continued to live the fashionable life "with a modish apartment on Staten Island that featured avant-garde decorations and a huge Modigliani nude in the living room; they patronized the Stork Club and other nightclubs." [79]

If Jesse Jackson is a worthy subject of psychobiography, so too is Robertson. Torn between a domineering father and a devout mother and beset with worldly failures, Robertson began to feel the tug of the spiritual. His mother, Gladys Robertson, had become attracted to fundamentalist churches and itinerant ministers, to whom she donated money. She sent religious tracts to the young couple, "praying constantly for their salvation." [80] Her entreaties came at a time when Robertson was increasingly discontented:

> It was in that period that there was just this incredible emptiness in my heart and I was looking for something better. I tried it all. I had pleasure. I had philosophy. I had made good grades. I had traveled all around the world. . . . And what I wanted was just not in any of those things. And I didn't know what it was.[81]

Robertson began to consider the ministry, first, as Harrell recounts, with an eye toward respectability, "in the form of the gracious Protestant churches that lay easily amidst the corporate skyscrapers of the city." This Christianity "offered much to young Pat Robertson—culture, dignity, and perhaps, most important, a regular and comfortable salary." The senator might approve such a ministry, but his mother regarded it as a cop-out: "Her prayers had not been that her son would become a minister—she wanted him to be a Christian." The turning point came when Gladys Robertson introduced Pat to Cornelius Vanderbreggen, an itinerant preacher she had supported financially. At a fashionable restaurant in Philadelphia, Vanderbreggen "witnessed" to Robertson in classic born-again fashion, "opening his Bible in the midst of the elegant restaurant, guilelessly probing those private and innermost feelings that genteel Christians did not discuss with a stranger." [82]

As Erikson suggests in his biography of Luther, an inner emptiness often seeks meaning in an "all or nothing posture," in a total commitment that really "means it." This, apparently, describes what happened to Robertson. The day after he met Vanderbreggen, "he began laughing, rejoicing that he had been saved." Although Dede resisted, Robertson radically altered his life, relishing such gestures as pouring "a bottle of Ballantine Scotch down the drain." He plunged into the conservative evangelical world, meeting evangelists and fundamentalist preachers. He enrolled in the Biblical Seminary of New York and sought out encounters with fervent Christians. Along this journey he encountered people who emphasized the charismatic gifts, such as speaking in tongues, and at last he seemed to find a home among those whose lives showed they "really meant it" by their "reckless, even fanatical" devotion. Robertson was actually introduced to speaking in tongues by a Korean women, Su Nae Chu, who was the widow of a Presbyterian minister killed during the Korean War. Charismatic sessions with his fellow seminary students would last hours; to Robertson these were "the most intense spiritual quests I have ever seen."[83]

Robertson's spiritual journey ultimately took him back to Virginia, where in 1959 he purchased a defunct television studio for a pittance ($70) and began spreading the word. From these humble beginnings he launched the Christian Broadcasting Network (CBN), which pioneered modern television ministries. The flagship program of CBN, "The 700 Club," a mixture of news, interviews, prayer, and (in the past) faith healing, got its name from a 1963 fund-raising campaign in which Robertson persuaded seven hundred viewers to pledge $10 a month to sustain the operation. As the years passed, Robertson adapted to new opportunities, adding satellite capacity in 1977, then converting to a twenty-four-hour cable network four years later. CBN provided Robertson with a broadcasting base from which he developed the hugely profitable Family Channel for cable TV.[84] The Family Channel reruns "wholesome" old television programs ("Lassie," "Leave It to Beaver," "The Waltons"), which are edited for moral content. It found a ready niche among parents concerned about the content of contemporary programming. Indeed, Robertson discovered that wholesome values were very good business. The Family Channel generated so much cash that by 1989 the IRS demanded its divestiture from the tax-exempt CBN. Robertson and his son complied, and in the complicated and controversial financial dealings that ensued, they gained controlling shares in a corporation worth millions. By 1992 the Family Channel was grossing nearly $150 million in annual revenues.[85] Critics allege that Robertson built this profitable enterprise with religious contributions from "The 700 Club" faithful. Supporters, however, see an entrepreneurial genius in Robertson that sets him apart from other television evangelists. Whatever one's interpretation, Robertson's enormous financial success buoys his continued political aspirations.

Robertson's religious conversion catapulted him into a Pentecostal world typically the domain of the lower classes. Yet his eager acceptance of charismatic expression also placed him at the center of a paradoxical trend in American social life. The very religious practices that academics viewed as least adapted to modernity—supernatural religion emphasizing gifts of the spirit, faith healing, speaking in tongues—grew in popularity during the 1960s and 1970s, even as other secular trends continued apace.[86] Thus Robertson moved "down" in social status at the very time when such practices were appealing to large numbers of people turned off by the shifting sands of modernity. Robertson's life therefore enabled him to speak to the power of the conversion he touted. He had lived the high life, but he abandoned the false gods of pleasure, symbolized by the Manhattan clubs that he likened to "softly lit, upholstered sewers." [87]

Although Robertson's religious expression clearly served his spiritual hunger, one senses in the growing scope of the CBN enterprise that he was also able to satisfy the taste for worldly success that preoccupied his father. A curious tension exists in the art and architecture of Robertson's Virginia Beach headquarters. The CBN empire is liberally graced with paintings of early Americans, thus linking the Founders of the nation to Robertson, who traces his lineage to the first settlers in Jamestown. On the grounds are Regent University, a modest version of Jefferson's University of Virginia, and Robertson's house, a graceful edifice, complete with pastured horses, befitting a southern gentleman of the eighteenth century. Robertson's religious journey has taken him full circle, from southern gentleman to religious zealot and back to southern gentleman. The enterprise, with its colonial motifs and biblical murals, with its upscale technology and pietistic religion, seems almost an attempt to harmonize the disparate elements of Robertson's life.

In response to such psychological explanations Robertson sees only continuity and God's plan. Just as there is a line of continuity from the Old Testament to the New, there is continuity from the early Church to the Protestant Reformation and from the Reformation to the founding of colonies in the New World. Moreover, there is a providential destiny in the "secret kingdom" for every individual, and Robertson sees evidence in the success of CBN that his purpose is to provide the next link in God's continuous plan. Thus above the entrance to the broadcasting headquarters is inscribed the Great Commission—"to go and make disciples of all nations." And in the darkened glass of the high-tech studio that beams "The 700 Club" around the world floats the visage of an aging St. Paul, a haunting reflection of a painting that hovers in blessing over the enterprise. One person's psychological explanation is another's destiny from God.

As an increasingly influential born-again charismatic, Robertson was at the center of a political movement that burst on the scene in the late 1970s. Profound social changes threatened theologically traditional Christians. The secularization of society that Bryan had feared a generation before seemed to be proceeding swiftly among the carriers of modern culture. Yet people seemed to yearn for religious and moral truths as much as ever. These societal tensions set the stage for a populist reaction against the elites whose contempt for the "religion of the people" made them an easy target of the politics of discontent. Robertson's foray into politics was the culmination of more than a decade of populist religious and moral stirrings that fractured old party and ideological ties. Robertson had been a lifelong Democrat and did not switch to the Republican party until the Reagan era. (In 1956 he had chaired Adlai Stevenson's campaign on Staten Island.) With the New Christian Right the Republican party inherited a new constituency that made some blue bloods uncomfortable. GOP strategists capitalized on the discontent symbolically, but how much they were able or willing to provide substantively is open to question. By 1988, as one top Republican official put it, many evangelicals were feeling feisty. "Theirs was the unfinished agenda." And Robertson was ready to lead the charge.

In spite of the ultimate failure of Robertson's presidential campaign, it is important to remember that he succeeded in mobilizing new political participants who will continue to press for amelioration of their grievances.[88] Moreover, as Garry Wills aptly noted, Bush's campaign for the presidency adopted elements of the cultural populism that Robertson had tapped;[89] these were devastatingly effective against Dukakis in the general election.[90] An analysis of Robertson's speeches and writings reveals why they fit within contemporary populism.

ROBERTSON'S CULTURAL POPULISM

As a charismatic Christian, Robertson took naturally to criticizing modern society. With its rejection of fixed moral principles, its celebration of the individual, and its acceptance of alternative lifestyles, liberal modernity seemed to undermine everything traditional wisdom taught was necessary for the good society. Moreover, Robertson found ammunition in the growing intellectual critique of the modern status quo, and his speeches and writing are sprinkled with references to Paul Johnson, Allan Bloom, E. D. Hirsch, and Paul Vitz. Thus despite the "feel good" themes promoted by Republicans in the 1980s, Robertson's speeches and paid media painted a dark picture of exploited children, poor schools, fractured families, and a vulnerable American economy. Those who responded to his message—many of them mobilized through churches or the parachurch networks of religious television—lived a world apart from many traditional business-class Republicans.[91]

In a speech announcing his potential candidacy, Robertson centered his criticism on the elite-led secularization that, in his view, undermined the foundations of society:

> We have permitted during the past twenty-five years an assault on our faith and values that would have been unthinkable to past generations of Americans. We have taken virtually all mention of God from our classrooms and textbooks. Using public funds we have begun courses in so-called values clarification which tend to undermine our historic Judeo-Christian faith. We have taken the Holy Bible from our young

> and replaced it with the thoughts of Charles Darwin, Karl Marx, Sigmund Freud, and John Dewey.[92]

Echoing Bryan's concern about moral relativism, Robertson charged that "instead of absolutes, our youth have been given situational ethics and the life-centered curriculum. Instead of a clear knowledge of right and wrong, they have been told 'if it feels good do it.' Instead of self-restraint they are often taught self-gratification and hedonism." If Bryan saw disturbing secular trends in the Jazz Age of the 1920s, Robertson saw their culmination in the antinomian "anything goes" morality that exploded in the 1960s and 1970s. His words ringing with the cadences of Old Testament prophecy, Robertson railed against the decadence of the age. "We have sown the wind—now we are reaping the whirlwind." [93]

Who is largely responsible for this sorry state of affairs? In true populist terms Robertson chastised the mass media and the cultural, legal, economic, and educational elites who control the powerful engines of economic life, socialization, and the law. About the law, Robertson said, "a small oligarchy . . . has been running this country for a long time and it has centered in the courts." [94] Comparing the Supreme Court with the Federal Reserve Board, Robertson elaborated on this theme:

> In essence we have two unelected elites which have enormous control over our destiny. One is our court. Five members of the court can make decisions which can radically alter the way we live, do business, educate our children, take care of our children . . . five members can do that. And the Federal Reserve, four members can do that.[95]

But the problem is not just the Supreme Court: the elite's flouting of tradition extends to the entire legal establishment dominated by liberal and secular values. Led by the American Civil Liberties Union, sympathetic judges have nearly succeeded in banishing the religious heritage of the nation. "A small elite of lawyers, judges, and educators have given us such a tortured view of the establishment of religion clause of the First Amendment of our Constitution that it has been called by one United States senator 'an intellectual scandal.' " [96]

In cultural affairs Robertson inveighs against the new-class elite that dominates the media, entertainment, and education. Echoing arguments made by neoconservative intellectuals about the disaster of the sexual revolution and the drug culture, Robertson seems incredulous that those who promoted through "liberal tolerance" divorce, runaway kids, astronomical teen-age pregnancy rates, the scourge of drug abuse, and the spread of AIDS should still be allowed to foist their failed solutions on the rest of the population. "The same liberal elites that gave us the problem deny the cause," which is that "human cruelty, human selfishness, alcoholism, drug addiction, and sexual promiscuity will always bring poverty and the disintegration of society."[97]

In education, Robertson argues, ageless wisdom has been replaced by the "new prophets" of the secular age: "The prophets of our generation are no longer the men of God. The prophets are the psychiatrists, the social scientists ... the heads of the learned departments at major universities ... these men of science are the new religion."[98] Special criticism therefore is directed at teachers unions, administrators, education colleges, and textbook publishers—whose embrace of "progressive education" made the schools "progressively worse" and deepened the problem of adult illiteracy. "The 'progressive education' advocated by John Dewey and his followers is a colossal failure and must be abandoned," Robertson states. "For our children's and our grandchildren's sake we must ensure that control of education is returned to their parents and caring teachers in local communities and taken away from a powerful union with leftist tendencies."[99] Clearly, Robertson capitalized on the growing populist revolt against the public school establishment, which was reflected in support for vouchers by inner-city blacks and others. Robertson's message was simple but compelling: "Our kids are owed—we owe them—a crime-free, drug-free, disciplined school environment, and we owe them learning in how to read and write; we owe them the transmission of our cultural values, and we owe them literacy skills."[100]

If Robertson makes the education establishment sound conspiratorial, his analysis comes from a simple conviction: all children and all illiterate adults have the capacity to learn, and if they are not learning, something must be wrong with the method used. The greatest tragedy, to Robertson, is the failure of public education to equip poor children for the future. He cites the experience of the renowned Chicago teacher Marva Collins, who makes extraordinary demands on ghetto children and has them reciting the classics by the seventh grade.[101] He credits his own initiative, Operation Heads Up, a literacy program emphasizing phonics and a huge vocabulary base, with teaching hundreds of thousands of functional illiterates to read and write. Discussing his Sing, Spell, Read, and Write program, Robertson claims

> I can guarantee that a child can learn to read, whether that child is Hispanic, black, American Indian, or Cambodian ... I can teach that child to read and write with fluency in English in thirty-six lessons. Guaranteed, 99%. We had one child in Pittsburgh who was reading at second-grade level. After twenty days, that child began reading at the seventh-grade level. I have seen little black children in Chicago, little fellas four years old, stand up and read a book. Tremendous. They were so excited, they didn't know what to do. I've seen them take newspapers and read words that would be jaw-breakers for most adults, read

> with fluency because we taught them the syllables and phonics ... because that's the way our brains work.[102]

Federal money is misspent, Robertson argues, if it merely supports the latest educational fad instead of focusing on the basics. Using volunteers and his phonics approach, Robertson claims that he can teach literacy for $8 per child or adult; thus with a fraction of the money spent by the federal government all the twenty-seven million functional illiterates in the United States could be reached if the right method were used. Why, then, does the educational establishment shun proven methods? The answer, to Robertson, is that these powerful interests have too much invested in the status quo to want change. He recounted that one school system in Selma, California, which served primarily children of Hispanic migrant workers, employed his Sing, Spell, Read, and Write curriculum as a demonstration project:

> They [the children] didn't have any education. They all spoke Spanish, and the school system had those children reading with considerable fluency at the end of the year. Yet with that demonstration project, the powers that be in the education system in California say, "No way. That would make us change our system, and we're not going to do it." [103]

If Robertson's message reflects a growing cultural populism in the United States, his concerns also echo populist views about large economic institutions. We will look at these less familiar views in the next section.

ROBERTSON'S CRITIQUE OF BANKERS

Since the founding of the American republic, populists have feared and distrusted the big banker, the paramount symbol of economic power at odds with the common folk. The cultural divide in colonial America between "locals" and "cosmopolitans" was often shaped by the money question; local farmers had an almost paranoid fear of being drawn into the web of commerce and debt in which they might lose their independence and self-reliance.[104] The debtor, they believed, was the slave of the lender, subject to his whims. The bondage was doubly to be feared because banks mysteriously manipulated the supply of money. This fear fit closely with religious beliefs, which cast debt in spiritual terms as contrary to the Protestant virtues of thrift and stewardship. After the Revolutionary War populists in the states often advanced debt relief and paper money schemes, much to the horror of cosmopolitans such as Alexander Hamilton, who sought to build a commercial empire based on the liberal use of credit. This money issue dominated the administration of Andrew Jackson, and his battle with the national bank, and blossomed again in the Populist era. In the late nineteenth century farmers found themselves repaying steep loans with deflated dollars, a product of the power of the large banks to restrict the money supply. Effective interest rates might at times approach 100 percent, thus encouraging the diverse calls for monetary expansion through silver coinage and the like.

In Pat Robertson we hear pronounced echoes of this struggle—a visceral reaction to the abusive and manipulative power of large financial institutions. Commenting on the savings and loan debacle, for example, Robertson remarked pointedly, "We shouldn't have to bail out the greed and the fraud of people in high finance." He expressed fear that a similar bailout will be demanded by large banks that made imprudent loans to developing countries. "They'll come in for funding through the Federal Reserve, and the taxpayers will have to pick it up again. And I think that is morally wrong. I think they should be accountable for their actions." [105]

Robertson's views go beyond these immediate issues to an ongoing fear of financial manipulation. In *The New World Order,* he uses intensely populist language to denounce the money trust, monopoly bankers, money barons, the capitalist cartel, and the "Establishment." [106] In his reading of history, powerful bankers hold citizens and businesses in bondage and can even capture governments needing cash as well:

> The money barons of Europe, who had established privately owned central banks like the Bank of England, found in war the excuse to make large loans to sovereign nations from money that they created out of nothing to be repaid by taxes from the people of the borrowing nations. . . . So monopoly bankers had two major goals. First, they sought to control the creation of money and the underlying political power of a nation. Second, they needed to encourage actions that would result in large-scale government deficit spending and debt creation at compound interest rates, paid for by taxes.[107]

Powerful European financial interests, he argues, tried to saddle the new nation with a private central bank, which Andrew Jackson wisely abolished. But the money barons persisted until they succeeded a century later in creating the Federal Reserve Board, which poorly serves the public interest. After surveying the failures of the Federal Reserve Board over the past half-century, Robertson sarcastically remarks, "So much for the benefits of a privately owned, and to my mind unconstitutional, central bank." Moreover, the Federal Reserve's creation "shows what incredible damage can be done to the banking system and the economy in general if a central bank has the power to shrink the money supply, force the default of loans, and collapse weak banks."[108]

Part of Robertson's outrage is directed at the apparent amorality of banks that pursue profit no matter what the end. Speaking in 1986 of his dream that communist tyranny would one day end, he called for the United States to "make our goal that no longer will communist tyranny be financed by loans and credits from bankers and industrialists in the free world." Not only did such loans prop up the communist dictators, but they co-opted the bankers as well. He chastised Western bankers who opposed the Polish Solidarity movement "because they were afraid that democracy in Poland would imperil their loans to the Communist government ... there's something inside of me viscerally that is opposed to that kind of greed and hypocrisy."[109]

This reaction to bankers, one senses, may stem as well from Robertson's own experience as a businessman. Speaking of the influence of the large banks, Robertson paints a vivid insider's picture:

> The power is subtle but incredibly intense. In high finance, all it takes is a quiet word from the right person to destroy the future of any public company that is carrying substantial debt.... The coup de grace is always administered in a paneled, deeply carpeted environment in the most genteel of tones. "I'm sorry, but our loan committee does not believe that this is a bankable proposition." "Our loan committee has voted not to renew your company's annual line."[110]

The influence of this "money trust," Robertson fears, extends into the large media organizations that shape mass opinion. Because banks manage vast trust funds, they exercise enormous leverage over the corporations in which they invest. Robertson echoes a familiar complaint heard on the left:

> It is my understanding that the major New York banks, and the trust funds that they manage, have substantial stock holdings in the New York Times Corporation, CBS, ABC, General Electric (which owns NBC), the Washington Post Company, the Times Mirror Corporation, and the Dow Jones Company (which publishes the *Wall Street Journal).* These corporations, and hundreds more industrial corporations, cannot afford to have demand loans called, credit lines canceled, essential expansion loans denied, their credit standing impugned, or a bear raid on their stock.... This awesome power—tantamount to the power of financial life and death—accounts for the fact that there never is a critical article about David Rockefeller ... in the major national media.[111]

Sounding decidedly left-wing, Robertson concludes that "the Establishment has built a network of interlocking corporate and bank boards in every phase of American life ... which control close to 60% of the total financial assets of the United States." [112] Such enormous power is alarming because of the increasing integration of world financial markets. Robertson looks at the Trilateral Commission, designed to increase economic and political cooperation between the United States, Japan, and Western Europe, and sees the velvet hand of the money trust satisfying its self-interest to the detriment of the public interest:

> The money barons are getting much closer to control of the world's economy than even they may have believed was possible. . . . Consider what would then happen if, in a Trilateral world, the central bank of Europe, the central bank of Japan, and the central bank of the United States began to coordinate their efforts, or even to merge. If that happened, some twenty-one people, possibly as few as three people, could control the money and credit of essentially the entire world.[113]

ROBERTSON AND THE TRADITION OF POPULIST PARANOIA

As we have seen, Robertson's analysis of high finance edges into what critics of populism see as its paranoid tendencies. Of course, one does not have to be paranoid to view with concern the power of large financial institutions. But with Robertson we enter a conspiratorial world of secret cabals operating behind the scenes toward goals more sinister than financial manipulation. In this he conforms to what Richard Hofstadter has called the paranoid style of American politics.

When George Bush proclaimed a "new world order" Robertson detected the ascendancy of a one-world, occult conspiracy whose origins could be traced back at least two hundred years. To Robertson this new world order conspiracy involves the destruction of national sovereignty, the abolition of private property, the "elimination of traditional Judeo-Christian theism," and rule by an elite that considers itself superior. He traces the origins of this conspiracy to the Illuminati, an eighteenth-century European secret society, which supposedly infiltrated the Masonic Order, sparked "satanic carnage" during the French Revolution, inspired the utopian thinking of the Marxists, and guided the nefarious designs of international bankers. Only by understanding the origins of this cabal, according to Robertson, can we appreciate the "commonality of interest between left-wing Bolsheviks and right-wing monopolistic capitalists." [114] Thus the international communist conspiracy is only a part of a broader movement that included the capitalist likes of Baron Rothschild, Cecil Rhodes, John D. Rockefeller, Andrew Carnegie, and J. P. Morgan.

Even more astonishingly, this conspiracy links the Council on Foreign Relations, the Federal Reserve Board, the State Department, the

Trilateral Commission, New Age religion, Masonic rituals, and occult signs on the U.S. dollar bill. Robertson concludes, "The New Age religions, the beliefs of the Illuminati, and Illuminated Freemasonry all seem to move along parallel tracks with world communism and world finance. Their appeals vary somewhat, but essentially they are striving for the same very frightening vision." Although Robertson qualifies some of his assertions, or poses them as questions, the conspiratorial tone remains. Commenting on the strange eye atop the pyramid on the dollar bill, Robertson sees clear evidence of the Masonic veneration of the Egyptian god Osiris. Then he adds, "Is it possible that a select few had a plan, revealed in the great seal adopted at the founding of the United States, to bring forth, not the nation that our founders and champions of liberty desired, but a totally different world order under a mystery religion designed to replace the old Christian world order of Europe and America?" [115]

No doubt many conservative Christians, who welcomed Robertson's advocacy of their concerns about moral decline, family breakup, and secularization of public schools, had no idea that in his mind these cultural trends are part of a grand conspiracy that includes communists, occult religionists, and "captains of wealth." Robertson tries to convince his readers that it all makes sense in light of the Christian understanding of Satan's seductive power. Just as there is a secret kingdom that penetrates the visible world with miracles from God, so there is a secret evil force that competes for earthly reign. Imagine for a moment, Robertson implores, how Satan might go about subverting healthy institutions and people. What better way than to draw people into an innocuous-sounding fraternal organization like the Masons:

> To my mind, there is no more monstrous evil than to bring public-spirited, often churchgoing, men into an organization that looks like a fraternal lodge, then deliberately mislead them until they are solid members. Then move them up thirty degrees to the place where they are ready to learn that Satan is the good god waiting to liberate mankind, and the Creator of the Universe (Yahweh, Elohim, Adonai) is, in their theology, the malicious prince of darkness.[116]

Robertson said that he wrote *The New World Order* in a short, intense period of time, which may give us a glimpse of how his mind works in a less reflective mode. We are left wondering how this well-read, intelligent man could seriously suggest that an Illuminati-inspired, occult and economic conspiracy might have been behind the assassination of Lincoln. What we see in Robertson is the darker inclination of populism, its capacity to degenerate at times into paranoid visions of evil cabals against "the people."

TENSIONS IN THE REPUBLICAN COALITION

Conspiracies aside, Robertson's critique of "liberal" elites in economics, education, law, and entertainment struck a chord in his followers, many of whom feel their values are flouted every day in the modern culture. Moreover, Robertson offered a populist, moralistic analysis of American society's ailments: selfishness, greed, and sexual irresponsibility are exploited by elites who care nothing for sustaining the foundations of a good society. What was needed, Robertson felt, was for the great mass of God-fearing citizens to rise up and say "no more." In this, we again hear an echo from an earlier day, when Bryan argued that the lack of community spirit is the ruin of society.

If Jackson diluted his populism with concessions to the antinomian left, Robertson had to make common cause with entrepreneurial enthusiasts in the Republican coalition who had little sympathy for his moral agenda and less for his economic views. No friend of unfettered capitalism, Robertson supported boycotts of stores that sold pornography and of advertisers that promoted sex and violence on TV. He criticized individuals and companies that make money in immoral ways. He charged that Time Warner's record division profits from heavy metal and rap music that blatantly incites violence and sexual abuse.[117] Not restricting himself to lifestyle issues, he criticized financial elites for "stock manipulation, blatant greed, and corruption."[118]

This less than favorable attitude toward capitalism did not go unnoticed. The *Wall Street Journal* featured several articles exploring Robertson's "off-beat" economic views. Most critical was an op-ed piece in 1988 by David Boaz, vice president of the libertarian Cato Institute, who labeled Robertson's economic views "crackpopulism." Boaz detected in Robertson a clear pattern of "hostility" toward credit, bankers, and the rich. He argued that Robertson was no friend of private enterprise but was an "heir of the populists," who promoted simplistic solutions to economic distress. Robertson's support for debt forgiveness was but another in a long line of "crackpot" populist ideas, such as Bryan's free coinage of silver, Father Coughlin's deliberate inflationism, and Huey Long's share-the-wealth scheme. In the 1988 campaign, Boaz concluded, Robertson competed with Jesse Jackson for the "crackpopulist" vote.[119]

Robertson's withering critique of individualistic notions of freedom, however, contained an insight about the dynamics of a free-capital market. He argued that "economic individualism" and the "radical consumerist view" lead to a "glorification of the self and to conspicuous self-gratification." He detected a worship of the self in "advertising, popular psychological therapy, and entertainment."[120]

Unlike many fellow conservatives, Robertson consciously linked this pathology with capitalist tendencies:

> It was Joseph Schumpeter who pointed out that the doctrine of Marxism was essentially theological in nature, identifying the proletariat as the chosen people and the state as the ultimate ecclesiastical authority. But . . . the doctrine of capitalism is no less theological, only in this case the god of this new secular religion is the self.[121]

Scholars of fundamentalism often argue that religious conservatives are unaware of the true sources of their angst.[122] Shorn of its fixation on conspiracies or crackpot solutions, Robertson's thought contradicts this view. He recognizes the atomistic potential of excessive individualism. He acknowledges the perils of modern capitalism unchecked by communitarian norms or moral codes. At least some of his followers, moreover, share these concerns.[123]

If Jackson made opposition to drugs respectable on the left, Robertson only marginally succeeded on the right in legitimating criticism of libertine advertising appeals, business practices, and corporate structures that may undermine traditional values. What has held the fragile conservative coalition together is the fact that evangelicals object, if for reasons different from those of other Republicans, to the heavy hand of the national government, to the bureaucratic public schools, and to the agenda of the left generally.

POPULIST CONVERGENCES: CULTURE AND ECONOMICS

We have seen that there may be more than superficial similarities between Jesse Jackson and Pat Robertson, a proposition likely to dismay partisans on both sides. But let us explore these similarities more deeply and consider how they relate to our broader discussion about how populists criticize the excesses of liberal culture.

FAMILY

A concern that preoccupies both populist leaders is the status of the American family. To Jackson and Robertson healthy families are the foundation of society. Both see the family in crisis. Likening the family to a society's economic base, Jackson spoke of the "destruction of personal infrastructure," thus comparing family decay to the nation's rotting bridges, roads, and industrial plants. "As our children die daily from drugs, liquor, babies making unhealthy and unwanted babies, violence and suicide, we need to give youth an alternative purpose and vision of their future in America." [124] Sen. Daniel Patrick Moynihan, D-N.Y., had endured decades of scorn for his report on the crisis in the black family,[125] but Jackson's writings and speeches mirror Moynihan's analysis: Strong families, good habits, and civilizing influences are critical for any struggling ethnic group to succeed. This insight explains Jackson's seemingly odd blend of radical economic demands and individual restraint throughout his adult life. To Jackson the two are intimately linked. As he put it, "The issue for black and non-white people is to discipline their appetites in such a way that they can demand respect of large corporate giants who control the production and distribution of the marketable items in this nation." In other words, successful demands require a selfless discipline. "If we are to lift ourselves out of this morass, we must go from the superficial to the sacrificial." [126] Thus "boundless liberalism" unwisely seeks freedom without moral restraint, affluence without work and self-discipline, and hedonistic pleasure rather than service to the community.[127] We hear these themes frequently from Robertson.

These themes are increasingly being heard at meetings of black denominations. At a 1991 meeting of the National Baptist Convention USA, the largest black denomination in the country, speaker after speaker called for a return to traditional morals and biblical truths. External threats such as racism and joblessness may set the stage for despair, one speaker noted, but they should not be used as scapegoats: "men are responsible" for their acts; "sex outside marriage is unacceptable"; "self-control as an option should be stressed." After proclaiming the crisis of the black male, one young man laid part of the blame on black parents and adults. "We raise our daughters, but love our sons. They watch TV instead of study." The young speaker brought the twelve-thousand participants to their feet with this admonition: "If we say no to drugs, maybe our children will too. If we say no to drinking and driving, maybe our children will too. If we stick with our families, maybe our children will too. . . . Redefine your manhood in terms of your ability to provide for your family, instead of your sexual prowess. . . . If we do that, maybe our children will too!" [128]

Pat Robertson also sees the American family under siege, undermined by no-fault divorce, irrational welfare and tax laws, and a popular culture that promotes immediate gratification. The nation is imperiled as a result. "Like it or not, the family is the foundation of our society. And in any society where the family begins to crumble, ultimately the cities crumble and then the states crumble and then the nations crumble. We must have a strong family image. But we haven't. The family is under attack." [129] Notably, Robertson spoke specifically to the black family and the threat a loss of the moral infrastructure would pose to the economic advancement of African Americans:

> For too long the wealth of black families has been drained by a welfare system that operated as though all the poor need is money. It is a system that forgot the critical importance of the values embodied in strong families—discipline, hard work, ambition and self-sacrifice, patience and love. It's easy to mock such values as bourgeois. But middle-class or not they constitute the spiritual foundation for achievement—the psychological infrastructure, if you will, for both personal growth and full participation in the world around us.[130]

Jackson and Robertson part company over the particular remedies to stop the decline of the family. Jackson emphasizes increasing government resources to low- and modest-income families; he proposes health care, day care, job training, scholarships, and the like, to be paid for by increased taxes on the wealthy. Robertson advocates tax relief to reduce the burden on families with children, a financial burden that he notes has grown dramatically. Both positions have become staples in the national debate about children and family policy.

NATURAL LAW

In the fall of 1991 the Senate confirmation hearings for Supreme Court nominee Clarence Thomas riveted the nation. Americans witnessed vivid allegations of sexual harassment by a compelling witness and a dramatic defense by the nominee. Almost lost in the process was an issue that many thought would take center stage in the hearings: Thomas's declared belief in the doctrine of "natural law." Before the hearings senators, columnists, and interest group leaders pored over Thomas's speeches and writings to discern what his commitment to natural law might mean. For a while the pages of the elite press were given over to unusual musings about an abstract philosophical concept and its historical origins, going back to St. Thomas Aquinas. Although Sen. Joseph Biden, D-Del., chairman of the Senate Judiciary Committee, parried with Thomas over natural law, the heavily coached nominee seemed to backtrack from his previous views. Thomas went so far as to declare that natural law had no place in judicial interpretation.

A casual viewer was left with the impression that natural law must be a peculiar notion, perhaps even a dangerous one. Is natural law really that peculiar? Is it embraced only by conservatives who dread change and reactionaries who fear democracy? Apparently not, because Jesse Jackson joins Pat Robertson in asserting that natural law is the grounding of ethical behavior and societal organization. Both Robertson and Jackson believe that universal moral laws govern individuals and societies, however differently such a grounding might be interpreted.

Robertson's views on natural law come as no surprise. Before and after his fling in presidential politics, Pat Robertson was an evangelical minister who affirmed timeless moral truths. In large measure, it was this quality that so appalled liberal observers of his campaign. They detected in his evangelism the specter of a "morally intrusive" statecraft flowing from his embrace of natural law. AIDS activists, for example, denounced the view held by some evangelicals that the disease is God's judgment on immoral lifestyles. To Robertson AIDS is only one example of the inexorable working of natural law. Note how he assigns responsibility for the violation of natural law by likening it to the most mundane of human laws:

> You are injured in the car. Did the city strike you and cause your accident? Well, you say ... of course not. I caused it myself.... But there was a law there, wasn't there? And you broke the law. You drove through the red light, which was a warning sign; and when you crossed through it, you got hit. Well, people in this country are violating certain moral laws and standards, and as a result, they're getting diseases.[131]

Surveying the modern landscape devastated by the AIDS epidemic, decaying family structures, children adrift, lagging achievement in education, and an eroding economic base, Robertson sees the inevitable consequences of a society straying from the principles of natural law. When you sow "moral decadence" you will "reap the whirlwind." But such views are not necessarily the exclusive province of the right. For three decades Jesse Jackson, one of the nation's most prominent progressive politicians, has expressed similar sentiments from the left. For example, in his moving eulogy for Don Rogers, Jackson outlined his understanding of natural law and the consequences of violating it. Jackson's words closely parallel Robertson's views:

> Even today, if we can hear and comprehend, he [Rogers] is still teaching the profound lessons of life—teaching natural law; teaching that you can't break the law of gravity, you can only prove it; teaching that you must live, and possibly die, with the consequences of your choices; teaching the value of the high road ... teaching us that all of us have sinned and fallen short of the glory of God; teaching that the wages of sin are death.[132]

Both men call upon the public schools to incorporate "character education." They routinely criticize the media for promoting hedonistic values and regularly challenge young people to learn that one must sacrifice "short-term pleasure for long-term gain." In every case, both Jackson and Robertson implicitly link natural law with character attributes that they deem of timeless worth and validity.

Interestingly, Jackson applies natural law in his critique of American rock music, a common target of Robertson and his followers. Jackson damns what he considers destructive messages. This is how he develops the critique:

> [A popular] song eventually closes on this line: "How can it be wrong if it feels so right?" Now that's an interesting proposition, because a whole lot can be wrong with something, even though it feels right. That's just like saying how can not doing homework be so wrong when it feels so right? How can not developing my mind be so wrong when it feels so right? If you go further in school, you will learn the philosophy called "Heathenism." And it deals with short term pleasure and long term pain. You remember this: The laws of convenience lead to collapse, and the laws of sacrifice lead to greatness.[133]

Jackson's sentiments are echoed by Robertson: "Instead of a clear knowledge of right and wrong, [our children] have been told 'if it feels good, do it.' Instead of self-restraint they are often taught self-gratification and hedonism." [134]

Long before Tipper Gore raised the issue of rock lyrics, Jackson was there, steadily denouncing the spiraling seduction, violence, hedonism, and indolence pummeling the young. He denounced sexually explicit lyrics, singling out specific albums and stating flatly, "We must call pornographic music what it is—child abuse." Jackson's criticism extends to the mass media. "Television is no better. This season's programs may have slightly less violence on them, but the sexual exploitation has increased. They even have a name for it; they call it 'T and A.' " [135] As any viewer of "The 700 Club" knows, these sentiments resound with Robertson, who censured the "T and A" formula in terms almost identical to Jackson's.

It may be easy to dismiss such sentiments as prudish. But to Jackson the issue is not prudery but morality, a morality grounded in timeless principles. To him the "anything goes" mentality of the era undermines the fight against injustice and poverty. Today's generation is imperiled by the "law of convenience"; its flouting of natural law will leave it impoverished, addicted, miserable, and unprepared for the battle against poverty, racism, and war. Moreover, Jackson argues, without the moral compass of natural law today's youth have no basis even to join the fight. This broader concern is the link that Jackson perceives between music that is libertine and that which is patently racist and sexist. In one speech, for example, Jackson denounced a Mick Jagger song entitled "Some Girls," which ends with the line "Black girls just want to get f—— all night—I don't have that much jam." Without moral boundaries, Jackson believes, pop music produces misogynist and racist lyrics that coarsen the sensibilities of our young.

Jackson's "puritanical" side is better understood when we recall the morally nurturing and parochial environment in which he was reared. In his community parents, ministers, and teachers taught the individual—with firm conviction—the "right" way to live. Enter a black church or church convention today and you will hear the same message. But an understanding of this side of the African American experience often eludes the "knowledge elite."

Like Jackson, Robertson believes that decadence originates from an ethical flabbiness that denies timeless truths. "Instead of absolutes, our youth have been given situational ethics and the life-centered curriculum." And Robertson echoes the criticism of popular culture. "Our motion pictures, our television, our radio, our youth concerts, with a few outstanding exceptions, seem to have a single message—God is out, casual sex, infidelity and easy divorce, the recreational use of drugs . . . are in. . . . We have sown the wind—now we are reaping the whirlwind."[136]

Unsafe Sex and Moral Authority

Another way that Robertson's and Jackson's understanding of natural law comes out is in the highly charged web of AIDS, safe-sex programs, and condom distribution to minors. To Robertson "safe sex" is an oxymoron and a delusion. Not surprisingly, he joins other conservative Christians in denouncing safe-sex educational programs and condom distribution in the public schools. These programs, he believes, will undermine moral codes and religious values. As a result sexual activity among the young will increase, causing unwanted pregnancies and disease. Moreover, the same "sex experts" who a generation ago claimed that condoms were notoriously unreliable now tell teen-agers that safe sex in an era of AIDS means using condoms, not practicing abstinence and fidelity. Such advice is almost criminal because it will inevitably result in more deaths of young people. Adults, in short, must not abandon their moral authority to guide the young in ways that are healthy for them, body and soul.

Jackson's views are more nuanced than Robertson's, but he, too, is troubled by contemporary attitudes toward sex. Speaking a few years before the AIDS epidemic entered the public consciousness, Jackson made this prophetic statement: "Our children are being programmed into premature heat, and the results are a teen-age pregnancy epidemic and rampant venereal disease. . . . This 'intercourse without discourse' is jeopardizing the welfare of this and future generations." Later, Jackson commented on the revelation that basketball star Earvin "Magic" Johnson had contracted the AIDS virus. While the "experts" rushed to capitalize on the publicity by emphasizing the need for AIDS awareness and safe-sex education, Jackson felt something was sadly missing. Interpreting Johnson's illness in terms of safe sex "was popular, but it wasn't right." To Jackson sex without love and commitment, which leads to unwanted babies and other tragedies, was the real unsafe sex.[137] Jackson went on "Arsenio Hall" to share this view, and he addressed the Rainbow Coalition in these terms:

> Not long ago our hearts were made heavy when one of the greatest athletes of our day or any day, Magic Johnson, said I have contracted HIV virus.... At first he said it was unsafe sex, but upon second thought he concluded it was deeper than that, and it is. It is deeper than that. We now are looking at a kind of ethical collapse, moral degeneracy.... There must be a revival of a sense of ethics, of spirituality, a sense of care.[138]

Characteristically, Jackson links sexual morality with a host of other issues. "You're looking at a combination of unsafe sex, unsafe drugs, unsafe guns, unsafe study habits, unsafe prayer life, unsafe family values. Add them together and it's called at-risk behavior, which leads to tragic and not magic consequences." [139]

Where Jackson parts company with Robertson and other conservative Christians is in his faith in sex education. To be sure, he advocates a strong dose of moral training and discipline, but he firmly believes that children must have sex education and that it can include the moral dimension. In part, this view arises from the sense of crisis that he feels. He recalls giving a speech at a high school in Washington, D.C., at which he noticed a large group of young children:

> I went to a school in Washington about a year ago. I saw about a hundred little kids, maybe two years old, three years old, little tots.... And I was glad that ... some little day care school had brought their children in.... Except [I learned] that these kids were the children of the juniors and seniors of the high school.[140]

Jackson describes his visit to a hospital that cared for sixty babies, all weighing less than two pounds. The hospital called them "boarder babies." Their mothers had registered under false names, given birth, and then abandoned their babies. Many of these babies were addicted to drugs or infected with AIDS. Given the magnitude of this crisis, with these babies sure to perpetuate the cycle of poverty, Jackson favors sex education with "sex discipline" in the schools to help prevent further tragedy. He observes that condoms, within this context, take on a different meaning. He is comfortable, then, applying ethics to the situation.[141] Robertson, on the other hand, doubts that the sex education establishment can ever seriously incorporate "sex discipline" or advocacy of abstinence into their schemes. He notes that liberals, such as Rep.

Pat Schroeder, D-Colo., tried to scuttle the one federal program that works—abstinence education—bowing to pressure from gays, liberal educators, and so-called sex experts. These differences aside, however, both Jackson and Robertson freely state that "the wages of sin is death."

THE FOUNDATIONS OF EDUCATIONAL EXCELLENCE

One of the clearest connections between natural law and public policy can be seen in the concern both ministers have for educational excellence. In numerous speeches during his days with Operation Push, Jackson identified these impediments to educational excellence: the loss of moral authority, moral decadence, mass media diversion, crisis of effort, and parental detachment. On every charge, one can imagine Robertson shouting a fervent "amen." In developing his themes, Jackson dovetails with "conservative" concerns:

- Loss of moral authority:
  For without the reestablishment of moral, not merely legal, authority by educators, we cannot effectively challenge this generation to achieve its potential and become a greater generation. There must be a revival of moral authority.
- Moral decadence:
  There is no such thing as value-free education. Nonvalues are values, but they are values leading to social decadence and decay. The death of ethics is the sabotage of excellence. A steady diet of violence, vandalism, drugs, a teen-age pregnancy epidemic, alcohol, and TV addiction have bred a passive, alienated, and superficial generation. The challenge is to close the economic and education gap, and moral decadence diverts one from the goal of catching up. . . . A generation lacking the moral and physical stamina necessary to fight a protracted civilizational crisis is dangerous to themselves, their neighbors, and future generations. . . . If we allow our children to eat junk, think junk, watch junk, talk junk, and play with junk—don't be surprised when they turn out to be "social junkies." We do reap what we sow.
- Mass media diversion:
  Whether we as educators know it or not, we are competing for the attention of our children's minds—and we are losing to the mass media. . . . Quantitatively, the mass media has greater access to our children's minds than the historic socializing agents (home, church, and school) combined—and qualitatively its impressions are deeper. . . . These entertainers and celebrities have tremendous power and influence on our children's minds, and they must be challenged to accept responsibility that is in proportion to the power they have. We cannot stand idly by and allow them to divert an entire generation through a superficial understanding of life and the world.
- Crisis of effort:
  We are also confronted with a loss of the will to study and struggle.

> We need a revolution of values and priorities if we are going to turn the situation around.... For what does it matter if the doors of opportunity swing wide open and we're too drunk to stagger through them?

- Parental detachment:

> Parents are the beginning and foundation of it all.... Parents are the only adults whose first priority and vested interest is the child.... Parental involvement in the education of our children is absolutely essential and must be creatively planned rather than allowed to occur as an afterthought.... Parents are the first teachers and the real enforcers of their child's conduct. They have the power to guide their child's study habits. Parents provide love, care, chastisement, and discipline and are the important models in the child's formative years. In short, parents are the only element that can demand total accountability from the school and the child.... Presently this most vital element is massively detached from our schools.[142]

There is little here that Robertson would disagree with and much that he has echoed frequently. Indeed, one of the complaints of conservative Christians is that the educational establishment—with its jargon and "experts"—erects barriers against true parental involvement. Moreover, Jackson started Operation Push, designed to inculcate sound educational habits in the young, whereas Robertson founded Operation Heads Up, focused on literacy. Robertson, in fact, made education one of his central issues. Chastising the nation for its complacency, he called for a major effort to erase functional illiteracy. But whereas Jackson stresses the need to double national funding for education, Robertson, deeply suspicious of the capacity of the public school establishment to address the crisis, looks to a different remedy. Spending more money on bloated educational bureaucracies will not solve the problem, he believes. Educational bureaucrats, protective of their positions and enamored of the latest intellectual fad, fail to see the simple truth that Robertson contends we have known for years—people learn to read and write by memorizing and learning phonics. These differences aside, both leaders link educational excellence to discipline, hard work, and delayed gratification. Failure to appreciate natural law, they argue, undermines educational achievement.

CHARACTER

Both Jackson and Robertson view "character," a term wonderfully premodern in its connotations, as a key to success in life. The lack of character encapsulates much of what the two candidates believe is wrong with American culture. Both candidates have called upon the schools to enhance "character education." To both leaders the inculcation of such timeless traits as honesty, discipline, integrity, diligence, and courage is neither controversial nor an imposition; rather, it is essential for success in school and in life.

To Jackson, the champion of society's most vulnerable, there is a special poignancy to such ageless wisdom. He challenged those "left out" of the dream through discrimination or poverty to cultivate even greater strength of character to sustain them in the struggle. As he put it in 1978, "The times we have made progress are when the victim has accepted the necessary discipline and sacrifices to survive against the odds." [143] A decade before so-called black conservatives mounted their own attack on debilitating victimology,[144] Jackson criticized the "dependency syndrome," which seduced the oppressed into waiting for "salvation from without." He continued, "If we depend upon some forces from Washington to shut off the TV and to increase our commitment to literacy in Watts, it is not likely to happen." The poor must develop stronger characters because they start life behind. "When we challenge our youth—who are behind in this race, and who have these chains on their ankles—to run faster, we are saying that because they are behind and because they are in a climate of hostility, they cannot follow a philosophy of hedonism." Perhaps upper middle class white kids can "afford" to experiment with drugs, promiscuity, and excessive television. Poor kids and minorities do not have that luxury. "Because we are behind in the race, we cannot afford the luxury of 18,000 hours of TV by the age of fifteen. . . . To be victims of a premature pregnancy epidemic because sex feels good is a luxury we can't afford. . . . If marijuana and cocaine and angel dust do not serve as a stimulus to close that gap, we cannot afford the luxury of the decadence of drugs." [145]

Like John Wesley in another age, Jackson chastises the powerful who ignore justice for the oppressed, while challenging the dispossessed to change their lives to be worthy of the struggle. And in doing so, he has been berating modern culture longer than many of the figures on the religious right. Perhaps what he saw as debilitating elements eating away at the most vulnerable members of society were a forecast of what would later sweep over the broader culture, especially among the young. As drugs, sex, apathy, family breakdown, and lagging educational achievement began to permeate the broader society, a chorus of voices rose to take up the challenge. How different things might have been, Jackson might say, had we taken seriously the insight of the gospel's message. "Blessed are the poor"—because sometimes the poor serve as a bellwether that the "nonpoor" ignore at their peril.

Debt Relief and the Year of Jubilee

Finally, we note the similarities between Jackson and Robertson on the question of debt and its burden on society. Since the nineteenth century populists have championed easy credit and debt relief, condemning banks with a vengeance. Government debt was often viewed as doubly pernicious because it transferred wealth from average citizens to wealthy bond holders and it would become a burden for future generations. Not surprisingly, Bryan and other populists leveled jeremiads against deficit spending: "A man who murders another shortens by a few brief years the life of a human being; but he who votes to increase the burden of debts upon the people of the United State assumes a graver responsibility." [146] Viewing the rapid rise of the national debt, Robertson echoed Bryan. He charged that deficit spending was patently immoral, especially in the 1980s, because the debt grew rapidly in a time of peace and plenty. "We have become the first generation ever to plunder the patrimony of its children and grandchildren. We have robbed them to pay for our wasteful excesses." [147] Jackson, too, denounced the accumulation of debt, especially by the federal government in the 1980s, as immoral and a drag on future economic vitality. In his 1984 speech to the Democratic National Convention, Jackson heaped criticism on the Reagan administration's promise to balance the budget. "Under President Reagan, the cumulative budget deficits for just his four years in office will be virtually equal to the total budget deficits from George Washington to Jimmy Carter." As a consequence, Jackson argued, less money would be available for productive investment, higher interest rates would sap economic growth, and the United States would be increasingly dependent on foreign capital.

Notably, both leaders offered similar remedies, although Robertson's was more radical. Jackson, in framing his "invest in America" message, called for debt relief as a necessary precondition to further productive investment. Tillers of the soil should be afforded special consideration. "Ranchers and farmers have fed America and the world. They deserve mercy, a moratorium, a restructuring of their debt." On the international level, too, Jackson viewed debt as debilitating for economic growth, trade, and prosperity. "Saddled with billions in debt, these [developing] countries have been forced into economic austerity as a condition for further credit. The result is a drastic reduction in their imports, and a drastic reduction in our exports. The resulting slowdown helps neither the debtor nor creditor." The remedy, Jackson argued, is "an international plan for debt forgiveness, relief, and rescheduling." [148]

For Robertson the theme of debt relief took shape as one of his most controversial ideas: the Year of Jubilee. No issue received such ridicule, and no issue was, Robertson believed, so misunderstood. The term "Jubilee," which comes from the Old Testament Book of Leviticus, refers to a fifty-year cycle in Israel in which all debts were to be canceled (though it is not clear that it was ever implemented). As early as 1981 Robertson touted the idea of a constitutional amendment dictating periodic debt relief. Over time his prescriptions became more sophisticated as he backed "some systematic provision for the cancellation of debt on a world wide basis." Robertson sees great wisdom in the Jubilee principle because it recognizes a central truth about economics: the compounding of debt. "The same principle of compounding which can bring about enormous wealth and prosperity can also bring about insupportable debt and bondage." [149] Robertson contends that a fifty- to sixty-year cycle operates in the economy and that biblical prophets understood its dynamics. As holders of capital aggressively lend their money, debt begins to grow; with compounding interest the burden doubles, then triples, and so forth, until there is a collapse. Not only does this compounding of debt undermine the economy of a society, but it concentrates wealth and power, as debtors become captives of lenders. "And the Bible contains a solution to the problem of excess accumulation of wealth and power. It is the Year of Jubilee." Robertson had ample evidence that by the early 1990s we had reached the point of insupportable debt burden. Within a decade the federal debt had tripled, a burden magnified by the debt owed by corporations, consumers, and developing countries. Worldwide debt, he noted in 1991, was "$25 trillion and it's moving toward $30 trillion . . . and it's going to collapse." [150]

Robertson's embrace of the Year of Jubilee was denounced as "crackpot," even by evangelical Christians. Indeed, one Christian writer compared Robertson with socialists, anarchists, left-wing liberation theologians, and radical evangelical groups such as Sojourners in his suggestion that debt be forgiven.[151] Robertson argues that one way or another debt relief will happen, so why not make it systematic and thoughtful rather than the outcome of an "economic blowout." This is how he defended his position:

> Well, the truth is that the Year of Jubilee is coming about. I said that there were two things we need to do. One was that . . . we need to mark the [farm] debt down to the appraised value of the underlying assets. That wasn't a very radical proposal, because that's what happens when you foreclose on a guy. You take his money and property, sell it at auction, then write the loan down to that much. I thought that instead of bringing about all this pain and anguish, why can't we do that? The other thing is that Third World debts are never going to be paid off . . . so why don't we write them down, or write them off and start over again? That's what the Bible did and they didn't have these terrible economic collapses. . . . But again that seems radical.[152]

Without such reasonable measures, Robertson argued, the compounding of debt will ultimately cause economic collapse and depression. "You'll have a Jubilee. Either there'll be a crash, there'll be hyperinflation, or there'll be debt relief. There's always one of these three things that takes place every fifty or sixty years in our economic cycle. And it's going to happen whether we like it or not." [153]

On economics more broadly, the two ministers also have similar religiously inspired visions that are critical of a capitalist market with no moral limits. Jackson harshly rebukes corporations that shun any responsibility toward the communities harmed when they close plants or send jobs abroad. He argues that the enormous tax breaks routinely received by companies to locate facilities in certain areas are akin to welfare benefits. He believes these incentives create a moral obligation that companies must repay, like "workfare" for welfare recipients. Left to their own devices corporations are tempted to take the benefit and run. They should not be allowed to do so. "I believe in workfare," Jackson said, "I believe in corporate workfare." [154]

Although criticism of capitalism comes more naturally from the left than the right, it also is heard from Robertson, who voices the concerns of traditional conservatives about greed. In his writings and speeches the objects of his criticisms have ranged from the robber barons of the nineteenth century to the "I've got mine, to heck with you" attitude of today.[155] Long before writing his most recent, conspiracy-filled book, Robertson had this to say: "Unbridled capitalism must be restrained, or people will get too much money and too much power and will use it to oppress others. . . . Just as the coercive utopianism of Communist materialism is not of God, neither is a capitalist materialism—based on the amassing of riches for personal gain, with disregard for the afflictions of the needy—right." [156] No wonder the *Wall Street Journal* was horrified.

SUMMARY

As Americans were buffeted in the 1980s by economic and cultural changes of global dimensions, Jackson and Robertson responded with populist cries for jobs and moral renewal. While others were celebrating the "liberal individual" on the left or on the right—in the arts or in economics—Jackson and Robertson spoke a traditional language of obligation, playing on the moral yearnings and economic insecurities of their followers. In spite of their differences, Jesse Jackson and Pat Robertson share a deeply held conviction: that moral failure underlies the problems of American society and politics. Indeed, Jackson would heartily agree with Robertson's assertion that the "crisis we face is a moral crisis." [157] This conviction is encapsulated in their twin criticisms of laissez faire economics and moral relativism in family life and culture. Both rebuke the rich for abusing their wealth; both chastise the media for promoting unwholesome family values. Both, ultimately, viewed their presidential campaigns as religious quests to "redeem the soul of America." [158]

We can perhaps learn an important lesson from our analysis: those whose vision is profoundly religious (and in that sense not strictly liberal and individualistic) tend to embrace a communitarian politics that cannot countenance the notion that some must be left out as the price of economic growth and will not lightly accept the pollution of community and family morals as the price of a free society. The moral dimension is what distinguishes a certain kind of modern populism from other forms of liberal and conservative politics. But to what extent does the American public share such populist sentiments? And to what extent did the campaigns of Robertson and Jackson tap the sentiment that existed? We turn to those questions in the next chapters.

NOTES

1. These statements by Jesse Jackson were taken from two sources: a speech delivered by Jackson to the Rainbow Coalition candidate forum, Washington, D.C., Jan. 25, 1992, and an interview with the author on a flight from Washington, D.C., to Dallas, March 12, 1992.
2. Pat Robertson's thoughts on debt are derived from an interview with the author, Virginia Beach, Va., August 8, 1991, but they are characteristic of his writings and speeches on debt and the Year of Jubilee.
3. Barbara A. Reynolds, *Jesse Jackson: America's David* (Washington D.C.: JFJ Associates, 1985), 32.
4. Edward Shils, "Totalitarians and Antinomians," in *Political Passages,* ed. John H. Bunzel (New York: Free Press, 1988).
5. Gail Sheehy, "Power or Glory?" *Vanity Fair,* January 1988, 46-55, 98-109.
6. Reynolds, *Jesse Jackson,* 23.
7. Garry Wills, *Under God: Religion and American Politics* (New York: Simon and Schuster, 1990), 224.
8. Reynolds, *Jesse Jackson,* 18-19.
9. Ibid., 19.
10. Jackson, interview with author.
11. See Marshall Frady's *New Yorker* series: "Profiles: Outsider, I—The Gift," Feb. 3, 1992, 36-69; "II—History Is upon Us," Feb. 10, 1992, 41-75; and "III—Without Portfolio," Feb. 17, 1992, 39-69.

12. Jackson, interview with author.
13. Wills, *Under God,* 225.
14. See Reynolds, *Jesse Jackson;* and David J. Garrow, *Bearing the Cross: Martin Luther King, Jr., and the Southern Christian Leadership Conference* (New York: Vintage, 1988).
15. Reynolds, *Jesse Jackson,* 83.
16. Wills, *Under God,* 227-228.
17. Ibid., 229.
18. Erik H. Erikson, *Young Man Luther: A Study in Psychoanalysis and History* (New York: Norton, 1962), 67.
19. Adapted from Reynolds, *Jesse Jackson,* 7, and combined with recent refrains.
20. Jackson, speech delivered at the 1988 Democratic Convention, Atlanta, Ga., July 19, 1988. See Frank Clemente and Frank Watkins, eds., *Keep Hope Alive: Jesse Jackson's 1988 Presidential Campaign* (Boston: South End Press, 1989).
21. Wills, *Under God,* 242.
22. James MacGregor Burns, *Leadership* (New York: Harper and Row, 1978).
23. Traveling with Jackson gives one a sense of what it is like to be a celebrity. Wherever Jackson goes he is besieged with well-wishers wanting handshakes, autographs, and photographs.
24. Gregory D. Squires, "Economic Restructuring, Urban Development, and Race: The Political Economy of Civil Rights in 'Post-Industrial America,'" *Western Political Quarterly* (March 1990): 201-217.
25. See Leon Dash, *When Children Want Children: The Urban Crisis of Teenage Childbearing* (New York: Morrow, 1989); and Jewelle Taylor Gibbs et al., *Young, Black, and Male in America: An Endangered Species* (Dover, Mass.: Auburn House, 1988).
26. Roger D. Hatch, *Beyond Opportunity: Jesse Jackson's Vision for America* (Philadelphia: Fortress Press, 1988), 18.
27. Jackson, interview with author.
28. Jesse L. Jackson, *Straight from the Heart,* ed. Roger D. Hatch and Frank E. Watkins (Philadelphia: Fortress Press, 1987), ix, 18.
29. William Jennings Bryan, *The First Battle* (Chicago: Conkey, 1896), 553.
30. See Jackson's 1984 Democratic National Convention speech in Jackson, *Straight from the Heart,* 3-18.
31. Ibid.
32. *Washington Post National Weekly Edition,* March 2, 1987.
33. Bryan, *First Battle,* 560.
34. Jackson, speech to the 1988 Democratic convention.
35. Bryan, *First Battle,* 543.
36. Jackson, *Straight from the Heart,* 3.
37. Bryan, *First Battle,* 126.
38. Jackson, *Straight from the Heart,* 16.
39. Bryan, *First Battle,* 542.
40. Ibid., 205.
41. Jackson, speech to the 1988 Democratic convention.
42. Jackson, speech, Jan. 25, 1992.

43. Ibid.
44. Bryan, *First Battle.*
45. Clemente and Watkins, *Keep Hope Alive,* 96.
46. Hatch, *Beyond Opportunity,* 29.
47. From Jackson's speech to the 1984 Democratic convention.
48. A good summary of the first half of the decade's most admired Gallup list can be found in Gary King and Lyn Ragsdale, *The Elusive Executive: Discovering Statistical Patterns in the Presidency* (Washington, D.C.: CQ Press, 1988). For the 1991 list, see *Emerging Trends* 14 (1992).
49. Robert Booth Fowler, *Unconventional Partners: Religion and Liberal Culture in the United States* (Grand Rapids, Mich.: Eerdmans, 1989).
50. Jackson, interview with author.
51. Ibid.
52. Ibid.
53. Frank Watkins, national political director, Rainbow Coalition, interview with author, Washington, D.C., May 1991. Described as Jackson's alter ego and closest aide, Watkins has been with Jackson since 1968.
54. Jackson, interview with author.
55. Jackson, speech, Jan. 25, 1992.
56. Norman H. Clark, *Deliver Us from Evil: An Interpretation of American Prohibition* (New York: Norton, 1976).
57. Jackson, *Straight from the Heart,* 176.
58. Sheehy, "Power or Glory?"
59. Jackson, interview with author. The draft of the speech Jackson gave at Harvard did not contain this discussion of the Ten Commandments. Instead, Jackson marked up his own copy and added the litany about the moral and ethical collapse.
60. Ibid.
61. Ibid.
62. Ibid.
63. Jesse L. Jackson, "How We Respect Life Is Overriding Moral Issue," *National Right to Life News,* January 1977, 5.
64. Colman McCarthy, "Jackson's Reversal on Abortion," *Washington Post,* May 21, 1988, A27.
65. One hears echoes of the Lincoln-Douglas debates, with the Jackson of the 1980s taking Douglas's position that slavery should be a matter of choice and the Jackson of the 1970s taking Lincoln's position that one does not have the right to do wrong.
66. Jackson, "How We Respect Life."
67. Jackson, interview with author.
68. Ibid.
69. Ibid.
70. Jackson, "How We Respect Life."
71. Jackson, interview with author.
72. Watkins, interview with author.

73. Manning Marable, *Black American Politics: From the Washington Marches to Jesse Jackson* (London: Verso, 1985).
74. Shils, "Totalitarians and Antinomians," 15, 28.
75. Robertson, interview with author.
76. Ibid.
77. David Edwin Harrell, Jr., *Pat Robertson* (San Francisco: Harper and Row, 1987), 22.
78. Ibid., 27.
79. Ibid., 28, 29.
80. Ibid., 29.
81. Ibid, 30.
82. Ibid., 31.
83. Ibid., 36.
84. See Jeffrey K. Hadden and Anson Shupe, *Televangelism: Power and Politics on God's Frontier* (New York: Holt, 1988).
85. A good summary of this background is found in Charlotte Allen, "God and Mammon: How Pat Robertson Serves Both," *Washington City Paper*, July 10, 1992.
86. Margaret M. Poloma, *The Assemblies of God at the Crossroads: Charisma and Institutional Dilemmas* (Knoxville: University of Tennessee Press, 1989).
87. Pat Robertson and Jamie Buckingham, *Shout It from the Housetops* (Plainfield, N.J.: Logos, 1972), 13.
88. James L. Guth and John C. Green, *The Bible and the Ballot Box: Religion and Politics in the 1988 Election* (Boulder: Westview Press, 1991).
89. Garry Wills, "The Power Populist," *Time*, Nov. 21, 1988.
90. Paul Taylor and David S. Broder, "Early Volley of Bush's Exceeds Expectations," *Washington Post*, Oct. 28, 1988, 1.
91. Guth and Green, *Bible and the Ballot Box*.
92. Robertson, speech delivered at Constitution Hall, Washington, D.C., Sept. 17, 1986, to open the petition drive for his presidential race.
93. Ibid.
94. Hubert Morken, *Pat Robertson: Where He Stands* (Old Tappan, N.J.: Revell, 1988), 41.
95. Ibid.
96. Robertson, speech, Sept. 17, 1986.
97. Ibid.
98. Morken, *Pat Robertson*, 40.
99. Robertson, speech, Sept. 17, 1986.
100. *New York Times*, Jan. 14, 1988, A20.
101. Morken, *Pat Robertson*, 71.
102. Ibid., 72.
103. Ibid.
104. Robert E. Shalhope, "Republicanism and Early American Historiography," *William and Mary Quarterly* 39 (April 1982): 334-356.
105. Robertson, interview with author.
106. Pat Robertson, *The New World Order* (Dallas: Word, 1991).

107. Ibid., 122.
108. Ibid., 129, 121.
109. Morken, *Pat Robertson*, 41.
110. Robertson, *New World Order*, 135-136.
111. Ibid., 135.
112. Ibid., 136.
113. Ibid., 130-131.
114. Ibid., 71.
115. Ibid., 185, 36.
116. Ibid., 185.
117. "Time Warner Promotes Presidential Assassination," *Religious Rights Watch: An Official Publication of the Christian Coalition*, August 1992.
118. Pat Robertson, *America's Dates with Destiny* (Nashville: Thomas Nelson, 1986), 221.
119. David Boaz, "Pat Robertson's Crackpopulism," *Wall Street Journal*, Feb. 10, 1988, 20. Other *Journal* pieces explored Robertson's opposition to the Federal Reserve Board and his criticism of supply-side economics. See Alan Murray, "Robertson, a Man of Unusual Economic Views, Expounds on Compound Interest, Disdains Fed," *Wall Street Journal*, March 7, 1988, 46; and "Jimmy Robertson," editorial, *Wall Street Journal*, March 4, 1988, 28.
120. Robertson, *New World Order*, 169.
121. Ibid.
122. Marshall Berman, *All That Is Solid Melts into Air: The Experience of Modernity* (New York: Simon and Schuster, 1982).
123. Robertson's Midwest coordinator, Marlene Elwell, headed a Detroit-based international organization dedicated to helping corporate officers integrate their Roman Catholic faith with their activities in the marketplace.
124. Clemente and Watkins, *Keep Hope Alive*, 96.
125. U.S. Department of Labor, Office of Policy Planning and Research, *The Negro Family: The Case for National Action* (Washington, D.C.: U.S. Government Printing Office, 1965).
126. Jackson, *Straight from the Heart*, 199.
127. Watkins, interview with author.
128. National Baptist Congress of Christian Education, National Baptist Convention USA, Oklahoma City, June 19, 1991.
129. *New York Times*, Jan. 14, 1988.
130. Pat Robertson, "The Wealth of Black Families," *Conservative Digest*, June 1987, 35-40.
131. Morken, *Pat Robertson*, 79.
132. Jackson, *Straight from the Heart*, 175.
133. Georgia May Swanson, "Messiah or Manipulator? A Burkean Cluster Analysis of the Motivations Revealed in the Selected Speeches of the Reverend Jesse Louis Jackson" (Ph.D. diss., Bowling Green State University, 1982), 173.
134. Robertson, speech, Sept. 17, 1986.
135. Jackson, *Straight from the Heart*, 200.

136. Robertson, speech, Sept. 17, 1986.
137. Jackson, interview with author.
138. Jackson, speech, Jan. 25, 1992.
139. Jackson, interview with author.
140. Ibid.
141. Ibid.
142. These quotations are taken from a speech that Jackson considers to be representative of his educational philosophy. See Jackson, *Straight from the Heart*, 198-202.
143. American Enterprise Institute, "A Conversation with the Reverend Jesse Jackson: The Quest for Economic and Educational Parity," American Enterprise Institute, Washington, D.C., May 16, 1978, transcript.
144. Shelby Steele, *The Content of Our Character: A New Vision of Race in America* (New York: St. Martin's, 1990).
145. American Enterprise Institute, "Conversation with the Reverend Jesse Jackson."
146. Bryan, *First Battle*, 77.
147. Robertson, speech, Sept. 17, 1986.
148. Clemente and Watkins, *Keep Hope Alive*, 95-96, 58.
149. Morken, *Pat Robertson*, 59, 54.
150. Robertson, interview with author.
151. John Robbins, writing from an evangelical Christian perspective, refers to Robertson's Jubilee as a "zany, immoral, and disastrous policy proposal." John W. Robbins, *Pat Robertson: A Warning to America* (Jefferson, Md.: Trinity Foundation, 1988), 80-84.
152. Robertson, interview with author.
153. Ibid.
154. Jackson, speech, Jan. 25, 1992.
155. Pat Robertson and Bob Slosser, *The Secret Kingdom* (Nashville: Thomas Nelson, 1982), 24.
156. Pat Robertson, *Answers to 200 of Life's Most Probing Questions* (Nashville: Thomas Nelson, 1984), 194-196.
157. Harrison Rainie, "Robertson's Grand Design," *U.S. News and World Report*, Feb. 22, 1988, 15.
158. In numerous speeches and in interview statements, both ministers spoke of redeeming the soul of America.

4

The Role of Churches in the 1988 Presidential Campaign

In the 1980s two groups of Americans—blacks and white charismatics—felt passionately that their grievances were not being addressed through conventional interest group action. In this chapter we examine the ways in which church networks and religious charisma helped leaders to translate that discontent into presidential crusades. These crusades endured into the 1990s as distinct factions struggling for influence within the political system.

What united the diverse groups of activists interviewed and observed for this study was their sense of discontent, even desperation. Many expressed the populist complaint that they were kept at the periphery of cultural and economic life in the United States. This pattern is especially striking because these people, as political activists, tended to be better educated and more affluent than the average supporters of the two ministers. From well-dressed, apparently middle-class black followers of Jesse Jackson, one heard a litany of economic woes, racism, violence, and collapsing family structures. "Every thirty-eight seconds babies are having babies. We fill jails but cut scholarships. . . . I see twenty-four-year-olds selling drugs in the neighborhood, refusing to move. They're doomed." Jackson spoke often of this sense of crisis. "Our babies are dying at a rate greater than that of Bangladesh. With roughly the same population, four times more young blacks in America are incarcerated than in South Africa."[1] More surprising perhaps is that white followers of Pat Robertson expressed equally passionate discontent. "The schools are a failure—we're raising incompetent adults." People were "hurting in their homes, in their schools. The moral fiber of the nation was slipping." Robertson, echoing these sentiments, argued that evangelicals had abandoned the earth "to people who have frankly been destroying everything they stand for."

"They are now coming to realize," he suggested, "that if this country breaks apart with moral decay not only are they in trouble and their children are in trouble, but possibly the whole world is in trouble." [2] One of the most vivid expressions of this sense of being at the periphery was made by Gary Bauer, a Christian conservative ally of Robertson's: "I find a lot of reasonable people who feel under siege. Their perception is that they're living in a hostile country, that everything they believe is under persistent attack." Speaking before the Christian Coalition, he declared that nothing less than a "civil war" over American culture is being fought.[3]

Discontent, however, does not guarantee political engagement. Indeed, scholars have puzzled for decades about the relative quiescence of people who "ought" to be rebelling, or at least organizing to protect their interests.[4] Why do some people fail to register their discontent through political mobilization? One view suggests that some cultures promote a fatalistic resignation in the face of misfortune, misery, or oppression. Life is a vale of tears that human will and action cannot change.[5] Another set of theories contends that the manipulation of powerful symbols of state authority or the existence of dominant ideologies so intimidates lowly individuals that they are effectively silenced.[6] A third theory suggests that collective action is inherently difficult, especially for the less well heeled.[7] Those with the most to gain through collective action are the hardest to organize: they have the least money available for political struggle and thus are the most tempted to be "free riders" by letting others fight for them. Sheer practicability is yet another dimension. Physically exhausted by the demands of work and families, mentally drained by financial stress, marital problems, time commitments to children, or job frustrations, many people simply have little in time, money, and energy left to devote to politics. Thus absence of hope, intimidation, economic barriers to collective action, and scarcity of resources inhibit those with grievances from seeking redress through political action.

So powerful are these forces that winning social movements are the exception rather than the rule. It is not surprising that some of the most successful models in American history, such as the abolitionist, temperance, agrarian, migrant worker, and civil rights movements, drew heavily from churches and religious leaders. To a greater extent than in other Western societies, religion has proved remarkably durable in the United States—the "nation with the soul of a church." In spite of secularizing trends, 70 percent of all Americans are church members, with 40 percent attending church, synagogue, or mosque in any given week. Indeed, far more people belong to a religious community than to any other private association, union, or group, making religion a key point of entry into the collective society. As one black Baptist pastor noted of his fellow pastors, "We can reach five times more people at 11:00 on Sunday morning than all the other black community organizations combined."[8] Members of churches, moreover, are far less elite than joiners of other civic and political organizations, and they contribute disproportionately. Scholars have documented for years that working-class and poor Americans contribute a far greater share of their income to churches than do those with greater means. This generous giving enables church organizations to operate an impressive array of charities, hospitals, and educational institutions. Churches, therefore, possess what social movements most demand—resources and a means of reaching the masses. Of course, religious commitment may be tepid in some communities, and many churches resist politicization for good reason. But when church networks can be mobilized, they are genuine political resources—especially valuable in a culture that inhibits collective action.

THE CHURCHES AND COLLECTIVE POLITICAL ACTION

Throughout much of American history the individualism celebrated in folklore and political theory was restrained by religious, moralistic, and communitarian social contexts and norms.[9] Nineteenth-century populists, sensing the breakdown of these norms in the rise of the robber barons and the acceptance of social Darwinism, sought to protect their communities through political action. By the middle of the twentieth century, however, a new set of broad economic, technological, and social forces were radically altering the delicate balance between individual autonomy and community. These new forces were not so easily categorized as those of the Gilded Age. The postwar generation saw the advent of incredible mobility, cosmopolitan education, mass communication, and the triumph of the international marketplace. Sprawling suburbs, obsessive television audiences, and the youth culture are symbols of this emerging society of individuals uprooted from traditional ties to family, village, and church.

Many Americans, consequently, now have relatively loose ties to political parties, unions, neighborhoods, and churches. This "loose boundedness," although a logical result of mobility and freedom, strips citizens of effective avenues for cohesive group action.[10] True leverage in politics comes when people enjoy some collective solidarity, but solidarity is undermined by the atomistic trends manifest today. Moreover, an individualistic political culture, with its emphasis on rights versus obligations and sacrifice, frustrates effective leadership.[11]

The postwar era that saw these dramatic social changes also witnessed major political developments. The most important is the decline of parties in the electorate—one of the great sea changes in contemporary politics. Voters simply do not have the emotional ties to parties they once did; fewer than half routinely vote. This change has momentous implications for our political system, contributing to a popular disengagement from politics. On a practical level, it has affected campaigning and political mobilization. Richard Fenno quotes the lament of one member of Congress about campaigning in an atomistic milieu: "It's a mystery to me. I go there and all I see are row after row of mobile homes and apartment houses. It's just a collection of shopping centers. . . . It's not a community. They have no Rotary Clubs or groups like that. It's just a bunch of houses. . . . I don't know how you would campaign there." [12] Politicians, like the one quoted here, who could not adapt to the new candidate-centered era, were replaced by entrepreneurs more comfortable with contemporary demands.[13]

Collective political action, as a consequence, is far more difficult, expensive, and easily fragmented today than in the past. Even churches are affected by these trends; pluralism is more pronounced and mobility saps congregational solidarity. The degree of Jackson's and Robertson's success testifies to the continuing political salience of religious networks despite adverse trends.

A relatively rich area of sociological research can help us understand the implications of this blend of religion, culture, and politics. Resource mobilization theories suggest that successful political efforts depend upon the availability and wise use of resources, such as organizational networks and entrepreneurial leadership. Adherents of this school argue that the difference between political movements lies in the ability of leaders to marshal resources (time, money, energy, followers) and make wise strategic decisions that maximize political clout.[14] But resource mobilization theories, at least as they are interpreted, often do not go far enough in addressing the other impediments to collective action—fatalism, intimidation, atomism, and the free-rider problem. Doug McAdam suggests that social movements require a change in the expectations of potential activists and followers, what he calls "cognitive liberation." [15] As we will see, churches and religious traditions both provided Jackson's and Robertson's campaigns with resources and also liberated many followers from cognitive habits debilitating to political action.

Churches, and especially charismatic religious leaders, offered hope as an antidote to the fatalism that can pervade low-status groups. The Jackson campaign exhibited an ecstatic quality that defies rationalist explanations and helps explain the sacrifices made by many of its followers. In July 1988, during the Democratic National Convention in Atlanta, a large auditorium with giant TV screens was set up for visitors who were unable to secure passes to the convention hall next door. As Jesse Jackson gave his address, one noticed the emotional response of the sea of black faces, all glued to the giant screens. The people rose to their feet again and again in response to their leader's prophetic challenge to society. At a National Baptist Convention meeting in Oklahoma City, similarly, Jackson's magnetic quality was evident. He began softly, "Jesus loves me, this I know," then described the failures of political leaders in biblical terms. He concluded with a roaring, mesmerizing chant that brought the crowd of twelve thousand to its feet, shouting and clapping. When all had settled down, Jackson performed the "altar call" for the unsaved to come forward. "Please, pastors," he intoned, "don't lead your flock astray." Finally, with his spiritual job completed, Jackson led another, secular, altar call to raise thousands of dollars to pay off campaign debts and succor his Rainbow Coalition operation in Washington, D.C. "Anyone who can donate $100 come forward now." What appeared to be several score individuals, including the entire clerical leadership of the convention, came forward. Jackson went on to $50, then $25, then any amount, until the entire crowd was filing in front of the dais to place cash and checks in the huge baskets provided. Clearly, religious charisma played a role in mobilizing and fund raising.

Robertson, too, was able to elicit a religious devotion in his supporters. Observers noted that they lifted their arms "in the charismatic posture of praise" at his rallies, uttering cries of "Praise the Lord" during his speeches. Their cars sported religious bumper stickers, and their lapel pins read "I Found It!" and "Praise the Lord." [16] Their earnestness and political naïveté seemed to call forth a generosity of spirit from normally hard-boiled journalists, who were relentless and withering in their coverage of Robertson but gentle and often sympathetic to his followers.[17] Robertson backers hailed from churches with such names as Praise Assembly, Abundant Life, Shield of Faith, Holy Spirit Harvest, and Higher Ground Christian Fellowship. Although not necessarily lower class, as earlier Pentecostals typically had been, these modern charismatic Christians did not enjoy high status in American society, and they knew it. They were "tired of feeling like religious and cultural refugees in their own country," and the promise of "one of theirs" in the presidency elicited an extraordinary response. As one chronicler put it, "Robertson supporters respond to his almost every statement, even those on such relatively neutral subjects as phonics, with an emotional fervor that is shocking and somewhat frightening in its intensity. They clearly are worried about what they see happening in their country, and they are scared about what it is doing to their children." [18] Keenly aware of the negative stereotypes many elites have of them, they nonetheless emerged from separatist cloisters that reflected a fatalism about the sinfulness of the broader society. Thus in 1988 they were imbued with a renewed hope, which Robertson kindled, that their concerns would be heard and their religious heritage affirmed in the broader society.

The solidarity that emerged from the church networks overcame the intimidation factor. Followers of Jackson and Robertson spoke frequently of the ways in which they were encouraged to participate by ministers and active lay persons; they spoke of how they joined like-minded partisans in praying and planning. These efforts contributed to a sense of esprit de corps outside the influence of dominant ideologies. Journalists might scoff at Robertson, and Republican regulars might call the insurgents names, but Robertson followers were buoyed by their shared context, by their discovery of each other, and by the intoxication of battles won. Similarly, while other Democratic constituencies might weigh the viability of candidates in determining their support, Jackson supporters operated in a shared cultural context that was intensified by the campaign.

Religious imagery can serve as a powerful means of calling the faithful to rise above selfishness, to transcend weariness, to overcome temptations of letting others fight the struggle. Ministers have a natural ability to mobilize resources—that is what they do week in and week out to keep their parishes going. Even in poor neighborhoods churches can thrive by extracting pennies from paupers and thereby shaming the better off to do likewise. The gospel account of the widow's mite, indeed, served as a key symbol in Jesse Jackson's fund-raising efforts. But in both Jackson's and Robertson's campaigns subtle and not so subtle peer pressure and moral suasion operated through the churches.

In summary, political mobilization, never easy, has become progressively more difficult in contemporary politics. Certain segments of religious America, however, run counter to depictions of the United States as a mass society of relatively unconnected individuals and thus offer collective bases for political mobilization. Different though they are in a number of respects, black congregations and conservative charismatic churches have one thing in common: they are central to the life of their members. When ministers speak, parishioners listen; when the church makes demands, members respond. Churches became vehicles for expressing popular discontent because they are places where people can "make common cause with one another," [19] gain self-confidence, overcome inertia, pool resources, and move out to do battle.

THE CHURCHES AND PARTY POLITICS

American political parties, unlike others around the world, choose presidential candidates through a relatively open process of electoral appeals to average citizens, not just to party elites.[20] Delegates to national nominating conventions function largely as bound agents of voters, and the convention resembles a coronation that ratifies the decisions of a mass electorate. Thus candidates must raise vast sums of money quickly, enlist thousands of volunteers, and build organizations in fifty states—all in the interest of reaching millions of voters in a crazy-quilt system of state primaries and caucuses. Moreover, an advance team must plan and coordinate daily campaign events for the candidate whose travel may encompass several states in a single, bone-jarring eighteen-hour day. This plebiscitary system puts a premium on tangible political resources such as money, volunteers, and media exposure. It also requires intangible assets such as intensity, commitment, and energy—resources both Jackson and Robertson enjoyed. The enormous resources necessary to mount a presidential campaign can evaporate quickly, however, as donors and activists abandon perceived "losers" to board the front-runner's bandwagon. Strategic players—such as big contributors, activists, interest group representatives, party leaders, and political action committee directors—do not back unconventional candidates who have little chance of electoral success.[21] Unique among the 1988 candidates, Jackson and Robertson could rely on sources of support, notably church networks and charismatic appeal, that were relatively independent of these strategic calculations. Their campaigns could pursue objectives long after other candidacies had folded.

The two means of selecting national convention delegates—caucuses and primaries—differ radically in how they facilitate penetration by the discontented. In the primary a mass electorate must be mobilized, a task largely achieved through the mass media, since most people get their cues from television rather than from the community contexts of family, village, and parish that operated in the past. In a caucus system, on the other hand, a small, well-organized cadre can overwhelm existing party networks. Primaries tend to attract average party voters, while caucuses draw ideologues and zealots. Although some scholars may pine for the good old days of party pros running the show through precinct caucuses and conventions, the reality is that no barriers can be erected against fervent, well-organized outsiders. "Party regulars," who supported the likes of George Bush, Michael Dukakis, and Bill Clinton in the past two presidential campaigns, can be thankful that caucuses are used in a minority of states, because both Jackson and Robertson magnified their natural support in caucus states. This is due in part to the intensity of their followers and in part to their church-based organizational assets. The primary, then, became the chief means of blunting outsider takeover of the presidential convention delegation.

Even in primary states, however, churches are tempting sources of political resources—money, forums, volunteer networks, a leadership cadre. Jackson and Robertson both capitalized on the churches in 1988, but so did other candidates. Dukakis's "ethnic" appeal to Greek Americans, which was a valuable fund-raising and mobilizing resource, was facilitated by Greek Orthodox congregations. Other candidates, too, sensed the possibilities of church networks and made attempts to capitalize on them. Bush's organization, as we will see, employed a strategy of co-opting the evangelical vote with direct appeals to evangelical leaders and followers long before Robertson announced his bid. Jack Kemp aired advertisements on Christian radio stations. Paul Simon, an active Lutheran layman, spoke frequently at congregations. And Bob Dole's organization trumpeted Elizabeth Dole's evangelical roots. Seasoned political operatives began speaking of churches in language reminiscent of the way their predecessors had spoken of precincts. A Bush lieutenant referred to "Robertson churches," "Dole churches," and "Bush churches." A Dukakis aide lamented the way Jackson's churches effectively operated as precinct organizations, "shutting us out" of the process. Although this pattern was less pronounced in the 1992 campaign, Clinton campaigned often and effectively in black churches. And Bush continued to exploit evangelical networks, agreeing to an interview by Pat Robertson on "The 700 Club" shortly before the Republican National Convention.

What has caused this phenomenon? Candidates are responding to the demands of campaigning in a relatively individualistic cultural context, one bereft of the collective institutions that once brought people together. In spite of church-state concerns, therefore, political mobilization through congregations is attractive. Jackson and Robertson were unique because they arose from and made appeals to distinctive religious communities where discontent was simmering, harvesting voters who felt their grievances had not been heard.

JESSE JACKSON AND THE BLACK CHURCH

African Americans, in spite of their social and religious diversity, share a defining experience in the legacies of slavery and discrimination. To be black in the United States was, and largely still is, to be different, to be "other," to live what W. E. B. Du Bois called the dual identity—black and American.[22] Even affluent, established black citizens can still experience the frustration of not being completely accepted by the white majority. In that sense they feel themselves on the periphery. This experience explains how even a professor holding an endowed chair at an elite university could capture his involvement in the Jackson campaign with the populist phrase, "Our time has come."[23]

In this context one of the ironic legacies of slavery and Jim Crow is that black churches emerged in the nineteenth century as the primary institutions "owned and operated" by the blacks themselves. Churches became the haven where African Americans could "be themselves," and the congregation served numerous community functions—a place to socialize, celebrate, mourn, and later to plan political marches and boycotts.[24] Jesse Jackson, acutely aware of this legacy, summarized it this way:

> The black church is the strongest independent, nongovernment-funded organization in the black community. . . . It's the most stable. It's where our leadership is trained. It's where our sense of dignity was taught, our sense of self-worth was taught. . . . Everything about society said that we were inferior, cursed, second class, secondary. But the church kept saying that we were God's children, not his stepchildren.[25]

Because of this legacy, Jackson knew, "our people tend to have confidence in the minister's point of view." Significantly, the black minister was the one community leader economically independent of the white power structure.

Political mobilization through African American churches, because of this legacy, does not carry the divisive baggage it does in predominately white congregations. To be sure, before the civil rights movement the black churches were cautious, even conservative, as ministers sought to protect and steward the unique position of the church in the community.[26] But once the potential for political mobilization was realized in the 1960s, through such organizations as the Southern Christian Leadership Conference, there was no turning back. Gifted and ambitious young men like Jesse Jackson would seek the ministry knowing it offered enormous influence in the black community, both spiritually and politically. And in spite of dramatic social and political changes in the past three decades, the church remains the central institution today.[27] Thus, even with the rise in the numbers of black elected officials and professionals, black ministers retain enormous influence; they are true leaders with loyal followers. As one Vassar-educated black state senator put it, "When the preacher says give, I open up my purse."

The church clearly played the pivotal role in Jackson's emergence as the preeminent black leader in America and in his evolving role as itinerant prophet for the times. As we have seen, however, throughout the 1970s Jackson remained suspect among veterans of the civil rights struggle because of his "unseemly" drive to adopt the slain leader's mantle. He was also held in contempt by some leftist black scholars, who saw him as the reincarnation of Booker T. Washington, selling self-help and bourgeois values to young blacks in Operation Push, or worse, as a huckster for black capitalists. That Jackson would ultimately mount a credible presidential campaign was laughable to some and disturbing to others.[28] Moreover, even some sympathizers thought his 1984 campaign was quixotic and possibly damaging to Democratic chances against Reagan; so a number of prominent blacks did not endorse his bid in 1984. But Jackson understood, perhaps better than some elected officials, the potent force the black church continued to represent. Speaking from the pulpits of the land, Jackson circumvented established black elected leaders, many of whom supported Walter Mondale, and "beat 'em." [29] Speaking of why these officials then supported him in 1988, Jackson observed, "I was not in conflict with them; they were in conflict with their base. My premise was not to attack them but to keep serving." [30] His charismatic campaign eventually captured the attention of the media and sparked his growing popularity among the black masses.

So the black church, as Jackson himself noted, figured "prominently" in his decision to run for president in 1984, even when many black elected officials counseled him otherwise. Indeed, it was often ministers who urged him to run, assuring him of financial and moral support. As the Reverend T. J. Jemison, powerful bishop of the seven-million-member National Baptist Convention USA, put it, "The black caucus did not endorse him in 1984, but we endorsed him. In 1988 we endorsed him first, then the black caucus came on board, but they followed us. . . . Jesse comes to us as a brother, as a Baptist minister." [31]

The 1984 Presidential Campaign

Let us trace the process of Jackson's emergence in some detail. The idea of supporting a black presidential candidacy as a means of increasing leverage in the Democratic party had been discussed in black circles for years.[32] Confidants of Jackson began urging him to consider running as early as 1980. Longtime aide Frank Watkins, himself a white ordained minister, first suggested the idea of a Jackson run in 1979 and inserted "teasers" in Jackson speeches as early as 1982. The need, as Watkins described it, was to develop a "third force" in American politics—to establish independent leverage for blacks and other progressive voters.

The critical flash point was the mayoral election of Harold Washington in Chicago in 1983. As recounted by Watkins, Jackson was outraged that Ted Kennedy and Walter Mondale had endorsed the two white candidates in the Chicago race without even consulting black leaders in the community (who enthusiastically backed Washington). Washington's victory ignited the black electorate. But the behavior of "liberal number 1" and "liberal number 2," as Jackson contemptuously referred to Kennedy and Mondale, convinced him that blacks could not depend on white liberals to do their bidding any more.[33] Moreover, Jackson reasoned, black registration was still low in the South and elsewhere, and an increase of 25 percent could have reversed the 1980 presidential outcome in eight states. He crisscrossed the South in the summer of 1983, speaking at annual church conventions and individual congregations. He preached of poverty and oppression from pulpits and employed religious imagery in his registration drive. "Nails in our flesh," was his reference to violations of the Voting Rights Act of 1965, which, he argued, kept blacks from exercising their right of political participation. "Run, Jesse, run," a refrain that was put to music, was heard wherever he went.

Once he had made the decision to run, Jackson used the black church as the launching pad for his 1984 campaign. The Reverend James Holley, a longtime friend and seminary colleague of Jackson's, proudly observed that Jackson announced his candidacy from his church in Detroit, where a stained glass window now features Jackson along with other black religious leaders of the past.[34] Hundreds of other ministers would eventually be able to recall the time when Jackson came to town.

Jackson frequently acknowledged the importance of the church to his crusade. Speaking before the Holiness Church in Tyler, Texas, he quipped that while Mondale might have big labor, "We have Big Church." [35] And that was not far from the truth. Bishop Jemison roared his approval of Jackson at a convention of Baptist ministers: "I don't know if I speak for all Baptists, but I speak for so many, the number I don't speak for don't matter. . . . We are behind him [Jackson] in numbers, in spirit, and we are behind him in sugar [money]." [36]

Jackson's early campaign strategy was almost entirely church-based. The fact that there were so many churches, and that they were spread across the nation, buoyed Jackson strategists. "The word went out . . . that 40,000 black churches could raise $250 each for what some Jackson aides insisted could be a campaign war chest of $10 million." [37] Jackson spoke in churches daily, raised money in them, and developed a cadre of local and state leaders among the activist clergy.

Some journalists even argued that the black churches sustained Jackson psychologically, particularly in 1984 when his association with Black Muslim leader Louis Farrakhan turned things sour.[38] As the primaries continued,

> Jackson would turn to the black church more and more. . . . The black church—the traditional haven since slave days, where raids and boycotts and marches were planned and wounds were bound and the dead were mourned—would become Jackson's haven too, the source of some of his best crowds, the bulk of his money, many of his votes.[39]

Jackson viewed the church and its leaders as a sustaining moral force in the campaign. Ruminating about the role preachers played as mentors in his life, Jackson recounted how nervous he had been on the eve of the first presidential debate. He called upon a trusted preacher and mentor, Dr. Sam Proctor, who knew Jackson when he was a student at North Carolina A&T:

> I remember so well my first debate. I was very nervous in New Hampshire, back in '84. I did not know what to do. Couldn't go backwards and afraid to go forward. So I called Dr. Proctor to [pray] with me. Got some advice and suggestions. "Don't be nervous," he said. "These guys . . . senators, governors, know a code language which you will crack fairly soon. Even if they ask a question you don't know the answer to, listen well and pick up the assumption of the question and the predicate and take the moral high ground. Take the ethical position and you will beat 'em down every time. They're not used to takin' the moral high ground and the ethical high road."[40]

For Jackson this advice resonated deeply, touching both his spiritual sense and his political inclinations. Even as he might fall short of his own ideals, he came to speak of the "moral center" as the keystone of his campaign. To him that was his contribution, his "ministry."

The Perpetual Campaign

The 1984 Democratic convention, in a sense, set the stage for the 1988 campaign. Jackson employed religious themes in his convention speech, in part to ask forgiveness for his "low moments." Drawing upon the lyrics of an old gospel hymn, he pleaded, "Please be patient with me, God is not through with me yet." And then came the black gospel singer intoning the "master's hands." The delegates swayed and, for a moment at least, the convention was suffused with a religious ambiance that only Jackson could have achieved. His dramatic speech, the most watched portion of the Democratic convention, catapulted him into national prominence. Gallup surveys found that Jackson was one of the most admired men in America, third on the list after Ronald Reagan, his nemesis, and Pope John Paul II.

For the next four years Jackson ran what was effectively a perpetual campaign. He seemed to show up everywhere and stay in the news. But most important, he solidified his black support. And he did so not just through political efforts but through his ministerial role as well. Jackson was there in 1986 to deliver the eulogies for athletes Len Bias and Don Rogers. His eulogy for Rogers was vintage Jackson in its biblical cadences, offering solace to the family and making a prophetic call for a war on the scourge of drugs that had killed the athlete:

> I know that your hearts are heavy today. But I want to share with you this afternoon, as a friend and minister of the Gospel, to remind you that if you will but put your trust in God, even in your darkest hour, he is able to sustain you. . . . Even in the midst of tragedy, I am sharing with you in the spirit of Christian joy and celebration to remind you that for the Christian the tragedy of death has already been conquered by Christ's triumph over death. We serve a mighty, merciful, and loving God, and I know today that Don is at peace, having worked and served his purpose here on earth.[41]

This perpetual campaign touched people across the nation. One noticed how many convention delegates, local Jackson coordinators, and ministers spoke of Jackson in personal terms as a man they knew, as a leader who had earned their respect. For example, Jackson had spoken at one minister's parish, he had addressed another supporter's high school class, and he had "cut a tape" (a radio spot) during the reelection campaign of a public official. By 1988 Jackson was the undisputed leader of black America. As one scholar and activist remarked, "He just dominates black politics now." The black elite flocked to Jackson's second presidential bid, if not out of love for Jesse, then out of necessity to support the most popular figure in black America.

With this support as his base, Jackson was free to broaden his appeal beyond the black community. He hired Jerry Austin as his campaign manager. Austin, a political consultant with a Jewish Bronx background, brought coherent organization to the Jackson effort, hiring staff and developing a strategy. He consciously sought to transform the crusade from an African American struggle into a "populist" campaign.[42] But as a shrewd strategist he affirmed the importance of the black church, stressing the necessity of understanding its diverse denominations. The consequence was that Jackson's monolithic support from black voters in 1988, combined with a respectable 12 percent of the white vote, brought him nearly seven million votes, victories in thirteen primaries or first-round caucuses, twelve hundred delegates to the Democratic convention, and a negotiating position within the Democratic party.

Racial pride may have been Jackson's major appeal, but the churches were his organizational base and biblical cadences his rhetorical tool in energizing supporters. The fund-raising techniques used in 1988, for example, had been patented in 1984. They typically involved the hard sell in congregations. Collection plates were passed in a variation on the altar call ("Come forward now!"), often to provide Jackson with plane fare to his next stop.[43] Although some of this fund raising was probably a violation of IRS regulations on the tax-exempt status of religious institutions, it was very effective. Austin noted that because of Jackson's magnetism and the national organizational network of churches, the critical campaign need was money for airfare. "I concluded that the most important thing the campaign had to do was raise enough money to keep Jesse in the air." [44] As Jackson's campaign progressed, money flowed in from more conventional direct-mail solicitation, but the church money sustained Jackson in the critical early stages when other candidates were floundering.[45]

When Jackson organizers moved into a state, they began with the churches. Even in a place as improbable as Iowa, the black churches figured in the strategic calculations. "There are," Austin remarked with the consultant's eye to detail, "one hundred twenty-three black churches in Iowa." [46] Whether in state campaign headquarters or at the national convention, the leadership ranks of the Jackson organization swelled with ministers, a fact confirmed by others in the Rainbow Coalition. One mayor and gay delegate from California observed, "I wasn't used to the idea of starting a meeting with a prayer, but the Jackson meetings always start with a prayer—the reverends are in charge." [47]

Dukakis organizers also remarked on the importance of the ministerial connection. Early endorsements of Jackson by prominent ministers and associations, one Dukakis official noted, preempted organizing efforts by other candidates. As he observed, "In Ohio we wanted to do outreach, but the churches endorsed Jackson early. They shut us out. We wanted to have a meeting with a black state representative, but he wouldn't even meet with us." [48]

Although Jackson's second campaign attempted to reach beyond his core constituency, the churches remained vital forums, as a reading of 1988 news stories reveals: "Campaigning before cheering audiences at Baptist churches in Newark"; "The Reverend Jackson came to Ebenezer Baptist Church today"; "In a highly emotional address to the Shorter African Methodist Episcopal Church"; "In a speech from the pulpit of the Ward African Methodist Episcopal Church here"; "He returned to Cleveland and addressed a tumultuous rally at the Pentecostal Church of Christ." And so it went.

Customs in the black church facilitated the campaign. When black ministers travel they receive the hospitality of congregations wherever they go. A visiting minister often gives a guest sermon and receives in return the proceeds of a special collection, or love offering, to defray travel expenses. Not only did Jackson employ this strategy for fund raising, but his ministerial backers did so as well. The Reverend James Holley said that the Detroit Baptist Alliance sent ministers to other states to persuade wavering brethren to back the Jackson candidacy.[49] Bishops and ministers for Jackson traveled extensively in behalf of the campaign.

White secular supporters of Jackson frequently noted the religious character of the campaign. A white advance man for Jackson quipped that if asked what church he belonged to he would say "AME [African Methodist Episcopal] because that's the church I've been in the most this past year." He also maintained that churches were the critical component of advance planning for Jackson's visits. "There would be competition between ministers as to who would have his church featured by the Jackson visit, and then the pressure was on to generate the crowd." Given the network of black churches and ministers, there was "no problem in advance work getting a crowd. . . . The minister is out to prove himself as an organizer." He noted with amusement how the Dukakis organization had to expend precious money on organizing rallies and getting crowds. That was the easiest part of advance work for Jackson; the challenge was keeping him on time and protecting him from the crush of well-wishers.

National convention delegates also stressed the importance of black churches as strategic resources in the campaign. In interviews with black Jackson delegates, each told specific stories about church-centered fund-raising efforts, endorsements by prominent ministers and church associations, and campaign mobilization through local parishes. Indeed, while these black delegates stressed the church as the prime institution through which they gained entree to the system, nonblack delegates for Dukakis, Al Gore, and even Jackson emphasized their ties to unions, party organizations, educational associations, and interest groups. Thus for many blacks the church is precinct and interest group rolled into one.

Success on Super Tuesday

After respectable showings in Iowa and other states holding early caucuses or primaries, Jackson turned Super Tuesday—so named because of the huge numbers of delegates at stake—against the intention of its creators. The coordinated primaries in the South were intended to provide a "moderate" Democrat with a boost toward the Democratic nomination. Instead, Jackson thumped his rivals in the South Carolina caucuses just before the Super Tuesday primaries. On Super Tuesday, March 8, 1988, he claimed victories in Alabama, Georgia, Louisiana, Mississippi, and Virginia, winning 330 delegates, more than Gore (318) or Dukakis (259).[50]

Jackson's triumph on Super Tuesday rested on his undeniable gift for gaining free media coverage, a less chaotic campaign organization that kept him on the road, and the black church networks that exist in virtually every major city in the region. Even in places with relatively small black populations, churches could be a formidable resource. In Oklahoma City, for example, the Baptist Church Alliance comprises the fifty or so black Baptist congregations. The pastors of these churches meet weekly, mostly to discuss church issues and problems, but political issues are easily coordinated. Word of a visit by Jesse could spread rapidly, making advance work easy to accomplish. All that was required was a time and a place, and the crowd was guaranteed. During the Super Tuesday campaign, Frank Watkins made it his personal quest to magnify Jackson's effect outside his natural base in the South. He traveled to caucus states such as Nevada and "hit the black church network." According to Watkins's description of the process, all he had to do was meet with prominent black ministers and convince them they had the power to take over caucuses. With no understanding of the dynamics of caucuses, black ministers in predominately white states had not realized that turnout at caucuses is extremely small. As Watkins recounted it, "All they would hear is that in 1984 Gary Hart got 40 percent. They had no idea how few people that was. . . . So I appointed them coordinators, gave them targets—five people at this precinct, ten people at that precinct, and so forth." [51] Because of these efforts Jackson scored surprising showings in a number of caucus states.

From 1984 through 1988 Jackson increased his share of the vote, but not by as much as one might have guessed by the strength of his success.[52] Jackson's victories, it must be noted, rested in part on a growing detachment of whites from the Democratic party in the South, not necessarily on a huge turnout of black voters. As Penn Kimball observed, turnout in the 1988 Democratic primaries in some states was actually down from 1984 (because many whites voted in the Republican election), thus increasing the relative share of the vote by blacks. Because whites defected to the GOP in Alabama and Georgia, Jackson "won a larger slice of a smaller pie." [53] This pattern of white defection continued in the 1992 primaries, blemishing an otherwise promising black-white coalition supporting Bill Clinton's candidacy.

Perhaps the unique feature of Jackson's campaign was the use of forums, filled with gospel music, amens, and talk of Jesus. Although his organizers went out of their way to schedule Jackson at biracial events, especially on college campuses, he always came home to a black congregation. The climax of the service was a sermon by Jackson, replete with themes of the manger, the crucifixion, and the resurrection.[54] The gospel choirs, one insider recalled, "were a must." Because Jackson was notoriously late on campaign stops, some means of keeping exasperated followers from going home was a necessity. Holding the audience's interest was no problem since the campaign stops resembled extended revivals, with fiery sermons, the best music of the 1988 season, and strategic planning all in one. Not to be outdone in tapping Pentecostal enthusiasm, Jackson actively campaigned among blacks who shared Robertson's charismatic faith. Addressing a huge convention of the black Pentecostal denomination the Church of God in Christ, Jackson enjoyed the humorous contrast between straight-laced white Secret Service agents "talking in their sleeves" and twenty-five thousand "spirit filled" worshipers "shouting, running down the aisle, and jumping." [55]

JACKSON AND THE MICHIGAN CAUCUSES: THE CHURCH AS PRECINCT

A fascinating pattern began to emerge in Jackson's 1988 campaign: the idea of the "church as precinct." Nowhere did this pattern manifest itself as strongly as it did in Michigan, where Jackson scored a smashing victory that stunned party regulars across the nation. On the evening of March 26, national newscasts announced in excited tones that Jackson had just scored a 2-1 victory over Dukakis, 113,832 votes to 61,750, which gave Jackson a delegate edge in Michigan of 74-55.

To appreciate the role of churches in Jackson's triumph, we must look at the background. The Michigan caucuses placed a premium on strong local organization because the six hundred district boundaries had recently been redrawn, creating confusion about the new districts. Getting one's supporters to the right caucus site became the critical organizational task. Normally, organized labor would have organized caucus attendance, but in 1988 labor decided to remain more or less neutral. Moreover, in 1984 Detroit mayor Coleman Young had persuaded many ministers to ignore Jackson as being unelectable. But by 1988 Jackson had achieved enormous popularity with the clergy, some of whom "felt bad" for not having supported him in 1984.[56] His organizers thus were free to capitalize on the black church network.

Like Jackson's national effort, his success in Michigan was a blend of shrewd organizing and charismatic appeal. Although the Dukakis organization imported most of its sixty paid staff for the Michigan contest, Jackson's campaign relied on a small staff and an army of volunteers. Heading the effort was Joel Ferguson, a Lansing developer who had worked in the 1984 campaign and knew the Michigan political landscape. One of his first strategic decisions was to commit the campaign to collecting the signatures required for Jackson to be placed on the ballot rather than paying a fee (an easier route used by the other candidates). The effort was largely church-based and simple in design: pastors throughout the state were enlisted to solicit signatures, which became the pool from which volunteers and caucus goers were drawn. In one small county the coordinator met with thirty-five ministers and ceremoniously gave each a sheet of paper with ten lines for signatures. She told each pastor to collect the names of ten parishioners and then to ask each of them to collect more, a process that yielded 325 volunteers. Throughout the state such efforts yielded a list of 13,000 supporters and 5,000 volunteers.

Although black churches served as precinct organizations throughout the state, their effect was most dramatic in Detroit, with its large black population. Like many other industrial cities, Detroit had seen better times as its auto industry continued to decline. Not far from the much-touted Renaissance Center were boarded-up buildings in prime downtown locations. For more than two decades the city had reelected Coleman Young, but by the time of the 1988 campaign his hold on the community clearly was slipping. Not only had Young opposed Jackson in 1984, but he had the habit of making nasty comments ("The only thing Jesse Jackson has run is his mouth"). Frustrated by the economic plight of their parishioners and increasingly proud of Jackson, ministers by 1988 were ready to mount a major effort in his behalf, in spite of Young. But the campaign had to reach people, motivate them, and get them to the right places on election day. That effort was organized along church lines.

To understand the role of the churches, imagine scanning the yellow pages of the phone book and seeing page after page of ads for black congregations, many with photographs of the minister: Second Ebenezer Baptist Church, Greater Rose of Sharon Baptist Church, Ebenezer African Methodist Episcopal Church, Shalom Temple Pentecostal Church, and so on. Detroit has, by my count, 13 Christian Methodist Episcopal churches, 36 African Methodist Episcopal churches, 147 Church of God in Christ churches, and 300 black Baptist churches (the list continues for nine pages).

What made this network of churches so formidable was that it had an existing means of communication. The Reverend James Holley organized the church effort for Jackson in Detroit. As vice president of the Detroit Baptist Alliance, Holley knows all three hundred black Baptist ministers in the city. As he noted, the alliance meets weekly to discuss church matters, and in any given week as many as 75 percent of the ministers attend. "When the chemistry is right, as it was with Jackson," they are willing to coordinate a political initiative in addition to their churchly functions. In Detroit alone, the black Baptist ministers lead parishes comprising half a million members. Allied with other black congregations, a united black church network could literally deliver the city's black population in the same way that city machines used to do. Moreover, as longtime black city councilman Clyde Cleveland noted, these efforts were repeated across the state, culminating in the unprecedented endorsement of Jackson by two statewide ministers groups.

In 1988 volunteers were solicited, supporters were organized, and money was raised through these churches. When Jackson visited Detroit he would speak in one of the churches, and the ministers from all the other churches would generate the crowd. On the Sunday before the Saturday caucuses, the individual churches, corresponding to citywide neighborhood precincts, sponsored Jesse Jackson Day. "In one church they might have a young person read a Jackson speech"; in another some other activity would remind parishioners of the caucuses. Because Jackson was "one of us," the response was overwhelming. Through these networks Jackson supporters were barraged with information telling them where they should go to vote and how the procedure would work, and they were asked whether they needed a ride. This effort culminated in a massive get-out-the-vote drive. On election day Jackson received more than 90 percent of the vote in the two predominately black congressional districts encompassing metropolitan Detroit (compared with 40 percent four years earlier), even while doing respectably elsewhere in the state.

Todd Watkins, a top black staff member for Dukakis who worked in the Michigan campaign, categorically attributed the victory to neighborhood churches. Jackson's access to a network of neighborhood churches gave him a distinct advantage. Depicting an organizational approach by Jackson that was similar to that of Robertson, Watkins described how the process worked:

> The parish is an ideal unit for [political] organization. It's the same as a precinct. They [the Jackson supporters] would have a precaucus coffee at the neighborhood church, in a comfortable surrounding, and pass out stickers for Jackson. They would create strong peer pressure not to back down. Then they would bring a bus, and the minister, the "shepherd," would lead them to the caucus site.[57]

The smooth operation of the black church network allowed Jackson's staff to concentrate on the other prong of their strategy: broadening Jackson's appeal. As political scientist David Rohde observed, Jackson's campaign "targeted both the political-intellectual sector and the economically distressed sector of the white vote. He went to Ann Arbor, he went to the U.P [upper peninsula]. He went to places in the state where there was agricultural distress." [58] Thus Jackson sought to combine his popularity in university towns with his populist message elsewhere. For example, he traveled to the farm community of Homer to speak to two hundred skeptical white farmers. By the end of the speech Jackson had won many of them over with a message that blended old-time populism with the quest for racial common ground: "When the farmer is driven from his land and the lights go out, we all look the same." [59] Other observers noted this populist element. According to one news magazine Jackson generated "a political electricity that hadn't been seen or felt in years—a populist dream of black and white voters, their spirits kindled, finding common ground under a unifying banner of hope." [60]

The fact that the black church effort could operate almost autonomously aided the campaign in dealing with potential conflicts within the Rainbow Coalition. As Councilman Clyde Cleveland noted, the Detroit campaign organizers worked with the pastors separately from the other groups, such as the gays and the sizable Arab-American population. Thus while black ministers were coordinating Jesse Jackson Day, Cleveland was meeting with gay leaders and arranging speaking engagements for the candidate in the local Arab community (including one engagement in a mosque). In spite of these and related efforts on campuses around the state, Jackson's share of the nonblack vote was estimated at no more than 20 percent. His victory rested on a huge and well-focused black electorate.

In analyzing the Jackson phenomenon we must not discount the extraordinary gifts and energy of the man Richard Nixon called one of the best campaigners of the twentieth century. Nor should we forget the importance of black anger, hope, pride, and solidarity nor the affinity of white liberals for Jackson's economic and foreign policy messages. But even popular candidates cannot survive without strategic resources.[61] Followers must be mobilized, potential voters activated, forums scheduled, campaign workers recruited, and supporters solicited for donations of time and money. The black churches provided Jackson's campaign with the lion's share of strategic resources and moral support, especially in its early stages when those resources were most needed, freeing Jackson to do what he does so well.

DEMOCRATIC PARTY POLITICS AND RELIGION

It is not enough to say that Jackson "got the black vote" and some liberal white support. Instead, it is more accurate to say that his campaign mobilized the black vote (and a respectable part of the white vote) because churches sustained the effort. Failure to appreciate the religious dimension of the black experience, moreover, resulted in egregiously distorted analyses of Jackson's campaign. A *New York Times* editorial, for example, pronounced ex cathedra that religion was irrelevant to Jackson's triumph on Super Tuesday. In contrast, Jackson's top aide put it simply, "Without the black church there was no campaign." [62]

Jackson's campaign did reach out beyond his natural constituency, and the candidate found enthusiastic audiences on college campuses and in high schools, at farm meetings and in state legislatures. Jackson won support of populists such as former Texas agricultural commissioner Jim Hightower. Hightower described his commitment to Jackson in this way: "I kept waiting for a populist leader to arise. I didn't expect him to be black, but he is." [63] Jackson championed labor's cause at a time when unions were under siege, gaining him goodwill and even some improbable endorsements, such as that from the Iowa Teamsters Union. But in reaching out to white voters, Jackson also used the churches and spoke in "prophetic" terms. As Jerry Austin noted, he spoke frequently in white churches. "In fact, he raised money in a white church in Iowa." [64]

Some black scholars viewed the religious dimension of Jackson's crusades positively, arguing that the black church, as an authentic community institution, embodied the progressive and prophetic tradition of African Americans.[65] The Jackson campaign was also analyzed as a means of increasing the leverage of blacks in the Democratic party.[66] Some suggested favorably that Jackson was "adopted" by the left and transformed by it.[67] He "grew," in this analysis, because he shed some of his moral traditionalism to rally disparate progressive forces—minorities, union leaders, feminists, gays, socialists—to make a forceful attack on Reaganism. Others, however, criticized the reintroduction of religious charisma as a retrogressive element, drawing black politics away from more tangible gains won by the "mundane" but effective power of black elected officials. Adolph Reed contends that Jackson wrapped himself in the mantle of civil rights and religion as a way to stifle dissent. Religious charisma, Reed argues, is antidemocratic and mirrors the authoritarian nature of many black churches. Jackson's evangelical style of campaigning, Reed says, celebrated form without substance, protest without strategic gains; it was an outlet for discontent without a means of ameliorating that discontent.[68] Not surprisingly, Jackson disputes Reed's analysis, calling it ignorant "of our history." Where was Reed, he asked, when churches sustained the civil rights movement? Where was he when we "marched from Dexter Street Church in Birmingham to 16th Street Church in Montgomery" ? [69]

Jackson clearly championed the agenda of the left—economic redistribution, feminism, gay rights, environmental concerns, nuclear disarmament, and Third World advocacy. Because of this he attracted a number of left-wing intellectuals and policy analysts to his campaign. Among them were Robert Borosage, former director of the progressive Institute for Policy Studies; Ann Lewis, a Democratic consultant; Frank Clemente, a well-known advocate of converting military spending to jobs programs; and Jack O'Dell, a foreign policy specialist who Robertson charged was a "card carrying communist."

Jackson also reached out to ethnic groups outside the mainstream. His embrace of the Palestinian cause in 1988 fostered a particularly interesting new political dynamic. His smashing victory in Michigan reflected a growing alliance between blacks and Arab Americans—an alliance of church and mosque. Jackson was free to develop this relationship because he had written off any thoughts of winning more than a token Jewish vote. (His rejection of the Jewish vote clearly hurt him later in the New York primary, when New York City mayor Ed Koch said Jews would be "crazy" to vote for him.) The solidifying alliance between blacks and Arab Americans was evident at the Democratic National Convention. For the first time in American politics Arab Americans were given a highly visible national forum to air their concerns. Dr. James Zogby, close adviser to Jackson, orchestrated the debate over a proposed Palestinian plank at the convention, an unprecedented effort that disturbed Jewish leaders. Although Zogby and Jackson ultimately agreed not to bring the issue to a vote on the convention floor, the development spotlighted the heightening tensions between blacks and Jews.

Jackson's 1988 campaign illustrates how important the black constituency, and by extension the black church, is to the American left. But there are inherent tensions. Many black ministers are socially conservative, and the message in black churches is not always sympathetic to the left's agenda on the family, gay rights, abortion, and artistic expression. As one black woman on the Democratic National Committee put it, "You won't find a more conservative lot on social issues than black ministers. They want me home making babies." Activist ministers acknowledged that they do not agree with Jackson's stands on some issues. And black ministers are not alone in their cultural conservatism, as I learned in interviews with Jackson backers, some of whom were genuinely shocked when I mentioned that Jackson supported gay marriages. Jackson recognized that there was some "tension" between his moral message and some members of the male gay community who do not want to accept the consequences of sexual promiscuity.

Jackson was able to negotiate his way through this delicate problem by focusing on a combination of racial pride, religious identification, and, as we saw in Chapter 3, social conservatism (his antidrug message, his call for educational excellence, and his claim that pornography is child abuse). During a candidate forum sponsored by the Rainbow Coalition, Jackson denounced the "ethical collapse" and "moral degeneracy" rampant in America with a thunder unequaled by conservative evangelists. One of the ironies of the 1988 presidential campaign is that both Jackson and Robertson, at times, sounded remarkably similar in their chastisement of popular culture and in their calls for sexual responsibility, discipline and hard work in the schools, and temperance with drugs and alcohol. Indeed, Jackson insiders recalled that the "puritanical" Jackson did not like to see alcohol on the press bus. For those on the left, however, such oddities were irrelevant because Jackson alone championed their broader agenda.

PAT ROBERTSON AND THE CHARISMATIC NETWORK

Pat Robertson viewed his campaign as the culmination of a growing evangelical movement that began in the late 1970s—a movement of those on the "outside" trying to beat down the doors of power. Thus the realignment of conservative Christians to the Republican party is of utmost importance: "I would say between 1980 and 1984 roughly six million evangelicals and Southern Baptists switched from the Democratic party to the Republican party. It was an extraordinary political event." Robertson noted that Reagan mobilized the evangelical community with appeals to hot button issues such as prayer and family values. But he also suggested that "the Democratic party did everything it could to drive the evangelicals away. . . . Paul Kirk [former Democratic party chairman] blasted me and the evangelical Christians in a fund-raising letter which I use far and wide, but what he said was so scathing about the people who were his natural constituency."[70] Moreover, in 1988 Bush was viewed as being lukewarm toward the religious agenda and was considered a weak candidate at that. Thus 1988 seemed the magic moment for Robertson to parlay his leadership in the movement into a winning political crusade.

But while Robertson sought to lead a broad coalition of Protestant evangelicals and conservative Catholics into battle, his core constituency comprised a narrow band of filial charismatics whose religious practices set them apart from other believers. Charismatics stress intense religious experience, in contrast to many mainstream evangelicals, who look to rational explanations for faith. For charismatics such paranormal encounters as glossolalia, prophecy, miracles, and faith healing represent a form of protest against the modern emphasis on functional rationality and scientific explanations. Old as Christianity itself and rooted in earlier revivals, these practices came to be regarded as normative for a group of "spirit-filled" believers with the birth of the Pentecostal movement at the turn of the century. Embraced by blacks and whites alike, Pentecostalism was associated with the lower classes. But as denominations like the Assemblies of God grew, they attracted a wider spectrum of followers turned off by the shallowness of a purely material existence. Moreover, this "unquenchable thirst for the spiritual" led in the 1960s to a charismatic revival among independent churches and mainstream congregations, bringing Pentecostal practices to more affluent parishioners. By the 1980s the majority of the most popular televangelists emphasized spiritual gifts. On racial matters charismatics are known to be more tolerant and open than many other conservative Christians. And as Margaret Poloma's account of the Assemblies of God shows, they actively struggle to maintain charisma in the midst of forces that might undermine it.[71]

As founder of the Christian Broadcasting Network and host of "The 700 Club," Robertson had cultivated that constituency for years, blending upscale technology with charismatic faith. At its peak CBN reached sixteen million households a month, and "The 700 Club" logged four million prayer calls to volunteers minding the telephone banks.[72] This formidable reach suggested to Robertson that religious conservatives, if properly organized, could effectively take over the Republican party.

Yet Robertson's quixotic presidential campaign illustrates some of the limits of evangelical politics. Although Jackson could rely on overt political support from ministers and church organizations, Robertson had to approach his church base more delicately. He felt compelled, for example, to resign his commission as a minister, whereas Jackson continued to campaign as "the reverend." Because white theological conservatives held a longstanding suspicion of politics, Robertson had to rely on what has been termed a "parachurch" network. This charismatic network included viewers of religious broadcasting, religious activists identified through mailing lists, antiabortion activists, and lay members of specific congregations quietly willing to organize their fellow parishioners. Moreover, Robertson's major resource—his identification with an ardent religious movement ripe for political mobilization—severely limited his attempt to broaden his appeal beyond charismatic Christians. Throughout the campaign journalists and political cartoonists focused on the "peculiar" practices of Robertson's faith, even as he sought to cast himself more broadly as a businessman and broadcaster. As seasoned political reporter Jack Germond observed, "Most journalists think he is a nut . . . every bio piece will include the fact that he claims to cure hemorrhoids with prayer."[73]

What secular journalists did not understand was that many fundamentalists and evangelicals were also skeptical, even hostile, toward faith healing, speaking in tongues, and emotional worship. Robertson, consequently, found that his attempt to broaden his political base to include conservative religionists of all theological stripes was fraught with obstacles. In the Bible Belt, for example, Robertson failed to gain substantial support from Southern Baptists, in part because of theological differences but also because of Reagan's popularity (and by association Bush's) with that constituency.[74] Robertson said ruefully, "If evangelicals had supported me in the same way as blacks supported Jackson, I would be the nominee of the party."[75]

Robertson officially began his campaign by announcing in September 1986 that he would run if he obtained at least three million endorsing signatures in one year's time. The rationale behind this goal was both symbolic and strategic. Symbolically, it would embolden some closet supporters who would support him only if he had a realistic chance of winning. Substantively, given the relatively small number of voters participating in Republican primaries and caucuses in 1984, Robertson calculated that he could win with three million votes in a three-way split. The early effort to secure names on endorsing petitions was largely based in churches or promoted to "700 Club" viewers. Although some creative accounting was probably employed, the organization met its goal, indicating to Robertson that God once again had provided him with a sign to proceed.

The most successful aspect of the campaign was fund raising, a specialty of televangelists and religious broadcasters. Through direct-mail lists that included many ministers, evangelical associations, and faithful contributors to CBN, Robertson's staff raised millions. According to the final accounting of the Federal Election Commission, Robertson surpassed all other candidates in prenomination finance, raising and spending a remarkable $41 million in contributions and federal matching funds. In contrast, Bush—at $34 million—raised $7 million less than Robertson, followed by Dukakis at $31 million, Dole at $28 million, and Jackson at $27 million.[76]

This fund-raising success was rooted in Robertson's strong appeal to the charismatic segment of the evangelical camp. Surveys of Robertson's contributors confirm that they were distinguished from other Republican donors by their intense religiosity. Although generally affluent (as donors tend to be) they were less elite than other Republican activists and more likely to have moved "down" in status from mainline to charismatic churches.[77] Compared with other Republicans, Robertson donors had less education and held lower status jobs; one-quarter were either homemakers or blue-collar workers. Moreover, although Republican contributors tend to be male, nearly half of Robertson's contributors were female, more than twice the number typical for the GOP. These findings confirm that Robertson's cultural populists comprise a less elite, pietistic faction within the Republican party.[78]

Robertson's campaign built a formidable political organization of local and state leaders through its network of local pastors, antiabortion activists, and Christian broadcasting audiences. According to Robertson the strategy was aimed at building thirty-five state organizations. "We realized that our natural base ... was the church constituency. So we had a state like Iowa divided into congressional districts and subdivided into precincts, and in each precinct there were churches that we would work through." [79] Although it was admittedly a ticklish proposition, pastors were recruited to serve as precinct and congressional district coordinators. To capture the dynamics, let us look at the campaign process itself.

ROBERTSON AND THE MICHIGAN CAUCUSES: FROM GRASS-ROOTS TO PRESIDENTIAL CRUSADE

Robertson's campaign was tested in Michigan—the first battleground in the presidential sweepstakes. There, a very early and confusing process designed to reward party insiders was turned to his advantage. Michigan meant more than just the first foray, however; it played a pivotal role in focusing national attention on the candidate.

Some background will be helpful here. Long before his presidential intentions crystallized, Robertson had created the Freedom Council to pursue his political agenda. This effort coincided with a growing sense of crisis within a segment of conservative Christians. Fortunately for Robertson, his best Freedom Council organizer turned out to be a woman who had deep political roots in Michigan. The story of Marlene Elwell of Detroit nicely captures the currents of disquiet on the right.[80]

A devout Roman Catholic, Elwell was an unlikely Robertson ally. Yet as a veteran of antiabortion politics, she was passionately committed to political goals and was willing to engage in practical efforts to achieve them. Her political activism had begun in 1972, when she was a "homemaker ... a Catholic mother of five who recognized the reverence for life." Politically motivated to oppose a state referendum to legalize abortion on the Michigan ballot in 1972, she helped engineer its defeat. "The referendum was supposed to pass by a 2-1 margin, but through a great grass-roots effort it was defeated by a 2-1 margin." Catholics, as she notes, were the main force behind the defeat. Then came *Roe v. Wade* a year later. "We were in a state of shock," she remembers, because all the effort that went into the defeat of the referendum was undone overnight by the Supreme Court. Elwell became active in antiabortion politics, helping to form the Michigan Right to Life organization and hosting the first national Right to Life convention. A lifelong Democrat at the time, she would remain a registered Democrat until 1980, when the Republican party held its national convention in Detroit. Not wishing to let such an opportunity go by, she organized a prolife "impact committee" and worked to get an antiabortion plank adopted in the Republican platform. This success solidified her growing alienation from the Democratic party, which spurned her efforts, and she became active in Republican politics from that time on. In 1984 Elwell's talents as an organizer won her a position as field director of the Reagan reelection campaign.

In spite of publicity to the contrary, Elwell concluded that there was "a void of Christians involved, especially evangelicals, in 1984," at least in Michigan. After the 1984 election she sought a way to mobilize them. "I attended a Moral Majority meeting, but it was a lot of talk and no grass-roots organization. And they were so judgmental I couldn't embrace it." Then a black minister in Detroit passed her name along to the Freedom Council, which contacted her. As Elwell notes, at the time the Freedom Council was nonpartisan and enjoyed the support of some black ministers concerned with moral issues. (Robertson's campaign actually intersected with Jackson's through this church connection. One of Jackson's principal ministerial organizers in Detroit, the Reverend James Holley, agreed to introduce Robertson to a Detroit meeting because he knew Robertson well through his charitable work.)

Because grass-roots organization was the focus of the Freedom Council, Elwell signed up. "What they planned was what I wanted to do precisely—organizing grass-roots Christians." She traveled to Virginia Beach in February 1985. "But the national staff at the time, who shall remain nameless, were not too keen on me, because I was a Catholic and a woman. It wasn't till May that I got hired to be a congressional district coordinator for the Freedom Council." Events catapulted Elwell into greater prominence in the organization. "In June of 1985 Pat came in to do a national news program. They needed organizing. I did it, the advance work. Pat was impressed and thought I might make a good state coordinator. That didn't happen, again because I was a Catholic and a woman." Later in the year, however, the state coordinator presided over a poorly planned event, was fired, and subsequently was replaced by Elwell. She became state coordinator of the Freedom Council in January 1986.

Elwell insists that at the time she and others in the organization had no idea that Robertson would make a run for the presidency but that she chose to focus on involving conservative Christians in Michigan party politics in part because of timing. By May 1986 the process of selecting precinct leaders and convention delegates would have begun. The early Michigan campaign was designed to allow party leaders to deliver the state to Bush long before other candidates could get organized. But Elwell saw in the process an excellent venue through which to get Christians involved.

It worked this way. To become a precinct leader or convention delegate in Michigan, a person had to file for election and get on a primary ballot. Working through religious networks, Elwell concentrated on getting conservative Christians to enroll by the May deadline for the August 1986 party elections. Although most signed up for the Republican elections, Democrats were encouraged to run in their party as well. Helping to spearhead the drive was a young couple, Michelle and John Miller, who produced a cheap but effective training video to demystify the process and encourage "Christians" to file for the party slots. In homes across the state the video helped to recruit a cadre of new party activists, organized precinct by precinct. It was old-fashioned organization: appoint county and city coordinators and give them targets. The result was a resounding success, with nine thousand people across the state filing for party election. Republican regulars, who woke up facing the prospect of losing control of the party, were stunned. As Elwell put it, "The Bush people panicked. Every county clerk was reporting a flood of filings, and they were ours. We even filed them in the Democratic party."

The success of the filings altered the political landscape and forced a decision on Robertson. Elwell recalled, "When we did this we had no idea that he would run for president. But after the filings, people kept saying, 'Is he going to run for president?' The excitement was high." But because the Freedom Council had been established as a nonpartisan, tax-exempt organization, it could not serve as the vehicle for a presidential quest. "So we couldn't be the Freedom Council anymore. I think [Robertson's success in Michigan] helped to push him over." To Robertson the remarkable Michigan results were a confirmation of God's blessing of his candidacy. In a sense, what had begun as a grass-roots movement was transmuted into a presidential quest.

Matched with Elwell's organizational genius was Robertson's popularity with an ardent following. His Michigan forums, in this sense, resembled Jackson's: "In a patriotic, politically charged sermon to about eight hundred church members, television evangelist Pat Robertson said Sunday he is seeking 'a new vision of America' in which citizens ask God to guide their government." [81] One observer noted that "congregation members awaited Robertson with an hour of joyous singing," a report in which one could have substituted Jackson's name for Robertson's. Robertson received endorsements from ministers. And as Elwell said, "The crowds were tremendous."

The Bush campaign, hoping to salvage what it could, announced victory in the initial election of delegates in August 1986, though the reality was quite different. By the time of the February 1987 Republican state meeting it was clear that the superior Robertson organization had gained control of the state party machinery. Elwell observed simply, "This started a big war." The early skirmishes involved an alliance with Kemp. "Christians had never been involved before. We started out being nice. We could have taken every congressional district.... That wasn't our intention. Since we did not have the experienced people, we turned to the Kemp people [and] helped elect them as chairs ... they were party people." This temporary alliance gave Kemp more delegates than he would have received, and it shut out many Bush backers. Kemp supporters, in return, demanded that Bush apologize for calling Robertson's backers "kamikaze recruits." The *Detroit News* announced the results as headline news with the following story: "Delegates recruited by T.V. evangelist Pat Robertson apparently gained a plurality of the 104-seat Republican state committee—the party's governing body. Robertson leaders claimed 63 seats belong to them or their conservative allies." One well-known Detroit political commentator referred to Robertson as "Commander in Chief of the Michigan GOP." Robertson said of the triumph, "We saw the hand of God going before us in Michigan affirm our every step."[82]

What ensued was a raucous free-for-all, marked by court challenges, rump conventions, and a new Bush-Kemp alliance to replace the Robertson-Kemp one. The tide turned in early December 1987 in favor of the Bush forces. A favorable court ruling allowed twelve hundred officeholders and unsuccessful candidates (Bush party regulars) to be seated automatically at county conventions, which would meet in January 1988. This ruling gave the Bush organization enough power to cut a fresh deal with Kemp, whose national organization was beginning to sense the Robertson threat. Thus Bush was able to emerge with the majority of delegates to the national convention. Although they won the battle, Bush and his backers emerged bruised and bloodied.

REPUBLICAN PARTY POLITICS AND ROBERTSON'S CAMPAIGN

The infusion of new people into the Republican party was evident throughout the campaign. The big story of the Iowa caucuses, for example, was not Bob Dole's victory, but Robertson's surprise second-place showing, beating incumbent vice president George Bush. Engineered again by Marlene Elwell, now working as Midwest director, the Robertson campaign built itself quietly through church networks. The potential of such mobilization became evident during a party fund-raising event in Ames, Iowa—the so-called cavalcade of stars. Robertson's forces organized their following so well that he won the straw poll there, creating a tremendous publicity advantage.

Robertson caucus attenders in Iowa were largely newcomers, mobilized by friends from their churches. More than half of those interviewed were viewers of "The 700 Club." Many of them had met as a prayer group before attending the caucus. Some were prolife Catholics; most were from evangelical and Pentecostal backgrounds. Culturally, these newcomers viewed themselves as distinct from the Bush and Dole mainline Republicans, a characteristic epitomized by a young, prolife woman who had served as a precinct captain for Robertson. Exuding the excitement of a neophyte, she described how she had packed the caucus so that more than half were Robertson people, "whereas all Bush and Dole had were a few older men!" [83] She had organized the precinct drive through her church, the First Federated Open Bible Church in Des Moines, which, she said, was one of twenty charismatic churches headquartered in Des Moines.

Observers of the Robertson campaign in other states again corroborated the importance of churches as bases of this organizational effort. Jack Germond made these observations:

> Evangelicals are not united, but the church is the glue for the Robertson campaign. At the Florida state convention their participation was impressive. Almost everyone I talked to—forty-five to fifty people—had reenrolled as Republicans and paid $50 apiece to attend. They are a homogeneous group—united, disciplined.[84]

The cultural distinctiveness of this new group of Republican activists was evident throughout the campaign. Robertson supporters were fervently religious and deeply concerned about families, schools, and moral decay. Little resembling stereotypical "elite Republicans," some even wore blue jeans to party conventions. Surveys revealed that many Robertson supporters fit the Democratic profile, blue collar and female.[85] Among those attending a postelection reception for Robertson in Oklahoma were a janitor, a truck driver, and the owner of a car stereo shop. A major organizational challenge for Robertson supporters in some states, therefore, was getting Democrats to change their registration to Republican before deadlines, an effort that was not always welcomed by GOP regulars. Germond commented on this phenomenon:

> In the South the Bush supporters really are country club people, but the Robertson people are a notch below. Church is so important to them. There is a cultural gulf between them and the country club types. . . . The new registrations are mostly Robertson people.[86]

Among the many newcomers were prominent women, who formed the backbone of Robertson's organization and voting support (as we will see in Chapter 6). Criticized for his antagonistic views toward feminists, Robertson nonetheless attracted highly skilled women to his cause. These included Constance Snapp, the campaign's communications director and highest paid staffer; Mary Ellen Miller, director of the field organization; and of course Marlene Elwell. Women also served as state directors, precinct organizers, and fund raisers. Robertson appealed to religious, prolife women who felt unrepresented by feminists, and they responded with enthusiasm to his crusade in behalf of "family values." In spite of stereotypes about conservative evangelists, Robertson seems comfortable around assertive, intelligent women. Ironically, Jackson, who embraced the feminist agenda, appeared to have had some conflicts with prominent women in his campaign.[87]

The key to Robertson's success in mobilizing new activists was the organizational base of a network of large charismatic churches. One of the keenest observers of this phenomenon was a top Bush strategist assigned to court the evangelical constituency and, ultimately, to blunt Robertson. Doug Wead, former special assistant to the president for public liaison, described how the Bush organization monitored Robertson's efforts and discovered ways to check them. Combining sophisticated polling and tracking techniques with "spies" in Robertson's camp, Wead's staff discovered that the Robertson organization capitalized on his popularity with charismatics, many of whom belong to "superchurches," congregations with five thousand or more members. "His base was the Assemblies of God," noted Wead, "but they weren't aware of it." Given the small turnout at caucuses and even some primaries, these superchurches had formidable potential. "The pastor of a superchurch is, or could be, the equivalent of a county chairman. In some communities there are five churches, any one of which could take over the party organization." Yet whereas Jackson could openly court the membership of the black churches, Robertson had to work quietly to exploit this potential. "Robertson had a hard thing to do. He had to slowly build a cadre within the church, which could then get the pastor to go along—let them use the church building, place announcements in the church bulletins." The Robertson effort would start slowly, almost imperceptibly then, as the large churches were finally "captured," the campaign would mushroom. "Robertson's pattern was to double that of in the last week and then double again on the weekend before the vote. They did it four times."[88]

In caucus states this strategy was highly effective because it was so difficult for opponents to detect. Indeed, Robertson's support on election day in caucus states, such as Iowa, was double that of the projections made by polls. Studies show that this underestimation worked in the primaries as well, for both Robertson and Jackson. Larry Bartels and C. Anthony Broh show that public opinion polls in 1988 consistently "underestimated support for Pat Robertson" from 4.5 to 5.6 percent and for Jackson from 4.3 to 6.4 percent. These figures suggest the "special strength among voters who were not part of the traditional electorate." [89]

As to campaign strategy, the Robertson staff had two broad goals: one involved a close marriage with churches and the other did not. The first goal was to mobilize followers from the church networks to pack party meetings and caucuses; the second was to broaden Robertson's appeal to compete in primary states. The campaign was successful enough in achieving the first goal to cause apoplexy among Republican party regulars (as we will see in the next chapter). Party regulars were threatened because, as Robertson himself noted, "A caucus is not that hard to win." It may be tough to organize people to turn out at caucuses, "but if you have a dedicated core of people, they can win caucuses."

A big part of the story of the Robertson campaign, consequently, was not Robertson's own rise and fall but the infusion of his followers into the Republican party,[90] where they stormed caucuses and conventions. Robertson's early success in the first stage of delegate selection in Michigan sent the party into a protracted, year-long struggle. He went on to dominate the Hawaii caucuses; he won in Alaska, Nevada, and Washington; and he did respectably in Iowa, Kansas, and Minnesota. Even in primary states where Bush defeated him, his supporters packed party caucuses to elect delegates, draft platform statements, and control party machinery. In several states, including Arizona, Georgia, Louisiana, North Carolina, Oklahoma, Oregon, South Carolina, Texas, and Virginia, Robertson supporters flooded party meetings, igniting fierce clashes, even fisticuffs, with Republican regulars.[91] Subsequently, many Robertson loyalists were elected to state party slots, and a good number are running for local offices.

Robertson's supporters did indeed view themselves as distinct. As one prominent state leader said, "There is something special about us. I never thought I'd say this, but we do resemble the Jackson people, we are different." Several of the key state leaders and delegates were quick to add that their involvement was not solely tied to Robertson. One commented, "We are bigger than Robertson though . . . we have issues versus just party loyalty." Another supporter observed, "I notice that everyone tries to make the movement very personal to Mr. Robertson, but I think that's a mistake. The issues will remain long after the candidate has stepped away from politics entirely."[92]

If the first major objective of the Robertson campaign—packing caucuses—was reasonably successful, the second goal—broadening the Robertson appeal to compete in primary states—was not. To appreciate this failure one must understand the strategic analysis of the Robertson campaign officials, particularly that of Robertson and of his campaign manager, Marc Nuttle. Nuttle has served as chief consultant in more than 150 federal campaigns in all forty-eight continental states; he worked with the Republican National Committee and was field counsel for the Reagan campaign in 1984. He was described as "extraordinarily good, meticulous" by Jack Germond, who noted that at the time of the Iowa caucuses Nuttle had consistently delivered what he said he was going to do.[93]

According to Nuttle, the "transforming" potential of the Robertson campaign was rooted in the awakening of culturally conservative religious Americans during the past twenty-five years. Those who felt strongly about traditional religion were "left out of things in the 1960s—whether in politics or in the broader culture." But then the federal control of schools accelerated, and the government intruded into areas once the domain of families. "In 1968 Reagan burst on the scene, and this group emerged out of primordial ooze as a distinct entity, concerned about divorce, taxes on families." Nuttle thinks this broad trend has not yet peaked:

> Approximately 35 percent of the population is at least partly motivated in terms of how to vote, what to buy, what to watch on TV, by conservative moral values.... These people are desperately seeking guidelines that will help them decide how to act. They are tired of drugs, the failure of schools, value relativity. They will act on those values. As Madison Avenue begins to appeal to this group, as they did with blacks and Hispanics, they will become socially acceptable and more powerful.... Power sources, like the press, will have to pay attention.[94]

Robertson echoed these views, suggesting that his candidacy was the natural outgrowth of a "tidal wave shift of political interest in the evangelical world." He noted the historic reticence of evangelical Christians toward politics:

> In 1976 they weren't very politicized; they had stayed away from public life. But what has happened is that the government has gotten so large and the liberal philosophic point of view is so pervasive in government that it has invaded the church. And areas that normally were left to theological speculation, such as the origins of life and the nature of a man and his woman, the role of parents in childbearing and child nurture, the education of the young, the welfare of the poor, the

> needy—these were essentially church concerns for 150 years, and suddenly the government moved into this and then the churches were told, "Well, there is a separation of church and state and therefore you shouldn't be into this area." [95]

By 1980 evangelicals were no longer accepting this logic. Reagan galvanized them with "appeals to prayer in the schools, profamily values, strong defense against communism, antiabortion, those hot button issues." But, according to Robertson, "the evangelicals in America are so sensitized now to the political ramifications of what's being done to them that they really want to get into politics." [96]

Nuttle believed that Robertson's cultural message was potentially crosscutting—that it could appeal to Democrats, including Catholics and possibly even blacks, who were fed up with the collapsing moral codes. Robertson agreed, arguing that he might have been able to attract 25 to 30 percent of the black vote in a general election on a religious and moral basis. "They honored me," as a minister, "because they really love God deeply. We have many, many people, including Jesse's mother-in-law, who watch our show." Robertson even criticized fellow Republicans in their approaches to black voters:

> Well, they don't know how to talk to them. I'm not for affirmative action, I'm for what is called self-help and what is called individual initiative.... [So I fail] in terms of the litmus tests ... the black Democratic leaders put on their allegiance.... But there is another strain that touches black people which is the religious strain. They love Jesus and the Bible. So they will vote for somebody on those grounds, at least a percentage of them will. But if a Republican comes out and says, "I'm against affirmative action" and doesn't say anything else, he's lost them. He has no appeal to them.[97]

The cultural conservatism and religiosity of many blacks suggests that this analysis is at least plausible. Moreover, as Clyde Wilcox's research shows, a remarkably large number of blacks apparently watched Robertson's religious broadcasts in the 1980s and, as a group, viewed him more favorably than did whites.[98]

Robertson also spoke often of the need to build alliances with Catholics, but he achieved limited success on that front, in part because of sectarian differences. For example, his key campaign staff members in Texas, according to one backer, "were hostile to Roman Catholics," perceiving them "as a cult." Thus the insulated world of some Robertson backers made coalition building difficult.

Top Robertson staff had no illusions about the "negatives" attached to their candidate, and they used sophisticated market research to design a strategy to overcome them. They distributed thousands of video- and audiocassette tapes stressing his leadership and business capabilities.

Robertson began speaking of himself as a businessman and broadcaster, and he claimed that when journalists used the term "televangelist" they were making religious slurs. The campaign put out brilliant newspaper ads comparing prejudice against John Kennedy's religion with prejudice against Robertson's religion. These ads featured full-page photographs of Kennedy side by side with Robertson.

All strategies were designed to make Robertson socially acceptable. As Nuttle observed during the night of the Iowa caucuses,

> Robertson is the best speaker, captivating on video, exudes leadership, holds them spellbound. . . . There are a lot of closet Robertson supporters out there, but it is not socially acceptable to be for him. . . . The problem is religion. When it is socially acceptable to be for him, then watch out.[99]

Several things undercut the Robertson strategy. First, Bush proved tremendously popular as Reagan's loyal heir apparent. Robertson put it this way:

> I ran essentially as a continuation of what would have been called a Reagan legacy. I had a campaign aimed at Main Street as opposed to Wall Street. George Bush's appeal, I had thought, was more to the Wall Street internationalists. . . . The thing that I was not aware of [was] that George Bush was viewed as the successor of Reagan . . . and I mean Reagan could have run for creator in New Hampshire and won, and Bush came in under those circumstances.[100]

Second, the Bush organization was tremendously effective. Nuttle observed, "All the other candidates could not cut into Bush's base [which included many evangelicals]. His campaign was imaginative, creative, kept everyone at bay. They had awesome resources; it felt like running against the entire party." Doug Wead, working the other side of the fence, confirmed that analysis. Wead discovered that having a Bush supporter in one of those superchurches could inoculate it against Robertson mobilization. When the Robertson organization attempted to co-opt the pastor to allow a table with campaign literature or notices of meetings in church bulletins, it took only one Bush backer to request the same for his organization, and the church was effectively neutralized. Thus after Iowa, when Bush campaign manager Lee Atwater desperately called upon Wead to develop a plan in the South to blunt Robertson, Wead had his strategy ready. Employing an army of paid staff and volunteers, Wead identified 215 superchurches in the South that would serve as Robertson's organizational base. A Bush supporter was identified in each church and provided with instructions on how to check the Robertson impact. "We would schmooze pastors," too, Wead noted, not to gain the support of the members but to neutralize Robertson's effort. Bush's popularity with other evangelicals, especially Southern Baptists, would be enough to ensure his victory. Wead, too, spoke of churches as he would precincts: "We took out [neutralized] the First Assembly"; "the Dole churches stayed with Dole, and the Bush churches went to Dole and Robertson"; and so forth.[101]

The third element undercutting Robertson's strategy was the set of circumstances peculiar to the campaign itself. According to Nuttle's postmortem, a sequence of events conspired to undo the efforts to make Robertson socially acceptable. They happened at the most critical juncture of the campaign:

> A campaign is like a spring; you stretch it and stretch it until it finally catapults you into credibility. We were just about there, had gotten the negatives down from 45 percent to 32 percent with the general population and down to just 15 to 20 percent with our [evangelical] base.[102]

Then, just two weeks before Super Tuesday, in what must have been some of the worst timing in recent campaign history, Jimmy Swaggart fell from grace in a pathetic scandal involving a prostitute. Again, public doubts about the seamy world of televangelism were raised. Robertson then became mired in "slippery lips and misstatements" that undermined his credibility. Simultaneously, he had to deflect charges by former representative Pete McCloskey that Robertson's father had kept him out of combat in the Korean conflict. Robertson's libel suit against McCloskey was scheduled to be heard on March 8, 1988—Super Tuesday. As Robertson later recounted, he was faced with the Hobson's choice of diverting precious money and time to the lawsuit (thus undermining his Super Tuesday campaign) or dropping the lawsuit and creating the impression that McCloskey was right.

Robertson's lack of experience as a national candidate surely hurt him, as he later admitted. Asked what he had learned from the experience, he responded unequivocally, "I learned that there is no novice who can come up the first time into politics and get put into the highest office of the land. This is a game for professionals. The laws are set up for professionals, the rules are set up for professionals, and a novice doesn't have any more chance than a high school football player would have in the Superbowl."[103]

One of Robertson's biggest mistakes, as he noted, was not husbanding his money more wisely. "I spent way too much money at the beginning, not realizing I was up against a spending limit. This thing is very quick, and it's necessary to save most of your money for television. I did much too much work on trying to organize grass roots and I went away from my own strength, which is television." Much of that money was spent on the petition drive. "I spent $10 million getting the signatures. But when I finally got a bunch of signatures, they weren't as good as I thought they were to begin with. And then it was too late to do much about it; most of the money was gone, and when I got in the primary season it was too late." He concluded his musings by saying that if he did it over again, "I would save every cent I could get my hands on till two or three weeks before Super Tuesday and then let it go." [104]

Clearly, Robertson was not prepared for the media approach he would face:

> I am by nature a teacher. . . . I like to teach on television, which means you try and explain things to people. The press is not interested in explanations. They want short, snappy quotes. . . . They want you to say, "I'm against taxes. I'm for life or against it." They just want it real simple. . . . There is usually about thirty seconds on television, maybe forty-five, that you can get on, and you'd have to give them something that is quotable for the evening news and that is it. Same thing with the headlines. "George Bush is against taxes." You know, "Read my lips." That is the way America works.[105]

Robertson was also not prepared for the scrutiny. "Those people are out trying to trap you all the time. There is a mind-set of . . . let's get a scoop and let's catch him in an error." Indeed, his depiction of journalists was ripe: "The print journalists pride themselves on their grungy look and their booze at night . . . and whenever they come into the room it would be like Darth Vader just walked in. . . . And they have this feeling. Very few of them have an open demeanor about the world we live in. They have a cynicism." [106]

Within Robertson's staff there were grumblings that Robertson did not read his briefing books carefully and that he would not otherwise submit to the rigorous discipline of a campaign. The "funny facts" that dogged his campaign, which Robertson admitted were "gaffes," were a result. Robertson claimed to know of Soviet missiles in Cuba and of the location of hostages in Lebanon. The most infamous episode was Robertson's assertion that the Bush organization might have been behind the Swaggart downfall. "It was obvious Swaggart did it [employed a prostitute], so it was silly to claim Bush was behind it," concluded Nuttle. This event, of course, happened just when the campaign required strategic distance from the world of televangelism. As Nuttle put it,

> Jim and Tammy Faye [Bakker] and Oral Roberts had happened within fourteen months. People were wary, but took a "let's see" attitude. Then, at the time when Robertson's credibility was in question, we had about four "funny facts" and Swaggart, and we lost twenty points in negatives overnight; the spring sprung back.[107]

Thus the campaign fell far short of the fears of opponents and the expectations of supporters. Robertson's million votes paled in comparison with the total evangelical vote (a third of the electorate), and they were dwarfed even by the petitions of the three million supporters he purportedly secured before announcing his candidacy. Nevertheless, Robertson remains a highly divisive figure among Republicans.[108] Indeed, his campaign manager referred to him as "a little radioactive," and his state coordinator in Hawaii, who ran unsuccessfully for the legislature, complained that his association with Robertson put the label "far right" on him.[109]

Strategy aside, there was another dimension that probably transcended campaign tactics and even disastrous events. Robertson's affiliation with the charismatic branch of evangelical Christianity did not sit well with many Southern Baptists—who might agree with him on political and social issues but found his religious practices unsavory. As John Green and James Guth have shown convincingly, Robertson was never popular with members of the Southern Baptist Convention, a critical constituency in southern Republican politics.[110] The bewildering theological diversity of the evangelical world remained an impediment to Robertson's attempt to broaden his base. It was particularly disappointing to the Robertson campaign that he split the evangelical vote with Bush on Super Tuesday. Using a narrow definition of "evangelical," the *New York Times* reported that Robertson won only 45 percent of the evangelical vote on Super Tuesday, compared with Bush's 30 percent. Using a looser and more encompassing definition, Doug Wead found that Bush received fully half of the born-again vote.[111] Thus, although Robertson energized a particular segment of evangelicals, he may not have been the best vehicle for mobilizing a broad coalition of cultural conservatives, whose theological squabbles make an overtly religious appeal problematic. If the Jackson campaign illustrates the farthest extent to which the church can become political, the Robertson campaign illustrates some of the pitfalls.

SUMMARY

In trying to discern the deeper meaning of the political events of 1988, one is struck with the blend of religious imagery and populist themes in the two minister-led movements. Championing the "disinherited, disrespected, and despised," Jackson offered a religious justification: "Jesus was rejected from the inn and born in a slum." [112] Robertson, too, adopted christic and prophetic imagery in his campaign. What links the two admittedly different movements is a religiously inspired populist critique of elites whose greed or immorality exploits the common people. Both parties had to channel these populist energies. As we will see in the next chapter, Democrats at the state level skillfully incorporated the Jackson forces into their coalitions, while Dukakis and the party faltered at the national level. The reverse is true for Robertson's supporters. They caused fissures in state-level politics but were co-opted by campaign pros into Bush's national organization. We now turn to that story and the continuing legacy of the two crusades.

NOTES

1. Jesse Jackson, speech delivered to the National Baptist Congress of Christian Education, National Baptist Convention USA, Oklahoma City, June 19, 1991.
2. Pat Robertson, interview with author, Virginia Beach, Va., August 8, 1991.
3. Gary Bauer, quoted in David Briggs, "Radical Changes in Role of Religion in Public Life Leaves America in Crisis," *San Diego Union and Tribune,* Jan. 12, 1991, B7; and Bauer, speech delivered to the Christian Coalition, Virginia Beach, Va., Nov. 15, 1991.
4. Murray Edelman, *The Symbolic Uses of Politics* (Urbana: University of Illinois Press, 1964).
5. Michael Thompson, Richard Ellis, and Aaron Wildavsky, *Cultural Theory* (Boulder: Westview Press, 1990).
6. Edelman, *Symbolic Uses of Politics;* Peter Bachrach and Morton Baratz, "Two Faces of Power," *American Political Science Review* 57 (September 1963): 632-642.
7. Mancur Olson, *The Logic of Collective Action* (Cambridge: Harvard University Press, 1965).
8. Interview with author, Oklahoma City, August 1991.
9. See Barry Alan Shain, "A Study in Eighteenth Century Political Theory: Liberty, Autonomy, Protestant Communalism, and Slavery in Revolutionary America" (Ph.D. diss., Yale University, 1990); Bernard Bailyn, *The Ideological Origins of the American Revolution* (Cambridge, Mass.: Belknap Press, 1967); Gordon S. Wood, *The Creation of the American Republic* (Chapel Hill: University of North Carolina Press, 1969); J. G. A. Pocock, *The Machiavellian Moment: Florentine Political Thought and the Atlantic Republican Tradition* (Princeton: Princeton University Press, 1975); and Alexis de Tocqueville, *Democracy in America,* trans. George Lawrence, ed. J. P. Mayer and A. P. Kerr (Garden City, N.Y.: Anchor, 1969).
10. Richard A. Merelman, *Making Something of Ourselves* (Berkeley: University of California Press, 1984).
11. For a fuller description of this argument, see the introduction in *The Atomistic Congress,* ed. Allen D. Hertzke and Ronald M. Peters, Jr. (Armonk: N.Y., M. E. Sharpe, 1992).
12. Richard F. Fenno, Jr., *Home Style: House Members in Their Districts* (Boston: Little, Brown, 1978), 235.

13. See Alan Ehrenhalt, *The United States of Ambition: Politicians, Power, and the Pursuit of Office* (New York: Random House, 1991).
14. John D. McCarthy and Mayer N. Zald, *The Trend of Social Movements in America: Professionalization and Resource Mobilization* (Morristown, N.J.: General Learning Press, 1973); McCarthy and Zald, "Resource Mobilization and Social Movements: A Partial Theory," *American Journal of Sociology* 82 (1977): 1212-1241; Alain Touraine, *The Voice and the Eye: An Analysis of Social Movements* (Cambridge: Cambridge University Press, 1981); William Gamson and B. Fireman, "Utilitarian Logic in the Resource Mobilization Perspective," in *The Dynamics of Social Movements*, ed. John D. McCarthy and Mayer N. Zald (Cambridge, Mass.: Winthrop, 1978); Joseph Jenkins and Charles Perrow, "Insurgency of the Powerless," *American Sociological Review* 49 (1977): 249-268; Lewis M. Lillian, "Organization, Rationality, and Spontaneity in the Civil Rights Movement," *American Sociological Review* 42 (1984): 770-783; Aldon Morris, *The Origins of the Civil Rights Movement: Black Communities Organizing for Change* (New York: Free Press, 1984).
15. Doug McAdam, *Political Process and the Development of Black Insurgency, 1930-1970* (Chicago: University of Chicago Press, 1985).
16. See Kenneth D. Wald's excellent article "Ministering to the Nation: The Campaigns of Jesse Jackson and Pat Robertson," in *Nominating the President*, ed. Emmett H. Buell, Jr., and Lee Sigelman (Knoxville: University of Tennessee Press, 1991).
17. I was struck by this contrast when I interviewed Jack Germond. He admitted that many journalists, including himself, view Robertson as a "nut," but he went on to portray rather sympathetically the many Robertson supporters he had interviewed. Journalists found that, compared with elite, "country club" Republicans, the Robertson people were religious, family-oriented, and passionately concerned about schools, moral breakdown, and the like. (Germond, interview with author, Des Moines, Iowa, Feb. 8, 1988.)
18. Vickie Kemper, "Looking for a Promised Land: The Robertson Campaign and the Wilderness Experience," *Sojourners*, June 1988, 25.
19. Merelman, *Making Something of Ourselves.*
20. Leon D. Epstein, *Political Parties in the American Mold* (Madison: University of Wisconsin Press, 1986).
21. Gary C. Jacobson and Samuel Kernell, *Strategy and Choice in Congressional Elections* (New Haven: Yale University Press, 1983).
22. W. E. B. Du Bois, *The Souls of Black Folk* (Chicago: A. C. McClung, 1903).
23. Lucius J. Barker, *Our Time Has Come: A Delegate's Diary of Jesse Jackson's 1984 Presidential Campaign* (Urbana: University of Illinois Press, 1988).
24. C. Eric Lincoln and Lawrence H. Mamiya, *The Black Church in the African American Experience* (Durham, N.C.: Duke University Press, 1990).
25. Jesse Jackson, interview with author, flight from Washington, D.C., to Dallas, March 12, 1992.
26. Robert Booth Fowler, *Religion and Politics in America* (Metuchen, N.J.: Scarecrow, 1985).
27. Lincoln and Mamiya, *Black Church in the African American Experience.*

28. See Manning Marable, *Black American Politics: From the Washington Marches to Jesse Jackson* (London: Verso, 1985); and speech by Marable, University of Oklahoma, Norman, Spring 1990.
29. Jackson, interview with author. Adolph L. Reed, Jr., criticized this circumvention of black elected officials in *The Jesse Jackson Phenomenon* (New Haven: Yale University Press, 1986).
30. Jackson, interview with author.
31. Bishop T. J. Jemison, speech delivered to the National Baptist Congress of Christian Education, Oklahoma City, June 19, 1991.
32. Ronald Walters, *Black Presidential Politics in America* (Albany: State University of New York Press, 1988).
33. Frank Watkins, interview with author, Washington, D.C., May 1991.
34. Rev. James Holley noted that when his church took over a building previously owned by a white congregation, he had to decide what to do with the stained glass window featuring prominent white figures in American history. He decided to add prominent figures from the African American experience and included Jackson as one of the giants.
35. Quoted in Bob Faw and Nancy Skelton, *Thunder in America: The Improbable Presidential Campaign of Jesse Jackson* (Austin: Texas Monthly Press, 1986), 35.
36. Ibid.
37. Ibid., 30.
38. Ibid. Jackson was severely criticized in 1984 for his association with Farrakhan, and many commentators took him to task for not repudiating more forcefully Farrakhan's anti-Semitic statements. Jackson's highly publicized slur against Jews (he referred to New York City as "Hymietown") deepened the rift between Jackson's movement and Jewish Democrats.
39. Ibid., 122.
40. Jackson, interview with author.
41. Jesse L. Jackson, *Straight from the Heart,* ed. Roger D. Hatch and Frank E. Watkins (Philadelphia: Fortress Press, 1987), 174.
42. Jerry Austin, interview with author, Des Moines, Iowa, Feb. 8, 1988.
43. Gail Sheehy, "Power or Glory?" *Vanity Fair,* January 1988, 46-55, 98-109.
44. Austin, "Frontline" interview with Judy Woodruff, Feb. 7, 1989.
45. According to the Federal Election Commission, Jackson's 1988 campaign raised more than $27 million, a huge increase over his 1984 effort.
46. Austin, interview with author.
47. California delegate, interview with author, Democratic National Convention, Atlanta, July 1988.
48. Dukakis official, interview with author, Democratic National Convention, Atlanta, July 1988.
49. Holley, interview with author, Detroit, December 1991.
50. Penn Kimball, *Keep Hope Alive: Super Tuesday and Jesse Jackson's 1988 Campaign for the Presidency* (Washington, D.C.: Joint Center for Political and Economic Studies Press, 1992).
51. Watkins, interview with author.
52. Penn Kimball, *Keep Hope Alive,* notes that Jackson increased his overall

southern primary vote from 966,000 votes to approximately 1,400,000 votes, a respectable gain to be sure, but still modest because the majority of blacks did not vote. In spite of many favorable circumstances, electoral dealignment remains a sobering fact.

53. Ibid., 84.
54. See Sheehy, "Power or Glory? " Austin, interview with author; and Faw and Skelton, *Thunder in America.*
55. Watkins, interview with author.
56. Roger Martin and Eric Freedman, "Jackson's Formula in Michigan: Hard Work," *Detroit News,* April 3, 1988, 1A.
57. Todd Watkins, interview with author, Democratic National Convention, Atlanta, July 1988.
58. Quoted in Martin and Freedman, "Jackson's Formula."
59. Ibid.
60. Quoted in Kimball, *Keep Hope Alive,* 108-109.
61. See Stephen J. Wayne, *The Road to the White House,* 3d ed. (New York: St. Martin's, 1988); and Nelson W. Polsby and Aaron Wildavsky, *Presidential Elections,* 8th ed. (New York: Free Press, 1991).
62. "The Preachers and the Bully Pulpit," Editorial, *New York Times,* March 8, 1988, A30; Frank Watkins, interview with author.
63. Jim Hightower, speech delivered to the Rainbow Coalition, Washington, D.C., Jan. 11, 1992.
64. Austin, interview with author.
65. Cornel West, *Prophecy Deliverance! An Afro-American Revolutionary Christianity* (Philadelphia: Westminster, 1982).
66. Walters, *Black Presidential Politics in America.*
67. Marable, *Black American Politics.*
68. Reed, *Jesse Jackson Phenomenon.*
69. Jackson, interview with author.
70. Robertson, interview with author.
71. The Pentecostal movement is often traced to the Azusa Street Mission revivals, held in Los Angeles from 1904 to 1906, which sparked the formation of a number of Pentecostal denominations. See Margaret M. Poloma, *The Assemblies of God at the Crossroads: Charisma and Institutional Dilemmas* (Knoxville: University of Tennessee Press, 1989).
72. Richard N. Ostling, "Gospel TV: Religion, Politics, and Money," *Time,* Feb. 17, 1986, 62.
73. Germond, interview with author.
74. James L. Guth, "A New Turn for the Christian Right? Robertson's Support from the Southern Baptist Clergy" (Paper presented at the annual meeting of the Midwest Political Science Association, Chicago, 1989).
75. Robertson, speech delivered in Edmond, Okla., November 1988.
76. Figures from Harold W. Stanley and Richard G. Niemi, *Vital Statistics on American Politics,* 3d ed. (Washington, D.C.: CQ Press, 1992), 262.
77. John C. Green and James L. Guth, "The Christian Right in the Republican Party: The Case of Pat Robertson's Supporters," *Journal of Politics* 50 (Febru-

ary 1988): 150-165; and Guth and Green, "Robertson's Republicans: Christian Activists in Republican Politics," *Election Politics* 4 (Fall 1987): 9-14.

78. John C. Green, "A Look at the 'Invisible Army': Pat Robertson's Campaign Contributors (Paper presented at the annual meeting of the American Association for the Advancement of Science, San Francisco, Jan. 14-19, 1989).
79. Robertson, interview with author.
80. When Robertson was asked who should be interviewed for this book, he immediately volunteered Marlene Elwell, whom he considers his best organizer. I interviewed Elwell by phone in January 1992.
81. *Detroit News*, Feb. 9, 1987, 3B.
82. Lisa Schiffren, "Robertson Backers Victorious," *Detroit News*, Feb. 22, 1987, 3A; George Weeks, *Detroit News*, Sept. 13, 1987, 3D; Weeks, "Robertson Ready to Raise His Flag for GOP Contest," *Detroit News*, Sept. 16, 1986.
83. Robertson caucus attender, interview with author, Des Moines, Iowa, February 1988.
84. Germond, interview with author.
85. Harrison Rainie, "Robertson's Grand Design," *U.S. News and World Report*, Feb. 22, 1988, 16.
86. Germond, interview with author.
87. The prominence of women in the Robertson organization was noted by Hubert Morken, *Pat Robertson: Where He Stands* (Old Tappan, N.J.: Revell, 1988), 227. Elizabeth Colton, who served as press secretary to Jackson in 1988, portrayed Jackson as uncomfortable with her role to the point of being abusive. She also felt that Jackson sometimes ignored women on the campaign trail. Barbara A. Reynolds alludes to a vindictive streak in Jackson in her biography, though in her case she did not attribute it to gender. See Colton, *The Jackson Phenomenon: The Man, the Power, the Message* (New York: Doubleday, 1989); and Barbara A. Reynolds, *Jesse Jackson: America's David* (Washington, D.C.: JFJ Associates, 1985).
88. Doug Wead, interview with author, Washington, D.C., June 1989.
89. Larry M. Bartels and C. Anthony Broh, "The Polls—A Review: The 1988 Presidential Primaries," *Public Opinion Quarterly* 53 (Winter 1989): 573-575.
90. Duane M. Oldfield, "Pat Crashes the Party: Reform, Republicans, and Robertson," Working Paper 90-11 (Institute of Governmental Studies, University of California at Berkeley, 1990).
91. This list is based on interviews as well as reports in *Congressional Quarterly Weekly Report*, May 14, 1988, 1267-1273; and *Governing*, October 1989.
92. *Atlanta Journal and Constitution*, Dec. 25, 1988.
93. Germond, interview with author.
94. Marc Nuttle, interview with author, Des Moines, Iowa, Feb. 8, 1988.
95. Robertson, interview with author.
96. Ibid.
97. Ibid.
98. Clyde Wilcox, "Blacks and the New Christian Right: Support for the Moral Majority and Pat Robertson among Washington, D.C., Blacks," *Review of Religious Research* 32 (1990): 43-56. Wilcox expands on the evidence for

potential black support for Robertson in *God's Warriors: The Christian Right in Twentieth-Century America* (Baltimore: Johns Hopkins University Press, 1992).

99. Nuttle, interview with author, Feb. 8, 1988.
100. Robertson, interview with author.
101. Nuttle and Wead, interviews with author.
102. Nuttle, interview with author, Norman, Okla., June 10, 1988.
103. Robertson, interview with author.
104. Ibid.
105. Ibid.
106. Ibid.
107. Nuttle, interview with author, June 10, 1988.
108. Green and Guth, "Christian Right in the Republican Party."
109. *Washington Post National Weekly Edition*, Dec. 26, 1988.
110. Green and Guth, "Christian Right in the Republican Party."
111. Doug Wead, "The Vice President and Evangelicals in the General Election," *Twice Abridged*, April 15, 1988.
112. Jackson, *Straight from the Heart*.

5

The Assimilation of Religious Activists into the Major Parties

Although neither of the populist ministers won the presidential nomination in 1988, their crusades unleashed forces that will continue to influence American politics during the 1990s. Part of that legacy is seen in the formation of pressure groups—Jackson's Rainbow Coalition and Robertson's Christian Coalition—that, like other lobbies, pursue political objectives. But a more far-reaching legacy is the way that newcomers, mobilized by the campaigns, remain as an active cadre in party politics and elections. In a European context one can imagine these movements forming separate political parties. In the United States, however, the structure of the party system tends to channel protest movements into one of the two major parties. Political representation, then, depends to an extent on how this process works. In this chapter we focus on the broader legacy to see how the populist energies of the 1988 crusades are being absorbed into the Democratic and Republican parties.

PARTY STRUCTURES AND PRESIDENTIAL CAMPAIGNS

Unlike their European counterparts, American parties are regulated to enable average voters to participate in nominating party candidates. Thus at the presidential level "outsider" candidates can penetrate the relatively porous parties by mobilizing followers in state caucuses and primaries. Rather than forming a new party, movements tend to penetrate the fortress of one of the major parties. The parties experience intense internal struggles as newcomers vie for influence. Although most of the literature focuses on the contentious Democratic party, the Republican party is not immune to the internal strife associated with party factionalism, especially since conservative evangelical Christians have emerged as a feisty new constituency within the Republican coalition.[1]

One consequence of the porousness of parties is that activists soon become seasoned veterans. John Kessel discovered that state and local party officials and campaign activists almost entirely were holdovers from previous presidential campaigns. He concluded, "A presidential party is never completely taken over by the new arrivals who come into politics in a given campaign, [but it] never goes back to being what it was before a particular campaign either." The infusion of the Jackson and Robertson forces into party structures has far-reaching implications, because the "presidential party at any time is a residue of its past campaigns." [2] As movement leaders, Jackson and Robertson can claim to have influenced their respective parties more than many "regular" party candidates have done. The ideological complexions of the Democratic and Republican parties, along with their electoral fortunes, are thus being shaped by the politics of discontent.

CHRISTIANS VERSUS REPUBLICANS

Robertson's 1988 presidential campaign accelerated the assimilation of cultural conservatives into the Republican party. It did so by mobilizing charismatic Christians,[3] who joined fundamentalists and other evangelicals enlisted earlier. Charismatics are indeed a distinctive group of Republicans, with passionate concerns about the collapse of moral codes and the disintegration of the family.[4] Moreover, their self-perception conforms to our depiction of them as populists. Considering themselves to be on the periphery of cultural and political life in America, they view Republican party regulars as privileged insiders protecting their status. As Robertson put it, "We have been telling the Republican party, let us in or we will kick the door down." [5]

Such sentiments were not welcomed by party leaders, especially at the state level. The major effect of the Robertson mobilization, consequently, was a series of battles for control of party machinery in several states, including Alaska, Arizona, Florida, Georgia, Hawaii, Iowa, Michigan, Nevada, Oklahoma, Oregon, South Carolina, Virginia, and Washington. The process, which began during the 1988 campaign, continued through the midterm election cycle and into 1992, indicating that the Robertson crusade was more an ongoing movement than a failed presidential candidacy.

Ironically, the broad significance of the campaign become manifest even as Robertson's electoral fortunes were collapsing. Just as horse-race journalists were writing off the Robertson candidacy, more savvy commentators were detecting a churning in GOP politics unheard of in modern times. It was clear by May 1988 that Robertson backers across the nation had moved into influential positions in the Republican party. In Alaska, Hawaii, and Oklahoma Robertson supporters controlled the national convention delegations and took key party positions. In Nevada Robertson backers took command of the state Republican party organization, while in Louisiana they took more than forty seats on the state Republican committee. In Virginia, Robertson's home state, his backers became firmly ensconced in the party, with Robertson's son serving in an important party position. In some states, such as Georgia, Michigan, and North Carolina, strong Robertson contingents were ultimately outflanked by hardball tactics of the Bush organization teaming up with party regulars. Seasoned by such lessons, many Robertson supporters remained active in state and local politics, and a number of them ran for office. Many joined forces with other prolife activists in 1992 to battle an organized abortion-rights effort to alter the antiabortion plank at the Republican National Convention.

The process of assimilating Robertson newcomers into the Republican party has not been smooth. In the next section we will examine the turmoil that is taking place in a number of state parties.

The Battleground in the States

Pat Robertson's presidential bid was profoundly threatening to many "regular" Republicans, resulting in bitter clashes and name calling. The state GOP chair in Michigan, for example, said the Robertson contingent looked like "the bar scene out of Star Wars"; in South Carolina his counterpart termed Robertson supporters "Nazis." Described as "cockroaches from the baseboards of the South," they were likened to "Iranian zealots," and their gatherings were compared to "Third Reich pep rallies." Robertson followers, in turn, angrily castigated efforts to keep them out. "Gestapo tactics" was how Robertson's campaign manager described Bush attempts to forestall Robertson's win in Hawaii.[6]

Robertson newcomers sometimes depicted their struggle with party regulars in New Testament language—Christians versus Republicans—casting venerable GOP regulars in the role of Romans persecuting the early Christians. Marlene Elwell, Robertson's Midwest political director, repeatedly described the Michigan GOP battle in polarized terms: "At our state convention we had quite a few Christians there. In fact, we outnumbered the Republicans."[7] Many of these Robertson Christians came to Republican county and state conventions with their Bibles ready to witness, something "silk stocking" Republicans found distasteful.

Thus a decade after the rise of the religious right and Reagan's adroit appeals to both "enterprisers" and "moralists" in the Republican coalition, tension was still felt between populist outsiders and well-established insiders.[8]

The cultural gulf separating mainstream Republicans from the Robertson insurgents was nicely captured in a story told by Elwell, who understood the need to build bridges between the newly mobilized charismatics and the party faithful. She recommended that the Robertson delegates not antagonize the regulars needlessly. "One of the things that many of the Christians wanted to do was to take their Bibles to the convention floor. . . . And so I discouraged them. . . . But, you know, the zealous, they went with their Bibles." This led to the following altercation:

> After our first session . . . we were coming off the convention floor, and one of the party regulars came up to me, and he was all upset and he was huffing and puffing, and he said, "Marlene, I've got to speak to you." . . . So I tried to calm him down. And he said, "You and your Christians." And I said, "Gee, what's the matter?" And he said, "Well, I was right in the middle of the convention, and one of these guys comes and hits me right over the head with a Bible!"[9]

After apologizing, Elwell found the guilty Christian. Asked why he hit the Republican, the man responded, "Because right in front of me he said a curse word!" Elwell laughs when telling the story. Her point in relaying it to Christian Coalition members in 1991 was to stress to new activists that they must avoid mistakes made by Robertson newcomers in 1988, admonishing them to practice Christian charity in their politics.

The conflict between the "Christians and Republicans" began in 1986 and continued into the 1992 election. Robertson's upset victory in the early stages of the Michigan caucuses in 1988, for example, sent the state party into a year-long, chaotic struggle, complete with court challenges, rump conventions, name calling, and shoving matches. By 1989 the embattled state chairman claimed that he was able to "patch things up" with his former adversaries.[10] The battle disillusioned some of the newcomers, but others came back in 1992. Tensions still remain between the "silk stocking" Republicans and the "Christians."

In Georgia the struggle lasted almost as long as in Michigan. It included credentials fights, rump conventions, and intervention by the national committee. In part, the bitterness of the battle reflected the cultural gulf between the suburban Republican establishment and the pietist Robertson neophytes, many of whom were former Democrats. One district coordinator for Robertson claimed that most of the Robertson people were Democrats involved in the GOP for the first time. He noted that their contingent elected both the national committeeman and committeewoman. A Georgia county coordinator confirmed that, like himself, many of the Robertson people were former Democrats. A "700 Club" watcher, he acknowledged that his entry into politics two years earlier had been a direct result of the Robertson mobilization. He was delighted with the Robertson contingent's accomplishments in so short a time. "We brought 20 people to the county meeting in 1987. By 1988 we brought over 100 of the 130 there." The Georgians I interviewed argued that they brought with them the potential for realigning culturally conservative Democrats into the Republican party. One commented, "Most of the Robertson people were Democrats. Most—nine of ten—that I talked with were uninformed that [the Democratic party] was the abortion party.... Once they understand that Democrats are the party of gays and abortion, they will be Republicans." This assessment may be plausible, but Republican "regulars" in Georgia were unenthusiastic in welcoming the newcomers.

In North Carolina Robertson supporters, undeterred by his poor showing in the primary, stormed district conventions to select delegates to the state convention and influence the party platform. This time verbal brawling was accompanied by fist fights, which erupted when two Robertson-dominated delegations were disqualified at the Fourth District Convention. Buoyed by their strength at the district level, Robertson forces eventually were outmaneuvered in classic hardball politics. Sue Wyatt, who chaired Robertson's state organization, accused the state Republican committee of unfair practices, including a $150 fee levied on delegates to deter Robertson backers from attending the convention. Wyatt responded by calling a Robertson boycott. "By not participating in a process designed to abuse our delegates, we believe we are today making a positive protest that we hope will help deter similar behavior in the future." [11]

In the Kentucky primary on Super Tuesday, George Bush trounced Robertson by a 5-1 margin. Robertson came in a distant third with only 11 percent of the vote, not enough to win a share of the voting delegation to the national convention. Later that month, however, Robertson backers flooded Republican precinct meetings to select actual delegates and to draft the platform. James Barnes described the Robertson takeover in Lexington:

> By 9:45 on a bright Saturday morning here, a long line of party precinct officers was already waiting to file into the banquet room of the Springs Inn Hotel, the site of the county convention.... A party regular, observing the pleasant weather, said many of his political allies might be on the golf course or attending to yardwork. Looking over the right side of the banquet room, he asked, "Who are those people?" They were, it turned out, Robertson supporters, row after row of them,

> extending almost to the back of the room. In the front of their ranks sat Melinda S. Fowler, a young woman who led the Robertson forces in the 6th Congressional District.[12]

Barnes reported that the well-organized Robertson cadre first voted in its slate of names for the district convention (which would send delegates to the national convention), then swept all the posts for party positions. Whenever the votes were taken, Fowler would signal the cues to her contingent. Party regulars were exasperated:

> Tears streamed down her cheeks after Freda B. Meadows found out that she had been defeated for a seat on the . . . Fayette County Republican executive committee. For years, Meadows had been renowned for combing the Lexington telephone book to update the party rolls, but she had been caught in the undertow of the wave of supporters of . . . Robertson's presidential candidacy. Velma Marshall, consoling Meadows, gestured toward the party's newcomers and muttered, "It used to be you had to pay your dues." [13]

Criticized for this bloc voting, Fowler responded simply, "We had the numbers, and that's what matters."

From the perspective of the party regulars, the Robertson minions wanted power without paying their dues. Moreover, the pietistic fervor of these religious populists made them seem both dangerously fanatical and naïve to party veterans. A Republican leader in one state described the Robertson backers: "Many of them have a total lack of understanding of process, parliamentary procedures. They voted for the rules on the floor, and then complained all day. They are more paranoid." Like Robertson, some of his followers see God's hand in what others view as mundane political events. To the party faithful this explains why the newcomers fail to "play by the rules."

The gulf between the charismatics and the country club Republicans explains another peculiar result of the Robertson infusion. In several instances after Robertson backers had seized the party organization, regular financial backers simply stopped contributing, allowing the "official" party organization to become a shell. They created new political action committees or alternative mechanisms in place of the formal party offices. Robertson backers were left wondering what kind of party they controlled. Outsiders, it turned out, needed the established networks represented by the regulars.[14]

As momentum created by Robertson's campaign carried into the following years, this weakness became apparent. In January 1990 Nevada state chairman Steve Wark (a Robertson newcomer) narrowly survived a recall effort under party rules that required a two-thirds vote for removal. Critics in the Republican state committee alleged that he had failed as a fund raiser and that he and his supporters, because of their inexperience, had contributed to the defeat of former Republican senator Chic Hecht.[15]

In neighboring Arizona in 1989 Robertson backers joined forces with hard-core supporters of former governor Evan Mecham (known as "Evanistas") to write a state platform declaring the United States "a Christian nation" and asserting that the Constitution created "a republic based upon the absolute laws of the Bible, not a democracy." The embarrassing national publicity that ensued—including Barry Goldwater's remark that the party had been taken over by a "bunch of kooks"—delighted the Democrats. The marriage of convenience between the "Evanistas," many of whom are Mormon, and the Robertson fundamentalists did not last long, however. When Mecham announced his plan to run again for governor, some Robertson supporters resisted the idea. "Governor Mecham is a Mormon," fundamentalist leader Anneta Conant explained. "I find Mormonism a cult and not Christian." T. R. Reid reported that GOP politics in Arizona "have pitted Christians against Jews, Christians against Christians, fundamentalist Christians against Mormons, and Mormons against Mormons—while Democrats and neutral observers look on in disbelief." [16]

By 1991 Robertson insiders claimed they had taken over the Louisiana Republican party. They were encouraged by their success in enacting the nation's strictest antiabortion law. In an era of weak party organizations and candidate-centered campaigns, however, control is an elusive thing. Their favored gubernatorial candidate got lost in the showdown between David Duke and Edwin Edwards. And, although Robertson expressed concern about Duke's background, many of his voters backed the former Klansman and neo-Nazi, who garnered the lion's share of the white Protestant vote. Moreover, as one observer noted, a number of those attending Robertson's Christian Coalition meeting in November 1991 were disappointed that Duke had been defeated in the gubernatorial race; among them was Billy McCormick, chairman of the Louisiana Christian Coalition, who backed Duke. It was not an auspicious moment for the movement.[17]

In Robertson's home state, however, the outcome seemed to vindicate the newcomers' efforts. Robertson lost the 1988 Virginia primary, but that summer his backers fought tenaciously for delegate positions to the Republican National Convention. Led by Anne Kincaid, Robertson's Virginia coordinator, Robertson backers engaged the nominating committee at the Virginia state convention in a marathon negotiating session that ended at 5:00 one morning. Having already secured six delegates and eleven alternates, their persistence won them three at-large delegate seats and eleven more alternates. Kincaid, another of the many women who have emerged as leaders in the Robertson effort, pleaded with the committee, "We can't let these people work this hard and not have some of them get to be delegates to the national convention."[18] Firmly entrenched in the party by 1990, Robertson's backers joined old-time Republicans in a reinvigorated GOP. While Democratic governor Doug Wilder campaigned for the presidency, Robertson's organization helped Republicans make major gains in the state assembly.

OKLAHOMA AND THE AFTERMATH OF THE 1988 CAMPAIGN

Oklahoma is a good example of the complex processes of conflict and assimilation now taking place in the Republican party. With a pietistic tradition and a large population of culturally conservative Democrats, Oklahoma seemed an ideal spot for Robertson to make inroads. Fully 65 percent of the citizens identify themselves as evangelicals.[19] Because Oklahoma's delegates were to be selected in 1988 by a newly created primary on Super Tuesday, the primary would be a good test of Robertson's electoral potential beyond the caucuses, which were more easily dominated by his zealous supporters.

It is difficult to know how well Robertson might have done had his campaign not faltered, damaged by his misstatements and by events such as the Swaggart scandal.[20] The Oklahoma campaign was well organized, however, and gave Robertson his best primary showing. On Super Tuesday he took 21 percent of the vote, although he won no delegates. The closed primary clearly blunted his impact. It kept many conservative Democrats, who routinely vote Republican in presidential elections, from crossing over to vote for him. One of the challenges for the Robertson campaign had been to persuade conservative Democratic voters to change their registration ten days before the primary. Remarkably, several thousand people apparently did change their registration to vote for Robertson.[21] One Republican party leader flatly stated, "If there had been an open primary Robertson would have won and Bush might have come in third."[22] The Robertson campaign clearly brought newcomers into the Republican party. The question is, what impact did they have?

Because it had taken a major organizational effort to mount a credible campaign, the Robertson forces were well poised after the primary to turn their attention to party caucuses and conventions, where the party would select delegates to the national convention and draft resolutions for the state platform. Even though all but three of the thirty-three delegates were bound by the primary outcome to vote for Bush, the Robertson people dominated the district conventions and arrived with an estimated two-thirds of the delegates at the state convention, which was held shortly after Super Tuesday. Under party rules the Robertson forces could have locked out all party regulars and sent a delegation to the national convention in New Orleans composed entirely of Robertson loyalists. They could even have denied Henry Bellmon, who was then governor, a spot on the delegation. But after intense negotiations Robertson leaders and Tom Cole, Republican state chairman, cut a deal. Some slots were allocated to the party regulars, who supported Bush, while Robertson was ensured domination of the platform and the hearts, if not the votes, of the majority of the delegation. The process turned out to be amazingly smooth, in part because there were no great philosophical differences between the two factions and because several of the key Robertson leaders had been longtime party activists. Unlike the situation in Georgia, where the cultural gulf between Robertson pietists and country club Republicans spawned bitter fights, in Oklahoma many of the regular Republicans were evangelicals and sympathetic to the issues raised by Robertson, if not to him personally.[23]

The process of assimilation did not end with the November 1988 election. On February 25, 1989, the Oklahoma Republican party held its convention to elect a new state chair, and the Robertson newcomers played a pivotal role. The establishment candidate, state legislator Mike Hunter, was backed by the luminaries of the party—Governor Bellmon, Sen. Don Nickles, Reps. Mickey Edwards and James Inhofe, and most of the state legislative delegation. Hunter even won the support of two key Robertson leaders, who sent a letter to former Robertson supporters endorsing Hunter and counseling practicality and prudence.[24] Hunter was challenged by two Robertson backers: Tommy Garrett, Robertson's state coordinator (whose literature contained endorsements by Robertson and by national activists Tim and Beverly LaHaye), and Mike Morris, a former state legislator who had endorsed Robertson in the primary.

What occurred at the convention illustrates the unpredictability that newcomers bring to party politics. On the first ballot Hunter received the most votes (though not the majority required), Morris came in a close second, and Garrett ran far behind. With 117 votes of 1,600 separating the two top candidates, Garrett's 195 delegates became crucial. Eliminated from balloting, Garrett pledged to support Hunter (who he believed would serve the party better). But as he was walking to the podium to announce his endorsement, Garrett was besieged by his own supporters pleading with him to let them vote their consciences (and some implying that they would go against his endorsement of Hunter anyway). He deferred and walked away from the platform. Shortly afterwards Hunter was heard saying that Garrett had "welched" on his pledge. Thus freed, the bulk of Garrett's supporters (the hard core of the Robertson contingent) moved to Morris as the more "conservative" candidate. Morris won by 28 votes, an outcome that stunned party leaders. Democratic leaders expressed delight because they viewed Morris as an irrational reactionary. Morris did not disappoint them. By the end of 1989 he had become embroiled in a controversial jail-house meeting with extremist Lyndon LaRouche. He was forced to resign in December, when party officials, including former Robertson lieutenant Mary Rumph (now national committeewoman), criticized his liaison with LaRouche and his poor fund-raising ability.

Chastened by this episode, Robertson backers returned in force during the 1990 Republican gubernatorial election. In a close Republican primary election, Christian conservatives tipped the balance in favor of Bill Price, an antiabortion conservative, who won an unexpected victory against businessman Vince Orza, an abortion-rights moderate whose popularity among independents and Democrats would have made him a strong competitor against Democratic candidate David Walters. Price, however, lost badly to Walters. Republican party stalwarts such as former governor Bellmon blamed the influence of the religious right for the loss of the Republican governorship.

ROBERTSON INSURGENTS AND THE REPUBLICAN PLATFORM

With Bush's nomination secured early in 1988, Robertson delegates at state conventions focused on including their concerns in the Republican platform. Although it is easy to dismiss the platform as meaningless, party leaders take it seriously as a statement of party principles. In a number of states Robertson backers got what they wanted from platform fights. They were able to interject forceful critiques of secular trends in education and society into the platforms.

THE OKLAHOMA AND WASHINGTON STATE PLATFORMS

In Oklahoma, for example, Robertson activists dominated the platform. Various planks illustrate the extent of alienation felt by moral traditionalists. The 1988 platform called for a human life amendment, the closing of "bars, bathhouses, and bookstores where sexual activity occurs," aggressive AIDS testing, enforcement of obscenity laws, opposition to surrogate motherhood, support for the husband as head of the household, opposition to redefining the family to include homosexual marriage, and enactment of laws that affirm "Judeo-Christian values rather than humanistic philosophy." Many of the concerns focused on education, an area in which conservative parents feel most under siege. The detailed education proposals included the following:

- Support for tuition tax credits and educational vouchers.
- Endorsement of the teaching of the basics, including the "traditional cultural heritage of our country."
- Opposition to any "involvement of the NEA in the public school system concerning educational policy," because the "National Education Association is a teachers-educators union that advocates sex education, ERA passage, abortion, sex clinics, nuclear freeze, a humanistic curriculum, and opposes traditional value systems."
- A requirement ensuring the daily reciting of the Pledge of Allegiance.
- Opposition to "the current advocacy of Secular Humanism in any form in the public schools because it is a violation of the First Amendment."
- Opposition to "utilization of mind-altering techniques for public school students."
- Opposition to state-mandated sex education in the public schools.
- Opposition to school-based health clinics that undermine parental values by dispensing birth control and conducting abortion counseling.
- Insistence that AIDS education emphasize that "sexual abstinence outside of marriage and fidelity within marriage with a non-infected spouse are the only truly safe ways to avoid the sexual transmission of AIDS."
- Opposition to the teaching of values education, death education, and situation ethics.
- Opposition to the "New Age Movement philosophy, including reincarnation, mystical powers, Satan worship, etc., as introduced in the textbooks of our education system."
- Revision of textbook adoption procedures to be more responsive to local parents.
- Support for "legislation requiring proper and accurate historical accounting in school textbooks according to the federal Vitz report."[25]

This and similar state platforms in 1988, though ridiculed by Democrats and many commentators, were harbingers of things to come in the Republican party. In a number of states in 1992, Robertson insurgents and their evangelical allies dominated the platform proceedings to the point that even the most radical proposals received serious consideration. In Washington State, for example, an early platform called for the elimination of yoga, channeling, values clarification, and witchcraft in public schools and for a crackdown on sex on college campuses. Labeling homosexuality a "deviant lifestyle," it opposed allowing gays to adopt children, teach in schools, or take jobs as day care or health care workers. Party regulars, charging that the insurgents wanted a "theocratic party," called the platform "a document right out of the Dark Ages." One state representative opined, "I just wish they'd go away and start their own party." Some of the 1992 newcomers were a bit too zealous even for Robertson's 1988 veterans, who worked to soften the platform. Provisions referring to yoga and college sex, for example, were dropped.[26]

The 1992 National Platform

This religious influence ultimately shaped the 1992 national Republican platform, which moved decisively toward its most "hard line conservative" positions ever on abortion, homosexuality, pornography, and the prevention of AIDS.[27] Although not as radical as the platforms of some state conventions, the GOP platform adopted by the national convention in Houston in August 1992 embraced New Christian Right positions on public prayer, the nation's religious heritage, and "family values." The platform criticized the media's "assault" on traditional values. It asserted that the "unborn child has a fundamental individual right to life which cannot be infringed." It opposed "programs in public schools that provide birth control or abortion services." It opposed "efforts of the Democratic Party to redefine the traditional American family" and called upon "state legislatures to explore ways to promote marital stability." Denouncing "efforts by the Democratic Party to include sexual preference as a protected minority," it opposed same-sex marriages. It rejected "the notion that the distribution of clean needles and condoms are the solution to stopping the spread of AIDS," arguing instead for education that stresses "marital fidelity, abstinence, and a drug free lifestyle." It condemned "the use of public funds to subsidize obscenity and blasphemy masquerading as art" and called for a "national crusade against pornography" and removal of smut on military bases. It supported "the right of students to engage in voluntary prayer in schools and the right of the community to do so at commencements." Finally, it supported public vouchers to allow parents to send their children to the religious schools of their choice. Thus, despite much-publicized efforts of abortion-rights and libertarian Republicans, a network of religious activists, as the *New York Times* reported, ruled the convention floor.[28]

THE CONTINUING STRUGGLE WITHIN THE GOP

The Robertson insurgency exposed the cultural divide that separated elite, country club types from less elite, religious moralists. But the clashes that occurred were intensified by the nature of Robertson's core constituency. Robertson's core backers were not generic evangelicals (many of whom are now mainstream Republicans) but Pentecostals and charismatics who challenge modern decadence more vociferously perhaps than any other group. Pentecostal Christianity, with its roots in hard-scrabble rural poverty and blighted urban neighborhoods, attracted a high percentage of blacks and poor whites, who found solace in the gifts of the Holy Spirit, while the allure of modernity captivated their less fervent brothers and sisters. Although the charismatic movement is far more middle class and suburban than Pentecostal Christianity, culturally it has remained a phenomenon on the margins of elite society. Robertson backers spoke a language of "sanctification," "healing," and "baptism in the Spirit" that even many Southern Baptists found unnerving.

Surveys of delegates and financial contributors confirm the distinctiveness of the Robertson backers, who tended to be newcomers with strong moral concerns. In terms of party activity and loyalty, Robertson activists typically were classic "amateurs," while Bush backers predominately were longtime party "professionals." In Virginia, for example, 75 percent of Robertson's state convention delegates had been active in the party for fewer than five years, compared with 39 percent of the Bush delegates. In Michigan nearly 55 percent of the Bush state delegates had previously been very active in local campaigns, compared with only 21 percent of the Robertson newcomers. This lack of long-term involvement was reflected in party loyalty. Although 79 percent of Bush's Virginia delegates said they would "always support the party," only 39 percent of the Robertson delegates so responded. Michigan delegates were asked whether they "would stop working for the party" if they disagreed with it on a major issue. Only 19 percent of the Bush delegates agreed with the statement, versus 80 percent of the Robertson backers. As party activists, therefore, "Robertson supporters appeared, for the most part, to be political amateurs—intense, brash, politically unsophisticated, and motivated more by candidate and issue concerns than by partisan loyalty." [29]

Robertson's backers were also distinguished by their profoundly conservative views on moral issues, especially on abortion. Whereas only 15 percent of Bush's Virginia delegates said abortion was the most important issue to them, 63 percent of the Robertson contingent said it was. This finding is not surprising because Robertson organizers capitalized on antiabortion networks to mobilize followers. In Virginia, for example, 62 percent of Robertson's delegates belonged to an antiabortion group.

In cultural terms the Robertson activists were distinctive as well. A survey by John Green and James Guth found that Robertson's financial backers stood out among all the Republican groups as the most fervently religious, orthodox, family-oriented, and conservative on social issues. Demographically, they were uncharacteristic of Republican elites, with far more women and modest-income contributors than was the case for other Republican candidate groups. Indeed, as the mail surveys of contributors came in, Guth and Green reported the surprising number of contributors who listed such occupations as secretary, waitress, and the like.[30]

The tremendous grass-roots success of the newcomers was another element that contributed to the intense clashes within the party. That success, ironically, was rooted in the naïve strategy Robertson had used in his run for the presidency. Reflecting on the campaign in the fall of 1991, Robertson concluded that he had made fundamental strategic mistakes, one of which was spending huge sums of money early to build thirty-five grass-roots state organizations. He learned, however, that "you win primaries with television," and his campaign had failed to husband money to pay for Super Tuesday advertising. So, Robertson concluded, as a strategy to gain in the polls or to win delegates through primaries, grass-roots organizing was inefficient. Yet as a means of building a long-range movement, it was a perfect tool. To Robertson, of course, the outcome suggested that God did have a "plan" for the campaign, even though it was not for Robertson to win the presidency. The legacy of the campaign, as he put it, was its "children"—Christian activists, energized by the excitement of the presidential race, who have remained to win slots in the party, run for office, and hold future candidates' "feet to the fire" on the "profamily" agenda.[31]

Although Robertson's "invisible army" was smaller than he had hoped, the GOP did experience an infusion of morally concerned activists, who influenced the Republican platform and altered state party politics. This influx of newcomers caused tension, even fisticuffs, at county and state conventions around the country. Over time these tensions may recede as the more tactically pragmatic Robertson supporters become party regulars and the inflexible ones are nudged out or leave of their own accord. This is not to suggest, however, that party politics will return to the way they were before Robertson's campaign. On the contrary, religious moralists, tactically flexible as they may be, will continue to demand that the GOP not retreat from its embrace of their agenda, as some Republican candidates have done with abortion.

In fact, one of the major focuses of the Christian Coalition in 1992 was protection of the antiabortion plank in the national Republican platform against challenges by newly energized abortion-rights Republicans. In a number of state conventions in 1992 Robertson's Christian Coalition forces mobilized for the abortion fight. At the Colorado state convention, for example, the state chapter of the Christian Coalition took the lead in distributing slates of antiabortion candidates for national delegates. The coalition booth also ran a locally produced video featuring endorsements by luminaries such as University of Colorado football coach Bill McCartney, former senator Bill Armstrong, and legendary black restaurant owner Daddy Bruce.[32]

Faced with a rejuvenated abortion-rights Republican force led by consultant Ann Stone, Robertson loyalists aligned themselves with other antiabortion groups to do battle at the national convention. At the platform hearings in the spring of 1992, for example, Christian Coalition director Ralph Reed presented testimony that made it clear that Republican fortunes rested on a robust evangelical vote. According to Reed, some twenty-four million voters in 1988 identified themselves as born-again Christians or prolife Catholics, a pivotal bloc that provided Bush with nearly 90 percent of its support. To maintain the loyalty of these cultural conservatives, Reed argued, the Republican party must keep its antiabortion plank and adopt "family friendly" policies, such as educational choice and abstinence programs in the schools.[33] The fact that Christian Coalition members were getting themselves elected as delegates in 1992 ensured that this message was heard.

JESSE JACKSON AND THE DEMOCRATIC PARTY

Almost unnoticed in the voluminous news commentary on Jackson's campaign was the relative absence of state-level battles between the Jackson forces and other powers within the Democratic party. There were no reports of fist fights, rump conventions, or wholesale challenges of delegates, either in 1984 or 1988. Interviews with state and national party officials at the Democratic National Committee meeting in Washington, D.C., in the fall of 1989 confirmed that, while tensions arose occasionally, state party officials avoided the kind of intraparty battles that characterized the GOP. In part, this lack of divisiveness was due to the more formalized set of rules that govern the Democratic party and thus ensure the legitimacy of vote getters. Furthermore, as Jo Freeman has observed, the culture of the Democratic party is more open to organized demands by "outsiders" for a place at the table than is the Republican party.[34] But most important, blacks are an intensely loyal element in the Democratic coalition. Thus even Democrats who dislike Jesse Jackson can sympathize with his followers, a number of whom are party regulars and a key constituency in state-level coalitions. The advice given by the leader of one Dukakis state delegation conveys the approach of Democratic insiders to the Jackson followers: "This is a sensitive time for the Jackson people; you should be aware of this. We need them going full steam in the fall." [35]

Interviews with state and national party officials indicate that Jackson's two campaigns did indeed bring newcomers into party politics, though some remain skeptical.[36] James Ruvolo, chairman of the Ohio Democratic party and head of the National Association of State Democratic Chairs, noted that attendance at party functions in his state was "way up," in part because of the influx of Jackson people. Echoing John Kessel, Ruvolo contended that some of these new Jackson people will stay active in the party. Officials in Michigan affirmed this prediction. Jackson's victory in the Michigan caucuses activated a host of newcomers, who blended well with the existing party cadre. Clyde Cleveland, city councilman from Detroit, remarked that never before had there been such participation as that which occurred in the foregoing party caucuses. Commenting on Jackson's two campaigns, Willy Brown, redoubtable speaker of the California Assembly, also argued that Jackson had galvanized newcomers, though he expressed frustration that scholars were not paying attention. Jackson's "greatest impact is the number of new people he inspired to become a part of the process. We have new candidates because of him." But, Brown complained, "The remarkable thing is that no one is studying this. I have received no questionnaires on what clearly is the most significant movement in the eighties. But after the 1972 convention I was surveyed endlessly, and it was studied to the minutest detail." [37]

When disputes occurred between Jackson newcomers and party regulars, they were mild compared with the Robertson fracas. In Colorado, for example, challenges of credentials and disputes over delegate selection created tension between Jackson forces and supporters of other candidates. But the disputants could not accurately be described as party insiders versus outsiders. Odell Berry, a black supporter of Jackson and former mayor of a Denver suburb, mediated differences. The fact that a staff member for Rep. Pat Schroeder could work actively for Jackson, while her boss supported Dukakis, suggests that the party dynamic was not bitter. In South Carolina the Jackson forces so swamped the party that tensions arose between them and the old guard. Still, nothing occurred like the fights that we saw taking place in the Republican party.

As Jackson's support among black elites rose from 1984 to 1988, the newcomers found themselves joined by party regulars—black elected officials (many of whom had supported Walter Mondale in 1984) who facilitated the process of assimilation. Jackson's magnetism and his mastery of the grass-roots black church network made it imperative for other black leaders to fall in line, and they did. According to one publication, the list of 1988 black delegates to the National Democratic Convention read "like a Who's Who of black politics."[38] Thus when Jackson energized black voters and activated new party participants, a seasoned black leadership was available to negotiate the terms of that assimilation at state and local levels.

In California Jackson's effort was led by Willy Brown and Maxine Waters, a respected activist who was subsequently elected to Congress. Jackson's Ohio campaign was coordinated by a state senator. In Oklahoma the Jackson delegation was led by a woman well known to party leaders and elected officials. And so it went. Virtually all the nation's black mayors (with the exception of Detroit's Coleman Young), members of the Congressional Black Caucus, state legislators, county officials, influential ministers, teachers, university professors—the entire political infrastructure of black America—fell in line behind Jackson. Rivalries were suppressed and old wounds were healed as Jackson came to dominate black politics as no figure had since the heyday of Martin Luther King, Jr., in the early days of the civil rights movement.

By 1988 Jackson's commanding leadership in the black community gave him an overwhelming 92 percent of the black primary vote. He brought approximately 1,200 delegates to the Democratic convention (compared with the 465 votes he received at the 1984 convention). One effect of Jackson's campaigns, therefore, was a dramatic rise in black participation at upper levels of Democratic party politics and increased leverage within the party. The numbers of blacks selected as national delegates rose from 481 in 1980 (14 percent of the total) to 962 in 1988 (more than 23 percent of the total).[39] Many state and national party positions, moreover, were filled by black supporters of Jackson.

To be sure, there is disagreement about just how much Jackson's campaigns accounted for the broad expansion of the black electorate. Certainly, the onset of the Reagan years energized blacks politically, and a number of other leaders and groups also sponsored voter registration drives. One black representative suggested that, while Jackson's campaigns inspired black voters in his district, the Rainbow Coalition was less prominent in actual voter registration efforts than the local NAACP, the state Democratic party, and the representative's own campaign organization.[40] Still, Jackson's inspirational quality cannot be minimized. One study of the 1984 campaign indicated that 67 percent of the newly

Table 5-1 Voter Registration in Selected Southern States (Increase between 1980 and 1986)

	Whites		*Blacks*	
State	Increase	Percent	Increase	Percent
Alabama	107,000	6	159,000	45
Georgia	190,000	11	126,000	28
Louisiana	30,000	2	86,000	18
Mississippi	41,000	4	120,000	36
North Carolina	154,000	7	145,000	33
South Carolina	16,000	2	51,000	16

Source: Voter Education Project, Atlanta.

registered blacks said the Jackson campaign was an important influence on their decision to register.[41] The expanding black electorate in the 1980s provided Democrats with a major political resource. Seasoned Democratic leaders in the states were prepared to accommodate these new voters and activists, even if they had little use for Jackson personally.

One of the major stories in electoral politics in the 1980s, consequently, was how Jackson's campaigns fueled the rise in black voter participation. From 1980 to 1984 black registration soared and voting participation, up 2 million in just four years, surpassed white rates in some districts. As evidence of the church base of this infusion, the increase was particularly notable among women. In eleven southern states black registration increased by 1.3 million, up nearly 32 percent.[42] Although registration had dropped off slightly by 1986, it was still dramatically higher than in 1980.

The significance of these figures became apparent in the 1986 Senate elections. A mobilized black electorate in the South, combined with the low voter turnout typical of a midyear election, secured victory for five Democrats in closely contested races. After gaining up to 90 percent of the black vote, John Breaux of Louisiana won with 53 percent of the total vote, Terry Sanford (North Carolina) with 52 percent, Wyche Fowler (Georgia) with 51 percent, Richard Shelby (Alabama) with 51 percent, and Alan Cranston (California) with 51 percent.[43] Alabama dramatically illustrates the pivotal role of an increased black vote. Between 1980 and 1986 white registration increased 6 percent for a total increase of 107,000 voters, while black registration increased 45 percent for a total increase of 159,000 voters. (See Table 5-1.) Democrat Shelby defeated Republican Jeremiah Denton by only 7,000 votes of the 1.2 million cast, receiving an estimated 90 percent of the increase in black voting. Although Denton received the majority of the increase in white voting, sheer numbers were against him. Thus the black vote was decisive. To be sure, Jackson's mobilization was not the sole reason for the rise in black registration, but it played a big role.

Many southern Democrats now routinely rely on patching together an overwhelming black vote with a respectable 40 percent or so white vote for electoral victory, a formula that often eludes national Democratic presidential candidates.[44] Clearly, black voters cannot be ignored by these regional politicians, a plus for genuine political representation. Indeed, it is no surprise that the late Lee Atwater, as chairman of the Republican National Committee, called for a "command focus" by the Republican party to increase its share of the black vote to 20 percent, a feat that would have saved five Republican senators in 1986.[45] Northern black voting also soared, and early evidence showed a surge in the number of black officials elected in the wake of the 1988 campaign.

Jackson's campaign launched a number of figures into prominence in the Democratic party. Ron Brown, who had managed Jackson's convention operation, was elected chairman of the Democratic party in 1989; he brought several Jackson operatives with him into the staff at the Democratic National Committee. Maxine Waters, who was elected to Congress in 1990, promised to champion the agenda of the Rainbow Coalition. (In 1991 she vociferously opposed the congressional resolution giving President Bush authorization to use force in the Persian Gulf.) The biggest surprise of the 1990 election unquestionably occurred in Minnesota. In a frugally financed but creative campaign, Jackson's state coordinator, Paul Wellstone, emerged from obscurity to upset the incumbent Republican senator, Rudy Boschwitz. Wellstone promoted his candidacy among party elites, political action committees, and fund raisers at the Democratic National Committee meeting in Washington, D.C., in September 1989, but he was not even the first choice of party elites for the nomination, nor was he given any chance of unseating Boschwitz. But as Jackson's coordinator he had built a formidable organization that included farmers, union members, "movement people," and "gays and lesbians from Minneapolis." [46] With this organization in place, Wellstone went on to seize the Democratic nomination. In the general election he ran an energetic populist campaign on a low budget, relying on publicity gained by his traveling van. He aired humorous commercials in which he spoke fast because he "did not have the money of his opponent." Then, when a sizzling sex scandal unraveled the Republican governor's race just two weeks before the election, other Republicans, including Boschwitz, saw their support begin to collapse. Blessed with this fortuitous circumstance, Wellstone went on to be the only challenger in the nation to unseat a senatorial incumbent. Like Maxine Waters, he made himself a thorn in the side of the Bush administration, presenting Vice President Dan Quayle, as president of the Senate, with petitions that called upon the administration to resist going to war in the Persian Gulf. Wellstone's maiden speech on the Senate floor denounced the resolution granting the president congressional sanction to use force.

Jackson also salted a number of organizations with people activated by his campaign. From the Children's Defense Fund to the Institute for Policy Studies to the Democratic National Committee itself, Jackson backers have become a permanent fixture of Washington life.

At the state level, too, Jackson's mobilization probably enhanced the leverage of black party leaders and elected officials. Certainly, more black faces were seen at party functions. Seasoned Democratic politicians, familiar with coalition building, welcomed new voters loyal to the party and found ways to accommodate them. As a number of southern senators demonstrated, support from black voters could be gained without losing much white Democratic support. Moreover, data collected by the Joint Center for Political Studies suggest that after leveling off in the early 1980s the number of black elected officials surged again from 1984 to 1990. This increase indicates that Jackson's mobilization spurred the growth down the line. Interviews with black pastors who became involved in the early stages of Jackson's exploration in 1983 suggest that this mobilization was a conscious objective of Jackson's from the start. As one pastor noted, "We went to the Baptist convention in Memphis in 1983, and Jackson spoke. His point was, 'I may not win, but a sheriff will be elected somewhere, or a legislator.' " Adolph Reed criticized Jackson for undermining the black drive for the mundane but essential power of elected officials, but there is some evidence that the opposite is true. Jackson's mobilization seems not to have hurt the Democratic party in the states, and arguably it may have helped.

Black leaders hoped that an activated and enlarged black electorate would act as a magnet for candidates in 1992. With Jackson out of the race in 1992, Democratic candidates campaigned actively for black support, using the church network Jackson had energized. This is how Dan Balz described one of Gov. Bill Clinton's campaign events:

> Gospel music vibrated through the Cook Convention Center in Memphis as Clinton mounted the stage before 20,000 delegates to the convocation of the Church of God in Christ, a fast-growing black denomination with more than 3 million members nationwide. With a beaming Clinton at his side, Presiding Bishop L. H. Ford told his flock, "I cannot endorse him, but I can bless him." The next morning the Memphis Commercial Appeal carried the quotation and a picture of Ford and Clinton on the top of its front page.[47]

Such events became common fare in the 1992 presidential campaign, leading Jackson to quip, "If we can register ten million new voters, then you will see George Bush speaking in black churches and singing gospel music."[48] The candidate whose fortunes were most graced by black support was Clinton, whose comfort with the black gospel milieu aided his quest for black votes. Clinton frequented Pentecostal revivals in Arkansas, campaigned often in black churches, quoted Scripture, and sang gospel music.[49]

CHANNELING DISCONTENT: NATIONAL STRATEGIES IN THE 1988 CAMPAIGNS

The responses of Bush's and Dukakis's national organizations to the insurgent movements in 1988 contrasted markedly with what happened at the state level. Dukakis and his Massachusetts advisers had to deal not just with black voters (who were welcomed by state Democratic pros) but with Jesse Jackson, a task for which they were unprepared. The adroit management of potential conflict at the state level was very different from that at the national level, where the Dukakis staff struggled ineptly to accommodate the demands of Jackson and his followers. The reverse appears to be the case for the GOP. State-level Republicans were unprepared for the mobilization Robertson unleashed, but national GOP pros seemed at least to be able to devise strategies for dealing with the evangelical onslaught. Although the context changed in 1992, there are lessons to be learned from the story of how the national campaign staffs of the presidential nominees dealt with the insurgent challenges of the two ministers.

JACKSON AND DUKAKIS

Dukakis made token appeals to the black community, but in the primaries he largely conceded the black vote to Jackson. After securing the nomination, Dukakis seemed incapable of comprehending that Jackson viewed himself in unconventional terms, as did his followers. Through excruciatingly poor coordination, the Dukakis staff failed to inform Jackson of Lloyd Bentsen's selection as the vice presidential nominee. Jackson, to his great irritation, learned of the decision as he was besieged by reporters when he arrived at Washington's National Airport. This seemingly cavalier treatment of Jackson was profoundly insulting to his followers. Black leaders spoke angrily of "the phone call that was never made." Jackson continued to press Dukakis for "respect," but Dukakis did not know how to respond and retain his own stature.

Trying to be conciliatory, Dukakis welcomed Jackson as a key "player" on the "team." But he went on to say that "every team has to have a quarterback—that's the nominee—you can't have two quarterbacks,"[50] unaware that Jackson, as a gifted college athlete, felt he had been a victim of the prejudice that "blacks can't be quarterbacks."

The cultural gulf between Dukakis and Jackson manifested itself in tense negotiations at the Democratic convention in Atlanta. With the "party hanging by a thread," Jackson, Dukakis, and top aides tried to find some accommodation.[51] Under intense pressure from the mercurial Jackson, Dukakis agreed to provide the minister with a plane and give him a prominent role in the campaign and an enhanced future role in the Democratic party. But Dukakis failed to develop a coherent strategy for dealing with the Jackson forces in the general election, and public tensions erupted over where Jackson would campaign. The maladroit handling of Jackson apparently lessened the enthusiasm of blacks for the Democratic ticket. After a dramatic surge in black participation in 1984, black voting slipped in 1988, to the Democrats' detriment. Moreover, in the early stages Dukakis did not seize upon the populist economic themes of Jackson's message that might have energized Democratic voters.[52] The inept handling of Jackson, of course, indicated a more profound weakness in the Dukakis organization. State Democratic leaders expressed dismay, even contempt, at the "amateur hour" at the national level, thus substantiating the argument about the contrasting structural strengths of the two parties.

The Jackson movement also intensified tensions between blacks and Jews in the Democratic coalition. Many Jews feared Jackson, with his embrace of the Palestinian cause and Yasir Arafat, his "Hymietown" slur on New York, and his relationship with black Muslim leader Louis Farrakhan, who had described Judaism as a "gutter religion." This schism in the party threatened to erupt in 1988, and it continues to simmer. As one Jewish insider observed, "The Jackson candidacy did bring out black-Jewish tension, because he didn't denounce Farrakhan. . . . [But] Jews haven't left because they still have more influence than Jackson, are big contributors." Jackson's populism (and Robertson's) reminded some Jewish elites of the anti-Semitism spawned by the politics of discontent. Thus Jackson was compared with "a populist like Wallace," with his "rhetoric of resentment." Democratic chairman Ron Brown gained stature in Jewish circles through "his ability to keep the lid on Jackson." The Jewish insider said, "[Brown] is a good guy, an anchor. He kept it together when it could have exploded at the convention."[53]

When Jackson announced that he would not seek the Democratic presidential nomination in 1992, many Democratic party figures breathed a sigh of relief that the magnetic minister would finally be off the stage. Jackson, however, sought to remain a player by launching a campaign for what he called a new independent Democratic majority. Designed apparently to keep remnants of his 1988 organization intact as an influence in the party (if not at the convention), it never took shape. But Jackson continued his maneuverings through well-staged Rainbow Coalition meetings, personal appearances, and behind-the-scenes machinations. During the 1992 primaries some of his major supporters in New York, apparently with his blessing, backed former California governor Jerry Brown, who announced that he would like to have Jackson as his running mate. This move hurt Brown's standing among Jewish voters and proved a highly mixed blessing.[54]

ROBERTSON AND BUSH

On the Republican side, there was considerable disagreement early in the Bush campaign about how to deal with the evangelical constituency. Some underestimated its diversity, equating Jerry Falwell's and Pat Robertson's lack of broad appeal with grass-roots weakness. Others argued that the GOP could not snub the third of the population that was "born again," noting that many of those believers were Democrats who supported Reagan. The Bush campaign, it turned out, was big and diverse enough to pursue simultaneous, even contradictory, strategies. In contrast to the failure of their counterparts in the Dukakis camp, Bush lieutenants anticipated the Robertson effort, monitored its growth, designed strategies to blunt its impact, and co-opted its potential supporters. According to an internal campaign document, Bush staff in June 1985 had "predicted that Pat Robertson would be a candidate for the presidency and further, that evangelicals would successfully take control of the Republican party structure in many counties, congressional districts, and states across the country." [55] The evangelicals would be energized because "theirs was the unfinished agenda." Secular conservatives got what they wanted out of Reagan, but what did the cultural conservatives really get but lip service from the Great Communicator?

A quiet but thorough effort had begun in 1985 to arrange for Bush to meet with key evangelical leaders, to have him appear on Christian television programs, and to feature stories about him in evangelical publications. Doug Wead, an evangelical Bush aide, even wrote a puff biography detailing Bush's faith for Christian bookstores. Between 1985 and 1988 Bush was photographed with almost a thousand evangelical leaders. Remarkably, by 1987 information was filtering into the campaign that Bush was the second choice of Robertson supporters. "Robertson was bringing his own people to the process and the people he was bringing were predisposed to support us if we would only go after them." Thus in a November 1987 memo Wead wrote, "It's time for us to play the evangelical card seriously. It's time for us to take off our gloves and go after the evangelical vote." [56]

In a way, Robertson's early success was a blessing to the Bush organization. It shocked Bush operatives into recognizing that they could not snub the born-again constituency. As Wead put it, "The evangelicals are a contradiction to [Lee] Atwater. His vision of Republicans is a yuppie thing." After Iowa, Wead's credibility rose, and he was given free reign to implement the evangelical strategy.[57] This aggressive effort led to a robust born-again vote for Bush in the primaries and subsequently in the general election.

Illustrative of the sophistication of national GOP operatives is the way the Bush campaign handled workers and campaign staff of the rival Republican candidates after Bush won the nomination: they hired them. Consultants, campaign managers, regional coordinators, and state directors for Dole, Kemp, and Robertson were hired by the Bush organization.[58] According to one of Robertson's state directors, this process accelerated when James Baker took over the Bush organization. Virtually all of Robertson's top lieutenants were hired and then effectively shut up. Once hired, campaign workers were instructed to clear any statement to the press. Moreover, Robertson was recruited as one of the surrogate speakers for Bush, and he campaigned obediently and very effectively for the ticket.[59] In some cases Robertson's state organizations were placed at the disposal of the national campaign to staff phone banks and the like. The Bush people discovered, thanks in part to Robertson, that they could court the evangelical vote in ways that did not undercut their support among other important voting blocs, an approach the national Democratic ticket never mastered.

Republican operatives learned through focus groups that themes articulated by Robertson in the primaries—for example, the Pledge of Allegiance and the American Civil Liberties Union's "attack on religion"—were devastating when aimed at Dukakis, and not just among evangelicals.[60] In the general election Bush got more than 80 percent of the evangelical vote, an increase over Reagan's count.[61] Those voters included many culturally conservative Democrats. Not only did Bush blunt Robertson by courting the born-again vote in the primaries, but he benefited tremendously from cultivating that constituency in the general election.

After the election tensions flared in the fragile Republican coalition. Evangelical leaders increasingly complained about being used by the GOP with little to show for their support. Charging that out of "thousands" of presidential appointments, Bush had made only three that were associated with the evangelical movement, Robertson even intimated that he could support Lloyd Bentsen for president in 1992.[62] As an incumbent president, however, Bush was able to deflect or co-opt these pressures, and by the time of the 1992 campaign Robertson's Christian Coalition was solidly behind the president. Moreover, in the summer of 1992 the strategic situation seemed to increase the value of the evangelical constituency for Bush. When independent candidate H. Ross Perot cut into Bush's traditional Republican support, the Republican campaign focused on shoring up support among conservative Christians, especially through Dan Quayle's highly publicized attacks on "cultural elites" that flout traditional values. With an uncertain economy Bush was again led by events to play the "evangelical card."

At the state level, however, where Republicans are less skilled at coalition politics, the infusion of cultural conservatives into the Republican coalition remains fraught with potential snares. Some old-time Republican activists continue to ask with exasperation, "Who are these Robertson people anyway?" In 1989, in the wake of the Supreme Court's *Webster v. Reproductive Health Services* decision, which gave states latitude in regulating abortion, notable Republican candidates backed away from their antiabortion commitments, and national party leaders are struggling to keep fissures from opening wide. Neither party, ultimately, is immune to the political consequences of discontent in American society.

THE CONTINUING INFLUENCE OF JACKSON'S AND ROBERTSON'S COALITIONS

A pattern emerges in the assimilation of the Jackson and Robertson cadres into their respective parties. Far more than other candidates, these two ministers led social movements that continued to wield influence long after the 1988 election was over. Jackson and Robertson formed organizations dedicated to registering and mobilizing voters, educating supporters, and holding candidates of their respective parties accountable on issues of concern. Both focused their efforts on increasing leverage in their respective parties.

Robertson's Christian Coalition aimed to ensure that concerns of the Christian right were not slighted by Republicans, even while mobilizing new Christian voters for local, state, and national politics. The Rainbow Coalition, mostly through Jackson's personal intervention, organized marches on state capitols in Michigan and California to protest cutbacks in welfare programs, to register voters, and to remind wavering Democratic members of Congress that these new voters care about statehood for the District of Columbia. Both organizations held national coalition meetings on the eve of the 1992 campaign and followed up with events at the national party conventions in the summer. The Christian Coalition hosted a thousand people from around the country in November 1991; Vice President Quayle was a speaker. The drift of the meeting was the need to support and elect more of the right kind of Republicans. The Rainbow Coalition held a national meeting and candidate forum in January 1992, at which the five Democratic presidential candidates lavished praise on Jackson and his organization. Jackson, in turn, spoke approvingly of the five Democrats, contrasted them sharply with Bush, and offered not even a slight nod to the Republican party. In short, although Jackson and Robertson did not run for president in 1992, they and their backers demanded to be heard in their respective party coalitions.

THE CHRISTIAN COALITION

On the Republican side Robertson worked swiftly to solidify conservative Christian influence. He formed the Christian Coalition from the remnants of his campaign organization, hired a smart young Ph.D. to run it, and established the explicit goal of developing state chapters to mobilize "profamily" voters. Director Ralph Reed bragged that "the Christian Coalition is the fastest growing interest group in America." He remarked that its goal is nothing less than ensuring that "whenever a Republican candidate runs for office, he has to come to us." In Reed's analysis the first wave of the New Christian Right (led by Jerry Falwell) was valuable but strategically weak. "The Moral Majority was largely a paper tiger. It was made up of direct-mail consultants and a string of 'Nightline' performances by Falwell." [63] True grass-roots organizations, local political battles, and state politics—these, he suggests, make up the second wave, and they were ignited by Robertson's presidential campaign. Scholars, indeed, have noted that the battles have shifted to communities and states.[64]

The Christian Coalition, according to Reed, concentrates on three things: gaining national members, developing state chapters, and mobilizing sympathetic voters. By June 1991 its 250,000 donors were reported to have provided the organization with a war chest of $12 million. Designed to ensure a stable financial base, the national membership provides the state chapters with seed money; the state chapters in turn operate the voter mobilization program. The organization claims 210 chapters in forty-two states.[65] Reed's goal is to have organizations incorporated in all fifty states by the end of 1992 and to have paid staff in at least twenty states.

The motto of the Christian Coalition is "Think like Jesus, lead like Moses, fight like David, run like Lincoln." The last reference, Reed explains, is to Lincoln's formula for electoral success: identify sympathetic voters and get them to the polls. That is the concept of the coalition's voter mobilization program; it is "strictly a get-out-the-vote approach. We don't endorse candidates so that the candidates are not labeled Robertson's candidates. . . . Our approach is, you're a Christian, you're prolife, profamily; so get involved." The "genius" of this nonpartisan mobilization, Reed argues, allows the organization to "use a 'stealth' approach as opposed to the Falwell approach of media events, rallies, and endorsements." Reed describes the process:

> We do it quietly. We call voters, ask them about abortion, ask them about issues of concern to them, ask about party, get a presidential profile. When we identify them as profamily Christians, then we put their names in the computer file and send a voter guide or score card on the candidates' stands on the issues. Then three days before the election, we call and get them to the polls.[66]

The potential strength of the coalition, Reed contends, is its sharp focus. "We have a focused, market niche. . . . We target that slice of the electorate and maximize [its] potential. . . . We are an interest-advocate organization. We have the same kind of relationship that blue-collar voters had with unions. Christians never applied that technology before; now we are." By the end of 1991, after eighteen months of operation, the coalition had a million voters on computer tape. "If the growth curve continues, we will have ten million voters on computer tape by the end of the decade. That's a tenth of the voting electorate."

A test of the strategy of "flying below radar" occurred in the 1991 Virginia state elections.[67] The Christian Coalition was credited with aiding the Republican surge in the Virginia legislature. According to Reed, "We sent out 100,000 voter guides and made some 15,000 calls. This was far more than any party organization did. And in a state legislative race it's like a bomb dropping. . . . It was a great success. The Republicans came within two seats of controlling the state senate and made gains across the board."[68] Indeed, eight incumbent Democrats were beaten by antiabortion, "profamily" Republicans. Whether the coalition can achieve this clout outside Virginia remains to be seen. Still, an analysis in the left-wing periodical *The Nation* suggested that the Christian Coalition constituted nothing less than a "quiet revival" of the religious right into a formidable electoral faction in the GOP.[69]

Reed echoed this assessment, predicting that Robertson's 1988 campaign would "be for evangelicals what Barry Goldwater's run was for conservatives in 1964: a defeat that provided the seeds of ultimate triumph."[70] Hyperbole aside, it was clear by the summer of 1992 that religious conservatives had increased their influence in the party. Robertson backers and their allies held a third of the seats on the Republican National Committee as well as top party posts in at least ten states, including California, Florida, Michigan, and Texas. They also influenced a number of state conventions. At the 1992 National Republican Convention in Houston, Reed estimated that evangelical conservatives comprised 40 percent of the delegation. His organization alone, he claimed, had 21 of the 107 delegates on the platform drafting committee.[71]

Evidence of this influence was the spotlight on "family values" at the national convention. Sensing that this might be the wedge issue of 1992, Republicans orchestrated an effort designed to highlight different visions of the American family supposedly offered by the two parties. On Wednesday, August 19, Robertson and other speakers sought to paint the Democrats as the party of same-sex marriages, of children divorcing parents (with the help of "radical" lawyers like Hillary Clinton), and of parents' limited options in choosing schools for their children. Robertson even claimed that Bill and Hillary Clinton wanted to "destroy the traditional family and transfer its functions to the Federal Government." In contrast, speakers extolled Bush's devotion to God and family. With a stagnant economy undermining the Bush presidency, Republicans hoped that they could play the "values" card one more time. But Clinton seemed far more resilient to such attacks, preempting them as Dukakis never was able to do. He charged that the Republican party had been captured by the "extreme, intolerant right wing [of] Pat Robertson, Pat Buchanan, Jerry Falwell, and Phyllis Schlafly." And he quipped that attacks on Hillary made it seem that Bush was "running for First Lady instead of for President." He also carefully distanced himself from "extremes" in his own party, saying he had never supported same-sex marriages.[72]

Robertson felt vindicated by the party's apparent embrace of his agenda. But history deals its ironies. In 1988 Jackson supporters, buoyed by their growing clout in the party, had found their interests unfortunately tied to those of Michael Dukakis, a flawed standard bearer who was further weakened by his clumsy handling of Jackson. Then in 1992, with Jackson somewhat marginalized, the Democrats seemed poised to recapture the White House. In a similar twist of fate Robertson supporters flexed their muscles at the 1992 Republican National Convention only to see their fortunes bound with a weakened George Bush, who had to defend the potentially divisive planks they inserted in the platform.

The Rainbow Coalition

Jackson, too, sought to institutionalize his movement by forming a permanent Rainbow Coalition, headquartered in Washington, D.C. Like

Robertson's Christian Coalition, the Rainbow Coalition puts its major effort into voter registration and education. Its agenda includes support for same-day voter registration, District of Columbia statehood, civil rights, and investment in industrial infrastructure, job training, education, day care, and welfare. Unlike Robertson, Jackson remains the prime mover, traveling and campaigning with the intensity of a presidential candidate. The closest counterpart in the Jackson organization to Ralph Reed is Frank Watkins, national political director of the Rainbow Coalition. Although he is a longtime associate of Jackson, the shrewd but unassuming Watkins does not operate with the autonomy Reed seems to enjoy. He operates in the background, deferring to Jackson, quietly doing his bidding. Part of the reason for Jackson's continued involvement is that, while Robertson had to build a genuinely new organization, Jackson continues to rely on the existing network of black churches and his own celebrity to keep the organization afloat. Without Jackson, no Rainbow.

It is not clear how much the Rainbow Coalition sustains an independent grass-roots organization with state chapters. Still, the energetic and compelling Jackson almost constitutes a social movement by himself, especially in his ability to mobilize the national black church network. When asked about the role of churches in his Rainbow effort, Jackson responded, "Almost every Sunday I speak to one to three thousand people. It may be one church; it may be two churches. There is no other place where that many people gather weekly. Every Sunday, with rare exceptions, I'm in some church [giving the guest sermon]. . . . Or at an annual banquet. The church nurtures the people's spirits, day in, day out, week in, week out." [73] Implicit in his comment is that these guest sermons result in special collection plate offerings. Or, as Jackson put it at a Rainbow meeting, he continues to go "hopping and skipping through black churches," [74] where he raises Rainbow money through the black church tradition of the "love offering." With traveling money thus assured, Jackson traverses the nation to inspire and exhort blacks, union members, young people, and the economically dispossessed to register and "vote with a passion."

The Rainbow Coalition is more than the black constituency. Jackson's allies include labor union organizers, grateful for his support, Hispanic leaders, gays, feminists, prairie populists, peace activists, and advocates of national health insurance. Jackson joined them in their struggles when no one else would, and they reciprocate, often with contributions. But the coalition remains heavily dependent on the financial support of the black church and Jackson's personality. Jackson remains unabashed in his religious style. He leads Rainbow members in prayer, hands held; he denounces moral decadence; he quotes from the

Bible. But more fundamentally, he views his own role in profoundly religious terms. "My religion obligates me to be political." While acknowledging that it is "presumptuous" to call oneself a prophet, Jackson nonetheless sees himself as coming from the prophetic tradition. This, in part, explains his continuous travel at a pace barely less grueling than that of a presidential campaign. "The others are running for the nomination; I am running to change America." [75] He might as easily have said "redeem" America, because every facet of his political ministry is interpreted in biblical terms, even the most seemingly trivial or secular. Although Robertson seems to have deemphasized charismatic religion on "The 700 Club," Jackson is as enmeshed in a religious world as ever. Interpreting his politics in terms of the "living word," Jackson seems curiously more "religious" than Robertson at times. Thus it is a supreme irony that a minister and his broad church alliance have become the vanguard of the nation's progressive movement. When Democrats campaign with Jackson they learn to "talk the talk" and "walk the walk" of gospel populism.

Through tireless travel and exhortation, Jackson kept the Rainbow Coalition alive in 1992. Every one of the Democratic presidential candidates appealed for support from the Rainbow. They praised Jackson and echoed many of the populist economic concerns he had stressed in 1988—especially the "invest in America" theme, which was included in the 1992 Democratic platform.

For Jackson personally the 1992 campaign was frustrating. Democratic nominee Bill Clinton, in contrast to Dukakis, was able to appeal independently to black voters. This ability allowed him to distance himself from Jackson without losing black support—a turn of events that clearly irritated Jackson. Having secured the nomination in June, Clinton criticized Jackson for inviting black rap singer Sister Souljah to a Rainbow Coalition meeting.[76] Clinton viewed her comments about the Los Angeles riots as racist and incendiary. Jackson, in turn, chided Clinton and defended Souljah (though he himself had criticized some rap music in the past). This interchange recalled the kind of criticism Jackson had received in the Farrakhan incident in 1984. To critics, and even to some friends, Jackson seemed to grow increasingly petulant, sensing perhaps that he might lose influence in a more centrist Democratic party. The *New York Times* reported the following incident on the first day of the 1992 Democratic National Convention:

> Although Mr. Clinton called Mr. Jackson yesterday morning to thank him for his endorsement, Mr. Jackson was feeling so isolated and furious that he was reduced to dragging Tom Brokaw, the NBC anchorman, and Timothy Russert, the NBC Washington bureau chief, into a men's room for a 23-minute harangue after his appearance on

> "Meet the Press." Those eager to use the bathroom said the muffled conversation from the inside sounded emotional and centered on Mr. Jackson's grievances about what he perceives as shabby treatment at the hands of the Clinton camp.[77]

It was a sad chapter in Jackson's life.

POPULIST ASSIMILATION AND POLITICAL REPRESENTATION

Struggles within American political parties will continue to serve as barometers of society, registering the frustration felt by various groups. Clearly, both the Democratic and Republican parties experienced an increase in populist pressure in 1988, for reasons I have suggested: key constituencies felt their economic and cultural survival was threatened. Different as they are, blacks and white moralist traditionalists are similar in this respect. Each is a distinct, though vital, minority within its respective party coalition, and each sees itself as distinct. Moreover, each group is marked by a pronounced sense of unease, even crisis. The African Americans I interviewed at the Democratic National Convention, for example, spoke of poverty and unemployment and of a generation of young people lost to violence, prison, rising unemployment, lagging educational levels, and teen pregnancy. Some black ministers speak of rescuing only a "remnant" of vulnerable black youth as a realistic goal. Jackson spoke of visiting hospitals with dozens of abandoned crack-cocaine babies, of destructive violence sweeping the cities, of rootless children. Others in the Democratic coalition, while concerned by particular issues, did not feel such a profound sense of threat.

Similarly, in the Republican party the angst is felt by the moral conservatives, who see themselves—and especially their children—under siege from powerful secular forces, not the least of which is contemporary consumerism. Robertson supporters feel unappreciated by the national press, the government, and the educational establishment, and they are keenly aware of how they are viewed in elite circles. One Robertson national delegate said about her compatriots, "They pay taxes, take care of their families, are the heart of America, yet are being painted as fascists, right-wingers." Another national delegate expressed her sadness at the moral collapse of American society. "Our wonderful country is being taken away from us." Robertson reflects this sense of siege. At a private fund raiser shortly after the general election in 1988, he echoed the imagery, common among religious conservatives, of a "new civil war" over the soul of America.[78] One does not find such desperation among the business executives and elite professionals who form the core of the "enterpriser" branch of the party—those whose main political concerns are taxes and regulations. Thus it is not so surprising that one Robertson state coordinator would remark, "I never thought I'd say this, but we do resemble the Jackson people, we are different."

This intensity of feeling, as we have seen, magnified the voice of discontent, especially in caucus settings. One lesson of the 1988 campaign, therefore, is that party regulars should be thankful for the presidential primary.[79] Had the parties operated with caucuses alone, Robertson's leverage especially, but Jackson's, too, would have been enhanced. These outcomes are stunning reversals of the pattern suggested by traditional defenders of political parties, who long for the days of the caucus. But since caucuses cannot be closed today, they magnify the voice of the most intense voters and enable "outsider" candidates to penetrate the system. The success of both populist candidates in the Michigan caucuses shows that intense voters (mobilized by church networks) can infiltrate even those party structures explicitly designed to reward party insiders. Robertson's "God squad" stormed caucuses and party conventions nationwide in 1988 (even in states where Robertson had lost badly in primaries) and again in 1992 (when he was not even a candidate), dominating many party meetings and writing platform language. This outcome came as no surprise to Bush aide Doug Wead, who understood that large charismatic churches, if properly mobilized, could easily capture the local Republican party machinery.[80]

For Jackson, too, success in those states with small black populations (Alaska, Delaware, Kansas, Nevada, and Vermont) rested on his ability to mobilize liberal and black activists in caucuses. The caucuses probably magnified Jackson's vote, even in states with a sizable black population, such as Texas and Michigan. The broader, more moderate primary electorate blunted the gains of the insurgents, a fact keenly appreciated by party officials. In the wake of the 1988 campaign, moderate Republicans and Democrats supported a move to adopt primaries in several caucus states. As Duane Oldfield observed, three states where Robertson supporters packed caucuses—Michigan, Virginia, and Washington—have since switched to primaries with the blessing and support of moderate Republicans.[81] In Michigan many Democrats as well were happy to make the switch. Although both parties experienced an influx of newcomers, neither was taken over entirely.

Aware that influence comes from numbers, not just from intensity, both movements turned their attention in 1992 to voter registration drives and get-out-the-vote (GOTV) programs. Jackson announced an effort in 1992 to increase registration in the fifty largest cities by 25 percent (although it was not clear how this effort would materialize). The Christian Coalition continues to try to involve Christian conservatives in electoral politics. In a curious sense, voter mobilization—which parties used to do with a passion—is now viewed as the raison d'être of insurgents within the parties. Benjamin Ginsberg and Martin Shefter have noted that low voting rates in the United States reflect a kind of electoral demobilization in the system. Because each party controls a share of the government, the system lacks a "loyal opposition" devoted to mobilizing the electorate as its means of regaining power.[82] This task seems to have fallen to those constituencies within the parties that are least comfortable with the status quo. The discontented minorities in each party, different though they are, share the incentive to mobilize their electoral supporters.

One consequence is that the two populist movements act as checks on each other. Robertson backers worked vigorously in Michigan to help elect Republican governor John Engler by a razor-thin margin in 1990. In 1992 Jackson's forces mobilized to unseat the vulnerable incumbent. They staged marches on the capitol over welfare cutbacks, and they planned massive voter registration and GOTV drives. In Virginia, where blacks and moderate suburban residents elected Democratic governor Doug Wilder in 1990, Robertson supporters helped weaken his support in the state legislature. Throughout the country we see this dynamic. In one place the Rainbow vote tips the scales in favor of the Democrat; in another the evangelical white vote gives the Republican the advantage. Feverish registration drives by both sides ensure that neither party will dominate. Those fearful of gospel populism with its moralism and uncompromising language, with its unpredictable charismatic leaders, may find some Madisonian reassurance in this balance.

In terms of political representation, the tangible results of these populist crusades have been mixed. On the Republican side Robertson complained that Bush failed to reward loyal evangelicals with positions in his administration. "We've been shut out of this administration, and they know it," he charged.[83] Although conservative evangelicals provided Bush with at least a quarter of his support, Robertson and others feel taken for granted. "We're just used every four years to win elections." Conservative columnist Cal Thomas, recognizing this pattern, suggests that these people may eventually get wise and demand more for their support.[84] Occasionally, a direct effect can be seen. When Pat Buchanan was snapping at Bush's heels early in the 1992 presidential campaign, the president appeased the religious constituency by firing National Endowment for the Arts director John Frohnmayer, who was targeted by the Christian Coalition for "funding pornographic and blasphemous art."

But the commitment of many elite Republicans to the populist concerns of moral traditionalists remains tepid at best.[85] Many "enterprisers" in the party would be happy if the religious right's social agenda would just disappear. Abortion is a divisive issue, crusades over pornographic art make the Republicans look like a party of bluenoses, and talk of a cultural war between secular and religious forces is profoundly unsettling. Robertson's campaign opened fissures in the Republican coalition that Ronald Reagan had been able to hold together. President Bush, though not as adept as Reagan, assuaged the evangelical constituency with vetoes of abortion-rights legislation and antiabortion judicial appointments. The benefits that come with electoral success, therefore, do provide a balm for intraparty wounds. Should Bush lose the presidency in 1992, however, Robertson backers may find themselves blamed for pushing the Republican party out of the mainstream. Their success in capturing the platform machinery could be a mixed blessing.

JACKSON AND THE DILEMMA OF BLACK REPRESENTATION

To assess Jackson's influence, one must understand an enduring concern of black politics: the struggle to gain "independent leverage" in the political system. Like the populists of the nineteenth century, African Americans historically have been dependent on one political party. This dependency has left them vulnerable to being written off, taken for granted, or sold out.[86] For example, southern blacks were tied to the Republican party after the Civil War. For a while the arrangement was mutually beneficial. Black voting support ensured Republican electoral hegemony, and in return Republican policies during Reconstruction enabled blacks to elect a number of state and national representatives. When the GOP found it expedient to abandon black interests, however, African Americans had nowhere else to turn.

The infamous Hayes-Tilden deal is a powerful reminder of what can happen when blacks lack independent leverage. In the election of 1882 Democrat Samuel Tilden, who won 51 percent of the popular vote against Republican Rutherford B. Hayes, was one electoral vote shy of the majority needed for victory. A controversial commission, created to decide the outcome in four contested southern states, gave seventeen disputed electoral votes to Hayes, thus giving him the presidency. The legitimacy of his election in doubt, Hayes appeased the Democrats by agreeing to speed the end of Reconstruction, effectively paving the way for white domination. Sold out by the Republicans, black voters in the South were disenfranchised, black elected officials vanished, and Jim Crow apartheid lasted for eighty years.[87]

In the contemporary era, too, black scholars and activists have warned of the dangers of being taken for granted by the Democratic party. In 1972 black activists convened in Gary, Indiana, and discussed openly the possibility of forming a third party to increase their influence. A principal goal of the movement was to shake up the status quo in which Republicans write off the black vote and Democrats take it for granted. One strategy involved creating a voting bloc that could withhold support from the Democrats to keep them honest or that could throw support to selected Republicans in return for benefits.

Ronald Walters argues that Jesse Jackson's campaigns embodied a successful quest to enhance this independent leverage in the political system.[88] In one sense Walters clearly is right. Jackson's campaigns energized the black electorate, making it much less likely for the Democratic party to take it for granted. Votes by southern Democratic senators against Robert Bork's nomination to the Supreme Court in October 1987 illustrate the power of the black constituency. One aide to Sen. Sam Nunn, D-Ga., observed that the black grass-roots response to the Bork nomination was so overwhelming that the issue was put in dramatic terms: "If you want to be elected again, you must oppose Bork." Moreover, Jackson's campaigns probably elevated the concerns of many blacks—South Africa, the black underclass, the growing gap between rich and poor, the need for public investment—to greater national prominence. During the 1992 election Democratic candidates actively campaigned for black support.

On the other hand, the long-term goal of exercising leverage in both parties did not change with Jackson's candidacy. Some argue that Jackson missed a historic opportunity. Shortly after the 1988 election President Bush made overtures to Jackson, who was invited to the Oval Office. Conservative columnists simultaneously began floating the idea of a run by Jackson for mayor of the District of Columbia, then embroiled over the collapsing administration of Marion Barry. William Safire argued that being mayor would have challenged Jackson to develop administrative experience, giving him an opportunity to put his message into practice and keeping him in the limelight. In turn, the Republican administration could have funneled resources into the city. Jackson, in effect, was given the opportunity of benefiting from Republican attempts to demonstrate an interest in black America. At the same time the Democratic party would be under pressure to respond. Jackson at first seemed open to the idea of a run for mayor, having moved his Rainbow Coalition office to Washington and registered to vote there. But aides vehemently opposed the idea, arguing that it was a "setup" aimed at co-opting Jackson. Jackson confidant Frank Watkins said, "I argued that it was the dumbest idea since the Reagan administration made catsup a vegetable." [89] Ironically, that setup, according to Watkins, would have helped a "Mayor Jackson" make Washington, D.C., a showcase with generous federal help. Thus Jackson probably had it within his power—given the relative goodwill Bush enjoyed with blacks and their smoldering resentment of Dukakis's treatment of their leader—to forge links with the Republican administration that might have embodied the independent leverage sought by black intellectuals and activists. Safire put it bluntly: "He coulda been a contender." Instead, he chose to become "shadow senator" of the District of Columbia. The problem with this logic, Jackson loyalists argue, is that the "aristocratic" tendencies in the Bush administration likely would have made such an alliance ephemeral. With economic issues increasingly paramount, an "empowerment" conservative like Jack Kemp might offer blacks longer term assurances than "blue blood" Bush ever could.

Jackson remains a thorny problem for the national Democratic party. He cannot be ignored because of his continued charisma in the black community and his mighty rhetoric, again on display at the 1992 convention. But his prominence is still problematic. One highly placed Republican party official, for example, said this about Jackson:

> He is the preeminent leader of the hard left in America. In addition to blacks his constituency is anyone who thinks they are oppressed or have a grievance or feel locked out, any farmer who feels he should be in business for perpetuity. It is a populist message, and it is the heart and soul of the Democratic party. Cooler heads know he is unelectable, but 35 to 40 percent of the Democratic constituency like him.[90]

This official concluded that Jackson's prominence helps Republican presidential prospects.

Jackson's legacy clearly is a complex one. In the past he blended an egalitarian vision of economics and race with culturally conservative themes—opposing abortion, pornography, and the seductive messages of the mass media or decrying the lack of rigorous standards in education. One of his greatest legacies, however, may come from today's temperance issue—drug abuse—which he elevated to the forefront of the national Democratic agenda. One cannot underestimate the significance of his denunciation of drugs, especially in light of the party's recent history. With the McGovernite takeover in 1972, the Democratic party became identified with 1960s permissiveness—"sex, drugs, and rock and roll." As a Baptist preacher Jackson was never comfortable with the libertarian excesses of the counterculture, with its "boundless liberalism," its abandonment of the work ethic and sexual restraint, its attraction to psychedelic destruction.[91] While other Democrats were calling for the legalization of marijuana, Jackson crusaded against the scourge of drug abuse. Just as Bryan helped legitimize antidrink sentiment in his day, Jackson effectively brought a "temperance" message on drugs into greater legitimacy within the Democratic party. Led by Jackson's long-term and passionate involvement, Democrats, once viewed as "soft" on drug use, seized the issue and now routinely criticize Bush as insufficiently committed to the war on drugs. To Jackson the drug issue is another example of fighting for the "moral center" on an issue rather than for the expedient political center. "In 1984 people said you're crazy to take on that issue; it wasn't viewed as a major issue, not popular. Now we're fighting a war on drugs." [92] Helping to forge the national consensus against drug abuse may be one of Jackson's lasting legacies.

The exigencies of Democratic primary politics, however, expose the profound tension in Jackson's message—a tension he sometimes acknowledges.[93] In his presidential quests he increasingly championed the agenda of the cultural left in America.[94] Enhancing its influence, however, renders the party less palatable to culturally conservative Democrats, many of whom are evangelicals.[95] One southern delegate for Al Gore said in 1988, "If the party goes too far on gay rights and abortion, that's bad for us." Republican consultants, indeed, make hay characterizing the Democrats as captive of the "loony left" [96]—militant gays, radical feminists, and pacifists. One GOP party leader gleefully noted, "Democrats have become the party of the experimental lifestyle. . . . Good Christians wear the cross and Jews the star of David, but Democrats wear New Age crystals." To the extent that Democrats become associated with New Age politics, he argued, the party would be hurt in the eyes of the majority of citizens.[97] Thus, the argument goes, when Jackson and others tie the fate of blacks to the cultural left, they may push the party out of the electoral mainstream. Moreover, such a shift may undercut true representation of fervently religious blacks, whose economic progressivism often belies a more traditional set of moral views shared by many conservative whites.[98] African Americans, by some reckoning the most religious sector of American society, ironically find themselves wedded to an increasingly secular and socially liberal Democratic party.

Here, the dilemma of black representation converges with developments in the Republican coalition. Some people who once voted as Democrats on the basis of economics have joined the GOP on the basis of cultural conservatism. Robertson's campaign energized a fresh cadre of these evangelical voters and activists (some of them former Democrats) and solidified their attachment to the Republican party. The Republican coalition, however shaky, has been enlarged on the basis of this infusion. The Democratic party, in turn, has become more homogeneously liberal. If, however, economic issues define the terms of presidential politics, rather than the valence issues that cut against the left,[99] Jackson's influence may well strengthen a more competitive national party. The major focus of the Rainbow Coalition in 1992 was economic populism: reinvesting in America's industrial infrastructure and in American workers (through job training, education, health care, day care) and making sure the rich pay their fair share of such investment. Clinton skillfully played on these themes in his campaign against Bush. If the Democrats do become more competitive at the presidential level, black economic interests may well be enhanced.

In terms of political representation, however, this potentially agreeable outcome does nothing to end black dependence on one party for political representation. Ron Walters noted that disaffection with the Democratic party remains so high among some blacks that the Republicans might make real inroads if they tried.[100] Occasionally, Republicans attempt to fashion policies aimed at challenging Democratic hegemony among blacks. Republican initiatives include enterprise zones, tenant purchase schemes in public housing, and pilot programs that allow inner-city youth to escape dysfunctional schools by providing them with tuition for private academies. But sustained efforts by Republicans to fashion alternatives to liberal approaches are undercut by the temptation to play the race card, to pit blue-collar and middle-class whites against their black counterparts. Not only did Pat Robertson avoid such appeals, but he campaigned actively for black support. He featured blacks in his ads, supported blacks in intraparty battles with Republican regulars, and denounced liberals for failing the black family. Ironically, one does not often find such attention to black concerns from "moderate" GOP leaders.

Until Republicans abandon racially polarizing campaigns, African Americans will not vote in a way to create true independent leverage in the political system. Their influence will rest on circumstances.

SUMMARY

For many African Americans unswerving loyalty to the Democratic party has yet to redress the great unfinished business of the nation—to provide the sons and daughters of African descent with full participation in the economic and social mainstream.[101] Black representation, therefore, remains a profound dilemma for American society. Effective representation of black interests would likely merge some culturally conservative elements with a progressive economic and racial platform. Jackson articulates this culturally conservative view when he inspires young people with his message of religious hope, charity, discipline, sacrifice, and achievement—a message that resonates with white evangelicals, as we will see in the next chapter.

In this sense at least, the interests of conservative evangelicals and black Americans are not necessarily at odds. Black ministers preach a morally traditional message, and American blacks are as fervently committed to religion as orthodox white believers.[102] On the other side charismatic Christians, sometimes more racially tolerant than their fellow fundamentalists, consider themselves the caring hearts of the GOP; some, at least, are more economically progressive than their "country club" Republican allies. Yet political forces are pushing these two constituencies in opposite directions. From the standpoint of political representation it is not necessarily a cause for rejoicing.

NOTES

1. See William J. Crotty, *Political Reform and the American Experiment* (New York: Crowell, 1977); Leon D. Epstein, *Political Parties in the American Mold* (Madison: University of Wisconsin Press, 1986); Austin Ranney, *Curing the Mischiefs of Faction: Party Reform in America* (Berkeley: University of California Press, 1975); James W. Ceaser, *Presidential Selection: Theory and Development* (Princeton: Princeton University Press, 1979); and Nelson W. Polsby and Aaron Wildavsky, *Presidential Elections,* 8th ed. (New York: Free Press, 1991).
2. John H. Kessel, *Presidential Campaign Politics,* 3d ed. (Homewood, Ill.: Dorsey, 1988), 116.
3. Gallup Poll surveys show that 8 percent of all national respondents describe themselves as charismatic or Pentecostal *(Emerging Trends,* 1989). Corwin Smidt has further shown that, as a group, charismatics and Pentecostals possess a theological and political orientation distinct from fundamentalists and other evangelicals. See Smidt, "Evangelicals and the 1984 Election," *American Politics Quarterly* 15 (October 1987): 419-444.
4. John C. Green and James L. Guth have documented the Robertson contributors' emphasis on morality, which sets them apart from supporters of the other GOP presidential candidates and general contributors to the party. See Green and Guth, "The Christian Right in the Republican Party: The Case of Pat Robertson's Supporters," *Journal of Politics* 50 (February 1988): 150-165. My interviews with caucus goers and delegates corroborated their findings. The Robertson people, driven by moral concerns, are often unconventional Republicans—a janitor, a carpenter, a car stereo shop owner, and so forth. Garry Wills has argued that both Robertson and Jackson tapped the moral yearnings of many average Americans in a time of seeming cultural disintegration. See Wills, "The Power Populist," *Time,* Nov. 21, 1988, 60ff.
5. Pat Robertson, interview with author, Virginia Beach, Va., August 8, 1991.
6. Thomas Edsall, "Will Feuds Sink the GOP?" *Washington Post National Weekly*

Edition, June 15, 1987, 29; Doug Wead, "The Vice President and Evangelicals in the General Election," *Twice Abridged,* April 15, 1988; Michael D'Antonio, "Fierce in the '80s, Fallen in the '90s, the Religious Right Forgets Politics," *Los Angeles Times,* Feb. 4, 1990, M3; Marc Nuttle, interview with author, Norman, Okla., January 1988.

7. Elwell used this phrase in a speech to the Christian Coalition's Road to Victory conference, Virginia Beach, Va., Nov. 15-16, 1991. In the speech she referred frequently to "the Christians" when speaking of the Robertson followers.
8. The massive psychographic survey of the electorate conducted by the Gallup Poll for the Times Mirror organization revealed the cultural gulf between the two most loyal voting constituencies in the Republican party. On some social issues "enterprisers" were close to some of the socially liberal Democratic groups, while the "moralists" leaned toward the right, along with culturally conservative Democratic voters.
9. Elwell, speech, November 1991.
10. This claim is according to retiring Oklahoma Republican chairman, Tom Cole, who described his conversation with the Michigan chair. (Cole, interview with author, Oklahoma City, Feb. 25, 1989.)
11. Bob Benenson, "Robertson's Cause Endures Despite His Defeat," *Congressional Quarterly Weekly Report,* May 14, 1988, 1267-1273; Associated Press, "Robertson Backers Set North Carolina Boycott," *New York Times,* May 25, 1988, A24.
12. James A. Barnes, "Anatomy of a Robertson Takeover," *National Journal,* March 26, 1988, 824.
13. Ibid.
14. Duane Oldfield, "Pat Crashes the Party: Reform, Republicans, and Robertson," Working Paper 90-11 (Institute of Governmental Studies, University of California at Berkeley, 1990).
15. Mike Norris, "The Holy Wars (Continued)," *Campaigns and Elections,* March-April 1989, 9-10.
16. T. R. Reid, "Arizona Republicans Have a Sects Problem: Religious Strife Is Dividing the Party," *Washington Post,* Aug. 13, 1989, A6.
17. Joe Conason, "The Religious Right's Quiet Revival," *The Nation,* April 27, 1992.
18. Margaret E. Kriz and Christopher Madison, "Putting 'Feet' on Robertson's Political Prayers," *National Journal Convention Daily,* Aug. 17, 1988.
19. This number comes from surveys conducted for the Republican party and was supplied by Marc Nuttle.
20. Nuttle said negative perceptions of Robertson rose sharply immediately after Robertson's sequence of misstatements and the Swaggart scandal.
21. Oklahoma Election Commission.
22. An aide to Henry Bellmon, then governor of Oklahoma, told me that Robertson would have won in an open primary.
23. This account comes from interviews with delegates to the state convention, including Tom Cole.

24. One of the signers of the letter told me that as a longtime Republican she understood that "influence" in party politics is more valuable in the long run than domination.
25. The Vitz report attempted to provide documentation showing that textbooks slight religion and family issues. See Paul Vitz, *Censorship: Evidence of Bias in Our Children's Textbooks* (Ann Arbor, Mich.: Servant Press, 1986).
26. Jackie Calmes, "Tougher GOP Stance on Social Issues Reflects Surge of the Religious Right," *Wall Street Journal*, Aug. 20, 1992.
27. Ibid.
28. 1992 Republican platform, Aug. 13, 1992; Alessandra Stanley, "Like-minded Delegates See a Frightening America," *New York Times*, Aug. 20, 1992, A7.
29. Corwin E. Smidt and James M. Penning, "A House Divided: A Comparison of Bush and Robertson Delegates to the 1988 Michigan Republican State Convention," *Polity* 23 (Fall 1990): 127-138; John McGlennon, "Religious Activists in the Republican Party: Robertson and Bush Supporters in Virginia" (Paper presented at the annual meeting of the Midwest Political Science Association, Chicago, April 1989); and James L. Guth and John C. Green, "Robertson's Republicans: Christian Activists in Republican Politics," *Election Politics* 4 (Fall 1987): 9-14.
30. Green and Guth, "Christian Right in the Republican Party."
31. Robertson, interview with author.
32. I attended the Colorado State Republican Convention in May 1992 and observed the dynamics. Booths for antiabortion activists and abortion-rights advocates were a prominent feature in the convention hall.
33. Testimony of Ralph E. Reed, Jr., before the Republican National Committee platform hearings, Salt Lake City, Utah, May 26, 1992.
34. Jo Freeman, "The Political Culture of the Democratic and Republican Parties," *Political Science Quarterly* 101 (1986): 327-344.
35. As recorded at a meeting of the Dukakis contingent from one state's delegation.
36. When I remarked to former governor Jerry Brown, then chairman of the California state party, that Jackson mobilized new participants into party politics, he responded with a query, "Did he? Where's the evidence? " Even to such party pros as Brown the chasm between white and black experience remains salient.
37. Willy Brown, interview with author, Washington, D.C., September 1989. Brown also said that he met with leaders of the Rainbow Coalition to discuss ways of getting a grant to study the phenomenon of the Jackson movement and its effect on mobilization in the Democratic party.
38. Joint Center for Political Studies, *Blacks and the 1988 Democratic National Convention* (Washington, D.C.: Joint Center for Political Studies, 1988), 19.
39. Ibid., 108.
40. The representative engineered his own victory with a massive registration drive and voter mobilization effort coordinated through the black churches in his district. Jackson's campaign, he noted, inspired and complemented this effort, but the Rainbow Coalition was not organized sufficiently to

provide the actual mechanism for registration and get-out-the-vote drives. Although Jackson's visits were beneficial, the representative and other established black groups were the prime movers in that district. (Interview with author, Washington, D.C., June 1989.)

41. Thomas Cavanagh, *Inside Black America* (Washington, D.C.: Joint Center for Political Studies, 1985), 15.
42. Voter Education Project, Atlanta, 1986.
43. *Congressional Quarterly Weekly Report,* Nov. 8, 1986, 2805.
44. John Petrocik notes that Republicans in the deep South must poll at least 65 percent of the nonblack vote to be competitive. Thus as long as Democrats can poll better than 35 percent of the nonblack vote, they have the advantage. Ironically, then, a 60-40 Republican advantage among whites is not enough. Although a realignment of whites has occurred in the South, with Republicans heavily supported by whites, this realignment occurred simultaneously with the addition of a new electorate—the black vote—that compensated the Democrats for the loss of whites. See John Petrocik, "Realignment: New Party Coalitions and the Nationalization of the South," *Journal of Politics* 49 (May 1987): 347-375.
45. Lee Atwater, speech delivered at the Oklahoma Republican Convention, Oklahoma City, March 25, 1989.
46. Paul Wellstone, interview with author, Washington, D.C., September 1989.
47. Dan Balz, "For the Democrats, the Prized Black Vote Draws All Eyes," *Washington Post,* Nov. 20, 1991, A4.
48. Jesse Jackson, speech presented to the Rainbow Coalition, Washington, D.C., Jan. 25, 1992.
49. David Maraniss, "Clinton's Journey of the Spirit," *Washington Post National Weekly Edition,* July 13-19, 1992, 10-11.
50. Jack Germond and Jules Witcover, *Whose Broad Stripes and Bright Stars: The Trivial Pursuit of the Presidency* (New York: Warner, 1989), 348.
51. Ron Brown, quoted in ibid., 347.
52. Wills, "Power Populist."
53. Member of a well-established Democratic Washington law firm, interview with author, Washington, D.C., June 1989.
54. News reports noted the Jackson-Brown linkage and its effect on Jewish support. See Sam Roberts, "Jackson's Moves in New York Appear to Aid Brown," *New York Times,* March 31, 1992, A12; and Sidney Blumenthal, "The Survivor," *New Republic,* April 27, 1992, 15.
55. Wead, "Vice President and Evangelicals in the General Election."
56. Ibid.
57. Wead, interview with author, Washington, D.C., June 1989.
58. The Robertson organization, according to Nuttle, was effectively blended into the Bush campaign. See David R. Runkel, ed., *Campaign for President: The Managers Look at '88* (Dover, Mass.: Auburn House, 1989).
59. According to one Republican National Committee official, Robertson was a very effective surrogate, solidifying the hard-core religious conservatives for Bush.

60. Top Bush strategists assembled focus groups of average Democrats supporting Dukakis and found that issues such as the Pledge of Allegiance and the American Civil Liberties Union were extremely damaging. See Paul Taylor and David S. Broder, "Early Volley of Bush's Exceeds Expectations," *Washington Post*, Oct. 28, 1988, 1. Radio spots for Robertson in Iowa featured the Pledge of Allegiance and an attack on the ACLU's protection of pornography and hostility to public religion.
61. CBS News/*New York Times* poll, Nov. 10, 1988.
62. Gloria Borger, "For Conservatives, Breaking Up Is Hard to Do," *U.S. News and World Report*, Feb. 5, 1990, 26-27.
63. Ralph Reed, interview with author, Chesapeake, Va., August 1991.
64. Hubert Morken, "Religious Lobbying at the State Level" (Paper presented at the annual meeting of the American Political Science Association, San Francisco, September 1990).
65. Joseph Coccaro, "Robertson Finds Force in GOP Grass Roots," *Virginian-Pilot and the Ledger-Star*, June 21, 1992.
66. Reed, interview with author.
67. Conason, "Religious Right's Quiet Revival."
68. Reed, interview with author.
69. Conason, "Religious Right's Quiet Revival."
70. Quoted in Calmes, "Tougher GOP Stance on Social Issues."
71. Coccaro, "Robertson Finds Force in GOP Grass Roots"; and ibid. Reed's claim about the platform committee was relayed to me by a Virginia reporter.
72. Pat Robertson, "Excerpts from Speech by Pat Robertson," *New York Times*, Aug. 20, 1992, A12; Gwen Ifill, "Clinton Assails GOP Attacks Aimed at Wife," *New York Times*, Aug. 20, 1992, A12; Bill Clinton, interview with Tom Brokaw for the combined NBC-Public Broadcasting coverage of the Republican National Convention, Aug. 19, 1992.
73. Jackson, interview with author, flight from Washington, D.C., to Dallas, March 12, 1992.
74. Jackson used this phrase in talking with Rainbow Coalition members during an appeal for sustaining funds, Washington, D.C., Jan. 25, 1992.
75. Jackson, interview with author.
76. Gwen Ifill, "Clinton Stands by Remark on Rapper," *New York Times*, June 15, 1992, A10.
77. Maureen Dowd and Frank Rich, "Smooth Face of Party Can't Hide the Turmoil," *New York Times*, July 13, 1992, A9.
78. Robertson, speech at fund-raising event, Edmond, Okla., Nov. 12, 1988.
79. Duane Oldfield, who has wonderfully documented the effect of Robertson's mobilization on the GOP, forcefully made this point. See "Pat Crashes the Party."
80. Wead, interview with author.
81. Oldfield, "Pat Crashes the Party."
82. Benjamin Ginsberg and Martin Shefter, *Politics by Other Means: The Declining Importance of Elections in America* (New York: Basic Books, 1990).
83. Borger, "For Conservatives, Breaking Up Is Hard to Do."

84. Cal Thomas, "Republicans Rediscovering Benefits of Traditional Values," Syndicated column, *Daily Oklahoman*, Dec. 19, 1991, 18.
85. This was Marlene Elwell's assessment of the situation in Michigan. She concluded that the "silk stocking" Republicans have taken over the party as the Robertson forces retreated in disgust. (Elwell, phone interview with author, January 1992.)
86. Ronald Walters, *Black Presidential Politics in America* (Albany: State University of New York Press, 1988).
87. Carol Swain provides a broad historical review of black electoral representation and documents the swift collapse of black elected officials in the post-Reconstruction era. See Swain, "Changing Patterns of African-American Representation in Congress," in *The Atomistic Congress*, ed. Allen D. Hertzke and Ronald M. Peters (Armonk, N.Y.: M. E. Sharpe, 1992).
88. Walters, *Black Presidential Politics in America.*
89. Frank Watkins, interview with author, Washington, D.C., May 1991.
90. Republican official, interview with author, Republican National Committee, Washington, D.C., June 1989.
91. Watkins, interview with author.
92. Jackson, interview with author.
93. Ibid. When asked about conflict within his coalition between black ministers and antinomian elements (particularly a segment in the gay community that seeks liberated sexuality with no consequences), Jackson acknowledged that it existed.
94. *Washington Post National Weekly Edition*, May 2-8, 1988.
95. One of the most startling recent findings is that religious observance is now a key factor separating voters in the two parties. The more frequent the church attendance, the more likely the voter will be Republican, a pattern that holds for Roman Catholics and mainline Protestants as well as for evangelicals. This difference was not apparent before 1976, and it is an ominous trend for Democrats in light of the strong attachment of Americans to religion. See Thomas Edsall, "The GOP Will Have to Work to Get Back the Big Mo," *Washington Post National Weekly Edition*, Jan. 23-29, 1989.
96. This remark was made at a workshop organized by Rep. Newt Gingrich of Georgia for the Republican National Convention in New Orleans, August 1988.
97. Republican official, interview with author, Washington, D.C., June 1989.
98. Jackson probably articulated mainstream black sentiment more when he wrote passionately against abortion, linking *Roe v. Wade*, 410 U.S. 113 (1973), to the Dred Scott decision. See Jesse Jackson, "How We Respect Life Is Overriding Moral Issue," *National Right to Life News*, January 1977, 5. Blacks, far more than whites, support school prayer and are at least as conservative, if not more so, on issues of discipline in the schools, drugs, pornography, and abortion. See Allen D. Hertzke, *Representing God in Washington: The Role of Religious Lobbies in the American Polity* (Knoxville: University of Tennessee Press, 1988), chap. 5; and Clyde Wilcox, "Blacks and the New Christian Right," *Review of Religious Research* 32 (September 1990): 43-55.

99. Marc Nuttle, a top Republican consultant, argues that the American electorate is significantly right of center on a host of issues. Thus, even though conservative activists push the Republican party to the right (as Democratic activists push their party to the left), the conservatives have a much easier time moving to the center of national opinion in a general election campaign than do the liberals, who face an insurmountable distance without a major issue such as war or depression.
100. Ron Walters, interview with author, Washington, D.C., January 1992.
101. Walters, *Black Presidential Politics in America.*
102. George Gallup, Jr., "Religion in America, 50 Years: 1935-1985," Gallup Report 236, May 1985.

6

The Characteristics and Opinions of Jackson and Robertson Voters

Now that we have examined the two populist candidates and their activist backers, let us turn our attention to the average voters who supported Jackson and Robertson. What were they like? What made them distinctive from other voters? To what extent were they receptive to populist politics? We can imagine a "gospel populist" profile of these average voters that would include the following characteristics: a discontent with the state of society, a feeling that elites are against the people, a church-rooted communitarian concern for the consequences of individual greed or immorality, and a quasi-religious hope for charismatic leadership to redress grievances.

On a number of issues we find a striking convergence between Jackson's and Robertson's followers that illustrates the populist character of the two crusades. Survey research conducted in 1988 is one indicator of public sentiment and experience; its findings give us a glimpse into this dimension of American politics. In our analysis we will use data from two excellent surveys, the Super Tuesday survey, conducted during the 1988 primary season, and the American National Election Study (NES), a nationwide survey conducted before the 1988 general election.[1]

The NES contained the widest range of questions relevant to our analysis. This survey is interesting because it allowed respondents to name a preferred candidate in both of the two major parties, thus illuminating the potential overlap between Jackson and Robertson sympathizers. Contrary to what we might expect, the overlap was sizable, especially for the smaller Robertson sample. For example, about 75 percent of those who said that Robertson "would make the best president" of the Republican contenders also volunteered a favored candidate on the Democratic side. Of those, more than half (52 percent) named Jackson as their favored Democrat for president. When Robertson supporters who refused to list a favored Democrat are added to the total, Jackson still remained the favored Democrat by a wide margin (39 percent of all Robertson sympathizers favored Jackson among the Democratic contenders). This overlap, of course, creates problems for clean analysis.[2] In another sense, however, it does not contaminate the analysis so much as it corroborates the thesis that gospel populism cuts across conventional political categories.

The Super Tuesday survey is a valuable supplement to the NES survey for a number of reasons. It was structured to elicit mutually exclusive candidate preferences across party lines, thus allowing us to compare the more "pure" Robertson and Jackson partisans with those in the NES sample. Conducted in the heat of the primaries, it included a larger sample of Robertson supporters than did the NES (94 supporters versus 77), allowing us to verify some of the more striking findings. The Jackson sample in the Super Tuesday survey also more accurately reflected the racial composition of his total voter support (64 percent black) than did the NES sample (43 percent black). Despite these advantages, I could not rely heavily on the Super Tuesday survey because of the limited range of questions asked. Yet the compatibility of findings between the two surveys strengthens my confidence that I have touched upon unexplored dimensions in the electorate. All relationships discussed here are statistically significant unless otherwise noted.[3]

The following eight propositions, which originate from the thesis of this book, will guide our exploration in this chapter:

- That supporters of Jackson and Robertson shared a discontent with the state of society.
- That supporters of Jackson and Robertson expressed a common populist sentiment about elites.
- That, when compared with other candidate partisans, supporters of Jackson and Robertson represented distinctive groups.
- That despite ideological differences supporters of Jackson and Robertson shared notable similarities.
- That supporters of Jackson and Robertson were deeply religious and tied to tightknit churches.
- That supporters of Jackson and Robertson expressed forms of communitarian dissatisfaction with liberal, individualistic trends in society.
- That the two candidates represented a charismatic hope to their supporters.
- That populism cuts across ideological lines in American politics.[4]

We find varying degrees of evidence for each of these propositions. The national surveys suggest, for example, that Jackson and Robertson supporters were distinct and remarkably similar in their discontent, their view of elites, and their concern that the nation was on the wrong course. This finding lends support to the argument that the populism of the two ministers resonated with their followers and energized a distinct portion of the electorate. We find striking similarities that fly in the face of journalistic stereotypes. Notably, followers of Jackson and Robertson were predominantly female and were strikingly similar in their faith commitment, especially compared with followers of other candidates. This finding meshes nicely with our analysis of the role of tightknit churches in campaign mobilization. In other words, campaign strategies that focused on churches and religious networks were uniquely adapted to appeal to the profile of potential supporters—church-rooted women. We also find evidence that Jackson's and Robertson's supporters invested in the two leaders a kind of charismatic hope that leaped across partisan and ideological boundaries. Robertson supporters, supposedly on the far right, were far more likely to invest hope in the Reverend Jesse Jackson, supposedly on the far left, than were backers of Michael Dukakis, Al Gore, Bob Dole, or Jack Kemp. Thus the religious dimensions of charismatic leadership seemed to foster hope amidst discontent that transcended conventional categories. We now turn to the dynamics of support for "gospel populism" in the 1988 presidential campaign.

OPINIONS OF ELITES AND GOVERNMENT

Interviews with campaign activists for Jackson and Robertson suggest that of all the party activists in 1988 these two groups were uniquely discontented. To what extent were average voters similarly distinct in their appraisal of American society? The National Election Study asked respondents a series of questions that tapped their discontent, their perception of elites, and their feelings about the state of the nation.

One of the most revealing questions asked respondents whether things were "going well" in the country or not. Most Americans did not express deep discontent with the state of the nation in our 1988 snapshot (though by 1992 the public mood had turned more sour, indicating that our 1988 populists may have been a bellwether of things to come). Approximately 64 percent of those surveyed said that things were going at least "fairly well." Just as William Jennings Bryan with his populist rhetoric did not always square with voter experience, so modern-day

Table 6-1 Opinion on the Condition of the Nation

Question: "Let's talk about the country as a whole. Would you say that things in the country are generally going very well, fairly well, not too well, or not well at all?"

Respondents	*Well* [a]	*Not well* [b]	*(N)*
Populist groups			
All Robertson supporters	47%	53%	(76)
All Jackson supporters	52	48	(311)
Black Jackson supporters	42	58	(123)
Other groups			
All Bush supporters	76	24	(759)
All Dukakis supporters	60	40	(512)
Black Dukakis supporters	62	38	(66)

Source: Compiled by the author from data in the American National Election Study, 1988 Pre- and Postelection Survey, Inter-University Consortium for Political and Social Research.

[a] The column combines responses of "very well" and "fairly well."

[b] The column combines responses of "not too well" and "not well at all."

populists often overestimate the discontent they seek to exploit. The "disinherited, despised, and the damned" often do not make a majority. Indeed, even a slight majority of blacks said things were going at least fairly well in 1988.

When we examine supporters of various candidates on this question, however, we find the greatest negative sentiment among supporters of Jackson and Robertson. On the Republican side 76 percent of the Bush supporters, versus 47 percent of the Robertson backers, felt things were going well. On the Democratic side 60 percent of the Dukakis supporters, versus 42 percent of the black Jackson supporters, were optimistic about the nation. (In discussing the NES questions, I have separated out the black Jackson supporters, who were his core backers and who illustrate most graphically the populist profile.) On this question we see a striking convergence of black Jackson supporters and Robertson backers, in contrast to other voters. Among the backers of major candidates in both parties, only a majority of the Robertson and black Jackson supporters felt the nation was not fundamentally on the right track. Notably, there was even a significant difference between black voters who supported Jackson versus those who supported Dukakis; black supporters of Dukakis were far more upbeat about the nation. (See Table 6-1.)

Table 6-2 Perception of Public Officials

Question: "I don't think public officials care much about what people like me think."

Respondents	*Agree* [a]	*(N)*
Populist groups		
All Robertson supporters	60%	(73)
All Jackson supporters	59	(279)
Black Jackson supporters	66	(102)
Other groups		
All Bush supporters	44	(660)
All Dukakis supporters	52	(446)
Race		
Blacks	60	(210)
Whites	49	(1,486)

Source: 1988 National Election Study.

[a] The column combines responses of "agree" and "strongly agree." Respondents could also mark "no opinion," "disagree," and "strongly disagree."

Clearly, there is some link between the populist rhetoric of Jackson and Robertson and the sentiments of their followers. This relationship comes out strongly when we look at voters' perceptions of elites. Among Republicans, Robertson supporters expressed the greatest discontent with elites; among Democrats, Jackson supporters expressed the greatest discontent. For example, 60 percent of Robertson's supporters agreed with the statement, "I don't think public officials care much about what people like me think," compared with 44 percent of Bush's supporters (see Table 6-2). Again Robertson supporters resembled blacks, 60 percent of whom agreed with the statement, compared with whites, only 49 percent of whom agreed. On the Democratic side, there appeared to be little difference between Dukakis supporters and Jackson supporters, but when we control for race we find that 66 percent of black Jackson backers agreed with the statement, versus 51 percent of the white Dukakis supporters and 54 percent of the white Jackson supporters.

As separate groups, Robertson supporters and black Jackson supporters resembled each other more than any other set of candidate backers. Perceptions of which elites are at fault may differ profoundly between the groups, but the populist profile emerges nonetheless.

Table 6-3 Opinion on Big Interests and Government

Question: "Would you say that the government is pretty much run by a few big interests looking out for themselves or that it is run for the benefit of all the people?"

Respondents	*Benefit of all*	*Few big interests*	*(N)*
Populist groups			
All Robertson supporters	14%	86%	(70)
All Jackson supporters	22	78	(273)
Black Jackson supporters	18	82	(102)
Other groups			
All Bush supporters	43	57	(627)
All Dukakis supporters	35	65	(423)
White Dukakis supporters	36	64	(354)

Source: 1988 National Election Study.

One of the best indicators of populist sentiment is the perception of large institutions. Historically, populists saw themselves as representing the "little guy" against powerful interests. The NES survey asked this question: "Would you say that the government is pretty much run by a few big interests looking out for themselves or that it is run for the benefit of all the people?" The majority of Americans polled said that a few big interests run the government, indicating that populist rhetoric might resonate broadly in certain instances. Indeed, that assumption was embodied in Bush's 1988 campaign strategy, which portrayed Dukakis as a captive of snobbish Harvard elites. Still, there were some dramatic differences between candidate groups, as we see in Table 6-3.

These differences suggest a deep populist sentiment among the Jackson and Robertson supporters. Again, Robertson supporters and black Jackson supporters registered the strongest agreement with our populist profile. Indeed, black Jackson supporters were significantly more populist in their appraisal of government than were blacks generally. Robertson supporters, remarkably, were nearly unanimous in their populist response. To be sure, these two groups may differ profoundly on which big interests run things. Still, the depth of discontent in both camps helps to explain why the two campaigns resembled social movements and why Jackson and Robertson did so well in caucus states, where the intensity of their backers magnified their political impact.

We must remember that although Robertson backers expressed populist discontent the broader evangelical community did not. Consistent with other surveys, more than a third of the respondents in the NES survey considered themselves "born-again" Christians. Yet on questions of discontent, perception of elites, and so forth, this group was indistinguishable from the total population. Thus, although Pat Robertson hoped to appeal broadly to the sizable conservative Christian community, his candidacy appeared instead to attract a distinct subset whose discontent set its members apart even from fellow religionists. To a lesser extent Jackson's followers shared that characteristic. Keeping in mind that the NES survey was conducted in the fall of 1988 after Dukakis had secured the nomination, we see that those voters who still preferred Jackson tended to be more pessimistic about the direction of the country than those who expressed preferences for other candidates. Notably, blacks who preferred Dukakis seemed less populist than those who remained loyal to "Jesse."

FEELINGS ABOUT CHARISMATIC LEADERSHIP

If backers of Robertson and Jackson were more likely to feel things were not going well in the nation, they might, according to our populist profile, invest greater hope in a charismatic leader to redress the crisis. We do not have good data on this point, in part because comparable questions were not asked about all candidates in the surveys. My interviews and observation suggest that a tremendous (at times millennial) hope was invested in Jackson and Robertson by their followers, a hope rooted in religious imagery and based on the fact that the two leaders spoke eloquently to their followers' anxieties.

The NES survey asked a series of provocative questions about the respondents' perceptions of the candidates—questions about whether the candidate made them feel "afraid," "angry," "hopeful," or "proud." Neither Dukakis nor Bush provoked strong sentiment either way, and Jackson did not make as many people afraid or angry as one might expect. Jackson elicited much stronger feelings of pride and hope than did either Bush or Dukakis (see Table 6-4). Of course, tremendous pride and hope was felt by his own supporters, especially by blacks. Remarkably, Robertson supporters were the most likely of the other candidate groups to say that Jackson made them feel hopeful and proud.[5] Indeed, more Robertson supporters said Jackson made them feel hopeful and proud than did supporters of Michael Dukakis, Al Gore, or Richard Gephardt. This result is surprising because members of theologically conservative denominations tend to oppose liberal civil rights policies and affirmative action. And there is often deep animosity between civil rights activists and religious fundamentalists. The most plausible ex-

Table 6-4 Feelings about Jesse Jackson

Respondents	*Makes you feel hopeful*	*Makes you feel proud*	*(N)*
Populist groups			
All Robertson supporters	64%	58%	(77)
All Jackson supporters	86	83	(313)
Black Jackson supporters	93	97	(126)
Other groups			
All Bush supporters	39	39	(756)
All Dukakis supporters	50	49	(510)
White Dukakis supporters	44	43	(421)
White Gore supporters	29	35	(168)
Total national sample	46	46	

Source: 1988 National Election Study.

planation is that Jackson's ministerial persona and the biblical cadences of his speeches—coupled with his traditional messages about sexual responsibility, drugs, and educational excellence—appealed to those cultural conservatives who responded to Robertson's candidacy.[6] Indeed, Robertson himself has written favorably of Jackson's message to young people.[7]

There is evidence that considerable respect went in the other direction as well, though not to the same degree. The much-documented "negatives" attached to Robertson, for example, were far less pronounced among blacks than among whites. On a thermometer scale of 0 to 100, with 0 "cool" and 100 "warm," 63 percent of all whites recorded cool responses (below 50) to Robertson, compared with 48 percent of blacks.[8] Similarly, Jackson supporters were less likely to view Robertson negatively than were other groups of candidate backers of either party. The following are percentages (by candidate preference) of those recording cool, or negative, responses to Robertson in the Super Tuesday survey: Dukakis, 69 percent; Gore, 63 percent; Dole, 54 percent; Bush, 46 percent; and Jackson, 44 percent. Again, conventional ideological categories do not explain why the "far right" candidate would be viewed less negatively by supporters of the "far left" candidate than by all those in the middle.[9]

This question revealed tension within the Democratic party as well. White supporters of Gore were the least likely of the Democratic groups to say Jackson made them hopeful or proud. Indeed, of all the candidate groups, Gore supporters expressed the greatest fear of Jackson. One plausible explanation is that Gore's supporters were concentrated among Democratic southerners, who felt more threatened by Jackson and his movement than did Republicans.

For those wedded to conventional notions of left versus right, these findings may seem paradoxical. Yet across the ideological spectrum hope was invested in leadership that carried with it the charisma of spiritual identification. To a pietist Robertson supporter, Jackson spoke a familiar gospel language of Easter promise and "hope in the morning." A close reading of Jackson's speeches shows a remarkable consistency, depth, and eloquence in religious imagery that many evangelicals could identify with. Similarly, Robertson's campaign evoked an evangelical and charismatic theme of racial harmony flowing from the spirit of God. Robertson put his black cohost in charge of "The 700 Club," opened his petition drive in 1986 with a black gospel choir in Constitution Hall, announced his candidacy in a ghetto neighborhood in the Bronx, put black faces in his advertisements, and featured support of prominent black evangelists. His supporters even backed black candidates in Republican intraparty skirmishes.[10] At a spiritual level Robertson's message was that in Christ there is neither black nor white.

If race remains the great crucible for the United States, these religious dimensions deserve scrutiny. The cultural divide that separated Dukakis, the secular technocrat, from Jackson, the black prophet, can be explained in part by religious dynamics. The strange and conflicting tactics in the GOP also arise in part from this mix of religion and race. Republicans wish to increase their share of the black vote, hoping to avoid electoral disasters such as the loss of the Senate in 1986 (yet they cannot seem to resist the temptation to use race baiting to gain white votes). For Republican strategists such as the late Lee Atwater this desire means the GOP must appeal to an emerging black middle class—a more affluent and probably more secular group of blacks—on the basis of economic self-interest. Robertson, on the other hand, appealed to the evangelical and moral dimensions of the black experience. He and his campaign manager both understood his potential appeal to black voters and ran the campaign on the theory that blacks might be an important constituency in a general election.[11] Ironically, in the 1988 campaign it was not "right-wing" Robertson but "centrist" George Bush who exploited racial polarization, fear, and hatred.[12]

RELIGIOUS BELIEFS

Religious faith resists easy pigeonholing: Is it the opiate of the oppressed or the liberator of the poor? Protector of privilege or

Table 6-5 Religious Practices and Beliefs

Respondents	*Religion important* [a]	*Pray several times a day* [b]	*Watch religious programs* [c]	*Born again* [d]	*Religion provides guidance* [e]	*Believe Bible's inerrancy* [f]	*Biblical literalist* [g]
All Robertson supporters	97%	58%	69%	76%	68%	82%	75%
Black Jackson supporters	93	55	67	63	64	68	68
All Bush supporters	79	31	30	42	47	51	36
White Dukakis supporters	78	26	28	37	42	47	19

Source: 1988 National Election Study.

Note: Boldface indicates the response recorded in the corresponding column.

[a] Question: "Do you consider religion to be an important part of your life, or not?" **(Important,** not important)

[b] Question: "About how often do you pray—**several times a day,** once a day, a few times a week, once a week or less, or never?"

[c] Question: "In the past week did you watch or listen to religious programs on radio or TV?" **(Yes,** no)

[d] Question: "Do you consider yourself a born-again Christian?" **(Yes,** no)

[e] Question: "Would you say your religion provides some guidance in your day-to-day living, quite a bit of guidance, or **a great deal of guidance** in your day-to-day life?"

[f] Question: "Here are four statements about the Bible, and I'd like you to tell me which is the closest to your own view. Just give me the number of your choice." (1) **The Bible is God's word and all it says is true;** (2) The Bible was written by men inspired by God, but it contains some human errors; (3) The Bible is a good book because it was written by wise men, but God had nothing to do with it; (4) The Bible was written by men who lived so long ago that it is worth very little today.

[g] For comparison purposes these responses from the Super Tuesday survey are included: (1) The **Bible is the actual word of God and is to be taken literally,** word for word; (2) The Bible is the word of God but not everything in it should be taken literally, word for word; (3) The Bible is a book written by men and is not the word of God.

challenger of the status quo? Sustainer of democracy or threat to pluralism? Our purpose is not to resolve these dichotomies, but, as we shall see, there is evidence that faith remains an important element of contemporary populism. This should not surprise us because, as we have seen, populism throughout American history has contained a religious element in its rhetorical style and organizational base.

The NES survey questioned respondents about the importance of religion, orthodoxy, and religious experience. General responses reconfirmed that most Americans are religiously rooted and fairly orthodox in their views. Jackson's and Robertson's partisans, however, were strikingly distinct in the depth, intensity, and degree of orthodoxy.

Table 6-5 compares the responses of Robertson, black Jackson, Bush, and white Dukakis backers to a number of questions about religion. We find a notable similarity between Robertson's supporters and Jackson's black supporters. I have broken out black Jackson and white Dukakis voters because they reflected more closely the core backers of the two candidates in the primaries and also because such a comparison provides a sharper, more meaningful contrast.[13] The NES asked respondents whether religion was important to them or not. Nearly 78 percent of the national sample said religion was important. Given the strength of this response, we would not expect to find much difference between groups of candidate supporters, and we do not. From Bush to Gore, Dukakis to Jackson, supporter groups hovered around the 80 percent range in responses. Two groups, however, registered near-unanimous sentiment about the personal importance of religion: black Jackson supporters (93 percent) and Robertson supporters (97 percent).

Supporters of these two contemporary populist leaders also adhered to a distinctly pietistic religious practice. Another question asked respondents how often they pray, from "several times a day" to "never."[14] Half the respondents indicated that they prayed at least daily, but 30 percent said they prayed several times a day, an indication of religious practice beyond the routine dinner-time invocation. Not surprisingly, Robertson supporters were the most likely to say they prayed several times a day, but black Jackson supporters averaged nearly equivalent responses. Indeed, a strong majority of black Jackson supporters and Robertson backers said they prayed several times a day, in contrast to all other candidate supporters, whose positive responses on that question hovered at approximately a third. White Jackson supporters were indistinguishable from other Democratic groups, indicating that Jackson's black support was distinct on religious lines.

Another question asked whether religion provided guidance in the person's day-to-day living. In the national sample nearly 47 percent said religion provided "a great deal" of guidance (as opposed to "quite a bit" or "some"). Supporters of Bush, Dole, Kemp, Dukakis, and Gore were near the national average in their responses to the question, but black supporters of Jackson and Robertson backers were distinct and apparently similar in the intensity of their religious conviction. Approximately 68 percent of the Robertson supporters and 64 percent of the black Jackson supporters said religion provided a great deal of guidance in their day-to-day lives.

It is important to note that black evangelical religion is unique in American history for its emphasis on prophetic and liberationist messages. Thus questions about the importance of religion, prayer, and guidance do not necessarily tap into differences between black and white religionists. Nonetheless, religion is extremely important to followers of the two ministers and thus corroborates the populist profile. Moreover, we can begin to understand why Jackson's ministerial role was so critical in his presidential bids. African American voters apparently are people of deep faith and religious practice, and they likely responded to Jackson's religious message as well as to his political one.

A kind of religious orthodoxy also brings the two populist groups together. One of the most interesting similarities between Robertson's backers and Jackson's black supporters was the extent to which they watched or listened to religious broadcasts. The survey asked whether the respondent had watched or listened to a religious program in the past week. Approximately a third of the national sample said "yes" (a notable finding in itself). Most candidate partisans registered comparable rates; however, 69 percent of the Robertson backers and 67 percent of the black Jackson supporters said they had watched or listened to religious programming, figures far above those for the other candidates. Given that religious broadcasting is dominated by evangelical or charismatic expression, it is likely that the black Jackson supporters and Robertson backers watched the same kind of programs. Indeed, as Clyde Wilcox discovered, a third of the blacks in Washington, D.C., watch "The 700 Club," 13 percent regularly.[15]

We find the greatest difference between white Jackson supporters and black Jackson supporters on this question—a difference of 35 percentage points—because Jackson's white supporters were indistinguishable from the general population. No doubt this pattern helps to explain why blacks as a group are more likely to view Robertson positively than are whites.

Black Jackson supporters and Robertson backers were also more likely than other groups to be "born again" and to adhere to a literal view of the Bible or a belief in biblical inerrancy. Recalling our exploration of Bryan and nineteenth-century populism, we see here the possibility that populism can take both morally conservative and economically progressive forms, each supported by traditional religious practice. For American blacks, most of whom supported Jackson, support for progressive politics is not inconsistent with pietistic religion.[16]

Both the National Election Study and the Super Tuesday survey asked whether respondents considered themselves born-again Christians. Approximately 35 percent of the respondents in the NES survey said "yes," 50 percent said "no," and the remaining responses were missing or unrecordable. When only "yes" or "no" responses were tabulated, the figures recorded were 41 percent "yes" and 59 percent "no."[17] Breakdowns by candidates were strikingly distinct. In the NES sample the top two groups were black Jackson supporters and Robertson backers, with only the Gore group even close. In the Super Tuesday sample the same pattern emerged, although the numbers were higher overall.

Some interesting wrinkles can be seen in the Super Tuesday findings. A gulf appeared between Dukakis's supporters (his Super Tuesday voters were even less evangelical than his national group) and Gore's backers (who were strongly born again). Still, compared with the other candidates, Jackson and Robertson received the greatest share of their total support from born-again voters.

The same pattern emerges when we look at the respondents' view of the Bible. Robertson supporters and black Jackson supporters adhere to a more orthodox view of Scripture than do backers of other candidates. The two surveys asked slightly different questions about the Bible. The National Election Study asked respondents to indicate which of the following statements was closest to their own view (the numbers in parentheses indicate the percentage of the national sample selecting that response after unrecordable responses were excluded):

1. The Bible is God's word and all it says is true (49 percent).
2. The Bible was written by men inspired by God, but it contains some human errors (41 percent).
3. The Bible is a good book because it was written by wise men, but God had nothing to do with it (6 percent).
4. The Bible was written by men who lived so long ago that it is worth very little today (2 percent).

This question tended to elicit the respondents' beliefs about biblical inerrancy, the view that Scripture is the true word of God. Most candidate groups were close to the 50 percent mark on this question, conforming to the national average; however, 82 percent of Robertson's supporters and 68 percent of Jackson's black supporters affirmed their belief in biblical inerrancy.

The Super Tuesday survey gives additional insight here. Unlike respondents in the national survey, Super Tuesday respondents were concentrated in the southern Bible Belt. They were asked about biblical literalism, the belief that the Bible is to be taken literally, word for word, a view that scholars have shown to be distinct from the more broadly held belief in inerrancy. Adherents of biblical inerrancy can still believe that the Bible must be interpreted and that humans can make errors in understanding its meaning. Literalists, however, eschew conscious interpretation and take the Bible as literally true, word for word. (These distinctions often demarcate evangelical from fundamentalist believers.) The results of the survey revealed the extent to which Jackson's and Robertson's supporters shared a literal view of Scripture. Super Tuesday voters were asked which of the following statements most closely described their feelings about the Bible (the numbers in parentheses indicate the percentage of the total sample indicating each response):

1. The Bible is the actual word of God and is to be taken literally, word for word (39 percent).
2. The Bible is the word of God but not everything in it should be taken literally, word for word (53 percent).
3. The Bible is a book written by men and is not the word of God (8 percent).

When we break these results down by candidate preference, we see the orthodoxy of Jackson and Robertson supporters. Only among the Jackson and Robertson supporters did a majority of the respondents take the literalist position. The orthodoxy was even more pronounced among Jackson's black supporters, who resembled Robertson pietists in the South. This Super Tuesday finding reinforces the conclusion that a religious gulf (in addition to a political one) separated Bush's supporters from Robertson's and Dukakis's from Jackson's.

To summarize, we see a consistent pattern of religious conviction and orthodoxy among the supporters of Jackson and Robertson. Moreover, the religious similarity between Robertson supporters and black supporters of Jackson is striking, as is the likeness between Bush supporters and white supporters of Dukakis. Apparently, the religious overtones of the nineteenth-century populists reverberate in our supposedly secular age, as modern-day Bryans appeal to a distinct group of fervent voters. To be sure, racial pride was central to Jackson's candidacy, but evidence from the surveys suggests that even among blacks there were differences. Dukakis's black support, for example, was less pious than was Jackson's black support. This examination of the religious dimensions of populism suggests that something other than "mere politics" was operating in the 1988 campaign.

Table 6-6 Candidate Preference by Gender

Respondents	*Male*	*Female*	*(N)*
Populist groups			
All Robertson supporters	30%	70%	(77)
All Jackson supporters	37	63	(314)
Black Jackson supporters	28	72	(126)
Other groups			
All Bush supporters	46	54	(764)
All Dukakis supporters	40	60	(517)
Total national sample	43	57	

Source: 1988 National Election Study.

Note: Respondents could also express preferences for a candidate in the other party.

GENDER, RACE, AND CLASS

The populist mobilization in 1988 drew support from distinct segments of the electorate. Jackson and Robertson supporters, as a group, more typically were female, minority, and working class when compared with backers of the two ministers' primary opponents. In these and in other ways Jackson and Robertson supporters resembled each other.

The most dramatic example of this similarity was the gender gap among candidate supporters. Women respondents outnumbered men by about 55 percent to 45 percent.[18] When we break down the results by candidate preference and by race, we find that certain groups of women responded uniquely to the populist cultural and economic messages of the two ministers. Fully 70 percent of Robertson's supporters and 72 percent of Jackson's black supporters were female (see Table 6-6.).

The Super Tuesday survey is an interesting complement to the National Election Study. There were more male voters in the sixteen Super Tuesday states than in the national sample (51 percent), but Robertson supporters were disproportionately female (61 percent), as were Jackson's supporters (56 percent). These results suggest that the black electorate in the South is far less heavily female than nationally, reflecting important cultural differences. Other distinct patterns emerged. Bush appealed disproportionately to male voters on Super Tuesday. Not only were 57 percent of his supporters men, but the majority of all Republican male backers supported him, in contrast to GOP women, the majority of whom supported others, primarily Dole and Robertson.[19] This pattern was especially advantageous to Bush because men outvote women in the South.

It is important to place these findings in context. If we can believe the NES survey, Jackson's disproportionate support from women in the national sample was due to the fact that nearly 70 percent of the black electorate is female.[20] Thus Jackson's huge support from the black community gave him a predominately female voting base. Dukakis, in fact, actually drew a greater percentage (and a greater raw number) of white women to his candidacy than did Jackson. We must remember that on the Republican side the vast majority of women (and men) expressed preferences for candidates other than Robertson, who appealed to a relatively narrow, if fervent, segment of the evangelical community. Still, the disproportionate response of women to Robertson's candidacy suggests that his message about the breakup of families, the crisis in public education, and the victimization of children resonated with women, or at least with a group of women especially anxious about the drift of secular society.[21]

A gender dimension also emerges when we compare Kemp and Robertson supporters. Commentators in the primaries suggested that Kemp and Robertson, as "conservatives," were competing for the same support from the GOP right wing. Survey results suggest, however, that their supporters were distinct. Kemp's national backers were far more likely to be male (61 percent) and Robertson's female (70 percent). Robertson also appealed more to blacks than did Kemp, and his backers were more fervently religious. Kemp enjoyed support, it would seem, from the "enterpriser" wing of the conservative movement. Tactically, Bush effectively preempted Kemp's potential support just as he did the born-again vote. Neither Robertson nor Kemp could cut deeply enough into Bush's popularity among moralists or enterprisers to keep the nomination from him.

Although support for Robertson and Jackson was heavily female, responses to questions about women's role in society were markedly different between their backers. Jackson's black supporters were ardently feminist, a position toward which Robertson supporters were decidedly unsympathetic. The National Election Study asked respondents whether "women should have an equal role with men in running business, industry, and government" or whether "women's place is in the home." On a seven-point scale, 1 indicated complete agreement with the feminist position, 7 indicated complete agreement with the traditional position, and 4 was in-between. The majority of all respondents in both parties agreed with the feminist position, with slightly less than half marking 1 (complete agreement) on the scale. The supporters of the two ministers split dramatically: Jackson backers took the most feminist position of

Table 6-7 View of Women's Role

Question: "Recently there has been a lot of talk about women's rights. Some people feel that women should have an equal role with men in running business, industry, and government. Others feel that women's place is in the home. Where would you place yourself on [a seven-point] scale, or haven't you thought much about this?" [a]

Respondents	*Support equal role* [b]	*(N)*
Right-wing populist group		
All Robertson supporters	26%	(73)
Other groups		
All Jackson supporters	51	(296)
Black Jackson supporters	52	(113)
All Bush supporters	45	(734)
All Dukakis supporters	45	(494)

Source: 1988 National Election Study.

[a] On a seven-point scale, responses could range from (1) "Women and men should have an equal role" to (7) "Women's place is in the home."
[b] The column records (1), the most feminist response.

all candidate groups and Robertson backers the most traditional (see Table 6-7).

The racial element presented interesting crosscurrents as well. Robertson's relative popularity among black voters is notable. Other Republican candidates received only single-digit support from blacks, while 17 percent of Robertson's national backers were black. And, as previously noted, blacks as a group registered more "warm" sentiment toward Robertson than did whites. Blacks, of course, identify almost exclusively with the Democratic party, and more than 90 percent of black voters chose Jackson in the primaries. Yet many of those same black voters registered remarkable sympathy for Robertson in election surveys. In the Super Tuesday primaries, for example, almost one-third of blacks rated Robertson more warmly than all other white candidates (including Democratic ones). Still more telling, one-fourth of all blacks surveyed said Robertson was their favorite Republican candidate, while only 10 percent of whites responded similarly. Robertson's paradoxical support among blacks, as Wilcox demonstrates, is based in religious factors such as a belief in biblical inerrancy, a born-again experience, and a tendency to view religious programming. Apparently, a greater proportion of blacks than whites watch religious programming. Keenly aware of this fact, Robertson believed that he could have won as much as 25 percent of the black vote in a general election—more than twice what Republican presidential candidates tend to garner. Thus although many blacks would disagree with Robertson's positions on certain issues, Robertson felt he could appeal to black voters on religious grounds.

In some ways race defines the American electorate.[22] As a group black voters are more likely than white voters to fit our populist profile. Black voters are more likely than whites to express discontent with the direction of society, to feel that elites do not care what they think, and to view government as controlled by big interests. They consistently support more populist positions than do whites on issues concerning wealth, taxation, and social spending. In addition, as a group they are more likely than whites to be religiously rooted, pious, and orthodox in their beliefs.

Table 6-8 contrasts the responses of blacks and whites on questions about discontent and elites and notes the responses of black Jackson supporters and Robertson supporters. Blacks, as we see, are more pessimistic about the nation than are whites. In addition, the biggest gap between whites and blacks can be seen in a question that tapped feelings about equal opportunity. In contrast to whites, the vast majority of blacks agreed with the statement that the problem is "we don't give everyone an equal chance." Blacks who supported Jackson expressed greater populist responses than other blacks. Thus it appears that the least disenchanted group of blacks was the most likely to back other candidates. The comparison also illustrates how distinctive Robertson supporters were in their appraisal of the nation and, ironically, how similar they were to blacks generally and to black supporters of Jackson. Even on the equal opportunity question, an issue that resonates uniquely with the black experience, Robertson's white supporters were more likely than other whites to see the lack of opportunity as a problem.

Presumably, class also affects populist sentiment. Unfortunately, we do not have good data on this issue. Evidence suggests, however, that supporters of Jackson and Robertson were less elite than other candidate partisans. Respondents were asked to place themselves in one of eight categories, including lower class; average working, working, and upper working class; average middle, middle, and upper middle class; and upper class. Typical of Americans, hardly anyone listed lower class or upper class, but responses clustered in two categories, average working and average middle.[23] On the Democratic side the class dimension is most evident. Although 44 percent of those expressing a preference for a

Table 6-8 Populist Response by Candidate Preference and Race (Percentage of respondents)

Respondents	*Nation not going well* [a]	*No say in government* [b]	*Officials don't care* [c]	*Government run by big interests* [d]	*Don't give equal chance* [e]
Populist groups					
All Robertson supporters	53	53	60	86	57
Black Jackson supporters	58	61	65	82	87
Race					
Blacks	48	56	60	73	83
Whites	33	39	49	66	47

Source: 1988 National Election Study.

[a] Question: "Let's talk about the country as a whole. Would you say that things in the country are generally going along very well, fairly well, not too well, or not well at all?" (The column combines responses of "not too well" and "not well at all.")

[b] Question: "People like me don't have any say about what the government does." (Possible responses were agree strongly, agree somewhat, neither agree nor disagree, disagree somewhat, disagree strongly. The column combines responses of "agree strongly" and "agree somewhat.")

[c] Question: "I don't think public officials care much about what people like me think." (Possible responses were agree strongly, agree somewhat, neither agree nor disagree, disagree somewhat, disagree strongly. The column combines responses of "agree strongly" and "agree somewhat.")

[d] Question: "Would you say the government is pretty much run by a few big interests looking out for themselves or that it is run for the benefit of all the people?" (For the benefit of all, few big interests.)

[e] Question: "One of the big problems in this country is that we don't give everyone an equal chance." (Possible responses were agree strongly, agree somewhat, neither agree nor disagree, disagree somewhat, disagree strongly. The column combines responses of "agree strongly" and "agree somewhat.")

Democratic candidate identified themselves as "average working class," 58 percent of Jackson's supporters (and 63 percent of his black supporters) so identified themselves. On the Republican side the differences did not emerge as statistically significant, yet Robertson's supporters appeared the least elite of the GOP partisans.

This pattern came out more noticeably in the Super Tuesday survey. One question asked simply whether the respondent's family income was less than or more than $30,000. A large majority of Jackson's and Robertson's supporters recorded family income under $30,000, with higher percentages than any other group of candidate backers (see Table 6-9). This disparity in income may help to explain the tension that

Table 6-9 Candidate Preference by Income

Respondents	*Income under $30,000*	*(N)*
Populist groups		
All Robertson supporters	62%	(91)
All Jackson supporters	60	(135)
Other groups		
All Bush supporters	44	(464)
All Dukakis supporters	54	(123)
All Gore supporters	51	(74)

Source: Super Tuesday survey.

erupted during the campaign between Robertson newcomers and Republican regulars.

That this mixture of race, gender, and religion affects people's responses to Jackson and Robertson should not surprise us. Gallup Poll surveys of the nation consistently record differences between the sexes and races on the basis of religion. In the 1990 Gallup survey of the nation, for example, women and blacks were far more likely to say religion is very important to them than were men and whites (see Table 6-10). Of those responding that religion is very important, a gap of 15 percentage points was found between men and women and a gap of 24 percentage points between blacks and whites. Thus when populist ministers launch crusades, we see a disproportionate response from women and blacks.

ECONOMIC VIEWS AND CULTURAL ATTITUDES

We have seen the similarities between the populist supporters of Jackson and Robertson in 1988. We will now look at the ways in which contemporary populism has split into right-wing and left-wing versions. In the nineteenth century populists were likely to blend progressive economics with conservative views on cultural issues such as sexual restraint, temperance, and the like. Although contemporary populists converge somewhat in their views on these concerns, Jackson's supporters (especially his black supporters) usually fit the economically populist profile, while Robertson's backers tend to be cultural populists.

The National Election Study asked a series of questions about personal finances and the economy. Black supporters of Jackson, not

Table 6-10 Importance of Religion by Sex and Race
(Percentage of respondents)

Question: "How important would you say religion is in your own life: very important, somewhat important, or not very important?"

Respondents	*Very important*	*Somewhat important*	*Not very important*
Male	48	32	18
Female	63	28	9
White	53	32	14
Black	77	17	4

Source: Gallup Survey of the Nation, 1990, as reported in *Emerging Trends,* April 1991.
Note: Percentages may not equal 100 because of rounding.

surprisingly, were the most likely to have experienced economic distress and to view matters pessimistically; Bush supporters were at the opposite end. Robertson backers were less optimistic than Bush backers but were not as pessimistic as Jackson supporters. One question, for example, asked whether the respondent had been hurt or helped by the "Reagan administration economic program." Nationally, the sentiment was almost evenly balanced, with a quarter recording "hurt," a quarter recording "helped," and the remaining half saying it made no difference. Differences among supporters of all candidates were not great, even across party lines, except that backers of Bush and Gore were disproportionately upbeat, while black supporters of Jackson were gloomy about their personal experiences under the Reagan program. Only 6 percent of the black Jackson supporters said that the Reagan economic program had helped them; 44 percent said it had hurt.

Reagan's presidency, as we saw in Chapter 4, energized the black electorate and helped infuse Jackson's candidacy with its remarkable fervor. Here, in part, we see why. Many of Jackson's backers, especially his black supporters, experienced the Reagan years as a time of personal economic loss, and few saw gains. In contrast, Bush voters (and many Gore supporters) experienced bullish years, suggesting that a retrospective evaluation was being made of the Reagan era. Robertson supporters tipped the scales in a slightly negative direction, with more having been hurt than helped. Thus Robertson's implied criticism of Reagan economics (especially of deficit spending) would have made sense to many of his followers. Still, the marked similarity we found earlier between Jackson and Robertson backers does not exist here.

Table 6-11 View of Reagan Economy

Question: "Is the economy better, no different, or worse as a result of Reagan's policies?"

Respondents	*Better*	*No different*	*Worse*	*(N)*
Left-wing populist groups				
All Jackson supporters	22%	46%	32%	(283)
Black Jackson supporters	9	53	38	(111)
Other groups				
All Robertson supporters	39	33	29	(70)
All Bush supporters	56	34	10	(685)
All Dukakis supporters	29	44	27	(452)
All Gore supporters	51	30	18	(165)
Total national sample	41	39	21	

Source: 1988 National Election Study.
Note: Percentages may not equal 100 because of rounding.

When asked whether the Reagan economy had been good for the nation, more respondents answered optimistically than when personal finances alone were considered. In the 1988 NES survey approximately 41 percent of the respondents said the economy was better as a result of Reagan's policies, 39 percent said it was no different, and 21 percent said it was worse (see Table 6-11). Some people apparently thought Reagan's economic policies were good for the nation even though their personal situation had taken a turn for the worse. Again supporters of Bush and Gore were the most bullish on the Reagan years, with more than half saying the economy was better as a result of Reagan's policies. Only 9 percent of the Jackson backers said the economy was better, and 38 percent said it was worse as result of Reaganomics.

This assessment of the Reagan economy is revealing. No doubt many of those preferring Gore, especially those in the South, backed Bush against Dukakis in the general election, and we can see why: they were uniquely optimistic about Reaganomics. Conversely, Jackson backers were pessimistic in their assessment of the Reagan era. The same pattern emerged when respondents were questioned about unemployment. Approximately 53 percent of black Jackson supporters said that unemployment was worse as a result of Reaganomics, and only 16 percent said it was better. Reverse the numbers, and you have the profile of Bush supporters: 52 percent said unemployment was better, 17 percent said worse. Robertson supporters, though not as upbeat as Bush supporters, were close to the national average. The point is that Jackson did not rally all economically discontented voters to his candidacy, but his supporters were disproportionately gloomy in their assessment of the economic state of the nation.

Was the populist outburst in 1988 the result of short-term economic forces? Apparently not. One question in the National Election Study looked at short-term changes by asking whether the respondent's personal finances were better or worse than they were three years ago. Except for Bush supporters, whose short-term economic fortunes were disproportionately rosy, there were no statistically significant differences between the other candidate groups. Most Americans did not see their short-term economic situation deteriorate, and a healthy 42 percent saw improvements. The more pessimistic assessments apparently tapped into long-range expectations and perceptions.

If Jackson supporters were more pessimistic about the economy than other candidate groups, they were correspondingly more inclined to support government efforts to help the poor and unemployed, a pattern typical of black voters. Just as nineteenth-century populists called for public efforts to redress economic inequality, contemporary backers of Jesse Jackson supported such measures. Robertson backers were the least conservative of the Republican groups on this question, a finding not so startling when we remember that his supporters were the least elite of the Republican candidate groups. Still, Jackson's backers most closely conform to the populist economic profile.

On a host of questions, as other surveys have shown, African Americans are economic progressives—concerned about unemployment, hunger, and poverty—and they are willing to see taxes (especially taxes on the rich) used to ameliorate inequality. In this sense, they are the true modern heirs of nineteenth-century populists and progressives, who challenged the assumptions of social Darwinism.

When we turn to cultural matters, however, Robertson voters emerged as distinct in their populist critique of contemporary culture. If Jackson backers are not sanguine about the economic benefits of the free market, Robertson supporters are no less critical of the free market in terms of morals and lifestyles. Each group, in its own way, criticizes the ascendant liberal order.

Several questions in the National Election Study touched on cultural discontent and attitudes about morals and lifestyles. What we find is that general public sentiment was mixed and not altogether consistent; sometimes traditional attitudes were dominant, other times liberal. Robertson supporters, however, either were more consistently conservative or they responded with greater intensity. For example, one question asked whether there should be more emphasis on traditional family ties;

Table 6-12 View of Traditional Values and Newer Lifestyles *(Percentage of respondents)*

Question: "This country would have fewer problems if there were more emphasis on traditional family ties."

Question: "Newer lifestyles are leading to the breakdown of society."

Respondents	*Stress family ties*[a]	*Newer lifestyles lead to breakdown*[a]
Right-wing populist groups		
All Robertson supporters	70	65
White Robertson supporters	74	71
Other groups		
All Jackson supporters	44	35
Black Jackson supporters	40	34
All Bush supporters	45	38
All Dukakis supporters	48	36
Total national sample	48	37

Source: 1988 National Election Study.

Note: While other respondent groups hovered close to the national average, only the Robertson groups were different to a statistically significant degree.

[a] Possible responses were "strongly agree," "agree," "neither agree nor disagree," "disagree," and "strongly disagree." The column records responses of those "strongly agreeing."

respondents were asked to place their answers on a five-point scale (strongly agree, agree, neither, disagree, strongly disagree). Apparently, this question touched apple-pie feelings of the respondents. Approximately 48 percent strongly agreed, and 34 percent agreed. There were no statistically significant differences between the groups of candidate backers, except for the Robertson group, 70 percent of whom strongly agreed. Although a large majority of the electorate agreed (in principle) about traditional family ties, Robertson backers felt more strongly than other groups about this issue. (See Table 6-12.)

Respondents were also asked whether "newer lifestyles are leading to the breakdown of society" and were given the same five-point scale for responses. Of those who answered the question, approximately 73 percent agreed (37 percent agreed strongly), a remarkable public embrace of "traditional values." Again no distinct differences between candidate groups were noticeable, except for the Robertson backers, whose responses were nearly unanimous and intensely felt. Indeed, 92 percent of the Robertson backers affirmed the statement, with 65 percent agreeing strongly. The point is that Robertson's profamily message, and his implied castigation of alternative lifestyles, was not necessarily unpopular; his supporters merely felt more intensely an opinion that many Americans share. Jackson supporters were not distinguishable from the national sample, nor were other candidate groups.

The Super Tuesday survey confirmed these basic patterns and brought forth some additional findings. Although Robertson supporters again disproportionately agreed that newer lifestyles lead to societal breakdown (72 percent agreeing), Dukakis's Super Tuesday supporters emerged as the most liberal group (57 percent disagreeing). To be sure, Bush's deep support on Super Tuesday meant that his candidacy attracted a large number of supporters across the cultural spectrum. Thus while Dukakis's narrower support was comparatively more "New Age" and Robertson's was more traditional, Bush's larger tent probably attracted sizable numbers on both sides of the cultural divide. The distinctiveness of Robertson's supporters, compared with those of other candidates, again emerged strongly.

If Americans appeared traditional on questions of "family ties" and "alternative lifestyles," they responded more liberally to questions about tolerating different moral standards and adjusting morality to fit the times. It is tempting to conclude that although most citizens believed "new morality" is leading to societal breakdown they were nonetheless willing to tolerate it. Yet the ambiguity of wording on this question probably influenced respondents' answers. "Tolerance" is imbued with positive connotations; after all who wants to appear intolerant? At any rate, approximately 60 percent of the public agreed that "we should be more tolerant of people who choose to live according to their own moral standards." Only 42 percent of the Robertson supporters responded positively, however, and 45 percent disagreed. Once again Robertson backers were the only group of candidate supporters who differed significantly from the national average on this question.

Another question asked whether respondents agreed with the statement that "we should adjust our view of moral behavior" to the changing times. The public was ambivalent on this question, with 49 percent agreeing, 41 disagreeing, and 10 percent neutral. Robertson supporters were not as ambivalent; 61 percent disagreed (51 percent disagreed strongly). Again Robertson supporters emerged as the most strongly traditional group. In contrast, only 31 percent of black supporters of Jackson disagreed with the statement (see Table 6-13).

We find the same pattern on attitudes to issues such as abortion and homosexuality. The National Election Study asked respondents which

Table 6-13 Opinion on Adjusting Moral Views

Question: "The world is always changing and we should adjust our view of moral behavior to those changes."

Respondents	*Disagree*[a]	*(N)*
Right-wing populist group		
All Robertson supporters	61%	(72)
Other groups		
Black Jackson supporters	31	(101)
All Bush supporters	42	(659)
All Dukakis supporters	37	(447)
White Gore supporters	53	(156)

Source: 1988 National Election Study.

[a] The column combines responses of "disagree" and "strongly disagree." Respondents could also mark "strongly agree," "agree," and "no opinion."

one of the following statements best reflected their view on abortion (the numbers in parentheses are percentages of the total sample agreeing with that statement):

1. By law abortion should never be permitted (13 percent).
2. The law should permit abortion only in case of rape, incest, or when the woman's life is in danger (33 percent).
3. The law should permit abortion for reasons other than rape, incest, or danger to the woman's life, but only after the need for the abortion has been clearly established (19 percent).
4. By law a woman should always be able to obtain an abortion as a matter of personal choice (36 percent).

Although Americans are ambivalent on the question of abortion, with a majority neither willing to ban it entirely nor to allow it unconditionally, Robertson supporters are the most heavily weighted toward the restrictive end. Indeed, approximately 72 percent of Robertson's supporters would either ban abortion or restrict it to cases of rape, incest, and threat to the mother's life. Several other findings also emerged. Sentiment on abortion, for example, was roughly the same across party lines, providing a stark contrast to party platforms that push the extremes. Moreover, 20 percent of Jackson supporters would ban abortion outright, a higher percentage than any of the other candidate groups except Robertson's. This percentage was the same for Jackson's black supporters and white supporters, indicat-

Table 6-14 Views on Abortion

Respondents	*Never permit*	*Permit conditionally*[a]	*Woman's choice*	*(N)*
Right-wing populist group				
All Robertson supporters[b]	36.0%	49.0%	14.0%	(77)
Other groups				
All Jackson supporters	20.0	43.0	37.0	(311)
All Bush supporters	12.0	53.0	35.0	(757)
All Dukakis supporters	14.0	51.0	35.0	(511)
Total national sample	13.0	51.5	35.5	

Source: 1988 National Election Study.

Note: Percentages may not equal 100 because of rounding.

[a] The column combines the middle two responses, which would accept legal abortion only under certain conditions.

[b] While other respondent groups hovered close to the national average, only the Robertson group was different to a statistically significant degree.

ing that a significant subgroup of his supporters held very conservative views on abortion. The general pattern holds, however: Robertson backers were disproportionately traditional on the abortion issue. (See Table 6-14.)

The survey also asked respondents whether they favored or opposed laws to protect homosexuals against job discrimination. The public was deeply divided on this issue, with 52 percent in favor of antidiscriminatory laws, 44 percent against, and 3 percent answering that "it depends." Robertson backers were not so divided; 64 percent opposed such laws. (See Table 6-15.)

Again Robertson supporters were the most conservative on this issue (with white Gore supporters somewhat conservative). Jackson supporters, especially his black voters, were decidedly liberal. There is obviously a racial dimension to this question that appears to touch concerns about discrimination and equal treatment uniquely salient to blacks. Even Robertson's black supporters, who were not generally distinct from his white supporters on most issues, diverged dramatically here. Similarly, Jackson's black supporters as a group were more liberal than his white backers on this question. Still, it is important to note that the issue tends to polarize. Almost a third of Jackson's black supporters opposed laws to protect homosexuals from discrimination, not taking advantage of the middle category that registered ambiguous feelings.

Table 6-15 Opinion on Protecting Homosexuals

Question: "Do you favor or oppose laws to protect homosexuals against job discrimination?"

Respondents	*Favor*	*Depends*	*Oppose*	*(N)*
Right-wing populist groups				
All Robertson supporters	35%	1%	64%	(66)
White Robertson supporters	26	2	72	(53)
Other groups				
Black Robertson supporters	75	0	25	(12)
All Jackson supporters	58	3	39	(260)
Black Jackson supporters	67	1	32	(97)
All Bush supporters	50	3	47	(606)
All Dukakis supporters	56	3	41	(405)
All Gore supporters	40	5	55	(148)

Source: 1988 National Election Study.

The surveys spotlighted some revealing dimensions about the southern electorate. In 1988 Gore supporters, concentrated in the South, emerged as a relatively conservative group (culturally, racially, and economically). They serve as a good surrogate for the white southerners so elusive to Democratic presidential candidates in the past two decades—voters that Bill Clinton sought to bring back into the Democratic fold in 1992, when he selected Gore as his running mate. These white Gore supporters were more elite, male, upbeat on Reaganomics, and suspicious of Jackson than were Robertson supporters. If the Jackson campaign capitalized on discontent, racial pride, and religious hope in the black community, the Robertson campaign mobilized charismatics and pietists who do not necessarily fit the stereotype of the southern white conservative (with its racial overtones). This was especially true of Robertson's national support, which included blacks, working-class folk, and whites who said Jesse Jackson made them feel hopeful. One way to understand this apparent paradox is to note that Pentecostals and charismatics, who formed the core of Robertson's support, were relatively progressive among evangelicals on racial issues. Indeed, historically, some Pentecostal churches were biracial, and a number of charismatics are more comfortable working side by side with fellow black religionists than are many other whites.

SUMMARY

Let us crystallize our findings about the followers of the two gospel populists. In 1988 the typical Jackson voter was black, female, working class, and a born-again Christian. She was church rooted, a viewer of religious broadcasting, orthodox in belief, both pietistic and prophetic in her understanding of Scripture, progressive on economics and civil rights, and a feminist. The typical Robertson supporter was white, female, working class to middle class, and a born-again Christian. She was church rooted, a viewer of religious broadcasting, orthodox in belief, pietistic, conservative on cultural issues, cool to feminists, and an admirer of Jesse Jackson. These two groups may diverge on opinions about women's rights, abortion, and economics, but they share a religious world view, a perception that elites are not listening to them, and a pessimistic assessment about the course of the nation.[24]

On a theoretical level I have suggested that contemporary populism, echoing the views of earlier populists, expresses a communitarian critique of our ascendant individualistic society. We find some evidence for this assertion, though certainly more research is necessary. Robertson supporters, for example, seemed especially concerned about the consequences of the liberal cultural marketplace, with its lack of moral certitudes, its sanction of alternative lifestyles, its disruption of family integrity. As conservative Christians, Robertson supporters also affirmed the idea of individual responsibility, and in that sense they were individualists. Yet modern individualism, as expressed in popular culture, emphasizes the unrestrained and (some would say) irresponsible individualism of hedonism. Thus the emphasis on individual responsibility is firmly rooted in communitarian norms. In the cultural realm, therefore, we find some corroboration that Robertson appealed to those who believed that the individual should be constrained by timeless religious truths. Jackson's backers, though often sharing this belief, criticized more sharply the consequences of a liberal economic marketplace, with its unconcern for the distribution of wealth and silence about the poor. Thus whereas Robertson backers sanctioned public, communitarian efforts to enforce moral norms in the cultural arena, Jackson supporters backed government programs to soften the effects of the marketplace.

Finally, our contention that a kind of populism in the electorate cuts across the ideological spectrum finds some support. It is not surprising that many citizens on the right and the left express discontent with elites in populist fashion; however, we find a richer vein of populism here, a populism anchored in religious conviction and community concern. We find that groups as apparently disparate as white pietists and blacks resemble each other far more than we might have imagined. Our analysis also confirms that the populist heritage in American politics has to some degree bifurcated, leading to distinct economic and cultural strains represented by Jackson and Robertson. Both camps, however, contain a trace of the other branch. Some of Jackson's African American backers expressed culturally conservative views rooted in traditional religion, and some of Robertson's supporters no doubt shared his critique of economic elites and bankers. Yet the harmonious blend of piety and protest in nineteenth-century populism is heard today as a somewhat discordant duet shaped by partisan and ideological notes. Thus in one campaign cultural discontent may rise to prominence; in another economic issues may predominate.

Nonetheless, one can argue plausibly that there is a kind of ideological consistency that emphasizes both dimensions of the populist critique of liberal society. It is to that argument that we now turn.

NOTES

1. The Super Tuesday survey was conducted between January 17 and March 8 in the sixteen states that held primaries on March 8, 1988. The primaries were in southern or border states except for those in Massachusetts and Rhode Island. The American National Election Study was administered between September 6 and November 7, 1988, well after the primary battles were over. (American National Election Study, 1988 Pre- and Postelection Survey, Inter-University Consortium for Political and Social Research.)
2. Because I was interested in broad national sentiment, not just opinions of activists, I relied on the following candidate preference questions from the NES: "This past year several candidates ran for the Republican presidential nomination. Which one of these candidates do you personally think would make the best president, or don't you have an opinion on this?" and "Which one of these Democratic candidates do you think would make the best president, or don't you have an opinion?" Although not all respondents gave a preference in both parties, many did, thus complicating the analysis. Given the small national sample of Robertson supporters (77 respondents), I chose not to try to isolate what some might view as "pure" Robertson supporters or to use only Robertson Republicans. Unless otherwise noted all relationships hold even when we remove black voters who listed Robertson as their favored GOP candidate (17 percent of this total), meaning that responses for white Robertson backers vary only slightly from those of all Robertson backers.
3. I have chosen to employ relatively straightforward percentages and breakdowns, using chi-square and standard residuals to test for statistical significance rather than more elaborate statistical procedures. Because my intent is merely to indicate some measures of sentiment, not to test hypotheses, the

use of these modest statistical tools seems appropriate.

4. These propositions could have been stated as hypotheses, to be tested rigorously. Given the limitations of the data, however, I chose to abide by the spirit of science and seek merely corroborative evidence for the propositions that I hope will spark further explorations. Too often social scientists overreach the quality of their data.
5. This finding corroborates Garry Wills's contention that it was the middle that exploited race animosity in the 1988 campaign, not the so-called extremes represented by Jackson and Robertson. See Wills, *Under God: Religion and American Politics* (New York: Simon and Schuster, 1990).
6. It is important to note that Robertson's Super Tuesday voters were less favorably inclined toward Jackson than was the sample in the NES survey. In the Super Tuesday sample approximately 49 percent rated Jackson negatively, or "cool," on a "feeling" thermometer scale (0-100). No doubt some will claim that the findings in the national survey are contaminated by the inclusion of the overlap group. I am inclined to think two things: first, that southern supporters of Robertson are distinct from those elsewhere, particularly more affected by racial politics, and second, that the national overlap provides a glimpse of dynamics hidden by the mutually exclusive candidate preferences contained in the Super Tuesday sample.
7. Pat Robertson, *The Plan* (Nashville: Thomas Nelson, 1989), 30.
8. The question was structured so that respondents were told that a score below 50 indicated that they felt cool, or negative, toward that candidate.
9. The classic explanation for this phenomenon is Phillip Converse's theory about the public's lack of ideological constraint. Insightful as his formulation is, my analysis suggests that a kind of ideological consistency can be found in religious piety and populism. I do not doubt, however, that many of those who feel warm to both Jackson and Robertson do not fully comprehend the extent to which the two ministers differ on a number of issues. See Phillip Converse, "The Nature of Belief Systems in Mass Publics," in *Ideology and Discontent*, ed. David Apter (New York: Free Press, 1964).
10. Clyde Wilcox, "Religion and Electoral Politics among Black Americans in 1988," in *The Bible and the Ballot Box: Religion and Politics in the 1988 Election*, ed. James L. Guth and John C. Green (Boulder: Westview Press, 1991), 168.
11. Interviews with Robertson and his campaign manager, Marc Nuttle, revealed these philosophical and strategic assumptions. Robertson remarked that GOP presidential candidates can seek a respectable black vote, but if they do not understand the religious dimension they will never succeed.
12. Wills made this argument in *Under God*. My viewing of campaign tapes and interviews independently confirms this judgment.
13. One problem with the NES survey is that many of those blacks who listed Dukakis as their favored candidate in the fall probably supported Jackson in the spring primaries. Since blacks as a group are more religious than whites, especially among Democrats, this fact would tend to inflate the religious profile of the Dukakis supporters. It makes sense, therefore, to break down the sample into black Jackson supporters and white Dukakis supporters,

because these represented a more meaningful comparison of the core supporters during the primary season.

14. The question included five possible responses: "several times a day" (30 percent in the national sample), "once a day" (25 percent), "a few times a week" (18 percent), "once a week or less" (18 percent), and "never" (8 percent). Very few Americans never pray (or admit that they never pray).
15. Clyde Wilcox, "Blacks and the New Christian Right: Support for the Moral Majority and Pat Robertson among Washington, D.C., Blacks," *Review of Religious Research* 32 (September 1990): 43-56.
16. Black support for liberal positions on economics, civil rights, welfare spending, defense spending, and international relations is well documented. Blacks are less consistently liberal on social issues such as abortion, drugs, gay rights, and pornography.
17. The 35 percent born-again figure is probably closer to the mark than the other figures, but the NES survey followed the technique of tabulating the recordable answers, thus slightly inflating the figure to 41 percent.
18. In the total survey women outnumbered men 57 percent to 43 percent, but when respondents were grouped by candidate preference we see less of a gap, suggesting either that women were less likely to express preferences or that men were more likely to express preferences in both parties (which the survey format allowed) For those expressing Democratic candidate preferences, the gender gap was 56 percent female and 44 percent male, compared with 53.5 percent female and 46.5 percent male on the Republican side.
19. Of all those expressing Republican preferences in the sixteen Super Tuesday states, 56 percent of the men, versus 44 percent of the women, favored Bush.
20. It is possible that survey methods oversampled women among blacks, but the well-documented crisis of the black man in America suggests that the black electorate is heavily female, even if not to the extent suggested by the NES survey.
21. An alternative explanation, which my colleague Ron Peters likes for its simplicity, is that women are more likely than men to watch religious TV and therefore were more likely to support Robertson. Although television may be a factor, my own research indicates that actual concerns and issues were important.
22. Thomas B. Edsall, *Chain Reaction: The Impact of Race, Rights, and Taxes on American Politics* (New York: Norton, 1991).
23. Only two-tenths of 1 percent of respondents said they were lower class, and only one-tenth of 1 percent said they were upper class.
24. We should not allow these profiles to become stereotypes. Many of the Robertson supporters I met on the campaign trail, for example, were young women, "modern" in dress and demeanor, but still generally fitting our profile. Similarly, Jackson's deep support in the black community included not only middle-aged black women but younger professional women (who also tended to fit much of the profile).

7

The Crucible of Liberalism and the Challenges of the Future

Populism, which has been described as the "eternal attempt of people to claim politics as something of theirs," [1] was at the core of the campaigns of Jesse Jackson and Pat Robertson. To the candidates their presidential campaigns were God-ordained, moral quests to represent the hurting, frustrated, anxious voices of people often ignored in calculations by elites. To the followers of these candidates the campaigns embodied an ecstatic moment in which their lives and yearnings rose to prominence. More like continuing social movements than campaigns, the two crusades endured after other candidacies had folded. The Rainbow Coalition and the Christian Coalition continue to pursue "economic justice" and "moral renewal" into the 1990s.

In a literal sense, populist movements usually fail.[2] They fail when unrealistically exalted visions hit the wall of reality. They fail when the chasm widens, as it easily can, between discontent and remedy. In another sense, however, they may succeed in the long run—at least in part. The issues they raise may be addressed by conventional politicians and by the dominant parties seeking votes. The concerns they voice may be legitimated as historians, scholars, and intellectuals become alerted to fevers in the body politic. With the Jackson and Robertson movements, the process of assimilating populist themes and concerns has begun.

The 1988 presidential campaign signaled trends that would affect the nation into the 1990s. From 1988 to 1992 surveys revealed an increasingly testy electorate, alienated or angry with politics as usual.[3] A 1990 CBS News/*New York Times* poll found that 77 percent of the population believed "government is run by a few big interests looking out for themselves." This was the highest percentage recorded in the quarter-century that researchers have used that measure of public alienation. This same voter discontent crested in a term-limitation movement that gave incumbents reason to run scared. Clearly, politics as usual was unacceptable to many citizens.

Writers, consultants, and political figures picked up on these populist themes. Echoing Robertson, Vice President Dan Quayle repeatedly denounced "cultural elites" in the 1992 campaign. Similarly, conservative Paul Weyrich called for a "new populist agenda" that would recognize citizen concerns about "cultural breakdown, a loss of the moral standards and ideals of excellence that make society function." [4] Kevin Phillips, on the other hand, echoed Jackson in his prophetic warning about the yawning gap between rich and poor in America, predicting populist outrage at the new plutocracy that arose during the Reagan years.[5] Another conservative, Charles Murray worried that a new politics of caste might emerge in America as the breach widened between the top 20 percent and the rest of the nation. Murray feared that the growing influence of the highly skilled, coupled with the abandonment of the underclass, might create a conservatism on the Latin American model—in which the powerful use government to "preserve mansions on the hills above the slums." [6] Democratic nominee Bill Clinton picked up these themes, charging that President Bush only looked after his millionaire friends. Even Quayle, as road tester of campaign ideas for the Bush administration, toyed with a populist attack on the "astronomical salaries of corporate chief executive officers." [7] Others suggested that soak-the-rich populism had limits and that "knowledge elites" instead remained a potential target of populist wrath. After all, among the favored 20 percent are television producers, top bureaucrats, and professors.[8]

The problems with routine partisan politics also received attention. E. J. Dionne suggested that Americans have come to hate politics because the traditional fault lines in the two major parties fail to comport with the everyday lives and convictions of the people. Although conservatives defend the free market, they also want to affirm traditional values, which rely on government support. Similarly, although liberals built the welfare state, they shun any talk of the values it should promote or reward, especially the assumption of responsibility. "When it is suggested that the well-being of children [on public assistance] depends on how their parents behave, liberals often try to change the subject." In a sense, the libertarian elements of both parties keep them from treating seriously either the voters' concerns or the broader needs of the polity.[9]

The quest for community that animated Jackson's and Robertson's campaigns found expression in the emergence of a communitarian group of social theorists. Robert Bellah comes to mind, with his critique of corrosive individualism and his call for "communities of memory." [10] But the "dance with community," as Robert Booth Fowler puts it, now ranges across the political spectrum.[11] There is even an attempt underway to fashion a set of communitarian remedies. Critical of the left-wing obsession with individual rights and entitlements and the right-wing glorification of unfettered markets, communitarians such as Amitai Etzioni, Mary Ann Glendon, and Daniel Yankelovich met in Washington, D.C., in November 1991 to offer specific proposals to renew the ethic of "reciprocal obligations," a theme popular with presidential candidate Bill Clinton.[12] Clinton even described his political vision in the puritan communitarian argot of the New Covenant, which captured his view that citizens who enjoy the benefits of society have a moral obligation to give something back.

POPULIST CANDIDATES IN THE EARLY 1990S

On the political front a variety of candidates felt the public pulse and attempted to capitalize on popular discontent. In 1990 maverick Democrat John Silber, president of Boston University, shocked the establishment by winning the Democratic gubernatorial primary in Massachusetts. His win was "shocking" because he, as a Democrat, spoke pointedly about the moral collapse of American society, the country's excessive materialism, the exploitation of children by television, and so forth. Columnist David Broder summarized the failure of the elite press to appreciate the power of Silber's populist message: "It's embarrassing to keep making the same mistake, as I and many others in the establishment press keep doing. Consistently, over more than two decades, we have underestimated the appeal of figures who mobilize public resentment of the political and economic elites." [13] Journalists described Silber as evoking "a kind of egghead populism," with his attacks on welfare dependency, "social engineering," and lax standards in schools.[14] Described as a "prophet of the politics of rage," Silber seemed well positioned for an upset victory, but at the last moment his campaign faltered.[15] He lost in the general election, in large measure because of intemperate, "shoot from the hip" remarks that alienated many blacks and women. In particular, he said he did not need to campaign in some black sections of Boston to "talk to a bunch of addicts." [16] And he implied that two-career couples who put their children in day-care centers were guilty of child neglect to support their "overweening materialism." By election day Silber had alienated enough traditionally Democratic voters to lose a close race to Republican moderate William Weld.

Silber's outrage had the potential of crossing political boundaries; instead, he allowed his campaign to degenerate into a kind of white male populism, presaging the presidential campaign of Patrick Buchanan in 1992. Our study of the populist crosscurrents in American politics suggests that Silber's intemperate tongue obscured the fact that his broader critique of society resonated widely, even with many of the blacks and women he insulted. For example, in his book *Straight Shooting*, Silber echoes Jesse Jackson's views on natural law, educational excellence, and cultural pollution in the mass media.[17] On the nurture of children, Silber's message even matched the cadence of Jackson's. "We had better prepare ourselves and them for reality—a reality that is infused with moral laws as surely as it is infused with physical laws; a reality in which there is no consumption without production, no freedom without defense, no self-fulfillment and no self-government without self-disciplined people who govern themselves." On the mass media, he was equally blunt. "Invaded by television, the home is no longer a sanctuary in which children are protected from the most sordid elements of human experience. The perverse, the sublime and the trivial are presented without moral differentiation, and the result is nothing less than a pollution of their sensibilities. Their minds—indeed, if I may use an old-fashioned term, their souls—are being trashed." Finally, on education Silber repeated Jackson's analysis of the factors undermining educational excellence: the decline of the family, erosion of respect for teachers, lack of high standards, and loss of moral focus in the curriculum.[18] These messages, unencumbered by racial undertones, might well have won Silber the governorship.

Other candidates succeeded in capitalizing on the anxious and angry feelings of voters. One of the most surprising was Democrat Harris Wofford of Pennsylvania, another former college president, whose "populism in tweeds" [19] vented anger at incumbents who seemingly have lost touch with the lives of middle-class Americans. Wofford ran against former attorney general Dick Thornburgh in a special Senate election in 1991 to replace Sen. John Heinz, R-Pa., who died in a plane crash. As Pennsylvania secretary of labor, Wofford had discovered the importance of health insurance to middle-class workers, and he hammered the issue home. His upset victory over Thornburgh brought to bear the economic side of contemporary discontent. Democrats sensed that they had found the Republican party's Achilles' heel.

In the same year we witnessed the spectacle of two different "populists" in the Louisiana gubernatorial election. Neither Edwin Edwards, flamboyant former governor, nor David Duke, former Klansman and neo-Nazi, presented a savory picture of populist politics. Edwards was heir to the "little guy" rhetoric and fast-buck corruption associated with Huey Long populism; Duke simply rekindled the mean politics of racial hatred. With the economy in shambles and voter anxiety rising, Louisiana was a fertile seedbed for resentment and blame; Duke harvested the bitter fruit. Edwards won the runoff, saved by an unusual alliance of blacks and business people who feared that Duke would shut down the state. The Louisiana race, in all its meanness and irresponsibility, provoked David Broder to express contempt for the "populist chic" infecting both right-wing and left-wing intellectual circles.[20]

The presidential campaign of 1992 brought forth a gush of populist expressions on the right and the left. David Duke, needing a job and an income, attempted to export his "whites' rights" message in a national presidential campaign. Hoping to exploit the aroused evangelical constituency, Duke began referring to himself as a born-again Christian, a claim disputed by one of his aides.[21] Duke's faith was questioned on "The 700 Club," with Robertson cohost Sheila Walsh expressing exasperation that people could not see through his phoniness. In a sense, while the populism of Jackson and Robertson was religiously rooted and communitarian, that of David Duke played on individual alienation. A man without spiritual or community roots, Duke appealed to kindred souls—like the pathetic young men from Dubuque, Iowa, featured in a *New York Times* photograph—whose sole identity seemed to be as "white people." [22] Our analysis of the religious wellsprings of populist discontent explains why Duke's base was narrower than many dire predictions had suggested.

The most formidable challenge in the Republican party in 1992 came from columnist Pat Buchanan, who sought to revive a kind of nativist, America-first conservatism, tinged with anti-Semitism and racism. In many states Buchanan drew support from former Robertson supporters, but there was a notable difference. Although Robertson's cultural concerns disproportionately were attractive to women, Buchanan's message of anger drew heavy support from men. Adopting, like Silber, a shoot-from-the-hip approach common among populists, Buchanan insulted many women and minorities. Although he drew a healthy 30 percent protest vote in many states in the caucuses and primaries, his future base may be more limited than he realizes. Moreover, his long-range effect may be less than Robertson's. Robertson received fewer votes than Buchanan, but he brought a distinct following into the GOP. Buchanan, instead, seemed driven to chase some members out of the party, especially neoconservatives.

On the left, too, candidates came forth with populist messages. Of the Democratic candidates in the 1992 sweepstakes, Iowa senator Tom Harkin campaigned as the economic populist, calling his party back to its roots, championing the "little guy," and castigating the Republican party in terms reminiscent of Franklin D. Roosevelt, William Jennings

Bryan, and Jesse Jackson. An unabashed progressive, Harkin fits a hardscrabble populist profile: his father, a coal miner, died of black lung disease; his mother, a Slovenian immigrant, died when he was ten. Having struggled his way up the ladder through grit and determination, he remembers where he came from. He makes no effort to hide his contempt for "George Herbert Walker Bush," calling the president's policies "bullshit." Harkin's natural identification with the underdog found intellectual justification in Kevin Phillips's populist critique of the Reagan years, which Harkin quotes with relish.[23] At the Rainbow Coalition candidate forum in January 1992, Harkin received the strongest ovations. "If you want a real Democrat," he roared, someone who will run right at the smug Republicans, "then vote for me." But Harkin's campaign illustrated the problem with a populism detached from the cultural discontent that also animates voters, many of them of modest means. Those in extreme economic distress do not constitute a majority, and they can feel stress in religious or moral terms as well as in economic ones. Harkin, a Roman Catholic, might have appealed more broadly to voters had he connected, for example, with many parents, whose economic concerns often blend with an equally salient struggle to maintain a wholesome environment for their children.

Former Democratic governor of California, Jerry Brown—once dubbed Governor Moonbeam for his New Age proclivities—began his presidential explorations with a "series of radio addresses on greed, corruption, and the country's moral crisis." [24] He transmuted himself into the candidate of rage against the system, at times competing with Buchanan for disenchanted voters. Governor Clinton, though not as strident as Harkin or Brown, also pitched a message about reclaiming politics and economics for average citizens.

Finally, the general election between Bush and Clinton reflected the twin populist dimensions examined here. A stagnant economy and poor job growth made Bush vulnerable to economically populist attacks by Clinton. Bush and his surrogates, in turn, fought back by portraying Clinton as captive of cultural elites. Beyond the two major parties, maverick businessman H. Ross Perot ignited a remarkable grass-roots movement when he offered himself as an independent "billionaire populist" for president, a mind-bending prospect indeed. Although Perot's unorthodox blend of ideas falls outside our study of religiously based populism, his presidential campaign clearly tapped into the populist disgust for the status quo. Clearly, for good or ill, populism was thriving in the 1990s.

LEFT-WING POPULISM, RIGHT-WING POPULISM, AND ELITES

Populism in the past typically combined economic and cultural critiques of elites. Today that heritage, to an extent, has split into left-wing and right-wing variants. One explanation for this split is that modern-day populists are contending with two different kinds of elites: those with economic power and those with cultural influence.

Undoubtedly, an economic elite exists and did very well in the 1980s. The Congressional Budget Office reported that from 1977 to 1989 the richest 1 percent of families received an astounding 60 percent of the total gain in after-tax income. One factor in this increase was compensation for top corporate executives, whose earnings jumped from about 35 times as much as the wages of the average worker in the mid-1970s to 120 times by the end of the 1980s.[25] The nation's wealth also became more concentrated, with the top 1 percent increasing its share of total assets. By 1989 that very rich group owned more assets than the bottom 90 percent of all households combined, leading one economist to conclude that "inequality is at its highest since the great leveling of wages and wealth during the New Deal and World War II."[26] Some economists caution that gains in income and wealth can reflect upward mobility, noting that when one tracks actual families there is considerable movement up and down. Others dispute this rosy picture, arguing that mobility is limited to one or two steps up or down the economic ladder.[27]

Viewing these numbers, Jackson blames Republican big business and the rich. But the emergence of the global economy and the high-tech revolution, which coincided with Reagan's supply-side policies, also played a part in the growing gap between rich and poor. Economically vulnerable citizens found themselves contending not with relatively easy targets like the robber barons of old but with a global marketplace in which they competed with the workers of Taiwan, Mexico, and Singapore. Although national tax and trade policies may have contributed to the problem,[28] nonetheless the new economic order profoundly undermined any progressive response to the conservative business era. For more than a decade economic progressives have struggled to offer a compelling alternative to the supply-side economic program, while the vulnerable fell further behind. The situation is ripe for populist outrage.

If there is an economic elite, thriving in the global village of "perpetual innovation,"[29] there is also a distinct, though related, cultural elite that thrives in the same environment. Social theorists contend that a "new knowledge class" or "verbalist" elite exercises influence over government bureaucracies, education, mass media, entertainment, and the arts—an elite with an increasingly global reach.[30] Read the newsletters of the religious right, and you will find a virtual obsession with the power of popular culture, as embodied by Hollywood, the rock music industry, and the mass media. Explore the pages of religious presses, and you will find a deep anxiety over the public schools and the perceived hegemony of the knowledge elite in determining what children learn and experience. Although often dismissed as paranoid or benighted, this cultural populism should be taken seriously because in many cases it accurately reflects the power of large institutions to pollute the moral environment.

Much is made of the rivalry between the new knowledge class—the people who produce network television, publish magazines, and manage education—and the business elite. But, for our analysis, the similarities are what matter: both the knowledge elite and the business elite are children of liberal individualism. The business elite embraces the ideology of the individual entrepreneur and the unfettered, consumer-driven free market. The knowledge elite also embraces the gospel of the individual but in cultural and moral terms rather than principally in economic ones. Members of the new knowledge elite are willing to regulate individuals for the sake of the environment or consumer safety, and some in the business community might tolerate state intervention on abortion. In neither case, however, do these elites articulate communalist vision.

Thus contemporary populists may be either economic or cultural populists, reacting to the apathetic responses of elites to their concerns. Each group of populists can plausibly claim that a distinct set of elites makes decisions that are harmful to their communities. Jackson speaks compellingly of the capitalists' power to shut down plants and shatter the very fabric of communities. Robertson demonstrates convincingly that the mass media, the entertainment business, and the education establishment represent an assault on the traditional moral values most Americans believe in, if not practice. In this sense, the two branches of populism reach the same conclusion: powerful individuals, operating in the liberal marketplace of ideas and consumer products, make decisions without concern for their effects on society. The response of liberals—both economic and cultural—is that the "public good" is an epiphenomenal result of individuals making choices for their own benefit[31] or that other mediating institutions must achieve what government cannot.[32] That may be, say the populists, but some individuals have so much economic power and wield so much cultural influence that the marketplace is a sham or at least imperfect. To right-wing populists, cultural elites determine what "moral swill" kids will be exposed to through pop music and commercial television. Elites even force taxpayers to fund works masquerading as art whose chief purpose is to demean everything ordinary people hold decent. To left-wing populists, in contrast, the 1980s represented a profound falling away from the vision of a caring national community, embodied in the New Deal, and an embrace of a neo-Darwinian competition (which Bryan had feared), pitting the working classes around the world against each other. Thus business interests are more unfettered than ever; they no longer operate within specific national boundaries, and they can shift operations across the globe at will as conditions dictate. Both kinds of populists decry the loss of high moral purpose that liberal thinkers themselves often acknowledge.[33] We will look now at the tensions between the liberal order and populism.

THE EFFECTS OF ASCENDANT LIBERALISM

In our quest to plumb the deeper historical tides that animate populists on both sides of the political spectrum, we are left with this question: Why now this simultaneous challenge to elites on the right and the left? The answer lies in the advent of powerful forces that appear uniquely disruptive to the economically vulnerable and the morally traditional. These forces include a capitalist free market that has reached global dimensions and an equally potent "free market" in popular culture, family life, education, the arts, and the mass media. In a sense, the modern age brought to fruition the enterprise of classical liberalism. But if liberalism has triumphed, it has left in its wake fresh challenges. Just as the collapse of communism undermined faith in the collective sharing of wealth, atomistic liberalism has sundered elements of our communal moral vision. Put another way, just as unfettered capitalism can undermine the idea of a "moral economy" (in which the vulnerable can make moral claims on the well-heeled),[34] so can it also undermine the "moral ecology" through its powerful engines of libertarian change so disturbing to cultural traditionalists. To use an environmental analogy, a "tragedy of the commons" results when powerful individuals are free to pollute the common culture.

There is nothing really surprising here. Even friends of marketplace liberalism concede that at times it offers a pallid secular grounding for moral obligation, community stability, and justice. What populism in the 1980s revealed is that religious sentiment often most cogently articulates these concerns. From the prophetic tradition of the black church on the left to conservative Christians on the right, a populist critique arose from the culture of tightknit church communities. These disparate strands of populism expressed their discontent with an ascendant liberal order that apparently leaves little room for moral stability or economic security. Let us explore this idea more fully.

In the summer of 1989 a young scholar named Francis Fukuyama dazzled the intellectual world with his thesis that "liberalism" as a grand philosophical idea had triumphed globally. With the collapse of the Marxist vision, no realistic alternative endured to challenge the liberal blend of capitalist economics, individual autonomy, and pluralist democracy. History, understood as a struggle between ideologies, would cease because no viable antithesis to the ascendant liberal order remained. Liberalism, simply, had won.[35]

Fukuyama used the term "liberalism" not in its narrow sense (as in "liberal Democrat") but in its broader, classical sense, as I use it in this book. Fukuyama's thesis, though denounced as simplistic, received some dramatic corroboration by the swift, earthshaking demise of communism. With astonishing alacrity former Marxist regimes embraced liberal free markets and political pluralism: walls came down metaphorically and physically. Fukuyama's thesis also helped to explain disparate events such as the emergence of the global economy, the collapse of moderate forms of socialism once popular in Western Europe, liberalization in the developing world,[36] and the era of Margaret Thatcher in Great Britain and Ronald Reagan in the United States (two figures who embraced the unfettered market and attempted to roll back their modestly "collectivist" welfare states). The 1980s marked a major hinge in history, not only in the United States but around the world.

Fukuyama was properly chided for distilling a complex array of ethnic, religious, economic, and political currents into a single sweeping thesis. (For example, his argument does not explain well the revival of ethnic strife around the world.) Still, his boldness pinpoints the central dynamic of modernity: liberalism seems to define the age. But if Fukuyama is right about the centrality of liberalism, his dependence on Hegelian dialectics keeps him from recognizing its implications. To him the triumph of liberalism will usher in a politics of bland tinkering, consumerism, and boredom:

> The end of history will be a very sad time. The struggle for recognition, the willingness to risk one's life for a purely abstract goal, the worldwide ideological struggle that called forth daring, courage, imagination, and idealism, will be replaced by economic calculation, the endless solving of technical problems, environmental concerns, and the satisfaction of sophisticated consumer demands. In the post-historical period there will be neither art nor philosophy, just the perpetual caretaking of the museum of history.[37]

Our examination of populism—limited though it is to a church-based movement in the United States—suggests that history may not end, as Fukuyama suggests, with acquiescence. The triumph of the liberal order instead will usher in the next phase of history, in which people struggle through the crucible of liberalism's weaknesses: its potentially corrosive individualism, its hollow moral core, its atomizing influence on communities, its disposition to cast the young adrift, and its ready abandonment of those unprepared for international competition. Politics will be manifested through disparate, often zealous attempts to compensate for the economic dislocation, cultural flux, and moral chaos regnant in modernity. In part, because he focused on political and economic liberalization, Fukuyama slighted the cultural strand in the liberal fabric. But we have seen how freedom practiced through individual autonomy and market choice can bring disruptive cultural change. Fukuyama's prophecy of citizen acquiescence thus rests on a faulty grasp of human nature—an assumption that people will go gently into that bland twilight, that religious, ethnic, and moral concerns will evaporate as we become global consumers—like oysters, all stomach, no soul.[38]

Lest we forget, the achievements of liberalism are breathtaking. For at least two centuries liberals have waged heroic battles against religious persecution, authoritarian government, monopolistic economics, and infringements on individual liberty. Understandably, liberal champions on the right and the left continue to fight those same foes. But liberalism's triumph reveals its problematic side: corrosive greed, consumptive consumerism, soul-less materialism, adult selfishness (and the resulting suffering of children), cultural triviality, moral relativism, a rotting community fabric, and a decaying set of civic institutions. Marx realized that the restless liberal order contained the potential to rip apart the fabric of communities and families. Politically, liberal culture contributed to candidate-centered politics, weakening parties, declining voting rates, and enervated leadership.[39]

Although these forces are particularly strong in the United States, we can discern similar patterns around the world. We see tension emerging in the newly freed societies of Eastern Europe. We notice that Pope John Paul II has shifted from the fight against totalitarianism to a concern for materialism, consumerism, superficiality, economic insecurity, the youth culture, the breakdown of families, and the atrophy of faith. We see it in the rise of Islamic fundamentalism, which attacks the decadence of liberal societies even while adopting economic and technological changes that could undermine the religious vision. If liberal forces are now driving history, the American experience may be instructive to the world. As the first "liberal" society, it has struggled with these conflicts all along, as we have seen in our review of American populist history. Even though elites in one form or another were liberals—suspicious of grand ideas, devoted to the individual definition and pursuit of happiness[40]—undercurrents of parochial, populist, communitarian, or traditional values operated, too. The interplay between liberalism and populism is a constant thread in American history.

Some see in the Reagan presidency a turn to true European conservatism, which emphasizes order, religion, and tradition undergirded by a robust state. Theodore Lowi makes this case, arguing that Reagan implemented his conservative agenda by transferring power to robust and intrusive state and local governments.[41] Perhaps. But when we look closely at the Reagan presidency, we see rhetorical support for moral conservatism actually accompanied by much "classical liberal" policymaking: deregulation of business, celebration of the free market, and promotion of an atmosphere of leveraged buyouts and golden parachutes, in which thirty-year-old investment bankers became chic in their shameless pursuit of wealth at all costs. The results of these policies are not conservative results: they are the analogue of liberal individualism in the cultural realm.

The "crucible of liberalism" describes the emerging politics of the 1990s. Liberal modernity is not something we oppose with an alternative ideology but something that we must struggle through—a test of our creativity, our compassion, our moral principles, and our civic institutions. How well societies and communities are forged in this crucible will determine their economic success, their goodness, and the extent of populist discontent among their citizenry. The challenge of political philosophy, as Aristotle observed, is to understand the tendencies of a regime in order to compensate for them. That is our challenge—especially in the United States, in some ways the most anarchic of liberal societies. If we abandon the underclass, if we let the working class slide farther down the ladder, if we continue to allow our young people to drift without challenge and meaning, if we permit moral pollution and corrosive individualism to further erode civic and family structures, we will be ill-equipped to compete with societies with stronger communal structures, such as Japan.

ECONOMIC CHANGES

The economic crucible of the liberal order became manifest in the 1980s as the global economy converged with the supply-side revolution. Supply-side economics offered an important insight but a faulty application. The insight was that pumping up domestic consumer spending, as the New Deal had done, makes sense only in a relatively self-contained economy. In the new international marketplace long-term investment, savings, and productivity are what matter. Instead of bringing those benefits, however, supply-side tax cuts and deregulation led to a consumer spending binge on foreign products; encouraged unproductive leveraged buyouts; and increased corporate, government, and consumer debt. Stories abound of the consequences of this decade of vanities. For example, the thriving small town of Ada, Oklahoma, found its economic lifeblood drained away when the profitable Brockway glass factory, the town's major employer, was closed. Although the plant was productive and profitable, its parent company was the victim of a junk bond leveraged buyout by a competitor.[42] Jesse Jackson sees in such events evidence of the failure of our society to negotiate the times.

Although President Reagan's policies may have hastened the trend, the income gap had been widening before the Reagan years, as the information age and the global economy shattered existing conditions. Less-educated, blue-collar workers once enjoyed middle-class lives through plentiful, high-paying industrial jobs and strong unions. That possibility is receding. Now workers must possess high-tech skills and nimble minds open to change and mobility. The difference in income between high school graduates (localists) and the college educated (cosmopolitans) widened dramatically in the past two decades, as the global marketplace, in a Darwinian sense, rewarded those "fit" for international competition. American workers now must compete with other workers around the world; capital and jobs are shuffled from one corner of the globe to another.

Robert Reich, discussing the implications of this "new reality," argues that the most economically successful people constitute a class of what he terms "symbolic analysts," those whose jobs center on analyzing and managing information. These symbolic analysts include software designers, computer programmers, business managers, top government bureaucrats, marketing professionals, international trade experts, mass media producers, communications specialists, systems analysts, consultants, engineers, lawyers, and professors. What unites these people is that they possess global skills. Reich notes that this favored 20 percent of the American population brings in more income than the other 80 percent combined. Even more ominous, from the perspective of the political economy, is that they have become detached from the lives, conditions, and communities of the rest of the population. This "secession of the successful" threatens the delicate bonds of communal solidarity. In America, Tocqueville argued a century and a half ago, those bonds meant that the well-off might help the less fortunate (by supporting public education, training, and infrastructure) in their own "enlightened" self-interest. But Reich fears that the suburban enclaves, gated communities, and private schools available to the top 20 percent belie a deeper secession: that these elites may come to have more in common with, and interact more with, their counterparts around the world than with people across the highway. Their fellow citizens may live in deteriorating neighborhoods, drive over crumbling bridges, send their children to failing schools, and suffer disproportionately the effects of dysfunctional family structures, but their professional associates live in Tokyo, Bonn, or Singapore.[43] The political economy of this new secession is reflected in increases in regressive payroll, sales, and lottery taxes (which fall on the bottom four-fifths of the population) and decreases in progressive income taxes borne by the top one-fifth. As enlightened self-interest becomes attenuated or harder to discern, investment in common infrastructure dwindles. The favored fifth hardly notices, however, because it has effectively seceded.

The high-tech revolution has introduced a new hierarchy of talent with some troubling implications for a democratic society. The quaint idea that strength of character might compensate for shortages of brainpower or elite education was nurtured in a previous era, when a strong back and willingness to work could secure a middle-class life and respect from political leaders. In the new meritocracy, however, "old-fashioned" character may be less important than elite education and global skills. Those who thrive in the global environment will be richly rewarded; the unprepared will fall further behind. Unfortunately, many of our citizens are unprepared for this reality. Among the reasons are poor political decisions and short-sighted corporate management. Educational standards collapsed, businesses failed to plan for long-term trends, and the government borrowed for short-term consumption rather than productive investment. In addition, the work ethic declined, family structures decayed, and the young drifted—which is another way of saying that we negotiated the modern crucible poorly. Both Jackson and Robertson spoke to this failure. Jackson sought to strengthen the commonweal so that more workers would be trained, more students taught, and more citizens prepared for the challenges of the age. Robertson sought to strengthen the moral ecology so that more families would remain intact, more children inculcated with proper values, and more citizens imbued with civic responsibility—cultural attributes equally important to economic success.

CULTURAL CHANGES

With the triumph of liberalism came an outburst of interest in the pathologies of modernity that highlight the cultural crucible of the times. From Andrew Oldenquist's "suicidal society" to Alasdair MacIntyre's "coming dark ages" to Christopher Lasch's "culture of narcissism" to John Diggins's "lost soul of American politics," we hear rumblings.[44] These voices question the social adequacy of liberal societies—at least when they are not sustained by religious mores or communal cultural habits.

Oldenquist, for example, depicts the pathologies of liberal modernity as a suicidal society, which is both a metaphor for social collapse and an empirical phenomenon. A hyperindividualistic society, he argues, is a suicidal one, because it undermines organs of social control, parental authority, and communal identity essential to the nurture of children. Today the young are not socialized in time-tested ways to see themselves as part of a social context with meaning greater than themselves. Instead, they are taught in a variety of ways that they must be autonomous individuals deriving meaning from their own choices, pursuing their own pleasure, marching to their own drummer. They are pummeled by the airwaves with messages of hedonism and individual fulfillment detached from traditional mores. In such a culture the young are captives of one another; they suffer anomie, rootlessness, dysfunction, and suicide. Oldenquist cites the shocking rise of teen-age suicide rates in the past two decades as symptomatic of a deeper malaise. "In 1897 the great French sociologist Emile Durkheim argued that the rise of individualism accounted for the great increase in suicide in nineteenth-century Europe. More specifically, a person's immunity to suicide is a function of the degree to which he is enmeshed in society."[45] Oldenquist agrees with Durkheim's remedy for high suicide rates:

> Thus, the only remedy for the ill is to restore enough consistency to social groups for them to obtain a firmer grip on the individual, and for him to feel himself bound to them. He must feel himself more solidary with a collective existence which precedes him in time, which survives him, and which encompasses him at all points. If this occurs, he will no longer find the only aim of his conduct in himself, and, understanding that he is the instrument of a purpose greater than himself, he will see that he is not without significance. Life will resume meaning in his eyes, because it will recover its natural aim and orientation.[46]

Jackson and Robertson both passionately share this analysis of society. To them our purpose in life is not hedonistic pursuit but God-ordained, sacrificial service. To teach the young otherwise constitutes a failure of society.

Along these same lines Lasch argues that the contemporary left and right are both morally bankrupt. Neither has a prescription for the consequences of what might be called "carnal capitalism."[47] The consumerist ethic that drives business thrives on whatever is titillating, cheap, shocking, alluring, and superficial. The historic tension between cultural conservatives and the entrepreneurial elite has increased as "capitalism came to be identified with immediate gratification" and thus "wore away at the moral foundations of family life." Lasch continues, "If conservatism implies a respect for limits, localism, a work ethic as opposed to a consumerist ethic ... a certain skepticism about the ideology of progress, it is more likely to find a home in the populist tradition than in the free-market tradition." Indeed, populists of the past "condemned modern capitalism for profoundly conservative reasons—because it required ... the progressive shattering of atoms of our social system." The left, on the other hand, is infected with an influential new-class outlook—"[impatient] with constraints imposed by the past, [believing] that personal and intellectual growth demands a repudiation of our parents, [eager] to question everything, the habit of mockery and irreverence."[48]

Not to be outdone in painting a bleak vision is Alasdair MacIntyre. MacIntyre likens our times to those of the late Roman Empire, when "men and women of good will" stopped trying to shore up the corrupt *imperium,* and turned instead to creating new communities where "both morality and civility might survive the coming ages of barbarism and darkness." To MacIntyre the "new dark ages" are upon us. Our task is to build "local forms of community within which civility and the intellectual and moral life can be sustained" during the coming barbarism of modernity.[49]

Overbleak, perhaps, but these analyses summarize for us the crucible of modernity. Lasch seeks a "haven in a heartless world," Bellah yearns for "communities of memory," Lears pines for "a place of grace," and Fowler seeks and sees "a refuge" in religion.[50] I do not want to imply that the dysfunctions of modernity are entirely liberal in origins. Many great liberal thinkers, including John Stuart Mill, argued that any society that promoted individual freedom had the power and the right to determine how the young were raised. Mill might agree with Oldenquist that it would be suicidal for any society based on individual freedom not to inculcate those traits in the young—integrity, duty, industry, sacrifice, communal identity, public spirit—which would ensure that as adults they would be productive and worthy citizens. As Tocqueville suggested, a liberal society may depend on "conservative" nurture of its young to remain free. This concern with children brings us to the essential point of the argument.

THE EFFECTS OF ATOMISTIC CULTURE ON CHILDREN

No issue so crystallizes the twin populist concerns—economic and cultural—as the future of the nation's children. As I followed the 1988 presidential campaign and its aftermath, observing and interviewing, the future of children emerged as the defining issue for Jackson and Robertson and their followers. Both candidates, who have long articulated their concerns about the young, have acted on those concerns. For more than two decades Jackson's main focus centered on speaking to school assemblies. He implored students to give up drugs and sexual obsessions, to study hard and develop strong character; he exhorted parents to invest greater interest and effort in the task of nurturing the next generation. In his campaign Jackson stressed the public investment required to improve life for young people. He deplored the weakening of the commonweal, which leaves many American children bereft of their most elemental needs—safety, health, nutrition, and education. He promoted his belief that there must be a renewed public spirit to ensure that parents have work and children have healthy places to learn and grow. "Investing in America" means, above all, spending money now on health care, day care, education, job training, and nutrition so that we do not have to spend even greater sums later on jails and welfare. In his 1992 address to the Democratic National Convention, Jackson eloquently implored the nation not to forget "our children."

Robertson, similarly, has focused his charitable and educational ministries on families and children. Talk to black ministers and you will find those with praise for Robertson's charity, Operation Blessing, and his educational program, Sing, Spell, Read, and Write. Designed to teach the basics of phonics, this educational initiative addresses the massive problem of illiteracy, Robertson contends, at a fraction of the cost of top-heavy or misdirected public school efforts.

More than anything else, Robertson hammered away at what he considers the colossal failure of American society with its youth. The erosion of families through divorce and illegitimacy steals from children the haven of security essential to educational achievement and success in life. The educational system fails to teach the basics, maintain discipline, and foster an appreciation of moral and ethical truths. The United States should treat its children better. "America owes its children a crime-free, drug-free, disciplined school environment." Had he not been burdened by inexperience and religious ideas that repelled some voters, Robertson might have cut deeper in his attempt to tap the moral yearnings of many Americans. His followers disproportionately were parents concerned about the secular environment imploding on their children. They merely felt more strongly sentiments that other Americans apparently share.

Jackson's denunciation of the media's exploitation of children, his call for character education in public schools, and his exasperation over the "ethical collapse" in society suggest that he, too, understood this public mood. His concern for these issues helps to explain why he was so admired by many Robertson supporters.

AN EMERGING CONSENSUS ON THE PROBLEMS

Here, too, in the emerging intellectual consensus about the needs of children we find vindication for the politics of discontent. In the past few years the plight of children in America has been examined in a flood of scholarly, popular, and government reports. The pictures presented in these reports conform, in many cases, to the critiques offered by Jackson and Robertson. Indeed, a consensus that crosses party lines and ideological boundaries appears to be emerging about certain aspects of the problem. Several notable books attest to this growing concern, as do several national studies.[51] The Carnegie Foundation for the Advancement of Teaching, for example, issued a report charging that the nation's children increasingly arrive at school unprepared, hungry, and insecure. Dealing with the educational crisis, it suggested, must begin with a recognition that "America has orphaned" many of its young. The report cites as a major culprit atomizing trends that undermine community support of young people. Ernest Boyer, president of the foundation, observed that children in the past enjoyed extended family roots and neighborhood support, which supplemented parental efforts and compensated for problems in the home. "Gradually, this protective ring was broken. Neighbors grew more distant, doors were bolted, friendliness was replaced by fear. . . . Relatives moved far away. Families became isolated and disconnected, struggling alone. . . . Modern life, which brought new options to parents, destabilized former certainties and weakened networks of support."[52] The Carnegie report called for public efforts as well as a change in the climate of family life.

Other studies corroborate Boyer's diagnosis. In January 1992 Victor Fuchs and Diane Reklis published an assessment of the nation's children. They concluded that America's children are worse off than they were three decades ago. They cite declining performances on standardized tests, a tripling of teen-age suicide rates, increasing incidences of homicide, worsening health problems (such as obesity), and rising poverty rates.[53] As scholars seek to explain this malaise, they identify both material and cultural factors that conform to the twin populist concerns. Material, or economic, explanations stress declining middle-class wages, intergenerational transfers from working parents to retired citizens, and the decreasing proportion of public investment in programs focused on youth.[54] One remedy would be a straightforward program of taxing and spending policies that would redistribute money from those without children to those with children. Cultural explanations stress family breakup, unwed motherhood, and an increase in "freedom" for children that amounts to abandonment.[55] One study, for example, found that the decline in the number of families headed by married couples in the 1980s accounted for half the increase in poverty.[56] Both kinds of deficiencies contribute to the weakening status of vulnerable children. Economic stress and joblessness hit children disproportionately, and children living in families without adult males lag far behind their peers in education and habits conducive to success.

Politically, we see this dual cultural and economic dimension as well. Jackson's concerns are reflected in the work of Marian Wright Edelman's Children's Defense Fund, a progressive Washington organization that lobbies for public investment in childhood and maternal care. Its interests include inoculations, nutrition, and health care. Robertson's concerns are echoed by James Dobson's Family Research Council, which champions the integrity of the family, while denouncing the moral climate and the tax burden on working parents.

THE NATIONAL COMMISSION ON CHILDREN

The worrisome decline in support for children was forcefully brought home in the final report of the National Commission on Children, published in 1991. Headed by Sen. John D. Rockefeller IV, D-W.Va., the commission sought testimony from experts and advocates throughout the nation and across the political spectrum. Its report, *Beyond Rhetoric: A New American Agenda for Children and Families,* is a remarkable document—passionate, eloquent, and direct—and it unremittingly documents the nation's failure:

> One in four children is raised by just one parent. One in every five is poor. Half a million are born annually to teenage girls who are ill prepared to assume the responsibilities of parenthood. An increasing number are impaired before birth by their parent's substance abuse. Others live amid violence and exploitation, much of it fueled by a thriving drug trade. . . . Too many children at every income level lack time, attention, and guidance from parents and other caring adults. The result is often alienation, recklessness, and damaging, antisocial behavior.[57]

The report brings together the material and cultural aspects of the problem in unusually urgent terms. Echoing Jackson, it calls for a strengthening of public programs to ensure that children are inoculated against disease, provided with proper nutrition, kept safe, and given an education that will allow them to compete in the changing world economy. The report also echoes Robertson's cultural concerns, urging a strengthened moral climate that would help the young resist self-destructive behavior such as sexual promiscuity, drug abuse, and violence:

> Today, too many young people seem adrift, without a steady moral compass to direct their daily behavior or to plot a thoughtful and responsible course for their lives. We see the worst manifestation of this in reports of violent and predatory behavior by adolescents.... It is evident in lifestyles and sexual conduct that indulge personal gratification at the expense of others' safety and well-being. It is revealed as well in a culture that ranks wealth and the acquisition of material possessions above service to one's community to the nation.[58]

In terms similar to Robertson's, the report chides the "rampant materialism among adults" that "fosters shallow ambitions in children and encourages them in empty, reckless, and sometimes dangerous pursuits." It chastises, as Jackson does, the media and entertainment industries that "glamorize drugs, sex, greed, and violence." It laments that "more children grow up without the consistent presence of a father in their lives." It calls upon parents to be vigilant monitors of their children's moral development, and it encourages public efforts to give parents more ability to control what their children are exposed to in the mass media. It deplores the fact that "from a very young age children today are increasingly exposed to images and messages that are extremely violent, gratuitously and explicitly sexual, and overly hostile toward and demeaning of women and minorities." It criticizes the violence in heavy metal music and cites serious studies about the harmful effects of a steady diet of violence in the entertainment industry. It notes that television "frequently presents children with values and messages antithetical to parents' most deeply held beliefs." It suggests a new commitment to providing young people with meaningful volunteer work as a means of their reclaiming a sense of purpose and meaning. Affirming the positive role of religion in sustaining a healthy moral climate for children, it notes that "teenagers who are religious are more likely to avoid high risk behaviors." In contrast to the "give 'em condoms" surrender of adult moral authority, it supports abstinence education. It unabashedly states that "there is no such thing as value-free education" and calls for a renewed commitment to teaching positive character traits. The report chides the timidity of textbook publishers and school administrators that produces the "perverse result ... that a major social institution entrusted by most parents with preparing children for adulthood is too often silent on critical moral and ethical issues." Finally, the report exhorts all Americans to "renew their personal commitment to the common good and demonstrate this commitment by giving highest priority to personal actions and public policies that promote the health and well-being of the nation's children."[59]

Although some may scoff at these exhortations, the report does what cultural conservatives and communitarians have demanded for two decades—it puts the majesty of the state firmly on the side of good sense. But the report also embraces the progressive concern about the need for public efforts to ensure a healthy material environment for young people. In some respects, the growing body of commentary and research suggests an emerging national consensus about the importance of the next generation. Notably, this consensus reflects a powerful criticism of the more extreme forms of laissez faire economics and cultural individualism. And if we accept Lowi's definition of liberalism as embracing greed and moral relativity, it directly challenges liberal ideology.

The anguish about children also suggests a political opportunity. A candidate who did nothing but emphasize the physical, economic, and moral security needs of children—looking to their future—would elicit a powerful response from the electorate. A Democrat who freely acknowledged the need for a healthy moral climate for children (expressing unease at the moral messages in some AIDS awareness and sex education programs), or a Republican who supported economic assistance programs for families and job guarantees, would likely find a crosscutting response from voters. Politicians might even discover that a redistributive politics—from those without children to those with children—is both sensible and feasible. Children could be the linchpin that brings fresh approaches to elections and governance, as politicians realize that our powerful emotional concern for our children allows us to respond to long-term solutions. When John Maynard Keynes remarked that in the long run we are all dead, he was not thinking as a parent or grandparent. Political figures who pay heed to the long-term health of the economy for the sake of our children, or to the long-term health of the moral environment, would have a formidable political resource.

More than anything else, the plight of children brings sharply into focus the tensions and paradoxes within liberal societies. What populists seem to be saying is something like this: Unless the young are provided with "places of grace" in the liberal maelstrom—havens of economic security, physical safety, and moral certainty—they will be hampered in their ability to weather the challenges of liberal freedom as adults. It is to that subject that we now turn.

THE PARADOXES OF LIBERALISM

An analysis of populist discontent in the United States points up the paradoxes of a liberal order. Liberal theory begins with the autonomous individual, a free atom floating in a state of nature, responsible for its actions, constrained only by voluntary consent to an "umpire government" created to protect liberties and mediate disputes with other free atoms. In actuality, however, the idea of the radically free individual is nonsensical or at least paradoxical. People are social creatures, molded by families, shaped by ethnic heritages and communities, constrained by religious mores, buffeted by economic tides, and socialized through a host of agents. Populists down through history seem far more comfortable with this understanding of human society than do their liberal counterparts. They accept the idea that society must play a strong role in shaping the moral and economic environment in which freedom is enjoyed.

One example of the paradox of liberalism is child rearing. In all healthy societies the young are socialized to lawfulness and taught that there is something larger than themselves to which they are duty bound. In the United States not long ago this socialization was mutually reinforced in families, schools, churches, Scouts, and Four-H clubs. We saw these influences in the early life of Jesse Jackson. The usual hypocrisy notwithstanding, children often heard the same messages—from McGuffey Readers, which taught lessons of courage, sacrifice, and duty, to youth organizations, which were founded on pledges of reverence and work, to churches that called for piety, moral restraint, and concern for others. Yet individual autonomy can become such a god in liberal societies that agents of socialization are undermined, casting the young adrift in their "freedom." Paradoxically, the supposedly utopian Summerhill, in which children are freed of adult restraint, becomes a hostile place for the young. Attempts to reconstruct the family along purely liberal lines, in fact, produce dystopian results. The young thrive when there are clear limits on freedom and clear messages about right and wrong, coupled with physical and emotional security.

Another example of the paradox of liberalism is the continuing strength of the military code. How is it that in the United States, by reputation the most individualistic and liberal of all cultures, a considerable portion of the population joins a rigidly hierarchical, duty-bound culture in which one pledges to obey superiors "unto death" in battle? Such a system is inconceivable for true liberal individualists, whose selfish code is perhaps best captured by the slogan "Nothing is worth dying for." The military, often vilified in the 1960s and 1970s, now offers a culture of order, discipline, and meritocracy that many blacks, especially males, find to be highly functional compared with the disintegrating environments they come from. Moreover, the military has been far more successful than civilian institutions in addressing such social problems as drug and alcohol abuse and racism because its hierarchy can enforce solutions. The military is today the most truly integrated social institution in the nation. Although our atomistic college campuses (with their clumsy attempts at multicultural understanding) are as segregated as ever, military bases around the world are places where blacks and whites work side by side, united by a common culture, speaking the same clipped language, taking orders from each other, recognizing (albeit with the usual grumbling) the meritocratic nature of advancement.

In economics, too, we see the paradoxes of liberal individualism. James Buchanan, a Nobel Prize-winning economist, calls for a rejoining of economics with its roots in moral philosophy. The free market, he argues, operates on the basis of an ethical and moral cement, not just through selfish instincts.[60] Although to Buchanan this cement involves such puritan virtues as honesty in trade and adherence to promises, one can go further and suggest that modern business practices have moral consequences: they can disturb the "community ecology"; they can produce moral pollution whose costs are borne by society. Consider violent television programming. Studies have shown that a diet of media violence increases aggressive behavior in children, with some suggestion that it may influence adults as well. Yet TV networks continue to produce violent programming.[61] Or consider what may seem a more benign example—beer commercials. In addition to promoting alcohol abuse, they present viewers with a hedonistic message at variance with healthy family life, childhood development, and other essential supports to society. The response of business is that viewers can choose not to buy the product, turn off the TV, and raise their children with values they cherish. True, they can. But using the community ecology analogy, people who do such positive things are not unaffected by the actions of others. As taxpayers and citizens, they bear the social costs of alcohol abuse or of dysfunctional children raised on a saturation diet of television—not to mention facing the very real physical threat of drunk drivers or violent individuals. The moral ecology can be polluted by business practice, something Robertson implicitly acknowledged in his criticism of Time Warner for selling Ice-T's infamous "Cop Killer" album.

The problem of political leadership is yet another paradoxical feature of liberal culture. Over the past decades political scientists have observed a sea change in our political system, notably the decline of political parties. Candidates once emerged from a relatively communal party context that stressed recruitment and deference; they now arise from a highly individualistic, candidate-centered milieu.[62] Politicians today at all levels of government are "political entrepreneurs"—in a sense, individualists—beholden largely to the organizations they have created. Deadlock, inefficiency, and fragmentation are common ills attributed to this new era. But the problem is deeper still. True leadership is inconceivable in purely liberal terms. To put it less starkly, the only kind of leadership compatible with liberalism is what James MacGregor Burns terms "transactional" leadership.[63] In other words, transactional leaders merely negotiate the bargains between free individuals and assemble the disparate coalitions on the basis of calculated self-interest. "Transforming" leaders—such as Lincoln, Roosevelt, and Churchill—on the other hand, draw upon moral and psychological dimensions that transcend bargaining and self-interest. Think for a moment of Winston Churchill, who took a dispirited people and fashioned them into the indomitable British who alone withstood Hitler. William Manchester argues that Churchill literally "transformed" the British people.[64] The idea that leadership can help people rise to their better angels presupposes that they have the psychological potential to be more than hedonistic liberal individualists. It presupposes that there is a higher moral code that all can recognize; a leader's job is to help people see it. Moral relativism allows no such possibility.

Among contemporary American leaders, Jesse Jackson consciously embodies this kind of transforming appeal. To Jackson this appeal is the very meaning of his life, his mission. He often measures his success by souls "transformed"—such as the former Klansman who marched against civil rights in Selma, Alabama, but who joined Jackson's presidential campaign. True leadership, Jackson believes, eschews the political center, striving instead to move the population toward the "moral center" of an issue. Throughout history, Jackson contends, the political center, the expedient, was often wrong, immoral. "Slavery was the political center, but it was not the moral center. Segregation was the political center but not the moral center." [65]

The very assumption of self-interested politics poses another liberal paradox. Witness the struggle of scholars of "rational choice" to explain collective group action. Even to pursue self-interest, they say, requires an ability to sacrifice for the good of the group, which will then pursue that self-interest collectively. How much simpler, it seems, to turn to a dimension of human life that transcends rational calculations. Consider these words in Jackson's speech to his delegates at the 1988 Democratic National Convention: "When you're too tough and mature to cry when you're hurting, I'll suffer with you. I'll die for you. I want you to suffer with me, and together our suffering will not be in vain." [66] Such a discourse of sacrifice and redemptive suffering—although it does not resonate with a culture of beer commercials, soap operas, and rock music, nor with a politics of PACs, consultants, and calculating ambition—nonetheless rings true to the ageless wisdom that we do not live by bread alone. We may, with help, rise to our better angels.

The lesson then is that liberal societies work best (or perhaps work at all) only when nonliberal underpinnings support them. Fukuyama recognizes this paradox, and it underlies much of Booth Fowler's trenchant work. In *Unconventional Partners,* for example, Fowler convincingly shows that liberalism depends on religion.[67] But where Tocqueville emphasized the religious mores that undergird a free society, Fowler argues that religion provides a necessary communitarian refuge from the competitive striving, skepticism, and moral shallowness of the liberal society. Without such a refuge liberalism might confront far more radical discontent and challenges. As it is, he argues, most Americans find in churches enough refuge, enough aesthetic harmony, enough moral certitude, and enough communitarian sharing to keep them going.

Exploiting the liberal paradox, Jackson and Robertson both called for a politics that was more exalted than a mere ratifying of interest-group bargaining, a polity greater than selfish individuals getting what they could from government. Jackson sought to inspire whites to see their common bond with blacks. Robertson called upon Americans to sacrifice for the next generation rather than squandering their inheritance. Each chided the other's party. Jackson reminded the Republican right that without mercy toward those left behind, without the kind of positive government that even paternalistic conservatives in Europe embrace, the "moral community" was an empty phrase. Robertson reminded the Democratic left that without traditional morals and strong families, all the liberal social programs in the world could not alleviate poverty or rescue the underclass. They both agreed on the need for traditional morals and strong families.

An analysis of populism helps us to see the connection between seemingly disparate manifestations of errant individualism.[68] How different are the thirty-year-old MBAs who see nothing unseemly about making millions of dollars plundering companies through leveraged buyouts from the cynical rock stars who exploit teen-agers with impunity? How different are the gay activists who insist on promiscuity as a right, regardless of consequences, from the television producers who exploit our worst instincts? Or how different are the artists who flout decency for its shock value from the advertisers who "push the edge of the envelope" for a buck? What each of these individuals is saying is that there are no moral limits; you must prove direct harm in the marketplace before you can stop us, and we have good lawyers. When "parochial" citizens express, however haltingly, communitarian aspirations for some control over the destiny of their children and their neighborhoods, they must be taken seriously. When workers in local communities ask for some semblance of economic security, they should not be dismissed. Politics urgently needs a renewal of vibrant, local community politics, combined with a national politics that acknowledges its value and nourishes its better lights. Unless this yearning for community, for moral order, and for a modicum of economic security and fairness can be accommodated in healthy ways, we will witness more of the dark side of populism, its potential for nativism and racism. Thus we must examine with greater scrutiny the emergence of "gospel populism."

THE SCOPE AND LIMITS OF GOSPEL POPULISM

Modernization, we were told, would bring the blessings of secular society, would free humanity from religious shackles. Religion would wither away. Yet on the eve of the millennium, religious faith continues to inspire many Americans, spilling over into politics across the ideological spectrum. Jackson and Robertson drew upon that faith to make their populist challenges to the system. Both emerge in this study, however, as imperfect vehicles for the movements they championed. It is appropriate, therefore, to explore the scope and limits inherent in religiously "anointed" leadership.

JACKSON AND THE POLITICS OF PERSONALITY

To some scholars religious populism on the right can be explained by theories of status politics as a desperate, but ultimately failing, quest to hold back the modern liberal tide. It is not so easy to explain how the disparate elements on the left in the United States were woven together by the most explicitly religious political figure since Bryan—the Reverend Jesse Jackson.

The voluminous literature on Jackson, along with his speeches, writings, and statements, confirms this judgment. Rooted in a strong tradition of black preachers who identified their people's struggle with the biblical narrative, Jackson has given thousands of speeches, virtually all laced with biblical allusions. Scriptural references emerge naturally in his conversation, his mind continually drawing connections between contemporary events and Christian truth. Jackson sees the Bible as a living history of the people of God. With a biblical understanding of time, he sees a simultaneity between the Exodus, the age of prophets, the life of Jesus, and the present era. The gospel did not happen long ago, but in a profound sense it is repeated in Hamlet, North Carolina, in Selma, Alabama, in Harlem, New York, and in Greenfield, Iowa. Wherever God's people suffer, there Jesus is, suffering. There we are called to be. While representatives of the religious right ultimately toned down their religious allusions to gain political acceptance, Jackson remains unabashed in his religious convictions and fervor. A leader on the religious right who suggested, as Jackson did, that our inner cities are collapsing because people have stopped obeying the Ten Commandments would be scorned by mavens of the elite press. Similarly, Jackson's condemnation of "Sodom and Gomorrah" sexual ethics never is featured on "Donahue" or criticized in the *New York Times* as imposing personal religious values. Perhaps the reason is that Jackson seems authentic; perhaps it is that he is black.

Jackson feels no need to tone down his spiritual side, even in political organizing. While hosting the Democratic presidential candidates in January 1992, he led his Rainbow Coalition of black leaders, union organizers, and rural populists—hands held—in prayer. He gave a characteristically prophetic address, denouncing the ethical collapse and moral degeneracy infecting the nation. He chastised Bush for ignoring the crucifixion of the dispossessed. He reminded the faithful that though it is dark in the evening, "joy cometh in the morning. . . . If the Lord is with us, of whom shall we fear?" Ending his address with Chronicles 7:14, a favorite passage of Robertson's, he proclaimed, "If my people, who are called by my name, humble themselves and pray and seek my face and turn from their wicked ways, then I will hear from heaven and will forgive their sin and heal their land." [69]

With a deep christic identification, Jackson sees his life as embodying a purpose that transcends his own selfish needs. "I am he who sent me," Jackson says. The issue is not "who I am" but "whose I am." Like Martin Luther King, Jr., Jackson has come to identify his role as being nothing less than that of redeemer of a sinful society. And herein lies the biblical quality of Jackson's life. Sinful in its racism, the society thus would be redeemed by a victim of racism. Sinful in its betrayal of the dispossessed, it would be elevated by one of the dispossessed. Smug in its secular achievements, technology, and material splendor, it would be called to judgment by an ebony prophet who saw beneath the facade to the deeper spiritual reality to "God's truths in history." "Surrendering yourself . . . you get bigger than yourself. Choosing to be selfless, you expand your life beyond the ordinary." Jackson sees his success, his notoriety, as a vindication of Paul's understanding of the gospel—to lose one's life is to gain it, to die to self is to live more fully. Jackson paraphrases the apostle, "He who loses his life in the great truth I offer shall find a greater life." [70] When critics accuse Jackson of failing to live up to that vision, he finds solace in the refrain of the spiritual: "Please be patient with me, God is not through with me yet." He bounces back, as one friend put it, because "Jesse not only believes in God, but he firmly believes God believes in him." [71]

As the masterful portrait by Marshall Frady shows, sometimes this religious vision inspires Jackson to rise to heights of courage and inspiration few can match. In the fall of 1990, when Saddam Hussein held Western hostages in the face of mounting military pressure by U.N. forces, the audacious Jackson traveled to the Persian Gulf on an errand of mercy. In tense negotiations with Saddam, Jackson secured the release of a plane load of hostages, possibly setting in motion what turned out to be a "wholesale exodus" of those detained in Iraq. With anxious passengers ready to depart, Jackson was besought by a woman (who had been hiding in a hotel room) to take her with him. He pleaded with the Iraqi authorities for hours to let her go, but they were adamant that she must stay because she had defied Iraqi orders. With the hostages ready to depart and tensions rising, Jackson thought of Jesus' parable of the one lost sheep. He decided that the woman must not be left behind. To ensure the safety of the other hostages, Jackson told the Iraqi authorities to let them depart but that he would remain behind, in effect offering himself as a hostage for the woman. Not wanting such an incident, the Iraqis finally relented; the woman was allowed to go. The denouement of the story, however, came when the hostages, including the woman, prepared for the last leg of their journey to freedom. As they rushed across the tarmac of the Kuwaiti airport to their plane, the normally limelight-seeking Jackson stayed back. Frady, surprised by this, edged over to get a better look. What he saw was Jackson, standing alone in the dark, weeping.[72]

Jackson represents, in a sense, the purest populism in America today, in his charismatic style and in his blend of religious piety, moral traditionalism, and progressive politics. There is great power in such a blend. One cannot understand the rise in black voting rates in the 1980s, or Democratic party politics in the 1990s, apart from Jackson's two presidential quests, which helped African Americans realize some of the promise of the 1965 Voting Rights Act. And one cannot understand those campaigns and Jackson's ongoing work apart from his religious charisma and church base.

No less than Robertson, Jackson sees "God's hand in history." No less than Robertson, he sees himself embarked on a divine quest to fulfill God's mission on earth. Amidst the complexities and contradictions of his life, one thing shines with dazzling clarity: To Jackson every public issue involves a moral dimension, ultimately religious. His role as prophet is to reveal that "moral center." When liberals complain about the mixing of religion and politics, they seldom target Jackson or his black church followers. They seldom complain when he argues that there is a Christian position on public policy issues. Yet with astounding creativity, Jackson finds the gospel in every nook and cranny of our political landscape. At times it sharply pricks our conscience. When a fire killed twenty-five people in a chicken processing plant in Hamlet, North Carolina, Jackson gave voice not only to the tragedy but to the moral failure as well. Even on mundane political issues, Jackson finds the gospel. Discussing the nation's need to invest in infrastructure, Jackson recounted in biblical language the story of a water-main break in Washington, D.C., that shut down a section of the city. "When the waters come, we are all in the same boat." Talking about health care, he reminded listeners that Jesus did not ask the woman whether she had insurance before he healed her of "the issue of blood." Amazingly, he usually pulls it off.

Jackson's incessant linking of issues with Christian imperatives, however, at times wears thin, illustrating one of the problems with his dependence on religious insight. He criticizes schemes that would encourage educational choice, which are supported by many inner-city blacks, through a strained reasoning about how Jesus suffered all the children.[73] Forsaking any hope of developing independent leverage in both political parties, he routinely compares Republican presidents to Pharaoh, Herod, and Nero. Imploring people to vote Democratic, he reminds them that Jesus rode into Jerusalem on a donkey, not an elephant.[74] Moving beyond the bounds of creative interpretation, Jackson referred to Mary the mother of Jesus as a "single parent" and made the holy family "homeless."[75] When his charisma is checked, Jackson can become petty and mean-spirited. Sensing his marginalization in 1992, Jackson courted Jerry Brown, dallied with Ross Perot, and chastised Bill Clinton. For years critics have noted that Jackson has an enormous ego constantly in need of stroking, that he is a haphazard administrator, and that he avoids the gritty task of tackling the problems he inveighs against. These attributes, too, suggest problems with religious charisma.[76]

Jackson's prophetic stance tempts him to see unambiguous, God-ordained solutions to human problems and injustice. He seems unaware of Reinhold Niebuhr's insight that at times God's intentions on foreign and domestic policy are not as clear as we might think, especially when trade-offs are involved. A populist identification with the "tillers of the soil" is one thing; envisioning a solution that does not entail massive farm subsidies (which often find their way into the hands of the wealthiest farmers while increasing prices and deficits) is another. Opposing defense spending is one thing; calling for U.S. force, if necessary, to restore the presidency of Jean-Bertrand Aristide in Haiti implies that some defense spending might be valuable in pursuit of justice. The temptation to offer "cheap prophecy" as an answer to complex issues can obscure the difficulties and trade-offs. At times

Jackson seems to have blinders. As critic A. M. Rosenthal asks, why does he not more vigorously reject Louis Farrakhan, whose virulent anti-Semitic influence now extends to college campuses? And how can Jackson justify his flirtation with unsavory foreign leaders—"Castro, Arafat, Qaddafi, the Ortegas, and Assad?" [77]

Thus Jackson's religious identification can be a source of great strength, but it also illustrates his temptation to identify his agenda with God's. Because Jackson aims so high— the very redemption of the United States—his personal failings seem particularly glaring. When he invited rap singer Sister Souljah to a Rainbow Coalition meeting, he surrendered to racial polarization, the divisive force his prophetic side fights against. When he reacted angrily and meanly to Clinton's criticism of the rap artist, exposing his easily bruised ego, he undermined his claim to articulate the "moral" position. Jackson at times seems at war with himself. Wanting to be recognized as the preeminent leader of black America, he is loath to criticize Farrakhan, Sister Souljah, or Al Sharpton. Yet he also strives to be the prophet of a generation, speaking a message that cuts across racial, ethnic, and class lines. Morally puritanical, he nonetheless forges a coalition with the cultural left that often shows contempt for puritanism. He agonizes about abortion but criticizes candidates who do not take the most extreme abortion-rights positions. In Jackson we see a classic problem with religious charisma: without checks or accountability, the ego becomes conflated with the religious persona.

Some important concerns about the relationship between church and state also arise from Jackson's religious populism. This study highlights a double standard in the way political efforts through black churches are treated (with impunity) compared with political efforts of other churches (with great scrutiny). The Catholic church in New York was sued over its antiabortion activities,[78] and the religious right frequently is accused of violating American norms separating church and state. Jackson's campaigns, however, induced many black churches and ministers to engage increasingly in overt partisan politics. To be sure, a deep historical legacy created and sustains a unique black church community and encourages political involvement. But Robertson is surely right when he suggests that political involvement is ticklish for white evangelicals but not for Jackson. "He went into black churches, raised money, took political offerings, had political rallies. They broke every regulation the IRS has and nobody paid any attention to it." Robertson claimed that had he done what Jackson did, "It would have been incredible; there would have been church tax exemptions being lifted all over America." [79] Perhaps the difference in the way the black church is treated reflects the extent to which our system works on the basis of informal accommodation, rather than on strict legality. For the government to descend upon the most important social institution in the black community, with its unique place in history, would seem to compound a history of injustice to African Americans. Such an accommodation, however reasonable it may be, does not diminish the hypocrisy of some "strict separationists" who selectively target only politically incorrect churches for their scrutiny.

Perhaps the deeper problem for the black church is the one identified by Tocqueville, but with a special twist. Because of its pivotal position in African American life, the church must take the lead in the crucial task—freely acknowledged by many ministers and scholars—of reestablishing the fabric of healthy family structures within the black community. Jackson's success at mobilizing black churches may entice other politicians to exploit that resource. To the extent that political effort diverts the church from its cultural role—creating healthy role models, building support systems for youth without parental guidance, and the like—it may undermine a critical mission. To Jackson and many other black preachers the political and the cultural cannot be distinguished. But allowing politicians, white or black, to co-opt such a valuable community institution for their own political agendas may delay a serious reckoning with the cultural crisis afflicting a segment of the African American community.

Robertson and the Politics of Insularity

Robertson's enormous success as a broadcast entrepreneur, university founder, and charitable organizer suggests genuine administrative and business acumen. His creation of the Family Channel as a wholesome alternative to prime-time television was both a brilliant financial move and a shrewd means of fighting the "war" over American culture. To his credit he has put money and energy behind charitable and educational programs that have won praise outside the evangelical world. On the political front he has succeeded in building the Christian Coalition into a genuine grass-roots organization that champions culturally populist themes and exercises considerable influence in the Republican party. Thus Robertson brings some strengths to his work not often associated with Jackson. Moreover, his concern about secular elites is not without foundation, as scholars have concluded that those with prestigious educations and professions do indeed form the secular vanguard of society.[80]

But we see in Robertson, as in Jackson, a tendency to conflate his personal agenda with God's plan. At times Robertson's moral jeremiad can seem compelling, as it did in Wichita, Kansas, when he joined protesters in chastising the doctor who performed third-trimester abortions (in a nationally advertised "business"). But it also can seem absurd, as it does when he links liberals with Satan and feminists with witchcraft. Robertson's understanding of prophecy as prediction also produces some troubling implications. He has foreseen stock market crashes that never occurred, and he repeatedly predicted (on the basis of prophecies in the Book of Revelation) that the Soviet Union would lead an army against Israel. His dependence on special religious powers of discernment apparently produces a kind of intellectual laziness, a habit of not letting facts get in the way of perceived insight. Moreover, Robertson uses his predictions to offer financial advice to "700 Club" members. And his newsletter oddly blends discussions of the coming kingdom with detailed investment advice —"This is a good year to purchase government T-bills and commercial paper."

Robertson's biblical literalism can take a disturbing turn as well. When asked on one "700 Club" program how God could have sanctioned genocide against the Midianites in the Book of Numbers, Robertson responded that sometimes God commands his people to "kill 'em all." His justification, moreover, was that such an extreme policy would prevent those killed from passing their wickedness to progeny who would likely be condemned to hell.[81]

Politically, Robertson tends to associate his personal fate with the divine plan. Responding to his early success in Michigan, he crowed, "The Christians have won!"[82] Moreover, his vision has become narrowly partisan. The splashy launching of the Christian Coalition in November 1991 often resembled a pep rally for right-wing Republican politics, thinly covered with a religious patina. The complaint is not that Robertson criticized federal regulation, taxes, gun control, and excessive litigation (those are legitimate issues for debate) but that he clumsily attempted to weave these technical and often secular concerns into a Christian "struggle for the soul of America." The sacred and the partisan were so merged that by the end of the conference Robertson's "Christian" followers were cheering announcements of Republican victories in state legislative contests. Oliver Thomas, counsel for the Baptist Joint Committee, conveys the partisanship that characterized the meeting: "Ralph Reed, the executive director of the Christian Coalition, was on the platform proclaiming the victories of the past year. Eight Democrats have been ousted from the Virginia Senate alone. In their place were prolife, profamily Republicans, most of whom were at the luncheon. Praise the Lord, said Reed." Thomas's statement that his own brother was a "Democratic officeholder and a fine Christian layman," was received with stunned silence.[83]

Since Robertson is pessimistic about the feasibility of any accommodation between conservative Christians and their perceived adversaries, he accepts the premise that a fierce "culture war" is now being waged in America.[84] Like any civil war there will be winners and losers. "Either we rule it or we will be subjects."[85] Although Robertson rejects theocracy, such statements hint of a latent and troubling Christian reconstructionism—the doctrine that believers should rule the government along Old Testament lines. Certainly, those who value crosscultural understanding cannot find comfort in talk of war, in which sympathy, along with truth, will be the first casualty.

Robertson's insulated religiosity, therefore, kept him from appealing to voters who might have shared his cultural critique of the times but who could not stomach his faith-healing ministry, his tendency to equate personal fortune with God's plan, or his paranoid musings about Freemasonry and the Illuminati. After his presidential campaign in 1988 Robertson retreated into the conspiratorial world of his subculture, obsessed with the language of the "new world order" in the same way previous generations had fixated on the "elders of Zion."[86] A nascent communitarian and Christian concern for the moral climate, which had emerged in his presidential campaign, seemed to lapse somewhat as he sought to wield influence in the Republican party. Robertson continued to rally Christian Coalition members on issues concerning abortion, pornographic art, the breakup of the family, and laxity in educational standards, but he tied that agenda, not altogether convincingly, to a "realist" foreign policy, laissez faire capitalism, and Jeffersonian individualism. Although Robertson's charismatic religion suggests that a godly plan guides the minute details of his life, his politics do not always seem to flow from that religious vision.

Finally, Robertson's crusade illustrates another sobering possibility: Populism, because it plays on discontent, can take an ugly turn. During the 1992 Republican National Convention, for example, one observer noticed that a Robertson state delegation cheered lustily as Houston police officers roughed up some gay rights demonstrators.[87] Evidence of a new and virulent strain of gay bashing convinces critics of the religious right that this kind of populism is indeed akin to the racist strain of a generation ago.

THE CHALLENGE OF CONTEMPORARY POPULISM

If a relatively positive portrait of religious populism has emerged in this study, we must remember that dangers and weaknesses loom as well. It is one thing to prophesy but quite another to come up with practical solutions in a complex, pluralistic, bureaucratic age. Before we celebrate church-based political mobilization, we should remind ourselves that it reflects the anemic state of the American political system. As Benjamin Ginsberg and Martin Shefter note, the two dominant political parties, content with their entrenched position in their respective branches of government, have largely given up on the kind of electoral mobilization that in the past channeled popular grievances.[88] Jackson and Robertson rushed into the vacuum left by this electoral weakening of parties. Thus we can view church-based voter registration and political mobilization as both a symptom of the civil malaise and an attempted cure.

The dependence of movements on the special religious lights of their leaders, as we have seen, may also lead to a troubling mixture of the sacred and the partisan. When Jackson compares Ronald Reagan to Pilate, George Bush to Nero, and Dan Quayle to Herod, or when Robertson implies that liberal politicians are in league with Satan, a dangerous line has been crossed, one that should trouble even the most generous accommodationist. Quayle, whatever his faults, hardly qualifies for the appellation "Herod of our generation." [89] And just because well-meaning Democratic politicians disagree with Robertson on complex policy issues, he should not link them with the prince of darkness. At the very least, one should approach these powerful religious images with humility.

Having acknowledged these dangers, I conclude that gospel populism in the 1980s and 1990s has much to teach us. A liberal political system must find ways to accommodate our concerns for economic security and moral stability, or we will continue to experience periodic outbursts of populist anger aimed at upsetting the repose of the smug and satisfied. Perhaps a rediscovery of the "forgotten ethic" of American populist communalism will help—an ethic simultaneously egalitarian and religious, democratic and morally nurturing.[90] Finding the practical contours of such an ethic will not be easy. But we should not be deterred from responding to the politics of discontent with authentic measures of hope.

NOTES

1. Peter Worsley, "The Concept of Populism," in *Populism: Its Meaning and National Characteristics*, ed. Ghita Ionescu and Ernest Gellner (London: Macmillan, 1969), 248. By cataloging diverse expressions of populism around the globe, international scholars have helped to define the scope and nature of populist politics. This fine collection demonstrates the enduring utility of the concept of populism as distinct from conventional ideological positions.
2. Ibid.

3. Michael Oreskes, "Alienation from Government Grows," *New York Times*, Sept. 19, 1990, A15; Michael Oreskes, "As Election Day Nears, Poll Finds Nation's Voters in a Gloomy Mood," *New York Times*, Nov. 4, 1990, 1; Phil Duncan, "The Lesson of Election Day: Angry Voters Want Action," *Congressional Quarterly Weekly Report*, Nov. 9, 1991, 3301.
4. Paul Weyrich, "Conservatism for the People," *National Review*, Sept. 3, 1990, 24-27.
5. Kevin Phillips, *The Politics of Rich and Poor* (New York: Random House, 1990).
6. Charles Murray, "The Shape of Things to Come," *National Review*, July 8, 1991, 29-30.
7. Kenneth T. Walsh, "The Retro Campaign," *U.S. News and World Report*, Dec. 9, 1991, 32-34.
8. Matthew Cooper with Dorian Friedman, "The Rich in America: Why a Populist Campaign against Them Has Its Limits," *U.S. News and World Report*, Nov. 18, 1991, 39.
9. E. J. Dionne, *Washington Post National Weekly Edition*, May 20-26, 1991.
10. Robert Bellah et al., *Habits of the Heart* (Berkeley: University of California Press, 1985).
11. Robert Booth Fowler, *The Dance With Community: The Contemporary Debate in American Political Thought* (Lawrence: University of Kansas Press, 1991).
12. Communitarian thinkers unveiled their platform at this conference and launched a journal, *The Responsive Community*. See Alvin P. Sanoff and Ted Gest, "Battling the Rights Wings," *U.S. News and World Report*, Nov. 25, 1991, 28-30.
13. David S. Broder, "Get the Point?" *Washington Post National Weekly Edition*, Oct. 1-7, 1990, 4.
14. R. W. Apple, Jr., "Erudition and Straight Talk by a Political Neophyte," *New York Times*, Oct. 9, 1990.
15. Fox Butterfield, "Politics of Rage Dominates Contest in Massachusetts," *New York Times*, Nov. 1, 1990, A1.
16. Broder, "Get the Point?"
17. John Silber, *Straight Shooting* (New York: Harper and Row, 1989).
18. These passages were quoted by Jenkin Lloyd Jones, "Candidate Campaigns for Moral Regeneration, Better Education," syndicated column, *Daily Oklahoman*, Nov. 4, 1990.
19. Sidney Blumenthal, "Populism in Tweeds," *New Republic*, Nov. 25, 1991, 10-15.
20. David S. Broder, "Making Bad Choices," syndicated column, *Norman Transcript*, Nov. 13, 1991.
21. Roberto Suro, "Aide in Duke's Campaign Quits, Questioning Religious Conversion," *New York Times*, Nov. 13, 1991.
22. The photograph by Mark Hirsch appeared in the Sunday *New York Times*, Nov. 3, 1991, 1, accompanying an article by Isabel Wilkerson, "Seeking a Racial Mix, Dubuque Finds Tension." The photograph showed four young men sporting T-shirts embossed with the letters *NAAWP* (National Association for the Advancement of White People). I say "pathetic" because to

identify oneself solely as a white person indicates a detachment from any other ethnic, religious, or community roots or traditions.

23. Sidney Blumenthal, "The Primal Scream," *New Republic*, Oct. 21, 1991, 22-25.
24. "Hotline, American Political Network," published by Doug Bailey and Roger Craver, 1991.
25. Sylvia Nasar, "The 1980s: A Very Good Time for the Rich," *New York Times*, March 5, 1992, A1.
26. Sylvia Nasar, "Federal Report Gives New Data on Gains by Richest in '80s," *New York Times*, April 21, 1992, A1.
27. See Paul Starobin, "Silver Linings," *National Journal*, April 11, 1992, 858-862.
28. This is the argument made by Donald L. Barlett and James B. Steele, *America: What Went Wrong* (Kansas City, Mo.: Andrews and McMeel, 1992).
29. Don Kash, *Perpetual Innovation* (New York: Basic Books, 1989).
30. The term "new class" was actually coined by dissident scholars in the communist bloc who saw in the party bureaucrats a new class, neither bourgeois nor proletariat but well-connected elites whose power flowed from the state. The term then became especially fashionable among such critics of the left as Daniel Patrick Moynihan and Jeane Kirkpatrick. It is a staple of neoconservative thought today. Peter Berger prefers the term "new knowledge class." See Peter Berger, *A Rumor of Angels*, expanded ed. (New York: Anchor, 1990).
31. Charles E. Lindblom, *Politics and Markets* (New York: Basic Books, 1977).
32. Michael Novak, *Free Persons and the Public Good* (Lanham, Md.: Madison Books, 1989).
33. Francis Fukuyama, "The End of History?" *National Interest* (Summer 1989), which was expanded into *The End of History and the Last Man* (New York: Free Press, 1992); and Theodore Lowi, Rothbaum Lectures, University of Oklahoma, Norman, November 1991.
34. Frances Fox Piven and Richard A. Cloward, *The New Class War: Reagan's Attack on the Welfare State and Its Consequences* (New York: Pantheon, 1982).
35. Fukuyama, "End of History?"
36. Samuel Huntington, *The Third Wave* (Norman: University of Oklahoma Press, 1991).
37. Fukuyama, "End of History? " 18.
38. This allusion is from Richard Hovey's play *The Marriage of Guenevere*, as quoted in Jackson Lears, *No Place of Grace: Antimodernism and the Transformation of American Culture, 1880-1920* (New York: Pantheon, 1981).
39. Allen D. Hertzke and Ronald M. Peters, Jr., eds., *The Atomistic Congress: An Interpretation of Political Change* (Armonk, N.Y.: M. E. Sharpe, 1992).
40. Theodore J. Lowi, "Before Conservatism and Beyond," unpublished manuscript, Cornell University, 1992; and Louis Hartz, *The Liberal Tradition in America: An Interpretation of American Political Thought since the Revolution* (New York: Harcourt, Brace, 1955).
41. Lowi, "Before Conservatism and Beyond."
42. "All Things Considered," National Public Radio, Dec. 10, 1991.
43. Robert B. Reich, *The Work of Nations* (New York: Knopf, 1991).

44. Andrew Oldenquist, *The Nonsuicidal Society* (Bloomington: Indiana University Press, 1986); Alasdair MacIntyre, *After Virtue: A Study in Moral Theory* (Notre Dame, Ind.: University of Notre Dame Press, 1984); Christopher Lasch, *Culture of Narcissism* (New York: Norton, 1991); John P. Diggins, *The Lost Soul of American Politics: Virtue, Self-Interest, and the Foundations of Liberalism* (New York: Basic Books, 1984).
45. Oldenquist, *Nonsuicidal Society*, 7.
46. Ibid.
47. My thanks to an old friend, Alan Merson, for this term.
48. Christopher Lasch, "Capitalism vs. Cultural Conservatism?" *First Things* (April 1990): 20, 22, 23.
49. MacIntyre, *After Virtue*.
50. Christopher Lasch, *Haven in a Heartless World: The Family Besieged* (New York: Basic Books, 1979); Bellah et al., *Habits of the Heart;* Lears, *No Place of Grace;* Fowler, *Dance With Community*.
51. Two of the books are Richard Louv, *Childhood's Future* (Boston: Houghton Mifflin, 1990); and David Blankenhorn et al., eds., *Rebuilding the Nest* (Milwaukee: Family Service America, 1990).
52. Ernest L. Boyer, "America Has Orphaned Its Young," *Los Angeles Times*, Dec. 8, 1991, M5. The Carnegie report is titled *Ready to Learn: A Mandate for the Nation* (Princeton: Princeton University Press, 1992).
53. Victor R. Fuchs and Diane M. Reklis, "America's Children: Economic Perspectives and Policy Options," *Science*, Jan. 3, 1992, 41-46.
54. "Beyond Jobless Figures, A Rise in Poor Children," *New York Times*, Nov. 26, 1991, A11.
55. Louv, *Childhood's Future*.
56. David J. Eggebeen and Daniel T. Lichter, cited in Chris Raymond, "Research Notes," *Chronicle of Higher Education*, Jan. 8, 1992, A8.
57. National Commission on Children, *Beyond Rhetoric: A New American Agenda for Children and Families* (Washington, D.C.: Government Printing Office, 1991), xviii.
58. Ibid., 343-344.
59. Ibid., 343-366.
60. Buchanan presented this analysis in a lecture at the University of Oklahoma, Norman, fall 1991.
61. Television networks have unveiled what may be a new low in the exploitation of violence. According to *Newsweek*, NBC has produced a new series—"I Witness Video"—that features camcorder footage of violent events. Episodes include footage of a policeman being kicked, stabbed, and shot to death; a car slamming into a pedestrian; an airplane crashing into a crowd; and a police shoot-out that ends with a bullet-riddled fugitive hanging from a car window, blood gushing from his head. The article concluded that "NBC's exercise in necro-shock comes from the pits of the porn trade. The word is snuff—and that rhymes with enough." (Harry F. Waters, *Newsweek*, June 15, 1992, 59-60.)
62. Alan Ehrenhalt, *The United States of Ambition: Politicians, Power, and the Pursuit*

of Office (New York: Random House, 1991).

63. James MacGregor Burns, *Leadership* (New York: Harper and Row, 1978).
64. William Manchester, *The Last Lion* (Boston: Little, Brown, 1983).
65. Jesse Jackson, interview with author, flight from Washington, D.C., to Dallas, March 12, 1992.
66. Jackson, speech to delegates, 1988 Democratic National Convention, in *Keep Hope Alive: Jesse Jackson's 1988 Presidential Campaign*, ed. Frank Clemente and Frank Watkins (Boston: South End Press, 1989), 218.
67. Robert Booth Fowler, *Unconventional Partners: Religion and Liberal Culture in the United States* (Grand Rapids, Mich.: Eerdmans, 1989).
68. The tensions between populism and liberalism are documented extensively by Christopher Lasch, who also draws upon republican historiography to discern sources of the populist critique of individualism. See Lasch, *The True and Only Heaven: Progress and Its Critics* (New York: Norton, 1991).
69. Jackson, speech to the Rainbow Coalition candidate forum, Washington, D.C., Jan. 25, 1992.
70. These quotes are from Marshall Frady, "Profiles: Outsider, II—History Is upon Us," *New Yorker*, Feb. 10, 1992, 66.
71. Quoted in Ernest R. House, *Jesse Jackson and the Politics of Charisma: The Rise and Fall of the Push/Excel Program* (Boulder: Westview Press, 1988), 17.
72. Frady, "Profiles: Outsider, III—Without Portfolio," *New Yorker*, Feb. 17, 1992, 58-69.
73. Jackson, speech to the National Baptist Convention USA, Oklahoma City, June 19, 1991.
74. Frady, "Profiles: Outsider, I—The Gift," *New Yorker*, Feb. 3, 1992, 52.
75. Jackson, speech to the Democratic National Convention, New York City, July 14, 1992.
76. House documents the administrative problems involved with charismatic leadership in *Jesse Jackson and the Politics of Charisma*.
77. A. M. Rosenthal, "Jesse Jackson's Message," *New York Times*, April 17, 1992, A17.
78. See Edward M. Gaffney, Jr., "The Abortion Rights Mobilization Case: Political Advocacy and Tax Exemption of Churches," in *The Role of Religion in the Making of Public Policy*, ed. James E. Wood, Jr., and Derek Davis (Waco, Texas: Dawson Institute of Church-State Studies, 1991).
79. Robertson, interview with author, Virginia Beach, Va., Aug. 8, 1991.
80. Wade Clark and William McKinney, *American Mainline Religion: Its Changing Shape and Future* (New Brunswick, N.J.: Rutgers University Press, 1987), 115.
81. Recorded in Gerard Thomas Straub, *Salvation for Sale: An Insider's View of Pat Robertson* (Buffalo: Prometheus Books, 1988), 358-359.
82. "Tax Free Candidate Endorsements," *National Journal*, Dec. 9, 1989, 2985.
83. Oliver S. Thomas, "Views from the Wall," Report from the Capital, January 1992, 7.
84. This language of the culture war is a staple of the scholarly and religious literature. See James Davison Hunter, *Culture Wars* (New York: Basic Books, 1991); Richard John Neuhaus, *America against Itself* (Notre Dame, Ind.:

University of Notre Dame Press, 1992); Robert Wuthnow, *The Struggle for America's Soul* (Grand Rapids, Mich.: Eerdmans, 1989); and James Dobson and Gary Bauer, *Children at Risk* (Dallas: Word, 1990).

85. Robertson, speech at fund-raising event, Edmond, Okla., Nov. 12, 1988.
86. Pat Robertson, *The New World Order* (Dallas: Word, 1991).
87. This story was relayed to me by a fellow professor who attended the convention.
88. Benjamin Ginsberg and Martin Shefter, *Politics by Other Means: The Declining Importance of Elections in America* (New York: Basic Books, 1990).
89. Jackson used this phrase in his speech to the Democratic National Convention, New York City, July 14, 1992.
90. Barry Alan Shain, "A Study in Eighteenth Century Political Theory: Liberty, Autonomy, Protestant Communalism, and Slavery in Revolutionary America" (Ph.D. diss., Yale University, 1990).

Suggested Readings

Ahlstrom, Sydney. *A Religious History of the American People.* New Haven: Yale University Press, 1972.

Almond, Gabriel, and Sidney Verba. *The Civic Culture.* Newbury Park, Calif.: Sage, 1989.

____. *The Civic Culture Revisited.* Newbury Park, Calif.: Sage, 1989.

Bailyn, Bernard. *The Ideological Origins of the American Revolution.* Cambridge, Mass.: Belknap Press, 1967.

Barker, Lucius J. "New Perspectives in American Politics." In *The National Political Science Review.* Vol. 1. Edited by Lucius J. Barker. New Brunswick, N.J.: Transaction, 1989.

____. *Our Time Has Come: A Delegate's Diary of Jesse Jackson's 1984 Presidential Campaign.* Urbana: University of Illinois Press, 1988.

Barker, Lucius J., and Jesse McCorry. *Black Americans and the Political System.* Boston: Little, Brown, 1980.

Barker, Lucius J., and Ronald Walters. *Jesse Jackson's 1984 Presidential Campaign.* Urbana: University of Illinois Press, 1988.

Barlett, Donald L., and James B. Steele. *America: What Went Wrong?* (Kansas City, Mo.: Andrews and McMeel, 1992).

Bartels, Larry M., and C. Anthony Broh, "The Polls—A Review: The 1988 Presidential Primaries." *Public Opinion Quarterly* 53 (Winter 1989): 573-575.

Bell, Daniel. *The Cultural Contradictions of Capitalism.* New York: Basic Books, 1976.

Bellah, Robert et al. *Habits of the Heart.* Berkeley: University of California Press, 1985.

Berger, Peter. *A Rumor of Angels.* Expanded edition. New York: Anchor, 1990.

Berman, Marshall. *All That Is Solid Melts into Air: The Experience of Modernity.* New York: Simon and Schuster, 1982.

Black, Earl, and Merle Black. *Politics and Society in the South.* Cambridge: Harvard University Press, 1987.

Boyte, Harry C., and Frank Riessman. *The New Populism: The Politics of Empowerment.* Philadelphia: Temple University Press, 1986.

Branch, Taylor. *Parting the Waters: America in the King Years, 1954-1963.* New York: Simon and Schuster, 1988.

Brinkley, Alan. *Voices of Protest: Huey Long, Father Coughlin, and the Great Depression.* New York: Knopf, 1982.

Broh, C. Anthony. *A Horse of a Different Color: Television's Treatment of Jesse Jackson's 1984 Campaign.* Washington, D.C.: Joint Center for Political Studies, 1987.

Bruce, Steve. *The Rise and Fall of the New Christian Right.* New York: Oxford University Press, 1988.

Bryan, William Jennings. *The First Battle.* Chicago: Conkey, 1896.

Buell, Emmett H., and Lee Sigelman. *Nominating the President.* Knoxville: University of Tennessee Press, 1991.

Burland, Philip B., and Ralph Lerner, eds. *The Founders' Constitution.* Chicago: University of Chicago Press, 1987.

Burns, James MacGregor. *Leadership.* New York: Harper and Row, 1978.

Butler, Jon. *Awash in a Sea of Faith: Christianizing the American People.* Cambridge: Harvard University Press, 1990.

Canovan, Margaret. *Populism.* New York: Harcourt Brace Jovanovich, 1981.

Cantrell, Gregg, and D. Scott Barton. "Texas Populists and the Failure of Biracial Politics." *Journal of Southern History* 55 (November 1989): 659-692.

Carter, Stephen L. *Reflections of an Affirmative Action Baby.* New York: Basic Books, 1991.

Cavanagh, James. *Inside Black America.* Washington, D.C.: Joint Center for Political Studies, 1985.

Ceaser, James W. *Presidential Selection: Theory and Development.* Princeton: Princeton University Press, 1979.

Clanton, Gene O. *Kansas Populism: Ideas and Men.* Lawrence: University of Kansas Press, 1969.

Clark, Norman H. *Deliver Us from Evil: An Interpretation of American Prohibition.* New York: Norton, 1976.

Clemente, Frank, and Frank Watkins, eds. *Keep Hope Alive: Jesse Jackson's 1988 Presidential Campaign.* Boston: South End Press, 1989.

Coletta, Paolo. *William Jennings Bryan.* 3 vols. Lincoln: University of Nebraska Press, 1964 for vol. 1 and 1969 for vols. 2 and 3.

Collins, Sheila D. *The Rainbow Challenge: The Jackson Campaign and the Future of U.S. Politics.* New York: Monthly Review Press, 1986.

Colton, Elizabeth. *The Jackson Phenomenon: The Man, the Power, the Message.* New York: Doubleday, 1989.

Converse, Phillip. "The Nature of Belief Systems in Mass Publics." In *Ideology and Discontent.* Edited by David Apter. New York: Free Press, 1964.

Crews, Mickey. *The Church of God: A Social History.* Knoxville: University of Tennessee Press, 1990.

Cunningham, Raymond. *The Populists in Historical Perspective.* Boston: Heath, 1968.

Dash, Leon. *When Children Want Children: The Urban Crisis of Teenage Childbearing.* New York: Morrow, 1989.

Diggins, John P. *The Lost Soul of American Politics: Virtue, Self-Interest, and the Foundations of Liberalism*. New York: Basic Books, 1984.

Dionne, E. J. *Why Americans Hate Politics* (New York: Simon and Schuster, 1991).

Dobson, James, and Gary Bauer. *Children at Risk*. Dallas: Word, 1990.

Donnelly, Ignatius. *Caesar's Column: A Story of the Twentieth Century*. Cambridge, Mass.: Belknap Press, 1960.

Du Bois, W. E. B. *The Souls of Black Folk*. Chicago: A. C. McClung, 1903.

Edelman, Murray. *The Symbolic Uses of Politics*. Urbana: University of Illinois Press, 1964.

Ehrenhalt, Alan. *The United States of Ambition: Politicians, Power, and the Pursuit of Office*. New York: Random House, 1991.

Eisenach, Eldon. "The American Revolution Made and Remembered: Cultural Politics and Political Thought." *American Studies* 20 (Spring 1979).

Epstein, Leon D. *Political Parties in the American Mold*. Madison: University of Wisconsin Press, 1986.

Erikson, Erik H. *Young Man Luther: A Study in Psychoanalysis and History*. New York: Norton, 1962.

Evans, Sara M., and Harry C. Boyte. *Free Spaces: The Sources of Democratic Change in America*. New York: Harper and Row, 1986.

Faw, Bob, and Nancy Skelton. *Thunder in America: The Improbable Presidential Campaign of Jesse Jackson*. Austin: Texas Monthly Press, 1986.

Fenno, Richard F., Jr. *Home Style: House Members in Their Districts*. Boston: Little, Brown, 1978.

Fowler, Robert Booth. *The Dance With Community: The Contemporary Debate in American Political Thought*. Lawrence: University of Kansas Press, 1991.

____. *Religion and Politics in America*. Metuchen, N.J.: Scarecrow, 1985.

____. *Unconventional Partners: Religion and Liberal Culture in the United States*. Grand Rapids, Mich.: Eerdmans, 1989.

Frady, Marshall. "Profiles: Outsider, I—The Gift." *New Yorker*, Feb. 3, 1992, 36-69; "II—History Is upon Us," *New Yorker*, Feb. 10, 1992, 41-75; "III—Without Portfolio," *New Yorker*, Feb. 17, 1992, 39-69.

Freeman, Jo. "The Political Culture of the Democratic and Republican Parties." *Political Science Quarterly* 101 (1986): 327-344.

Fukuyama, Francis. "The End of History?" *National Interest*. Summer 1989.

____. *The End of History and the Last Man*. New York: Free Press, 1992.

Gaither, Gerald H. *Blacks and the Populist Revolt: Ballots and Bigotry in the New South*. Tuscaloosa: University of Alabama Press, 1977.

Gallup, George, Jr. "Religion in America, 50 Years: 1935-1985." Gallup Report 236, May 1985.

Gamson, William, and B. Fireman. "Utilitarian Logic in the Resource Mobilization Perspective." In *The Dynamics of Social Movements*. Edited by John D. McCarthy and Mayer N. Zald. Cambridge, Mass.: Winthrop, 1978.

Garrow, David J. *Bearing the Cross: Martin Luther King, Jr., and the Southern Christian Leadership Conference*. New York: Vintage, 1986.

Germond, Jack, and Jules Witcover. *Whose Broad Stripes and Bright Stars: The Trivial Pursuit of the Presidency*. New York: Warner, 1989.

Gibbs, Jewelle Taylor et al. *Young, Black, and Male in America: An Endangered Species.* Dover, Mass.: Auburn House, 1988.

Ginsberg, Benjamin, and Martin Shefter. *Politics by Other Means: The Declining Importance of Elections in America.* New York: Basic Books, 1990.

Goodwyn, Lawrence. *The Populist Moment: A Short History of the Agrarian Revolt in America.* New York: Oxford University Press, 1978.

Greeley, Andrew. *The Denominational Society.* Glenview, Ill.: Scott, Foresman, 1972.

Green, John C., and James L. Guth. "The Christian Right in the Republican Party: The Case of Pat Robertson's Supporters." *Journal of Politics* 50 (February 1988): 150-165.

Guth, James L. "A New Turn for the Christian Right? Robertson's Support from the Southern Baptist Clergy." Paper presented at the annual meeting of the Midwest Political Science Association, Chicago, 1989.

Guth, James L., and John C. Green, eds. *The Bible and the Ballot Box: Religion and Politics in the 1988 Election.* Boulder: Westview Press, 1991.

——. "Robertson's Republicans: Christian Activists in Republican Politics." *Election Politics* 4 (Fall 1987): 9-14.

Guth, James L., Ted G. Jelen, Lyman A. Kellstedt, Corwin E. Smidt, and Kenneth D. Wald. "The Politics of Religion in America: Issues for Investigation." *American Politics Quarterly* 16 (1988).

Hadden, Jeffrey K., and Anson Shupe. *Televangelism: Power and Politics on God's Frontier.* New York: Holt, 1988.

Harrell, David Edwin, Jr. *Pat Robertson.* San Francisco: Harper, 1987.

Harris, Fred. *The New Populism.* New York: Saturday Review Press, 1973.

Hartz, Louis. *The Liberal Tradition in America: An Interpretation of American Political Thought since the Revolution.* New York: Harcourt, Brace, 1955.

Hatch, Nathan O. *The Democratization of American Christianity.* New Haven: Yale University Press, 1989.

Hatch, Roger D. *Beyond Opportunity: Jesse Jackson's Vision for America.* Philadelphia: Fortress Press, 1988.

Herberg, Will. *Protestant, Catholic, Jew.* New York: Doubleday, 1955.

Hertzke, Allen D. "American Religion and Politics: A Review Essay." *Western Political Quarterly* 41 (December 1988).

——. "Christian Fundamentalists and the Imperatives of American Politics." In *Religious Resurgence and Politics in the Contemporary World.* Edited by Emile Sahliyeh. Albany: State University of New York Press, 1990.

——. *Representing God in Washington: The Role of Religious Lobbies in the American Polity.* Knoxville: University of Tennessee Press, 1988.

Hertzke, Allen D., and Ronald M. Peters, Jr., eds. *The Atomistic Congress: An Interpretation of Political Change.* Armonk, N.Y.: M. E. Sharpe, 1992.

Hicks, John D. *The Populist Revolt.* Lincoln: University of Nebraska Press, 1961.

Hofstadter, Richard. *The Age of Reform.* New York: Vintage, 1955.

House, Ernest R. *Jesse Jackson and the Politics of Charisma: The Rise and Fall of the Push/Excel Program.* Boulder: Westview Press, 1988.

Hunter, James Davison. *American Evangelicalism.* New Brunswick, N.J.: Rutgers

University Press, 1983.
____. *Culture Wars.* New York: Basic Books, 1991.
Huntington, Samuel P. *The Third Wave.* Norman: University of Oklahoma Press, 1991.
Ionescu, Ghita, and Ernest Gellner. *Populism: Its Meaning and National Characteristics.* London: Macmillan, 1969.
Jackson, Jesse L. *Straight from the Heart.* Edited by Roger D. Hatch and Frank E. Watkins. Philadelphia: Fortress Press, 1987.
____. "How We Respect Life Is the Overriding Moral Issue." *National Right to Life News,* Jan. 1977, 5.
Jenkins, Joseph, and Charles Perrow. "Insurgency of the Powerless." *American Sociological Review* 42 (1977): 249-268.
Johnson, Phillip E. *Darwin on Trial.* Washington, D.C.: Regnery Gateway, 1991.
Kash, Don. *Perpetual Innovation.* New York: Basic Books, 1989.
Kelley, Dean M. *Why Conservative Churches Are Growing.* New York: Harper and Row, 1972.
Kessel, John H. *Presidential Campaign Politics.* 3d ed. Homewood, Ill.: Dorsey, 1988.
Kimball, Penn. *Keep Hope Alive: Super Tuesday and Jesse Jackson's 1988 Campaign for the Presidency.* Washington, D.C.: Joint Center for Political and Economic Studies Press, 1992.
Kleppner, Paul. *Continuity and Change in Electoral Politics, 1892-1928.* Westport, Conn.: Greenwood, 1987.
____. *The Cross of Culture: A Social Analysis of Midwestern Politics, 1850-1900.* New York: Free Press, 1970.
Kloppenberg, James T. *Uncertain Victory: Social Democracy and Progressivism in European and American Thought, 1870-1920.* New York: Oxford University Press, 1986.
____. "The Virtues of Liberalism: Christianity, Republicanism, and Ethics in Early American Political Discourse." *Journal of American History* 74 (June 1987): 9-33.
Kurland, Phillip B., and Ralph Lerner. *The Founders' Constitution.* Vol. 1. Chicago: University of Chicago Press, 1987.
Ladd, E. C., and Charles Hadley. *Transformations of the American Party System.* New York: Norton, 1975.
Landess, Thomas H., and Richard M. Quinn. *Jesse Jackson and the Politics of Race.* Ottawa: Jameson Books, 1985.
Lasch, Christopher. "Capitalism vs. Cultural Conservatism?" *First Things* (April 1990): 15-23.
____. *Culture of Narcissism.* New York: Norton, 1991.
____. *Haven in a Heartless World: The Family Besieged.* New York: Basic Books, 1979.
____. *The True and Only Heaven: Progress and Its Critics.* New York: Norton, 1991.
Lawrence, Bruce B. *Defenders of God: The Fundamentalist Revolt against the Modern Age.* San Francisco: Harper and Row, 1989.
Lears, Jackson. *No Place of Grace: Antimodernism and the Transformation of American Culture, 1880-1920.* New York: Pantheon, 1981.

Lemann, Nicholas. *The Promised Land: The Great Migration and How It Changed America.* New York: Knopf, 1991.

Levine, Lawrence. *Defender of the Faith.* New York: Oxford University Press, 1965.

Lienesch, Michael. *New Order of the Ages: Time, The Constitution, and the Making of Modern American Political Thought.* Princeton: Princeton University Press, 1990.

Lillian, Lewis M. "Organization, Rationality, and Spontaneity in the Civil Rights Movement." *American Sociological Review* 42 (1984): 770-783.

Lincoln, C. Eric, and Lawrence H. Mamiya. *The Black Church in the African American Experience.* Durham, N.C.: Duke University Press, 1990.

Lindblom, Charles E. *Politics and Markets.* New York: Basic Books, 1977.

Lipset, Seymour Martin, and Earl Raab. *The Politics of Unreason.* 2d ed. Chicago: University of Chicago Press, 1978.

Louv, Richard. *Childhood's Future.* Boston: Houghton Mifflin, 1990.

McAdam, Doug. *Political Process and the Development of Black Insurgency, 1930-1970.* Chicago: University of Chicago Press, 1985.

McCarthy, John D., and Mayer N. Zald. "Resource Mobilization and Social Movements: A Partial Theory." *American Journal of Sociology* 82 (1977): 1212-1241.

———. *The Trend of Social Movements in America: Professionalization and Resource Mobilization.* Morristown, N.J.: General Learning Press, 1973.

McDonald, Forrest. *Novus Ordo Seclorum: The Intellectual Origins of the Constitution.* Lawrence: University of Kansas Press, 1985.

MacIntyre, Alasdair. *After Virtue: A Study in Moral Theory.* Notre Dame, Ind.: University of Notre Dame Press, 1984.

McLoughlin, William G. *Revivals, Awakening, and Reform: An Essay on Religion and Social Change in America, 1607-1977.* Chicago: University of Chicago Press, 1978.

Maddox, William S., and Stuart A. Lilie. *Beyond Liberal and Conservative: Reassessing the Political Spectrum.* Washington, D.C.: Cato Institute, 1984.

Manchester, William. *The Last Lion: Winston Spencer Churchill.* Vol. 2, *Alone, 1932-1940.* Boston: Little, Brown, 1988.

Marable, Manning. *Black American Politics: From the Washington Marches to Jesse Jackson.* London: Verso, 1985.

Marsden, George M. *Fundamentalism and American Culture.* New York: Oxford University Press, 1980.

Mead, Sydney E. *The Nation with the Soul of a Church.* New York: Harper and Row, 1975.

Menendez, Albert J. *Religion at the Polls.* Philadelphia: Westminster, 1977.

Merelman, Richard A. *Making Something of Ourselves.* Berkeley: University of California Press, 1984.

Meyers, Marvin. *The Jacksonian Persuasion: Politics and Belief.* Stanford: Stanford University Press, 1957.

Miller, Perry. *Errand into the Wilderness.* Cambridge: Harvard University Press, 1956.

Morgan, Edmund S. *The Puritan Dilemma: The Story of John Winthrop.* Boston: Little, Brown, 1958.

Morken, Hubert. *Pat Robertson: Where He Stands.* Old Tappan, N.J.: Revell, 1988.

Morris, Aldon. *The Origins of the Civil Rights Movement: Black Communities Organizing for Change.* New York: Free Press, 1984.

Morris, Lorenzo, ed. *The Social and Political Implications of the 1984 Jesse Jackson Presidential Campaign.* New York: Praeger, 1990.

Neuhaus, Richard John. *America against Itself.* Notre Dame, Ind.: Notre Dame Press, 1992.

____. *The Naked Public Square.* Grand Rapids, Mich.: Eerdmans, 1984.

Nichols-Casebolt, Ann M. "Black Families Headed by Single Mothers: Growing Numbers and Increasing Poverty." *Social Work* (July-August 1988): 306-313.

Nisbet, Robert A. *The Quest for Community.* New York: Oxford University Press, 1953.

Noll, Mark A. *One Nation under God? Christian Faith and Political Action in America.* San Francisco: Harper, 1988.

____, ed. *Religion and American Politics: From the Colonial Period to the 1980s.* New York: Oxford University Press, 1990.

Norris, Mike. "The Holy Wars (Continued)." *Campaigns and Elections,* March-April 1989, 9-10.

Novak, Michael. *Free Persons and the Common Good.* Lanham, Md.: Madison Books, 1989.

Oldenquist, Andrew. *The Nonsuicidal Society.* Bloomington: Indiana University Press, 1986.

Oldfield, Duane M. "Pat Crashes the Party: Reform, Republicans, and Robertson." Working Paper 90-11, Institute of Governmental Studies, University of California at Berkeley, 1990.

____. "The Right and the Righteous: The Christian Right Confronts the Republican Party." PH. D. diss., University of California at Berkeley, 1992.

Olson, Mancur. *The Logic of Collective Action.* Cambridge: Harvard University Press, 1965.

Palmer, Bruce. *Man over Money: The Southern Populist Critique of American Capitalism.* Chapel Hill: University of North Carolina Press, 1980.

Pangle, Thomas L. *The Spirit of Modern Republicanism.* Chicago: University of Chicago Press, 1988.

Peters, Ronald M. *The Massachusetts Constitution of 1780: A Social Compact.* Amherst: University of Massachusetts Press, 1978.

Petrocik, John. "Realignment: New Party Coalitions and the Nationalization of the South." *Journal of Politics* 49 (May 1987): 347-375.

Phillips, Kevin. *The Politics of Rich and Poor.* New York: Random House, 1990.

Piven, Frances Fox, and Richard A. Cloward. *The New Class War: Reagan's Attack on the Welfare State and its Consequences.* New York: Pantheon Books, 1982.

Pocock, J. G. A. *The Machiavellian Moment: Florentine Political Thought and the Atlantic Republican Tradition.* Princeton: Princeton University Press, 1975.

Pohlmann, Marcus D. *Black Politics in Conservative America.* New York: Longman, 1990.

Pollack, Norman. *The Just Polity.* Urbana: University of Illinois Press, 1987.
——. *The Populist Response to Industrial America.* New York: Norton, 1962.
Poloma, Margaret M. *The Assemblies of God at the Crossroads: Charisma and Institutional Dilemmas.* Knoxville: University of Tennessee Press, 1989.
Polsby, Nelson W., and Aaron Wildavsky. *Presidential Elections.* 8th ed. New York: Free Press, 1991.
Preston, Michael, Lenneal J. Henderson, Jr., and Paul L. Puryear. *The New Black Politics.* New York: Longman, 1987.
Ranney, Austin. *Curing the Mischiefs of Faction: Party Reform in America.* Berkeley: University of California Press, 1975.
Reed, Adolph L., Jr. *The Jesse Jackson Phenomenon.* New Haven: Yale University Press, 1986.
Reich, Robert B. *The Work of Nations.* New York: Knopf, 1991.
Reichley, A. James. *Religion in American Public Life.* Washington, D.C.: Brookings Institution, 1985.
Reynolds, Barbara A. *Jesse Jackson: America's David.* Washington D.C.: JFJ Associates, 1985.
Riker, William. *Liberalism against Populism.* Prospect Heights, Ill.: Waveland Press, 1988.
Robbins, John W. *Pat Robertson: A Warning to America.* Jefferson, Md.: Trinity Foundation, 1988.
Robertson, Pat. *America's Dates with Destiny.* Nashville: Thomas Nelson, 1986.
——. *Answers to 200 of Life's Most Probing Questions.* Nashville: Thomas Nelson, 1984.
——. *The New World Order.* Dallas: Word, 1991.
——. *The Plan.* Nashville: Thomas Nelson, 1989.
——. "The Wealth of Black Families." *Conservative Digest,* June 1987, 35-40.
Robertson, Pat, and Jamie Buckingham. *Shout It from the Housetops.* Virginia Beach, Va.: CBN Press, 1986.
Robertson, Pat, with Bob Slosser. *The Secret Kingdom.* Nashville: Thomas Nelson, 1982.
Runkel, David R., ed. *Campaign for President: The Managers Look at '88.* Dover, Mass.: Auburn House, 1989.
Saunders, Robert M. "Southern Populists and the Negro, 1893-1895." *Journal of Negro History* 54 (July 1969): 240-261.
Schattschneider, E. E. *The Semisovereign People.* New York: Holt, Rinehart, 1960.
Shain, Barry Alan. "A Study in Eighteenth Century Political Theory: Liberty, Autonomy, Protestant Communalism, and Slavery in Revolutionary America." Ph.D. diss., Yale University, 1990.
Shalhope, Robert E. "Republicanism and Early American Historiography." *William and Mary Quarterly* 39 (April 1982): 334-356.
——. *The Roots of Democracy: American Thought and Culture, 1760-1800.* Boston: Twayne, 1990.
Sheehy, Gail. "Power or Glory?" *Vanity Fair,* January 1988.
Shils, Edward. "Totalitarians and Antinomians." In *Political Passages.* Edited by John H. Bunzel. New York: Free Press, 1988.

Silber, John. *Straight Shooting: A Course of Action for Our Troubled Times.* New York: Harper and Row, 1989.

Smidt, Corwin E. "Evangelicals and the 1984 Election." *American Politics Quarterly* 15 (October 1987): 419-444.

____. "Praise the Lord Politics: A Comparative Analysis of the Social Characteristics and Political Views of American Evangelical and Charismatic Christians." *Sociological Analysis* 50 (1988): 53-72.

Smidt, Corwin E., and James M. Penning. "A House Divided: A Comparison of Bush and Robertson Delegates to the 1988 Michigan Republican State Convention." *Polity* 23 (Fall 1990): 127-138.

Smith, Willard. *The Social and Religious Thought of William Jennings Bryan.* Lawrence, Kan.: Coronado Press, 1975.

Squires, Gregory D. "Economic Restructuring, Urban Development, and Race: The Political Economy of Civil Rights in 'Post Industrial America.'" *Western Political Quarterly* 43 (March 1990): 201-217.

Steele, Shelby. *The Content of Our Character: A New Vision of Race in America.* New York: St. Martin's, 1990.

Straub, Gerard Thomas. *Salvation for Sale: An Insider's View of Pat Robertson.* Buffalo, N.Y.: Prometheus Books, 1988.

Strout, Cushing. *The New Heavens and New Earth: Political Religion in America.* New York: Harper and Row, 1974.

Swanson, Georgia May. "Messiah or Manipulator? A Burkean Cluster Analysis of the Motivations Revealed in the Selected Speeches of the Reverend Jesse Louis Jackson." Ph.D. diss., Bowling Green State University, 1982.

Thompson, Michael, Richard Ellis, and Aaron Wildavsky. *Cultural Theory.* Boulder: Westview Press, 1990.

Tocqueville, Alexis de. *Democracy in America.* Translated by George Lawrence. Edited by J. P. Mayer and A. P. Kerr. Garden City, N.Y.: Doubleday/Anchor, 1969.

Touraine, Alain. *The Voice and the Eye: An Analysis of Social Movements.* Cambridge: Cambridge University Press, 1981.

Vetterli, Richard, and Gary Bryner. *In Search of the Republic: Public Virtue and the Roots of American Government.* Totowa, N.J.: Rowman and Littlefield, 1987.

Vitz, Paul. *Censorship: Evidence of Bias in Our Children's Textbooks.* Ann Arbor: Servant, 1986.

Wald, Kenneth D. "Ministering to the Nation: The Campaigns of Jesse Jackson and Pat Robertson." In *Nominating the President.* Edited by Emmett H. Buell, Jr., and Lee Sigelman. Knoxville: University of Tennessee Press, 1991.

____. *Religion and Politics in the United States.* 2d ed. Washington, D.C.: CQ Press, 1992.

Wald, Kenneth D., Dennis Owen, and Samuel S. Hill, Jr. "Churches as Political Communities." *American Political Science Review* 82 (June 1988): 531-549.

Walters, Ronald. *Black Presidential Politics in America.* Albany: State University of New York Press, 1988.

Wattenberg, Martin P. *The Decline of American Political Parties.* Cambridge, Mass.: Harvard University Press, 1986.

Wayne, Stephen J. *The Road to the White House.* 3d ed. New York: St. Martin's, 1988.

Weber, Max. *The Protestant Ethic and the Spirit of Capitalism.* New York: Scribner's, 1958.

West, Cornel. *Prophecy Deliverance! An Afro-American Revolutionary Christianity.* Philadelphia: Westminister, 1982.

Wilcox, Clyde. "Blacks and the New Christian Right: Support for the Moral Majority and Pat Robertson among Washington, D.C., Blacks." *Review of Religious Research* 32 (September 1990): 43-56.

——. *God's Warriors: The Christian Right in Twentieth Century America.* Baltimore: Johns Hopkins University Press, 1992.

Willner, Ruth Ann. *The Spellbinders: Charismatic Political Leadership.* New Haven: Yale University Press 1984.

Wills, Garry. *Under God: Religion and American Politics.* New York: Simon and Schuster, 1990.

Wilson, Charles Morrow. *The Commoner: William Jennings Bryan.* New York: Doubleday, 1970.

Wilson, William Julius. *The Declining Significance of Race.* Chicago: University of Chicago Press, 1980.

——. *The Truly Disadvantaged: The Inner City, the Underclass, and Public Policy.* Chicago: University of Chicago Press, 1987.

Wood, Gordon S. *The Creation of the American Republic.* Chapel Hill: University of North Carolina Press, 1969.

Woodward, C. Vann. *Tom Watson: Agrarian Rebel.* New York: Rinehart, 1955.

Wuthnow, Robert. *The Restructuring of American Religion.* Princeton: Princeton University Press, 1988.

——. *The Struggle for America's Soul.* Grand Rapids, Mich.: Eerdmans, 1989.

Zlomke, Susan. "From Private Interests to the Public Interest: A Neglected Theme in the Framing of the American Constitution." Ph.D. diss., Stanford University, 1991.

Index